MUSCLEMAG INTERNATIONAL

EXPLOSIVE GROWTH!

Everything You Ever Wanted To Know About Building Muscle

GERARD THORNE & PHIL EMBLETON

Published by MuscleMag International
5775 McLaughlin Road
Mississauga, ON
Canada L5R 3P7

Canadian Cataloguing in Publication Data

Thorne, Gerard, 1963-
   Explosive growth! : everything you ever wanted to know
about building muscle

Includes index
ISBN 1-55210-020-0

   1. Bodybuilding. I. Embleton, Phil, 1963- II. Title.

GV546.5.T476 200   646.7'5   C00-901105-6
Designed by Jackie Kydyk

10 9 8 7 6 5 4 3 2 1 Pbk

Distributed in Canada by
CANBOOK Distribution Services
1220 Nicholson Road
Newmarket, ON
L3Y 7V1
800-399-6858

Distributed in the United States by
BookWorld Services
1933 Whitfield Park Loop
Sarasota, FL 34243
www.bookworld.com

Printed in Canada

This book is not intended as medical advice, nor is it offered for use in the diagnosis of any health condition or as a substitute for medical treatment and/or counsel. Its purpose is to explore advanced topics on sports nutrition and exercise. All data is for information only. Use of any of the programs within this book is at the sole risk and choice of the reader.

ACKNOWLEDGMENTS

By the time writers get to their fifth book, there's a temptation to assume that those who helped out know who they are and publicly thanking them is no longer necessary. But a re-evaluation of such a thought process quickly brings us back to reality.

Once again to Bertha Thorne and John McCarthy for keeping the writing team of Thorne and Embleton on the correct financial path. In the murky waters of tax forms, invoices, and government red tape, it's nice to know we can rely on such sound advice.

To Rob King of Heavyweights (www.heavyweights.com), our sincere thanks for proofing the manuscript and offering suggestions.

To Jackie Kydyk and staff at MuscleMag International, our thanks for yet another outstanding job on putting this book together. And Jackie congratulations on the new addition to the family!

Our thanks to Gina Logan and Holly Burns at Formula One. We appreciate the opportunity to be associated with such a dynamic new company.

And finally to Robert Kennedy. Despite the horrendous year Bob had in his personal life, he still had time to keep in touch with regards to this book's creation. Hang in there Bob, and thanks once again for allowing us to contribute to MuscleMag International.

Our sincere thanks to you all.

Table of Contents

Foreword

by Robert Kennedy

In the early seventies I decided to make a number of road trips to gather material for MuscleMag International. I made road trips because flying was at that time, an expensive luxury I couldn't afford. In my dented 8 cylinder Ford tank, of which seven cylinders fired reliably, I drove through the rust belt of the Great Lakes region, stopping in the declining steel towns that were being battered by recession. I was checking out the local gyms, getting pictures of up-and-coming bodybuilders (you'd be amazed how much money you can make selling pictures of bodybuilders AFTER they've made the big time). Besides, I just liked talking to people and taking pictures. Still do. So it was more of an excuse to get out of the office. I had been told by one bodybuilder who had placed in the top five at a state-level competition to check out the gym he trained at in his old town. Since I was passing through the area anyway, I met him at a coffee shop and we walked to his club. In an era of fitness centers, air-quality technology, and an almost fanatical obsession with cleanliness, bright lights and open spaces, this training area would be difficult to comprehend. In the basement of a building that had been built around the turn of the century and was now, for the most part abandoned (except for the stray cats that could be seen through the broken windows), was the "iron dungeon" my new friend wanted to show me.

We descended a narrow flight of stairs illuminated by a single bulb that hung precariously from the ceiling and I immediately detected the unmistakable odor of rat urine. At the bottom my eyes desperately adjusted to the gloom. It was a large, almost cavernous room that ran the full length of the abandoned building. The walls were brick, and on one side there appeared to be a pattern of deep indentations. I later found out the basement had been used during prohibition by local gangsters to hide booze from Windsor, Ontario. The indentations were produced by a Tommy Gun, an old machine gun that was the weapon of choice in those days. An accident? A gun battle? An execution? No one remembered. No one seemed to care. The floor was uneven and bare, and cockroaches scurried away at the sound of our footsteps. There was one washroom, though that's being kind. If you ever see the opening scene in the movie *Train Spotting* it will give you some idea of what I'm talking about. The sink dripped, and the porcelain looked like it hadn't been cleaned for over 50 years. There were four other men in the gym. One was a laid-off steelworker, one was a grocery store clerk who had gotten heavy into the sixties and appeared to have stayed there, and they were both spotting a lawyer doing squats. The fourth man was the owner, a Vietnam vet with a deep scar across his chin, who walked around with an empty coke bottle in which he'd spit tobacco juice, though judging by the stains on the floor, his accuracy left something to be desired. And the equipment? At this point you're probably expecting me tell you about old car axles and buckets filled with bricks. The equipment was absolutely new! It was clean, it was polished, and when what little light there was shone on the weights, it radiated out like a lighthouse beacon. After being introduced to the owner, he just looked at my outstretched hand, spat into his bottle, and said, "Goddamn Limey Bastard! There goes the neighborhood!" and walked away. My new friend patted me on the back and said, "Good, he likes you! If he didn't he would have told you to leave." I was a bit put off at this point and asked, "And what if I didn't want to leave?" My friend replied, "He keeps a loaded shotgun by his desk. It has knotches in the stock." I was soon introduced to the rest, who were much friendlier than the owner. After taking lots of pictures, I left with the lawyer as he appeared to be the most articulate of the bunch, and I was hoping for some quotes.

Over lunch, I asked him why an affluent, professional like himself would train in such a dump. He was actually paying MORE than it would cost to workout at a gym that had luxuries, like toilet paper! His reply encapsulated the experience in the most eloquent way imaginable. "Yeah, the place stinks, and the owner isn't all there. One day he was really drunk and talked about it. Did two tours. Saw some things he just can't come to grips with... Most of the time he's polishing the weights. Did you notice how they shined? But when he lifts, he goes all calm. It's all about focus. My job, I've got to be thinking all the time. If my opponent does this in court, how do I counter? What if my client screws up on the stand? It's like my life is a non-stop chess game. If I go to one of those fancy gyms, I meet people from work or clients and my mind is back into overdrive. Or I see some chick I want to hit on and my hormones take over. Some nights I can't sleep because I'm so wound up from work. But when I go into that basement, all you can really see clearly are the weights. And when I wrap my hands around that steel bar my body comes alive and at that instant all that exists is me and this piece of metal, and my mind just shuts down and I lose myself in the moment. I can spend hours down there, and when I come out my body is sore but my mind feels totally recharged. It is strange, but out here, on the surface, I'm like some kind of drone, I just exist for work or to meet other people's expectations. But down there, in that basement gym, if only for a short time, I exist!" Losing yourself in the moment. This man had rediscovered the Zen Buddhism path to enlightenment. Japanese monks, living lives of brutal austerity, would focus, like our bodybuilders, on simple physical movements (such as using a bow and arrow), with the intent of disciplining the mind so as stop all conscious thought, and in this way find enlightenment. These monks spend years, their whole lives often, just practicing a simple physical movement. And that's what pure, hardcore bodybuilding was, and still is, about. The ultimate goals, get big, get strong are still there. But that real rush, that moment when your body takes over and the thoughts that have been crowding your mind are released, that moment of inner peace is the goal, even if it's only a transitory one.

This book is about pure hardcore bodybuilding. It's about existing in bodybuilding, with bodybuilding, for bodybuilding. The focus remains on three goals, get big, get strong and win . Doesn't matter how you do it, that's between you and your conscience. This book gives you the how, you provide the focus. If you're prepared to sacrifice comfort for survival, if you can ignore the world around you to stick to your goals, then this book is for you.

I went back to that "iron dungeon" a few years later. The neighborhood was experiencing an economic boom, and a brand new fitness center with the latest electronic gizmos, aerobics classes, and an eardrum splitting stereo system combined to make a very vibrant gym/pick-up spot. And the old place I told you about? It was gone. The building had been torn down and all that was left was a vacant lot. The owner had left town, for parts unknown. I sat back in my very comfortable, very new rental with the air conditioning blasting, and felt a tremendous sense of loss. I had witnessed the passing of an era. What was bodybuilding about anyway? After all these years I'm really not sure anymore. But I think the closest I've come to finding the answer was on a cold November morning in the basement of an abandoned building, in a gym run by a man who had seen too much.

Grab a barbell, and lose yourself in the moment.

Robert Kennedy, MuscleMag International

Preface

It's been nearly four years now since we released our first book, *MuscleMag International's Encyclopedia of Bodybuilding*. Yet as soon as that book hit the shelves, readers began requesting a follow-up book devoted exclusively to supplements and drugs. Our response was *Anabolic Primer* – probably the largest, most comprehensive book in its class. But the letters kept coming. It seemed Robert Kennedy's new *Oxygen* magazine had stimulated the female half of the population into wanting a book aimed at their needs. Once again it was back to the keyboard with the result being *BodyFitness For Women*. Despite the success of all three books, the one group that felt left out were the very individuals who really started the whole weight-training craze in the first place – HARDCORE BODYBUILDERS!

In a manner of speaking the book you hold in your hands is about 60 years in the making. From the days of John Grimek, Vince Gironda, and Steve Reeves, to today's behemoths represented by Paul Dillett, Nasser El Sonbaty, and Ronnie Coleman, hardcore bodybuilding has undergone a tremendous evolution.

Although no book is complete, we have done our best to pack just about every conceivable piece of hardcore information between the covers. We don't take up space talking about dumbells or barbells. The book assumes you are at the intermediate or advanced level and want to take things a step further. For those new to the sport, we suggest reading Arnold's or our Encyclopedias, or one of Robert Kennedy's excellent publications. Such books lay the foundation, while this one fills in all the details that are needed to be competitive in today's bodybuilding arena.

This book has two primary objectives; to gather together all the techniques and strategies relating to hardcore bodybuilding, and then show you how to incorporate them into your training. One of the themes running throughout the book is scientific credibility. No, we have no intentions of boring you with scientific mumbo jumbo. But in the last ten years researchers have finally accepted weight training as a legitimate form of exercise, and as such there is a substantial amount of research available to back up current training theories. Of course we also present advice from the sport's true "scientists" – the top pro and amateur bodybuilders you see in the bodybuilding magazines every month.

Another aspect to the book is neutrality. We don't subscribe to the notion that there's one "best" way to train. Everyone is different and what works for one may not work for another. And for a few lucky individuals, "all roads lead to Rome!" We have done our best to discuss as many different training styles as possible. At one end you have Mike Mentzer's one set to failure, heavy-duty style of training. On the other we find Arnold's high volume, 20 sets per bodypart routines. Falling in between are Charles Poliquin's and Dorian Yates' 6 to 10 sets per bodypart recommendations.

If there's one thing that separates our books from most others it's the inclusion of the drug issue. Like it or not, pharmacology is a part of modern bodybuilding. No matter how much you preach against a certain activity, there will be those who will engage in it. We think it makes far more sense to provide accurate information and let readers make up their own minds rather than spreading unfounded horror stories. Of course, since anabolic steroids are illegal substances in many countries, particularly the United States, you have to ask yourself whether becoming part of the drug war is worth it in exchange for a few extra pounds of muscle mass.

As much as we would like to claim that reading this book will put you on the Olympia stage, honesty prevents us from doing so. Only a select few have the genetics to go all the way to the top. For every Flex Wheeler, Dorian Yates, and Ronnie Coleman, there are thousands slaving away in gyms around the world that never rise above a local championship. We are confident, however, that everyone who follows the advice in this book can make great improvements in his or her physique. And we might add, a few genetically challenged individuals have occasionally made it to the top. Who knows, you may be one of them. You certainly have nothing to lose by trying.

Gerard Thorne
Phil Embleton
Fall, 1999

Introduction
What Is
Hardcore
Bodybuilding?

Nasser El Sonbaty and Flex Wheeler

"Many misguided beginners and intermediates ride that roller coaster. They never realize that 12 months of moderate training is better for size, strength, and growth than a year of on-and-off training. Consistency in the long run, is more important than intensity."

— Mat Wilson, *MuscleMag International* contributor commenting on one of the most important variables for success, consistency.

"Come on, one more. Don't go getting lazy on me. Let's bust some ass here!"
You hear it day in and day out. The yelling, screaming, and other polite words of encouragement echoing forth from squat and bench press racks all over the world. Welcome to the domain of hardcore bodybuilders. The blood, sweat and tears of pumping iron. You've paid your dues and struggled through those first few months of learning the basics. You've reached the point where getting down and dirty is a rite of passage and not something to be shunned. You are now a hardcore bodybuilder!

HARDCORE – A MUCH MALIGNED TERM

Dan Freeman

Just the word "hardcore" alone tells you, you are up to no good. Few terms conjure up the range of images as hardcore. If you don't believe us simply stick the term in front of such words as "supplements," "drugs," and "training." See what we mean? Hardcore signifies all-out, balls-to-the-wall, no bullshit, to the extreme. Hardcore bodybuilders don't hang out at health spas, take in Barry Manilow concerts, or derive most of their nutrition from "a light salad." On the other hand, hardcore bodybuilders are passionate about their training, highly knowledgeable, and some of the most dedicated athletes in the world. Yes we have two extremes here, but that's probably the best way to sum up hardcore – EXTREME!

HOW DO I KNOW IF I'M HARDCORE?

Although a few individuals can nail down the precise moment they started considering themselves hardcore bodybuilders, for most it was more of an evolution than a revolution. There is no magic moment to signify that you are now hardcore. For some it takes two months, while others need two years. And then there are the bulk of bodybuilders who never become hardcore. The term hardcore is as much a state of mind as a physical condition. Those few hours a week spent at the gym are only a fraction of what it means to be a hardcore bodybuilder. At the risk of contradicting ourselves, here are a few light-hearted symptoms to indicate that you have probably fallen into the hardcore category of bodybuilding.

11

Introduction – *What Is Hardcore Bodybuilding?*

You find yourself listening more to Charles Poliquin than Gene Simmons.

Those New Kids on the Block CD's have been replaced with Def Leppard and Iron Maiden.

You start doing barbell bench presses and use the Universal bench press for hanging your towel on.

Winstrol and Dianabol replace earlier conversations of Geritol and Gravol.

You put your copies of *Teen Beat* and *Seventeen* in the attic and replace them with *MuscleMag International, Flex,* and *Maxim.*

You practice flexing your calves while using the John.

Those beefy guys down in the far end start asking you to spot them.

Robert Kennedy phones you requesting a photo shoot!

This list is by no means complete and like most diseases, you don't need to have all the symptoms to be diagnosed. But if you possess three or four or more of the previous, then the odds my friend are good to excellent that you have hardcore fever. Great! Consider this book the cure. Over the next 400 pages or so we are going to "treat your illness" with just about every cure known. But unlike other diseases, our cures will only make things worse! Instead of losing weight you will gain weight. Instead of becoming frail and weak, you'll develop freaky strength and size. Instead of a diagnoses of "terminal" meaning your life will end prematurely, "terminal" in bodybuilding means you'll be trying to out-lift guys forty years your junior when you are in your sixties and seventies. Hardcore bodybuilding is the greatest disease in the world. Now let's show you how to live with it!

> **"In order to set up a foundation for gaining muscle mass you should optimize your lifestyle. For example decreasing stress levels, getting proper sleep, and keeping away from excess alcohol and recreational drugs, will result in an ideal hormonal base on top of which further changes can be made by optimizing training and diet."**
>
> – Dr. Mauro DiPasquale, regular *MuscleMag International* columnist commenting on what it takes to optimize strength and size gains.

Tho-mass Benagli and Enzo Ferrari

Aaron Maddron

Thomas Koller

BOOK ONE

THE ROAD TO HARDCORE

CHAPTER ONE

In the Footsteps of Legends

Rather than jump right into the heart of hardcore bodybuilding, we thought it best to give you a brief historical perspective on the sport. For our younger readers whose knowledge of bodybuilding consists of Arnold and the current Mr. Olympia line-up, rest assured the sport you are part of has a long and vibrant pedigree. When you step on stage at your first contest it may help you know that you are following in the footsteps of thousands of individuals, some of whom have been dead for thousands of years!

MILOS – PUTTING UP WITH THE BULL!

In many respects the first individual to use modern progressive resistance training techniques was the Greek strongman, Milos. According to legend, Milos started "training" using a small calf, which he carried around on his shoulders on a daily basis. As the calf increased in weight, so did Milos' strength. Finally as the legend continues, Milos strolled into the amphitheater on Olympic day carrying the full-grown bull on his shoulders. We'll never know if this is fact or fiction. Given the average weight of an adult bull is anywhere from 750 to 1000 pounds, it is conceivable, but just barely (keeping such an animal cooperative would take other skills, however!). Whether true or not, the important thing to draw from this story is that Milos (or the writer who first made up the story) had a knowledge of progressive resistance training thousands of years ago.

SPARTICUS KNEW BEST

As frequently happened in the ancient world, the Greek Empire had its day and was replaced by the next great dynasty, the Roman Empire. Modern bodybuilders can thank the Romans for creating what could be called the first training gyms. Granted the gladiators who trained there had a different viewpoint than their owners, but there's no disputing the fact that the Romans knew a thing or two about physical conditioning.

For those readers who spent history class asleep or fantasizing about the latest fitness model, let's give you a brief introduction to physical conditioning, Roman style.

To a generation raised on MTV and video arcades, it's hard to believe that at one time the primary source of entertainment for the average citizen was going to the theater and watching men fighting to the death with one another or wild animals. Rome's great landmark, the Coliseum, is proof of just how popular such spectacles were to Roman society. The "star" performers in such events were highly trained individuals called gladiators. Few people willingly volunteered for the job and most gladiators were drawn from the criminal population or conquered nations. To make sure the audience got their money's worth, each gladiator was given special training at a system of training schools. Here they received instruction in such disciplines as strength, flexibility, and weapons. In many respects gladiator schools were the first organized physical culture centers. The next time you hear a bodybuilder talking about being ripped, cut, or diced, politely remind him of what those terms meant to his counterpart 2000 years ago. Incidentally for those who seem captivated by ancient Rome, rent out the great 1950s movie, *Sparticus*, starring Kirk Douglas. After watching this movie that personal trainer at the gym won't seem half so bad!

No doubt many readers are wondering how ancient Rome and modern bodybuilding compare. Look at it this way, both gladiators and modern bodybuilders put long hours in the gym. Both used various forms of exercise to strengthen and enlarge the muscles. Both groups then put their muscles on display in front of large audiences. Granted the outcome of a bodybuilding contest usually differs from the main event at the Coliseum, but nevertheless, you had two groups of people being admired for their strength and power. Have things really changed that much?

Eugen Sandow

UNDER THE BIG TOP
The next group of individuals who contributed to the sport of modern bodybuilding were the old time strongmen who traveled around Europe with circuses in the 16th, 17th, and 18th centuries. After performing their great feat of strength, many of these portly gentlemen would strip down to nothing more than a fig leaf and flex their muscles. It's highly doubtful such characters sported muscular 20-inch arms, but they hold a special place in bodybuilding as they were among the first to add posing to their routines. They didn't just lift heavy objects. They actually showed the audience the muscles that enabled them to exert their great strength.

THE SANDOW EXPERIENCE
In the late 19th century a movement was started to try and halt some of the detrimental health issues of the industrial revolution. A few individuals who were years ahead of their time realized that while the new technology of the industrial revolution may be beneficial in terms of productivity, it was slowly destroying the health of a large segment of the population. A combination of increased pollution and decreased physical labor meant that more and more people were succumbing to health related problems. In response to this, a group of individuals called physical culturists, began preaching the benefits of regular exercise and healthy eating. From this movement emerged an individual whose name became synonymous with physical perfection – Eugen Sandow.

What separated Sandow from other strongmen and physical culturists was his almost flawless physique. Most of Sandow's contemporaries tended to be rather generous around the midsection (no doubt due to copious amounts of beer and sausage!). But Sandow sported a physique that exhibited a very small degree of bodyfat and was almost perfectly proportioned. Sandow's fig-leaf posing exhibitions became so popular that he was brought to America by showman extraordinaire Florenz Ziegfeld (the same Ziegfeld of the Follies fame).

Charles Atlas

It wasn't long before Sandow's physique became the standard by which other physical culturists were measured. In many respects he was the first true bodybuilder in that his fame was based as much on his physique as what he could lift. To honor Sandow's role in bodybuilding history, Joe Weider created a statue bearing Sandow's name, and each year it is given to the winner of bodybuilding's most prestigious prize, the Mr. Olympia.

THE WORLD ON HIS SHOULDERS

By the early 20th century physical culture exhibitions became a popular form of entertainment, so popular in fact that a businessman by the name of Bernan Macfadden published the first magazine devoted to the discipline, called *Physical Culture*. In 1903 he held the first contest called "America's most perfectly developed man." Suprisingly the winner received $1000, which at the turn of the century was worth nearly as much as the $100,000 awarded to the winner's of todays top contests. One of the winner's of Macfadden's contest was a young Italian immigrant named Angelo Siciliano. Angelo had a stroke of good luck early in his career as someone convinced him to change his name, and Angelo Siciliano became Charles Atlas!

Siegmund Klein

Few people remember or even know that Charles Atlas won the "America's Best Built Man" contest. But virtually everyone who has picked up a barbell knows Atlas as the person who popularized Dynamic Tension training. Recognizing that self-conscious teenagers were the biggest market, Atlas created an ad called "Don't kick sand in my face," and placed it in the backs of comic books. The ad shows a skinny teen being humiliated in front of his girlfriend by a "big bully" who kicks sand in his face. The bully decides not to hit the teen because he's "so skinny he may dry up and blow away." Our teen orders Atlas's Dynamic Tension courses and the next time he encounters the bully on the beach he uses his new, muscular physique to drop the bully with one punch. Now such advertising may seem tame by today's standards but by the mid-seventies this one ad had sold over six million courses of dynamic tension, and made Atlas and his descendants a considerable amount of money.

Dynamic tension involves contracting the muscles against an immovable object. The muscle contracts but doesn't change in length. The best example of this is clasping the hands together in front of the body and pushing inward. As both sides of the body produce almost equal force, there is little or no movement, but the triceps, chest, and shoulders, contract very forcibly.

John Grimek

What's ironic is that Atlas spent more time building his physique with standard barbell and dumbell exercises than dynamic tension techniques!

THE BEGINNING OF THE MODERN ERA

Besides Atlas the other significant physical culturist of the 1920s and 1930s was Siegmund Klein. Klein followed in Sandow's footsteps in that his physique was both strong and pleasing to the eye. In addition Klein was an outstanding athlete and never ceased to amaze audiences with his remarkable muscle control and flexibility.

In 1930, the American Athletic Union (AAU) held the first Mr. America contest, and through the efforts of Atlas, Klein, and others, physical culture gyms and contests sprang up all over the country.

The 1940 and 1941 Mr. America contests were won by John Carl Grimek. After Sandow, Grimek was probably the first modern bodybuilder in that his amazing feats of strength were secondary to his physique. Another great bodybuilder of the same time period was Clancy Ross who was one of the first to use weight training for building muscle more so than developing strength. Up to this point in time strength was the primary goal of weight lifters and any extra muscle was just a "side effect."

Steve Reeves

STEVE REEVES – THE EMBODIMENT OF PERFECTION

When lists are composed of the greatest bodybuilders of all time, the name Steve Reeves is always near the top. After winning both the Mr. America and Mr. Universe titles, Steve was cast as Hollywood's newest Hercules. With his perfectly proportioned physique, rugged good looks, and charismatic personality, Steve was the first bodybuilder to transcend the sport, and helped pave the way for guys like Arnold, Lou Ferrigno, and to a lessor extent, Sylvester Stallone. More than anything Steve proved that muscles could sell movie tickets and for a period in the 1950s he was the biggest star in all of Hollywood.

"Before Weider there was John Grimek who was the original pioneer of modern-day bodybuilding. Yes, there was Reeves, but when it came to pure slabs of massive thickly developed muscle, John was in a class of his own."

– Garry Bartlett, *MuscleMag International* columnist commenting on the death of John Grimek.

Reg Park

REG PARK – IDOL TO AN OAK!

With Reeves packing movie houses across the world, the door was left open for the next generation of bodybuilding stars. From South Africa came 6 foot two inch, Reg Park. Where Reeves placed the emphasis on proportions, Park was all size. Because of his height and size, Park was probably the first really big bodybuilder on the scene. Little did he know that his physique would be the focal point of a young Austrian kid named Arnold Schwarzenegger, who one day would blend Reeve's screen success and Park's brute size into an unbeatable combination.

Another bodybuilder of the 1950s who helped define the sport was native American, Bill Pearl, who won both the Mr. America and Mr. Universe titles. Now in his seventies, Bill still sports a physique that could hold its own at a major bodybuilding contest! Bill's a perfect example of absolute devotion to the sport and every morning around 4 a.m. he gets out of bed to hit the weights.

Still another famous bodybuilder of the fifties was Chuck Sipes, who not only sported one of the best physiques around, but also developed a reputation as the strongest bodybuilder around (much the same as Greg Kovacs these days).

THE GLORY DAYS OF MUSCLE BEACH

As the 1950s rolled into the '60s, California's reputation as body-building's heaven seemed secure, and the Garden of Eden was Venice Beach, Santa Monica. This stretch of beach was always a popular spot to see the most famous bodybuilders in the world, but it was Hollywood that immortalized the area with a series of "Beach Movies" staring Annette Funicello and Frankie Avalon. Later, Sharon Tate (tragic victim of Charles Manson's family) would make *Don't Make Waves*, which featured many of the sport's top stars including the Blond Bomber himself, Dave Draper.

Dave Draper

On any given day you could walk down "Muscle Beach" (as Venice Beach was becoming known) and see such greats as Rick Wayne, Freddy Ortiz, Harold Poole, Chet Yorton, Dave Draper, and Larry Scott, training in the outdoor weight area knows as "the pit."

The most dominant bodybuilder of the 1960s was Larry Scott. Larry became famous because of his outstanding arm development particularly his biceps. In short order he won both the Mr. America and Mr. Universe titles and then became the sport's first Mr. Olympia.

In 1965, Canadian immigrant, Joe Weider, publisher of *Muscle Builder Power* magazine (now *Muscle and Fitness*), created a contest to determine just who was the greatest bodybuilder alive. It would feature only those who won such titles as Mr. America or Mr. Universe and become a sort of Super Bowl of bodybuilding. Larry Scott fought off the sport's best and won the inaugural contest, and then proved it was no fluke by successfully defending his title the next year. The 1966 Mr. Olympia was significant as it featured a relative newcomer, Cuban defector, Sergio Oliva.

Larry Scott

THE TRUE BODYBUILDING MYTH

If Sandow had the first "ripped" physique, and Park the first massive physique, then the Cuban-born Sergio Oliva was the first bodybuilder who could truly be called "freaky." Even by todays growth hormone inflated standards, Oliva stands out. From his 28-inch thighs, to his 28-inch waist, to those 22-inch arms, Oliva's physique sent a shiver up the spine of competitors everywhere. So overpowering was his reputation that many in the game who had never seen Oliva in person, said he must be a "myth." The name stuck, and forever after Sergio Oliva became known as The Myth.

Sergio Oliva

Oliva easily won the Mr. Olympia from 1967 to 1969. In fact he won the 1968 title unopposed as no one dared challenge him. This all changed in 1969 when a young Austrian immigrant arrived on the scene sporting a physique that matched Oliva's and a personality that surpassed the Cuban's. Most of you have guessed by now that we are referring to Arnold Schwarzenegger, and his first Mr. Olympia appearance in 1969 was the start of a career that has seen few equals.

Arnold Schwarzenegger

CLASH OF TITANS

Few sports succeed without great rivalries. Baseball had Joe Dimaggio and Ted Williams. Boxing had Mohammed Ali and Joe Frasier. Tennis had John McEnroe and Jimmy Conners. And on it goes. When Arnold stepped on stage at the 1969 Mr. Olympia, it was the first time the Myth looked human. While a tad short of Oliva in the genetics department, Arnold's physique was nevertheless the equal of the great Cuban. But what gave Arnold the edge was his personality. Oliva appeared almost unsure and awkward on stage while Arnold brimmed with confidence and charisma. The judges awarded Oliva the 69 Mr. Olympia but most in the audience new it was just the start of something bigger and better.

The 1970 Mr. Olympia saw the pendulum swing from Sergio to Arnold, and for the Austrian Oak (a nickname given Arnold by writer and bodybuilder Rick Wayne) it was the start of his record run of six Mr. Olympia's and his future dominance of Hollywood.

Franco Columbu, Arnold Schwarzenegger and Jusup Wilkosz

It's no exaggeration to say Arnold redefined bodybuilding. He had both the physique and the personality to transcend the sport. Arnold was as comfortable mixing with Hollywood's social elite as posing against competitors on stage. Despite challenges from Lou Ferrigno, Franco Columbo, Serge Nubret, and Oliva again in 1972, Arnold dominated the Mr. Olympia from 1970 to 1975. It would be nearly ten years before another bodybuilder of Arnold's caliber stepped on the Olympia stage.

ZANE AND COLUMBU – A STUDY IN CONTRAST

After Arnold left bodybuilding to begin his equally dominant career in Hollywood, the sport's reins were passed to two individuals with opposing physiques; Franco Columbu and Frank Zane.

Like Arnold, Franco started his career in Europe winning both Mr. Italy and Mr. Europe. He first met Arnold in Germany in the mid-1960s and after Arnold immigrated to America in 1968, it was only a matter of time that the Sardinia-born Franco did the same. Franco was one of the most powerful

Franco Columbu

Frank Zane

bodybuilders in the sport, despite standing just five foot five. But that short frame carried 180+ pounds into combat and only for Arnold's presence probably would have won the Mr. Olympia on a number of occasions in the early 1970s. As it was, he won his class at the Olympia in 1975, and placed second to Arnold for the overall (at one time the Olympia was divided into two classes; above and below 200 pounds). When Arnold retired in 1975, the door was open for Franco and he won the overall Mr. Olympia title in 1976.

Frank Zane was a perfect example of how intelligence and dedication can sometimes make up for less than perfect genetics. Despite his five foot ten frame, Frank could never seem to develop the mass of bodybuilders the same height that regularly outweighed him by 20 or 30 pounds. Now most would accept this and move on to other pursuits, but Frank used a combination of intelligence and creativity to build what many consider to be the most perfect bodybuilding physique of all time.

Frank's chiseled 190-pound physique propelled him to three consecutive Mr. Olympia titles from 1977 to 1979, and showed a generation of bodybuilders that there was more to bodybuilding than great genetics.

INTO THE EIGHTIES

We would be remiss if we left the impression that the only great bodybuilders in the seventies were Arnold, Franco, Oliva, and Zane. The sport was growing by leaps and bounds, thanks to the documentary *Pumping Iron*, Arnold's promotion efforts, both in Hollywood and at contests, and the popular TV show, *The Incredible Hulk* featuring 260-pound Lou Ferrigno.

Lou Ferrigno

At the time Lou was the largest bodybuilder ever, standing six foot five, and weighing 260-270 pounds in contest shape. Lou won both the Mr. America and Mr. Universe titles, and placed third to Arnold and Serge Nubret at the 1975 Mr. Olympia. He skipped the 1976 contest but by all accounts was set to compete at around 280 pounds for the 1977 show when Hollywood began casting for a large bodybuilder to play the alter ego of scientist Dr. David Banner from the popular comic book series, *The Incredible Hulk*. Recognizing that show business had much more to offer than bodybuilding, at least financially, Lou jumped at the opportunity, and put his bodybuilding career on hold for nearly fifteen years.

Other great bodybuilders of the 1970s included Ken Waller, Mike Katz, Robby Robinson, Danny Padilla, Boyer Coe, Mike Mentzer, Roy Callender, Albert Beckles, Jeff King and Kal Salzimack. Most of these greats won the Mr. America, Mr. World, or Mr. Universe titles, and many continued their quest for the Mr. Olympia into the 1980s.

Robby Robinson

Mike Mentzer

The 1980s started with controversy as Arnold won the 1980 Mr. Olympia, held in Sydney Australia. But unlike his victories in the seventies, where in most cases he was the best, this time he was slightly off while some of his competitors were in the best shape of their lives.

Arnold came out of retirement after getting in shape for his first big Hollywood movie, *Conan the Barbarian*. With friends urging him on he came out of retirement and won the whole shebang. As would be expected, many accused the judges of giving the title to Arnold out of reputation and not the quality of his physique. It didn't help matters that such bodybuilders as Chris Dickerson, Boyer Coe, and Mike Mentzer, were in outstanding shape.

If the 1980 Mr. Olympia raised a few eyebrows, the outcome of the 1981 show was looked on by some as bodybuilding's version of the 1919 throwing of baseball's World Series by the Chicago White Sox. After five years in retirement himself, Franco Columbu duplicated Arnold's 1980 triumph by winning his second title in 1981. Franco clearly was not at his best as his legs were way below the standard of the other competitors, his posing routine seemed subdued, and to make matters worse, he sported a rather pronounced gynocomastic lump in one pec (the result of excess testosterone or anabolic steroids converting to estrogen). Once again Franco's weaknesses were highlighted by the outstanding shape of such competitors as Roy Callender, Danny Padilla, Chris Dickerson, and Tom Platz.

Chris Dickerson

Tom Platz

Lee Haney

FINALLY!

After placing second to Arnold and Franco in 1980 and 1981, Chris Dickerson had serious thoughts about retiring, but bodybuilding's first African-American Mr. America, decided to give it one more try. He was rewarded for his efforts by winning the coveted Sandow trophy in 1982, in London, England. The win didn't come easy, however, as such stars as Casey Viator, Frank Zane, and Tom Platz, were also in outstanding shape.

THE LION ROARS!

1983 was significant for two reasons; a relative newcomer named Samir Bannout won the title, and it featured the individual who would dominate the sport for the next eight years.

Samir Bannout originally hailed from Lebanon, and was nicknamed the Lion of Lebanon because of his fierce determination in the face of larger foes. Samir relied on Frank Zane's strategy of defeating larger opponents by displaying a physique of almost perfect proportions. His win was a popular one, but the show's third place winner, Lee Haney, seemed to get the most attention.

EIGHT IN A ROW

No less an authority than Arnold said after seeing Haney win the 1983 Mr. America, that he would be competitive on the Olympia stage in short order. But Arnold probably didn't expect Haney to break his own record of six straight Mr. Olympia's, or his record total of seven. But Haney did just that, starting in 1984 and continuing until 1991. Lee Haney won eight straight Mr. Olympia titles, and became the first bodybuilder since Arnold to be almost assured of first place before he even took to the posing platform. Such bodybuilders as Mike Christian, Lee Labrada, Rich Gaspari, and Berry DeMey, occasionally made things interesting, but they never managed to wrest the title from the 250-pound Atlanta native.

THE FAIRER SEX

Before moving into the 1990s we need to branch out and elaborate on the other major significant development of the 1980s, the emergence of female bodybuilding as a sport. The concept of women training with weights was not new, as such Hollywood greats as Marilyn Monroe did it back in the 1950s. But it would be the late 1970s before women's bodybuilding as a distinct sport became popular. And it would be primarily due to the work of one woman, Lisa Lyon.

While tame by today's standards, Lisa Lyon's physique was nevertheless primarily the result of weight training or "body building." Combining grace with great muscle tone, Lisa showed a whole generation of women that weight training would not masculinize their bodies.

Thanks to Lisa's efforts and the efforts of other women pioneers such as Doris Barrilleaux and Christine Zane, women's bodybuilding took off with the first Ms. Olympia being held in 1981, and won by Rachel McLish. Like Larry Scott at the 1965 and 1966 Mr. Olympia, Rachel successfully defended her title in 1982. The early eighties saw such female stars as Shelly Gruwell, Lynn Conkwright, Carla Dunlap, and Candy Csencsits, battle for supremacy and create the foundation of

Lisa Lyon

Carla Dunlap

the modern women's bodybuilding movement. From Mclish the title passed to Carla Dunlap, Kike Elomaa, and Cory Everson. Cory became the first "Arnold" of the sport, winning six straight titles from 1985 to 1990. She in turn was followed by Lenda Murray who won six of her own titles. The third dynasty seems assured with three-time and current Ms. Olympia, Kim Chizevsky, showing no signs of relinquishing the title.

THE BRITISH INVASION

Just as Lee Haney's reign of terror was coming to an end in 1991, his heir was stepping up to the batter's box. Like Haney's third place win in 1983, Dorian Yates' second place finish to Haney in 1991 signaled the beginning of his own dominance of the sport.

Dorian Yates' six Mr. Olympia wins established three things; it raised the bar from 245-250 pounds to 265-270 pounds; it meant the first time since Samir Bannout in 1982 that a non-American won the title; and it showed that a bodybuilder didn't need to live or spend a lot of time in southern California to win the Mr. Olympia title.

Yates became known as the working class Brit, because of his Birmingham, England background. He didn't fit the mold of the California beach blond bodybuilder with his massive 270-pound

Cory Everson and Carla Dunlap

physique either. But Dorian's six wins were significant as they established the new direction that the Mr. Olympia had taken. No longer could a 190-pound Frank Zane win the title. With the exception of Shawn Ray, Flex Wheeler, and Lee Priest, all of the top six Mr. Olympia placers in the last five years weigh 245 pounds or more. In fact the top bodybuilders of the last five years, Paul Dillett, Nasser El Sonbaty, Kevin Lervone, and Dorian Yates, all weigh between 250 and 280 pounds. And we should point out that Wheeler and Ray have added about 30 pounds to their physiques since turning pro.

Lee Priest

Flex Wheeler

Ronnie Coleman

RONNIE COLEMAN AND BEYOND

After winning the 1997 Mr. Olympia, Dorian Yates took his final bow and threw the title to the sharks nibbling at his heels. The 1998 title was significant as it was the first time in 14 years that someone other than Dorian Yates or Lee Haney had won the title. But it would not be one of the heavy favorites. Texas police officer, Ronnie Coleman emerged from the middle of the pack to become just the tenth person in bodybuilding history to win the Olympia title.

Coleman's victory was both popular and surprising. After six years of Yates, many felt guys like Nasser El Sonbaty, Kevin Lervone, Flex Wheeler, or Shawn Ray, would inherit the crown. But throughout 1998 Ronnie Coleman emerged to win a number of pro contests and in September walked away with the big one.

Since the first Mr. Olympia in 1965, a number of trends have developed with regards to bodybuilding. The first is the most basic – mass. Larry Scott won the first title weighing around 195 pounds. Sergio Oliva then raised the bar to 225-230. Along came Arnold and up it went to 240 pounds. Not counting Arnold's win in 1981, there was a period where the under 200 pound bodybuilders had a chance. But starting with Lee Haney in 1984, the Mr.

Olympia has become the domain of the big guys. Here's a weight by weight comparison of all ten Mr. Olympia's.

Larry Scott – 195
Sergio Oliva – 230
Arnold Schwarzenegger – 240
Franco Columbu – 185
Frank Zane – 190
Chris Dickerson – 185
Samir Bannout – 195
Lee Haney – 245-250
Dorian Yates – 265-270
Ronnie Coleman – 250-255

Jean-Pierre Fux

It's reached the point now that state and even city winners are weighing 240 pounds. And it appears things will only get worse (or better depending on your point of view!). Canadian Colossus, Greg Kovacs, won the Canadian Nationals and competed in the New York Night of Champions weighing 310 pounds! Guys like Nasser El Sonbaty, Paul Dillett, and Jean-Pierre Fux routinely go over 300 pounds in the off-season. If judging criteria doesn't change, the 2005 Mr. Olympia will weigh about 300 pounds, and his counterpart in 2010 will tip the scales at 320-330. It sounds farfetched, but this is where the sport is headed.

Besides the increase in size, the other major trend is a decrease in body fat percentage. From Larry Scott's eight to ten percent, to Arnold's six to eight percent, to Dorian's two to four percent, anything above five percent these days is considered fat! Many see this as a step backward, while others call it progress and evolution.

AND SO THE TORCH PASSES

When Robert Kennedy released his best-selling book, *Hardcore Bodybuilding*, in the early eighties, he knew that a few of the book's readers would eventually go on to become the next generation of bodybuilding superstars. Likewise we are confident that many readers of this book will step into the competitive arena, and a few will go far, perhaps all the way to the Olympia stage.

As you've seen, bodybuilding has a rich and exciting past. Like baseball, boxing, and the Olympics, we've had our ups and downs, but the sport is as popular as ever. So, in a manner of speaking you are walking in the footsteps of Milos, Sandow, Arnold, Haney, Dorian, and the others. We wish you well in this endeavor as you write your own chapter of bodybuilding history.

Greg Kovacs

CHAPTER TWO

Anatomy and Physiology

As you are going to be spending thousands of hours building those muscles of yours, we thought it fitting that you have some idea as to what exactly you are creating. Any engineer worth his or her salt knows the physical and chemical properties of the various building materials that go into his or her construction project. In many respects you are just like that engineer building a great bridge or high-rise office complex. Where would Star Trek's Mr. Scott or Lt. LeForge be without knowing the intricacies of the Enterprise's Warp engines!

In this chapter we are going to take you back to high school biology. No, there won't be any quizzes, and that pretty little blond is not sitting two seats in front of you. You are stuck with the authors. But we promise to do our best and make this lesson as painless as possible. As you'll discover the human body is not a random collection of parts. Everything is integrated and contributes to the smooth running of the whole organism. You may think you are working biceps, but we assure you the entire body is being stimulated, and not just the muscular system either. The cardiovascular, endocrine, and nervous systems, all come into play. Which incidentally is why bodybuilding (the activity not the professional sport) is such a healthy undertaking. Everything you read in this chapter is as important to body-building as sets, reps, supplements, and weight.

Christine Oakley

FOR MALES ONLY?

Chances are from your earliest days playing in the schoolyard, you've heard this line before. Muscles are what separate men from women, right? Wrong! Both sexes have the exact same muscular system, and while the average male is stronger than the average female, this only applies to Joe and Jill average on the street. Most women who regularly train with weights, can hold their own with the couch potatoes that characterize far too many men these days. So for you guys that don't regularly lift iron, don't underestimate that petite looking brunette over there. She may be able to kick your ass at the squat rack. And you know something, it's high time too!

MUSCLES DOWN AND DIRTY

Outwardly muscles are those long, lumpy, structures that hang off the body's bone structure (for the trivial types among you, "muscle" comes from the Latin "musculus" which means "mouse." The early anatomists thought contracting muscles looked like a mouse running underneath the skin). We say long as most muscles have a long dimension and a shorter one (i.e. length and width). But some muscles like the deltoids (shoulders) are pretty much the same length in all

Tho-mass Benagli and Enzo Ferrari

directions. In any case their main purpose is support, movement, and temperature regulation. Most people are familiar with the movement variable as that's what you do every time you hit the gym. But your muscles are also involved when you sit or stand still. In fact right now as you read this book, most of your muscles are contracting slightly to keep you in one position. And for those of you in northern climates, the shivering process you undergo in response to cold is one way the body helps stay warm. By causing small but numerous contractions, the vibrating muscles help raise body temperature.

NOT ONE BUT THREE

The body has three types of muscles; cardiac, smooth, and skeletal. The focus of this chapter will primarily be skeletal, although we'll touch on cardiac a bit later. As for smooth, suffice to say it forms the main constituent of many organs and internal structures. As an example the movement of food through the digestive tract is primarily due to smooth muscle contraction (called peristalsis). So while smooth muscle plays an indirect role in bodybuilding (all that extra protein needs to be digested!), it's not something that you focus on in the gym. Skeletal muscle on the other hand is what bodybuilding is all about, especially making it bigger and stronger.

SKELETAL MUSCLE

Fiendishly clever those anatomists naming the muscles that attach to the body's skeleton, skeletal muscles! But as simple as it sounds, that's where the name comes from. Physiologists also use the term striated muscle as skeletal muscles have a striated appearance when looked at them under a microscope. A third name is "voluntary muscle" as for the most part you have conscious control over their contraction and movement. You can't really speed up the smooth muscle contractions in the digestive system. Likewise the only way cardiac muscle contraction can be increased is by doing more exercise and increasing heart rate. But for the most part you can't "will" the heart to beat faster (we know the psychologists are arguing that you can increase cardiac muscle contraction. But this is in specially trained individuals who have learned to modify brain waves. For the purposes of this text, trust us, the heart is on its own!).

Roland
Cziurlok

STRUCTURE AND ORGANIZATION

As with most organs and structures, skeletal muscle has specialized cells called muscle fibers. The name fiber comes from their shape, which is long and cylindrical. Thus they look more like "fibers" than normal cells, most of which are oval.

Muscle fibers are themselves subdivided into smaller fibers called myofibrils, which are composed of thick and thin threads called myofilaments. The thick myofilaments are composed of large protein called myosin while the smaller myofilaments are composed of a protein called actin.

When viewed under a microscope, skeletal muscle shows a pattern of alternating light and dark bands. These bands are the result of the arrangement of the actin and myosin myofilaments. For convenience physiologists have called the dark areas A bands, and the lighter areas I bands. Running down the middle of the I bands is a thin dark line called the Z line. Don't worry too much about the different filaments, proteins, and bands, the important thing to remember is that the section of muscle from one Z band to the next is called a sarcomere; and this is where that all-important entity known as muscle contraction takes place.

SUPPORTING STRUCTURES

Muscles are not distinct entities that work by themselves. There are a number of other structures that play a role in muscle contraction and support. As they are the source of many injuries as well, we need to look at them in some detail.

TENDONS

Muscles are connected to other muscles or bones by long, tough bundles of dense connective tissue called tendons. The Achilles tendon that connects the calves to the heel bone is probably the best known tendon in the body. The biceps tendon that connects the lower biceps to the radius bone of the forearm is a close second. When a muscle contracts it pulls on the tendon which in turn pulls on the bone or muscle it's connected to. Despite bodybuilders and other athletes saying they "ripped" a tendon, in effect tendons rarely tear because of their strength. Instead the weaker point where the tendon connects to the muscle or bone usually lets go first. As we will see later where the tendon attaches on the bone plays a big role in muscle strength.

LIGAMENTS

Just as muscles don't connect directly to other muscles but by tendons, bones don't rest on other bones. Instead they are joined by fibrous connective tissue called ligaments. Although considered inelastic, that is unmovable, ligaments do allow a certain degree of movement at joints. Ligaments add structure and support to bones at joints and are very durable. When they do tear, there is considerable pain and swelling, and therapy and surgery is often needed to correct the problem.

CARTILAGE

Cartilage can be considered the shock absorbers of the body, as its main function is to prevent bones from rubbing against one another during movement. Cartilage is the site of many sports related injuries. We could write a whole book on knee cartilage alone. The intense knee pain experienced by many former athletes is the result of small amounts of cartilage coming lose and lodging between the femur and tibia. As the knee bends the cartilage acts as a sort of lock, both restricting movement and producing considerable pain. In bodybuilding the squat and leg press cause most knee-cartilage injuries. Which is sad really as these are two of the best exercises you can perform in the gym. But unfortunately many people throw technique out the window and bounce at the bottom of the movements. We'll say more on this later.

BURSAE AND TENDON SHEATHS

Like most forms of machinery the human body works best when the moving parts are surrounded by fluid. Bursae are sacks filled with a special type of fluid called synovial fluid that helps reduce friction wherever muscles, tendons, or bones move past one another. For want of a better term, bursae act as cushions.

Jay Cutler

Besides sack-shaped bursae, the body has evolved long cylindrical bursae called tendon sheaths. As the name implies tendon sheaths surround tendons and help reduce friction in areas that are undergoing constant movement such as the wrists, ankles, fingers, and toes.

MUSCLE CONTRACTION

It may seem ironic that in the quest to make your muscles bigger, they are in effect getting "smaller" every time you exercise them. But don't worry as this only applies at the cellular level. Physiologists explain the contraction of muscles with what has popularly become known as the sliding filament theory.

Those two proteins discussed earlier, actin and myosin, are arranged in bundles which are lined up across from one another. When a muscle contracts, the actin of one fiber attaches to the myosin of another fiber. The myosin then undergoes a conformational change (sort of like Dr. David Banner turning into the Incredible Hulk) which causes it to bend and drag or pull the adjacent fiber along. It then reverts back to its old form and detaches from the actin. The whole process repeats in a leap frog manner with adjacent fibers sliding past one another (you now see where the theory of sliding filament comes from – are these people original or what).

What we neglected to mention is that the whole attaching, sliding, detaching, is dependant on such ions (charged atoms) as calcium, sodium, and potassium. Many readers probably recognize these ions as electrolytes – those substances heavily promoted by sport's drink manufacturers. If the body is depleted of such ions then muscle contraction is impaired. The diuretics taken by bodybuilders to shed water and "rip" up also increase electrolyte excretion. Many a contest bodybuilder has cramped up backstage (Paul Dillett at least twice) and a couple have even died (Hans Sallmeyer, Mohammed Benaziza).

TYPES OF MUSCLE CONTRACTION

Physiologists have sub-divided muscle contraction into five main categories. The first three, twitch, treppe, and tetanus, have little or no application to bodybuilding.

The simplest, twitch, is a short duration, low force contraction that may or may not be noticeable. In many cases twitches can only be detected by advanced medical equipment. Most readers have probably noticed twitches while sitting down watching TV or reading a magazine. The forearms and thighs are the most common sites, but twitches can occur in any muscle. Those involved in severe accidents may experience twitching in the facial muscles.

Treppe involves a gradual increase in contractions until a steady tension is reached. After a short period of time the muscle fatigues (usually from calcium depletion) and the contractions cease.

Tetanus occurs when a muscle never gets a chance to relax between contractions. The condition of lockjaw is one such example. It is caused by a virus (bacteria) that interferes with proper muscular contraction of the jaw muscles. This is why you have to get that rather large needle in the butt if you are unlucky enough to have been bitten by a wild animal (no, pre-contest bodybuilders don't count).

Ronnie Coleman

ISOMETRIC VERSUS ISOTONIC CONTRACTIONS

We left these two till last as they have the most application to weight training.

The most common type of muscle contraction is called isotonic and involves the familiar shortening of the muscle as it contracts. When you do that set of biceps curls, the biceps muscles are contracting against gravity and shorten, thus drawing the forearm towards the upper arm. The name isotension comes from isos meaning equal and tonos meaning tension.

Isometric contractions occur when a muscle contracts against an immovable object. Pushing against a brick wall will cause the muscles in the legs and upper body to contract but no shortening occurs. The name comes from iso meaning equal and metron meaning length. Although we think of weightlifting being primarily isotonic, every exercise involves a combination of both. The muscle being exercised contracts isotonicaly, while many of the stabilizing muscles contract isometrically. In the biceps curl, the biceps contract isotonically, while the lower back and thighs (there are other muscles involved as well) contract isometrically.

Aaron Maddron

FIBER TYPES –
FAST AND SLOW TWITCH

Why is it that two seemingly identical individuals can end up dominating two entirely separate forms of exercise? Why is it that some individuals can bench 500 pounds for a single rep, but still only manage 315 for a couple of reps? Yet others can bang out 315 for ten strict reps but not come close to benching 500 for a single. The answer lies in the genetic make-up of each individual's muscles. What we are referring to here is fiber types – specifically fast and slow twitch.

Fast twitch muscle fibers are designed for rapid firing. The muscles of the eyes and hands are two such examples. Fast twitch muscles contain an over abundance of energy-producing organelles called mitochondria. They also have faster nerve conduction due to a large network of calcium-supplying sarcoplasmic reticulum. On the other hand fast twitch fibers tire easy as they have low levels of myoglobin, the primary oxygen-binding protein that increases the rate of oxygen diffusion into muscle fibers. Fast twitch fibers are found in muscles that are used for short bursts of power.

Slow twitch muscle fibers are designed for steady state, long term contractions. They do not tire as easily as fast twitch fibers. As they fire much slower than fast twitch, their calcium supply is lower. Conversely they have a large amount of oxygen-binding myoglobin to prolong their duration of contraction. The muscles of the lower back (spinal erectors) that keep us upright all day are primarily slow twitch.

Besides their physiological make up, fast and slow twitch muscles are different colors. As slow twitch muscle contains a proportionally larger amount of myoglobin, the muscle has a reddish color to it. On the other hand the lower amount of myoglobin gives fast twitch muscle a pale, white appearance. The terms "red" meat and "white" meat come from such myoglobin differences. Chickens cannot fly because their primary wing muscles (the breast) are mainly white, fast twitch muscle fiber. Conversely ducks, can fly long distances with the predominately red, slow twitch breast muscles. Your poultry eating will never be the same!

Finally, fast twitch muscle fibers take longer to recover from workouts than slow twitch. For example it may take a predominately fast twitch muscle like the hamstrings 72 to 96 hours to recover, while a slow twitch muscle like the soleus may only take 48 hours, and in some cases in as little as 24.

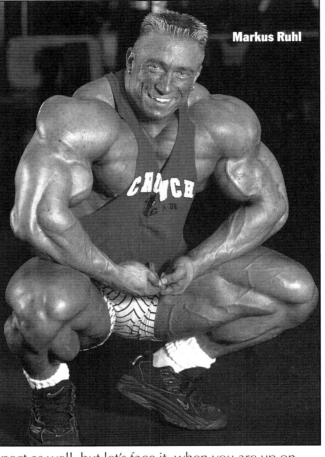

Markus Ruhl

MUSCLE GROWTH!

Unless there's something we don't know, chances are most readers are primarily interested in one thing – muscle growth!

Sure many of you want the strength aspect as well, but let's face it, when you are up on stage, who cares what you can lift. The judges certainly don't. They're only interested in your size, symmetry, definition, and how well you present it.

A few years ago we would have said that there is one theory to explain muscle growth. But alas things are a changing. Scientists now have good evidence to suggest a second theory to account for muscle growth. Within a few years there very well may be a third.

"Despite all the articles and advertisements to the contrary in muscle magazines and bodybuilding books, the fact is not everyone can develop a top level physique. Under the law of the land we may be equal, but it is obvious that some people are superior to others."

– Greg Zulak, *MuscleMag International* columnist telling it like it is with respect to the genetic element in bodybuilding.

HYPERTROPHY

Hypertrophy is defined as the increase in the size of a muscle because of an increase in the size of the individual muscle fibers. When a muscle is subjected to a form of resistance (i.e. lifting heavy weight) the muscle fibers, for want of a better term "break down." Over a short period of time they are repaired, but slightly bigger and stronger. This is an adaptive response that prepares the body for the next weight lifting session. Over a period of years the constant breaking down and building up results in much bigger and stronger muscles. At one time it was thought, that all things being equal (i.e. training, diet etc,), a person with few muscle fibers could never hope to build the same degree of muscle mass as someone more favorably blessed. But research carried out over the last five years gives hope to those genetically challenged!

> **"The great news is that you can do a lot with average genetics, especially if you are willing to stay in the race for the long term. The only reason that a trainer usually reaches his or her genetic potential, expressed in terms of size and strength, in roughly four or five years, is that most people get stuck in a pattern of always training with the same weight, the same exercises, and eating exactly the same way."**
>
> – Ron Harris, *MuscleMag International* contributor outlining how bodybuilding success is based on more than genetics.

Flavio Baccianini

HYPERPLASIA

It first started with animal studies, but then the same results were seen in humans. Researchers found that when cats were run through a period of resistance training, those animals that engaged in exercise not only had stronger muscles, but, and here's the important thing, showed evidence of increased muscle fibers. In other words, two became four so to speak. The animals' bodies modified the muscle fibers not only by increasing their size but also their number. Big deal you say, what about humans? Well, a 1996 study published in the *Journal of Applied Physiology*, found that 6 out of 11 test subjects (human subjects we might add!) showed an increase in the total number of muscle fibers after 12 weeks of resistance training.[1]

Researchers are not sure just how the increase takes place. The most popular theory is that some of the fibers initially present, split and become separate muscle fibers. This is feasible as muscle fibers are really cells after all, and most other body cells split or replicate all the time.

MUSCLE ANATOMY

Hopefully by now you are beginning to get an idea of just how complex human physiology really is. It's now time to start looking at the muscles as separate entities and how they relate to bodybuilding.

The human body contains approximately 430 skeletal muscles. We can't give you a precise number because even the world's top anatomists can't decide if a particular structure is one muscle or two. The human body evolved long before *Grey's Anatomy* came into being.

And it did so out of necessity not convenience. As might be expected we have no intentions of discussing all 430! Instead we'll look at the major muscle complexes in the human body.

NAMING

Anatomists use a number of different variables to name muscles. The following are the most common naming characteristics. Keep in mind many muscles are named by a combination of the following.

Shape – The early anatomists recognized that some muscles had geometrical shapes that could be easily seen. For example the large muscles of the upper back/lower neck had a trapezoid shape so they were given the name trapezius. The adjacent shoulder muscles had a deltoid shape, so, you guessed it, were called deltoids (deep stuff what!). Finally the gracilis muscle is named as such because of its long, slender shape.

Size – Some muscles are named based on their relative sizes compared to related muscles. The best examples of this are the gluteus maximus and gluteus minimus, and pectoralis major and minor.

Location – Muscles such as the supraspinatus and infraspinatus are named because of their positioning on the body. Supra means above and spinatus refers to the spine of the scapula (shoulder blade). The tibialis anterior is located in front of the tibia (lower leg bone).

Tho-mass Benagli

Attachment Sites – Most muscles are attached to bones and anatomists take advantage of this in their naming systems. For example the sternohyoid is attached to the sternum and hyoid bones.

Number of Heads – This is probably the most popular naming system and refers to the number of parts or "heads." The biceps have two heads, the triceps three, and the quadriceps four. The prefixes bi, tri, and quad, all come from the Latin, and mean two, three, and four, receptively.

Direction of Muscle Fibers – The names of some muscles indicate the direction of their fibers with respect to their attachment structures. For example the tranversus (across) and obliquus (slanted or oblique).

Shawn Ray

CLASSIFYING MUSCLES BASED ON ACTION

Besides the previous, anatomists use other terms to describe muscles. With the primary function of muscles being to cause movement, anatomists use various terms to describe what type of movement or action a particular muscle causes. The following table is a brief summary:

Muscle Type	Action
Flexor	Bending so the angle between the bones decreases
Extensor	Bending so the angle between the bones increases
Dorsiflexor	Bending the foot dorsally (toward back of foot)
Palmar flexor	Bending wrist ventrally (toward palm)
Plantar flexor	Bending foot at ankle toward sole of foot
Abductor	Movement away from center of body
Adductor	Movement towards center of body
Pronator	Turning forearm so palms face downward
Supinator	Turning wrist so palms face upward
Rotator	Turning around a longitudinal axis
Levator	Movement in an upward direction
Depressor	Movement in a downward direction
Protractor	Movement in a forward direction
Retractor	Movement in a backward direction
Tensor	Make a body part more rigid or tense
Sphincter	Reduces size of an opening

ORIGIN AND INSERTION

When a muscle contracts one of the attached bones remains stationary while the other moves with the contracting muscle. Although things are not as simple as that, for convenience we say the part of the muscle attached to the stationary bone is called the origin, and the part attached to the moving bone is called the insertion.

Jean-Pierre Fux

AGONISTS AND ANTAGONISTS

Just as a Shakespearean play contains agonists and antagonists, so too does the muscular system have the forces of good and evil. Anatomists use the term agonist to describe the muscle that is responsible for the desired movement. Curling the forearm upwards is primarily due to the contracting biceps so in this case the biceps are the agonists. In the same movement the opposing muscle, the triceps, relaxes, so we call it the antagonist. Unlike our Shakespearean analogy, the antagonist does not oppose the agonist but by relaxing, actually helps it.

By now many readers probably see the disadvantage of rigidly enforcing the terms agonist and antagonist. What happens when you do triceps pushdowns? In this case the triceps is the primary mover so it becomes the agonist, while the opposing biceps relax, so technically they are now antagonists. With the possible exception of the shoulders, most muscles work in pairs and such can be agonists or antagonists depending which is contracting and which is relaxing. Here are a few examples:

Biceps – Triceps
Chest – Back
Quads – Hamstrings
Abdominals – Spinal erectors

Notice we left the shoulders out. From a training point of view the deltoid muscles are probably the most unique in the entire body. Where most other muscles have opposites or partners, the deltoids stand alone. For an explanation we need to look at evolution.

The human muscular system evolved to help it move against gravity. Just about every plane of movement a human can move the body or move another object, a muscle system comes into play. But, and here's the key, humans did not develop large muscles to push downwards because gravity does it for us. We need powerful muscles to lift things up (the deltoids) but if we want to put that object down we drop it and good old Newtonian physics takes over. If you question our argument, the next time you're in the gym stretch your arms out straight and grab both handles of a cable crossover machine. Now push downwards. If you are lucky you may be able to push twenty-five or thirty pounds, but that's it. Conversely most readers can probably press a hundred pounds or more over their head.

LEVER SYSTEMS

Not counting the Bill Kazmier's and Manfred Hoebels' among you, we are confident most of you can't lift a car. Yet if we gave you a long crowbar, odds are you could lift the rear end off the ground. Such is the power of levers that even an average strength individual can jack up a one ton car and change a flat tire.

The human body is a marvel in engineering and for those of you who only see things in biological terms, your workouts are as much physics as physiology.

The movements of most skeletal muscles are accomplished through a series of rigid level arms pivoting around a fixed point called a fulcrum. Also acting on the lever and fulcrum are two forces 1) the weight to be moved, and 2) the applied force that moves or lifts the weight. In the human body the bones act as the levers, the joints as the fulcrum, and the muscles as the applied force. As the playground see-saw is perhaps the most well-known lever system, well use it as the prototype when describing the body's three types of lever systems.

Mike and Midajah O'Hearn

FIRST CLASS LEVER

In a first class lever system the force is applied at one end while the weight to be moved is at the other end. The fulcrum is located between the two. The farther the applied force from the fulcrum, the more weight can be lifted. This is why you can lift much more weight with a long crowbar than a short one. In the human body the pivoting of the cranium (skull) on the atlas is an example of a first class lever.

SECOND CLASS LEVER

In a second class lever the applied force is at one end, while the fulcrum is at the other. The weight to be moved is located in between. The closer the weight to be moved is located to the fulcrum, the more weight can be lifted. The common, everyday wheelbarrow is an example of a second class lever system. The best example of a second class lever in the human body is the calf muscle. The balls of the feet act as the fulcrum, while the applied force is represented by the calf muscles. In this case the entire body plus the weight stack resting on your shoulders (or knees) is the weight to be lifted.

THIRD CLASS LEVER SYSTEMS

This is the most common type of lever system in the body and involves having the weight to be moved at one end, the fulcrum at the other end, and the applied force close to the fulcrum. Lifting clay with a shovel is a perfect example of a third class lever. The next time you do biceps or hamstring curls you are making use of a third class lever. The applied force is generated by the biceps, the fulcrum is the elbow, and the weight to be moved is the forearm plus the barbell (or dumbell).

STRENGTH APPLICATIONS

Not counting a few frat parties you'd probably like to forget, chances are you use a screwdriver to remove the tops from most cans. When muscles use a lever system they gain what is called mechanical advantage or leverage. Not counting identical twins, everyone has different length bones and muscle attachments. This is why some smaller individuals can out-lift larger, more muscular people. They have better body levers. A muscle that has an insertion relatively far from a joint has more leverage than one that is attached close to the joint. It's the old long versus short crowbar scenario. An analysis of top powerlifters and Olympic lifters would show a proportionally greater number of mechanically advantaged individuals than the normal population. Most 123-pound individuals can't lift three times their body weight over their head – a feat that a couple of the best Olympic lifters have done. So the next time some muscularly-challenged individual right off the street out-lifts you on the bench press, don't take it personally. Odds are this individual owes his or her strength to an accident at birth – i.e. genetics!

OTHER REASONS FOR STRENGTH WITHOUT AN INCREASE IN MUSCLE MASS

We just looked at how the principle of levers allows a smaller individual to out-lift a larger, more muscular person. Besides levers, there are a couple of other variables that influence strength. Researchers have discovered that weight training can increase the coordinated firing of nerve motor units. A single motor nerve may control up to 1000 individual muscle fibers. The more motor units firing simultaneously, the greater the force generated. In a manner of speaking the muscle gets stronger not because of increased size but increased efficiency. It can do more with what it has available.

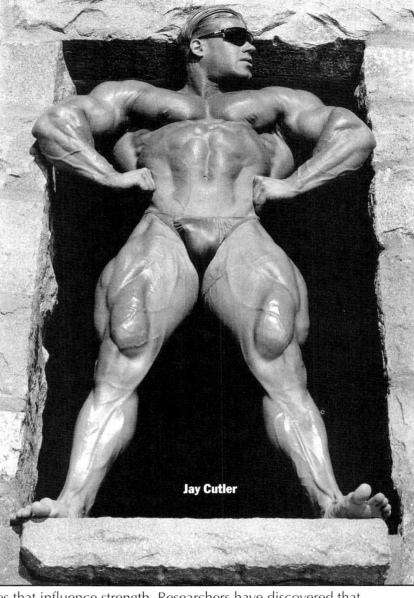

Jay Cutler

"I too have seen skinny little geeks challenge 300-pound monsters to a little arm wrestling competition and have been amazed that many times the little geek has won."

– Chris Confessore, *Powerlifter* and *MuscleMag International* columnist, commenting on the "size is not everything" scenario when it comes to strength.

A second variable for strength concerns the relationship between agonists and antagonists. As time goes on the body learns to decrease neural activity to the opposing muscle group. This means less resistance to the agonist or contracting muscle. What we have here is a case of the muscles getting stronger because the body "learned" how to get stronger.

A final mechanism of action to explain increased strength is neural activity. Muscles are controlled by electrochemical energy. The simple term is nerve stimulation. It has been found that regular weight training increases the amount of neural activity to the muscles. Further, changing the exercises every few weeks seems to keep increasing the degree of electrical activity, while performing the same exercises seems to decrease electrical activity.

THE MAJOR MUSCLES

Chris Cormier, Kevin Levrone, Ronnie Coleman and Shawn Ray

Earlier we mentioned that the human body contains over 400 muscles. For practical purposes we are going to discuss the major muscles that apply to bodybuilding i.e. the ones that do most of the lifting and score you the most points on stage. In many cases bodybuilders use abbreviated names when referring to some of the muscles. For convenience we'll use both the anatomical and "gym" name(s) (in brackets) in the following descriptions. And to keep things simple we will not use technical insertion and origin points when describing the muscles' location. For most bodybuilders are not concerned that the soleus attaches to the fibula and tibia bones and inserts on the posterior surface of the calcaneus tendon. Instead we'll give a general anatomical location (in the case of the soleus it's the lower part of the calf muscle that's located on the lower and outer edges of the tibia and fibula) as it relates to training. For those who wish a detailed description of muscular insertion and origin, we suggest either a copy of a first year anatomy text, or the bible of anatomy, *Grey's Anatomy*.

Soleus (lower calf) – The soleus is located on the lower and outer edges of the fibula and tibia bones of the lower leg. Its function is to plantar flex the ankle joint (i.e. point the feet away from the lower legs). To fully activate the soleus muscle the knees must be bent when flexing at the ankle joint.

Gastrocnemius (upper calf) – The gastrocnemius is located on the upper outer edges of the tibia and fibula of the lower leg. Its function is to plantar flex the ankle joint and flex the lower leg at the knee joint. To fully activate the gastrocnemius the legs must be kept relatively straight when flexing at the ankle joint.

Biceps femoris (hamstrings) – The biceps femoris is located on the back of the large femur bones of the upper legs. Its functions are to flex the lower leg at the knee joint, and extend the thighs at the hip joint.

Rectus femoris, Vastus lateralis, Vastus intermedius, Vastus Medialis, (Quadriceps, Quads, thighs) – All four heads are collectively known as the quadriceps and are located on the sides and front of the large femur bones of the upper legs. All four muscles extend the lower legs at the knee joint; and the Rectus femoris also flexes the thighs at the hip joint.

Rectus abdominis (abdominals, abs) – the abdominals run from the hip bones up to the lower ribs and sternum. The abs have numerous functions including flexing the lumbar (lower) spine, depressing the rib cage, and stabilizing pelvis during walking and running.

Pectoralis major (pecs, chest) – The pecs are connected to the clavicle (collarbone) and the sternum and ribs 1-6 on one end, and the upper humerus bone of the upper arm on the other end. The pecs adduct and rotate the arms medially.

Pavol Jablonicky

Latissimus dorsi (lats, back) – The lats attach to the iliac crest, thoracic and sacrel vertebrae, and upper humerus. The lats depress, rotate, and retract the scapulas (shoulder blades), as well as medially rotating the upper arms at the shoulder joint.

Trapezius (traps) – The traps attach to the occipital bone of the skull and vertebrae C7 (cervical) to T12 (thoracic) of the spinal column. The traps elevate, retract, and rotate the scapulas.

Rhomboids – The rhomboids attach to vertebrae between C7 and T5, and the medial border of the scapula. Their primary function is to retract and elevate the scapula.

Deltoids (delts, shoulders, front delts, side delts, rear delts) – The deltoids attach to the clavicle, scapula, and humerus bones. The front delts draw the arms forward (flexion), the side delts raise the arms to the side (abduction) and the rear delts draw the arms back (extension)

Biceps (biceps, bis) – Both the long and short heads of the biceps attach to the scapula at one end (origin) and the radius at the other (insertion). The biceps flex the forearm at the elbow, and supinate the forearm.

Triceps (triceps, tris) – The long head attaches to the scapula, while the lateral and medial heads attach to the humerus (origins). All three heads insert on the ulna. All three heads extend the forearms at the elbows.

REFERENCES
1) *Journal of Applied Physiology*, 81, 2004-2012, 1996.

Roland Cziurlok

CHAPTER THREE

Strength Training Principles and Concepts

This chapter can be considered a hodge-podge of advanced concepts and principles that make up the science of bodybuilding. A couple, like sets and reps, are common to most, while others like dynamic variable resistance and time under tension will probably be new to most.

Dan Freeman

> **"I'll let you in on a little secret. When it comes to developing muscle every system works. But it doesn't work forever. Eventually your body adapts to the method of lifting employed and gains stop. It happens whether you are using heavy duty, high sets/high reps, power training with heavy weights for low reps, or doing supersets, trisets, forced reps, or cheat reps. No one system works continuously."**
>
> – Robert Kennedy, *MuscleMag International* publisher and editor summing up the various training styles – they all work, and then they all don't work!

REPS

Probably the most fundamental variable associated with bodybuilding is the term "rep." In its simplest form a rep is one complete movement of an exercise. It involves both the upward lifting of the weight against gravity, and the downward resisting against gravity. Kinesiologists use the term positive or concentric contraction to describe the raising portion, and negative or eccentric, to describe the lowering portion. Bodybuilders have long focused on the raising positive half of reps, but in recent years the negative portion of the reps has been found to be just as important if not more valuable for developing strength and size. Later in the book we will be describing negative reps in more detail. Suffice to say negative reps allow you to use heavier weight than the positive portion. In other words you can lower more weight in a slow and controlled manner than you can lift in a positive manner.

> **"Personally I don't count reps because they're instinctive.**
> **I'm a big believer in using your instinct and intuition."**
> —Aaron Baker, top IFBB pro offering his views on reps.

Perhaps the most common question pro bodybuilders are asked at seminars is "how many reps should I do?" And the answer is, it all depends on your goals. If your primary goal is pure strength, then the suggested range is 3 to 5. Conversely if your primary goal is maximum size, then reps in the 8 to 12 range are generally recommended. But keep in mind there is a great deal of overlap between the two. In most cases when you get stronger, you will also gain some muscle mass. Likewise size increases are usually accompanied by strength increases. But there's another variable that must be considered as well, muscle fiber type.

Earlier we saw that muscles are composed of both fast and slow twitch muscle fiber, with each being geared towards different activities. As no one knows for sure just what their ratio of fast to slow twitch muscle fibers is, it may take some experimentation to find which rep range works best. Many great bodybuilders like Nimrod King and Serge Nubret, found that sets composed of 15 to 20 reps were more productive than those in the traditional 8-12 range. Others such as Dorian Yates, Michael Francois, and Casey Viator, obtained great results using heavy weight for 4-6 reps. It generally takes a couple of years for an individual to determine the best rep range suited to their individual genetics. As a matter of fact most bodybuilders find alternating high reps and low reps the most productive.

Aaron Baker

TIME UNDER TENSION

In recent years a different guide has evolved to determine the best rep range, this being the total time the muscle is under resistance or tension. Research has shown that to recruit the most muscle fibers, the muscle must be under tension for between 45 and 60 seconds. Such strength researchers and coaches as Dr. Wayne Wescott and Charles Poliquin use the term "time under tension" to indicate the duration of time a muscle is working against a given resistance. Charles Poliquin has also popularized the term "tempo" to integrate time under tension and number of reps.

"The optimum reps/set scheme is one that maximizes the important components of muscular fatigue, muscular density, cardiovascular density, and muscular endurance."

– John Parrillo, *MuscleMag International* columnist, commenting on the different variables that must be taken into account when designing a program.

Let's say you want to do ten reps on the bench press. This equates to approximately six seconds per rep (60 divided by 10 equals six). You have a couple of options of performing the reps in terms of speed. You can take two seconds to raise the weight, and four seconds to lower it, thus emphasizing the negative portion of the rep. You can do the reverse and raise it in four seconds and lower it in two seconds, thus emphasizing the positive portion. Or you can do an even three up, three down, and give equal consideration to both concentric and eccentric contraction. The two extremes of five and one, or one and five can also be done but lowering or raising the weight in one second drastically increases the stress placed on the tendons and soft tissues of the joint regions.

Another example would be to perform six-rep sets. In this case each rep will take approximately ten seconds. Conversely 20-rep sets will be done in approximately three seconds.

Curtis Leffler

So far we've divided tempo into positive and negative portions, but there's a third variable you can incorporate and that's pausing the weight. Besides raising and lowering the weight you can pause for a short time period at the top of the movement. If you decide to incorporate pausing into your routine it would look something like this on paper:

Bench press 3 sets of ten reps, 212 tempo
2 seconds raising
1 second pause
2 seconds lowering

SETS

In discussing reps we've made mention of sets without defining the term. Hopefully by this point in your bodybuilding career, you know that reps are combined into groups called sets. Next to reps, sets are the other fundamental term in bodybuilding and also the subject of their own confusion!

There are two schools of thought when it comes to how many sets of an exercise to perform during a workout. These two styles go by many different names, but for convenience we are going to use the terms "Classical" and "High Intensity."

"A number is just a number, and numbers can be deceiving. Like the scale weight of a muscular man at 180 pounds, compared to the scale weight of a fat man at 180 pounds, the number means nothing. The two may weigh the same but the visual effect is vastly different. Keep that in mind when deciding on sets and reps and listen to what your body is telling you along the way"

– Charles Glass, top trainer and *MuscleMag International* columnist outlining how getting fixated with numbers can have its drawbacks.

Jeff Poulin

THE CLASSICAL SYSTEM

The classical system of sets is by far the most popular training style in bodybuilding history. Virtually every top bodybuilder of the last fifty years has used the classical system. By classical we mean performing three or four sets of three or four exercises for each major muscle group during each workout. Everyone from Steve Reeves and Reg Park, to Arnold Schwarzenegger and Ronnie Coleman, used or uses the classical system of training. As the majority of this book is devoted to the classical system we will leave it at that and take a closer look at the high intensity style of training.

HIGH INTENSITY AND HEAVY DUTY

In many respects high intensity is the polar opposite to the classical system of sets. Instead of performing multiple sets and exercises for each muscle group, you do just one, all out, high intensity set to failure. That's it. Not one set more.

High intensity training owes much of its existence to the works and writings of Dr. Arthur Jones, inventor of the Nautilus line of equipment, and former Mr. America and Mr. Universe, Mike Mentzer.

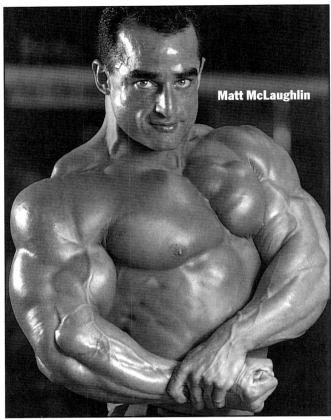

Matt McLaughlin

"At the time my reaction was "come on! What possible good could one set a week of squats do for you?" I quickly dismissed the man as a raving lunatic – and a bastard to boot."

– Mat Wilson, *MuscleMag International* contributor, not holding any punches in commenting on the one set to failure theory of training

Dr. Arthur Jones is one of the most colorful characters associated with the science of strength training. He's also one of the most knowledgeable. Even those who don't subscribe to Jones' theories grudgingly admit that his research has played a key role in highlighting the problems associated with overtraining.

Dr. Jones conducted a number of studies (primarily back in the late sixties and seventies) that compared high volume training (i.e. the classical system) with high intensity training (one set to failure). According to his research the high intensity style of training produced results just as significant as the classical system. Further he also discovered the classical system left many in a state of nervous and physical exhaustion; what sports physiologists now call overtraining. He even argued that those who did make progress on the classical system were not getting out of it what they put in to it. To use a business analogy, their investment far surpassed their returns.

Dr. Jones applied his theories to a new line of training equipment, which he called Nautilus; named after the squid-like marine creature whose shell resembled the primary moving part on his machines – cams. Nautilus centers sprang up all over the U.S. in the seventies, with members performing one set per body part during their workout. In and out the door in fifteen minutes, two to three times per week.

Despite making Jones a wealthy man, and despite making significant in-roads with the general population, high intensity training never caught on with hardcore bodybuilders. It would take someone bodybuilders could relate to, to make them stop and consider that maybe, high intensity training did have a place in bodybuilding.

MR HEAVY DUTY – MIKE MENTZER

It's no exaggeration to say former Mr. America and Mr. Universe, Mike Mentzer, has done the most to sell Jones' theories to bodybuilders. Mentzer refined and repackaged high intensity training and called it Heavy Duty. He did his "preaching" in his monthly article in Joe Weider's *Muscle and Fitness* magazine. He also wrote two very successful books, *Heavy Duty 1 and 2*. In recent years he was featured regularly in *Muscular Development* magazine.

Mike took Jones' one set to failure and modified it by having the individual extend the set past positive failure by including such advanced techniques as rest pause, supersets, and strip sets. If Jones was forceful about his theory, Mike was passionate. In fact his single-minded devotion to Heavy Duty is probably the main reason why he's not taken as seriously as he should be. Further, his articles in *Muscular Development* during the mid to late nineties, tended to dwell as much on philosophy as hardcore training. That's too bad as Mike's general philosophy that most beginner and intermediate bodybuilders are in a state of overtraining because of too many low intensity, high volume sets, is basically sound. With a few exceptions, most pro bodybuilders these days are doing fewer sets and exercises than their counterparts twenty or thirty years ago. Most recently, six-time Mr. Olympia, Dorian Yates, has said that Mike Mentzer's writings have heavily influenced him and he usually only does two exercises for 2 to 3 sets each. But, and here's perhaps the biggest argument to Mike's one set to failure ideology, there has never been a bodybuilder who won a top title while following Heavy Duty. A few may have switched to high intensity after years of the classical system. But no one has followed Heavy Duty from day one and went all the way to the top, and believe it or not, this includes Mike himself. During his competitive years in the seventies, Mike spent considerable time following the classical system of bodybuilding. It was only after he won the Mr. America and Mr. Universe titles that he started devoting more time to high intensity, both practical and from a marketing perspective.

Mike Mentzer

"I think a very advanced person can benefit from Heavy Duty training for short periods of time – especially when they've plateaued from their regular routine and are overtrained. But it's totally unsuitable for beginners. Yes you can take the volume thing too far but intensity is not the only factor influencing gains."

– Greg Zulak, *MuscleMag International* columnist, commenting on the role Heavy Duty training may play in bodybuilding.

Our stand on Heavy Duty is, it will probably work for most, but only for a short time period, say four to six weeks. Most who switch from classical to high intensity initially make progress because the extra rest allows them to recover from the chronic state of over-training they are in. But after a month or so, they bottom out on high intensity. In theory one set to failure may be sound, but it's just not practical for most. For one thing Mike's definition of to failure is far above the average bodybuilder's. Such stress can play havoc with the adrenal system. Another issue is that there is more to building a physique than all out muscle stimulation. It takes many sets and reps over long periods of time to hit all the different muscle fibers, not to mention the network of blood vessels and nerves that innervate such musculature.

A final consideration, and one Mike has agreed with, Heavy Duty is not fun! One all-out, ass-to-the-floor set for each muscle is downright painful. And while Mike argues that the extra time saved can be put to other useful endeavors, let's face it, spending an hour or two in the gym is part of the social experience that goes with bodybuilding.

TIME BETWEEN SETS – IS THERE A BEST REST INTERVAL?

The time you rest between sets is called the rest interval, and once again generalizations take precedent over specifics. Different goals mean different rest intervals. Individuals engaged in competitive sports will train differently than those working out for recreation. And then there's powerlifting, Olympic lifting, and bodybuilding.

Bruce Patterson

Before looking at rest intervals in more detail we should add that genetically gifted individuals or those who have their systems heavily modified with pharmaceuticals can probably follow just about any rest interval and make great progress. For such individuals all roads lead to Rome. But for the rest of us, the following guidelines should make your training as productive as possible.

IF YOUR GOAL IS STRENGTH THEN...

For those looking to maximize strength development, (i.e. increasing your one rep maximum), the general recommendation is to rest 3 to 5 minutes between sets. The rationale is that it takes approximately this length of time for full ATP and creatine phosphate supplies to return to maximum levels. Of course when we say primarily strength, keep in mind that there is bound to be some muscle hypertrophy associated with increased strength. But we doubt there's any reader who'll get too upset if they "accidentally" put on a few extra pounds of muscular bodyweight.

IF YOUR GOAL IS SIZE THEN...

The proper name for increasing muscle size is hypertrophy and primarily involves an enlarging of individual muscle fibers, and secondarily an increase in the number of muscle fibers. There is also evidence to suggest that fast twitch muscle fibers enlarge to a greater degree than slow twitch muscle fibers. Studies with olympic, power lifters, and bodybuilders show fast twitch muscle fibers twice as large as slow twitch muscle fibers in the same muscle. But don't bodybuilders, olympic and power lifters have different training styles and rest intervals? The answer is yes as bodybuilders usually rest 45 to 60 seconds between sets, while the other two groups wait 3 to 5 minutes. Does this mean both rest periods lead to identical results. Well yes and no!

The studies that found the difference in muscle fiber size also found that bodybuilders had enlarged fast and slow twitch muscle fibers, while Olympic and power lifters primarily had very large fast twitch muscle fibers only. No one is sure why the difference, but the guess is bodybuilders, because of their faster pace and increased aerobic activity stimulate both muscle fiber types.

So what we are left with is that both short (45 to 60 seconds) and long (3 to 5 minutes) rest intervals will produce almost equal sized muscles but of different sized muscle fiber ratios. Our suggestion is to experiment with both rest intervals.

Jamo Nezzar

IF YOUR GOAL IS POWER THEN...

Power is defined as strength over time and forms the basis of most sports. Such activities as wrestling, judo, and sprinting, require short bursts of power; while swimming, running, and rowing require a steady amount of power. Although few studies exist to recommend a precise rest interval, the volume of anecdotal evidence suggests that those involved in the former category of sports follow a shorter rest interval type of training. The reason is that short rest intervals help the body adapt to lactic acid buildup, the primary waste product associated with anaerobic exercise. That intense burning sensation you feel while doing squats is primarily the result of lactic acid. The same thing happens while running a 100-meter dash, or applying a wrestling move. This is why most strength coaches recommend following a 45 to 60 second rest interval during training. It conditions the body to lactic acid buildup, and improves the body's ability to remove it.

HOW OFTEN PER MUSCLE GROUP

Another concept that can lead to bewilderment is figuring out how often to train each muscle group. At one end of the spectrum we have the one session per week per muscle group. While at the other we find the 10 to 12 sessions or more per week devotees, popularized in Europe. Then we have the bulk of bodybuilders who hit each muscle group on average twice a week. The most important variable in determining training frequency is each individual's unique recovery system. It makes no sense to go back to the gym and train a muscle that has not recovered from the previous workout. Conversely waiting too long will only bring on excessive soreness but little improvement. Your goal when you hit the gym is to surpass the previous workout, whether by doing more reps with the same weight, using more weight for the same number of reps, or using the same weight for the same number of reps, but in a shorter time period. Many trainers and coaches these days use the term "optimal volume of training" to determine frequency of workouts, and not maximal volume. Ten high intensity sets will do more to stimulate growth and not drain the recovery system, than twenty sets of low or medium intensity.

MUSCLE MEMORY

Bodybuilders and other athletes know from experience that once they reach a certain level of size and strength, regaining that level after a layoff is far easier than getting there the first time. It may take you years to work up to a 300 or 400 pound bench press, but only a few months of consistent training to get back there after a few months off. The ability to regain lost strength and size faster after a layoff than it initially took to gain it, is called muscle memory. Physiologists are not sure of the exact mechanism of action but the best explanation seems to be the brain makes a template of the muscle's strength and size level and then files it away. It's much the same as building a house, a set of plans makes things much easier than drafting as you go. Many experts use muscle memory to explain why the one set to failure style of training seems to work better for those who have first built an appreciable amount of mass using the high volume classical system of training. Once the mass is built, holding on to it, improving on it, or regaining it, can be accomplished with far fewer sets than needed to build it in the first place.

Robby Robinson

Muscle memory is also something to keep in mind when debating as to whether or not to take a layoff. Many bodybuilders become so obsessed with size that they refuse to take any time off fearing they'll lose size and strength. This "fear of shrinking" usually leads to a state of over-training. This in terms leads to stagnation and in some cases a loss of strength and size! Ironic isn't it that the very thing that is believed to build size and strength can lead to its loss (we'll say more in the section on overtraining in the chapter on injuries).

Suffice to say taking a few months off will not lead to an appreciable loss of size and strength. And the small amount you lose can easily be regained because of muscle memory. A solid month of training will bring you back to about 90 percent of your pre-layoff level (assuming a four to six week layoff). The layoff will also do wonders for all those minor aches and pains which most bodybuilders have but can't seem to get rid off. In most cases they are the result of tendonitis, the cure for which is rest.

INDIRECT MUSCLE STIMULATION – THE SPILL OVER EFFECT

Indirect muscle stimulation, more popularly called the "spill over effect" was first recognized and written about by Nautilus inventor, Dr. Arthur Jones. Dr. Jones noticed that weight trainers who only performed a few basic exercises developed size and strength in all their muscles

Jean-Pierre Fux

groups, not just the ones being selected targeted by exercise. Jones used the analogy of throwing a rock into a pond and watching the ripples move outwards. Jones proposed that training one muscle causes an indirect growing effect on other muscles and that the bigger the muscle being worked the greater the "spill over effect." Performing heavy squats will increase arm size because the legs are fifty percent of the body's mass and they produce an enormous spill over effect. Likewise training the biceps stimulates the legs but to a much smaller degree because the biceps are proportionally very small as compared to the legs.

Without going too far out in left field, astronomers use much the same logic when searching for planets around distant stars. Even though they can't see the planets they know they are there because the planets' gravity causes changes to the star's orbit (astronomers use the term "wobble"). Granted stars because of their size have a bigger effect on planets than planets do on stars, but nevertheless a small body can effect a larger one. Are you still with us? Think of your legs, chest, and back, as stars, and the biceps, triceps, and individual shoulder heads, as planets. Training the bigger muscles has a greater effect on the smaller muscles than the other way around. What does this mean for bodybuilders? (you knew we'd get around to this sooner or later!) It means that to develop maximum size in all your muscles you should focus most of your energy on the basic exercises that stimulate the larger muscle groups. Busting your ass doing squats, barbell rows, and barbell presses will not only build you great leg, back, and chest muscles, but they also do wonders for the biceps, triceps, and shoulders.

A NEW LOOK AT EQUIPMENT

By the very nature of their inventories, modern gyms can be confusing and intimidating. In fact Romania's Vlad the Impaler (the real-life inspiration for Dracula) would probably be envious of the assortment of machinery housed in a large commercial workout center. Pulleys, cams, barbells, ropes, plates, equipment straight out of a medieval dungeon. And the outcome might be the same if used incorrectly – torture!

Despite the variety in shape, size, and method of operation, all forms of training equipment have one primary function, to provide resistance for muscles to work against. In the case of dumbells and barbells, the resistance is constant, while some of the newer machines increase or decrease tension with time (called variable). One of the most frequently asked questions in bodybuilding (and the pros can vouch for this) is which is the best type of equipment to use.

Liane Ohigashi, Matai Lorenze, Kristine Prall, Marc Troy Kenolio, Allison China

"A lot of old-school bodybuilders scoff at machines as being useless for adding size. Nothing could be further from the truth, especially in chest training. I believe some chest machines, particularly the Hammer Strength lines are superior to barbells."

– Ron Harris, *MuscleMag International* contributor adding his voice to the free weight machine debate.

There are five primary pieces of equipment you can use for training. Barbells and dumbells are the simplest and most common, and with the exception of some "glitzy" health spas, found in every gym. Cable machines have the weight stack attached to a series of pulleys and provide continuous tension on the muscle. Smith machines are sort of halfway between regular machines and barbells in that you have to put the weight on the bar like a barbell, but unlike a barbell the machine is balanced. Most gyms usually have one or more lines of strength training machines that target all the body's muscle groups. Some machines like Nautilus use a series of cams and chains to lift the weight. Hammer Strength is very simplistic and has the moving parts rotating on simple bearings and hinges. Finally such brands as Keiser rely on hydraulic power to increase or decrease tension.

Here are brief descriptions of some of the more popular types of training tools.

DYNAMIC CONSTANT RESISTANCE

Perhaps the simplest type of training, constant resistance as the name suggests involves no change in the tension over time. The direction of the movement may change, but the tension on the muscle remains constant over time. It is identical from top to bottom. Most free weight exercises and some machines are based on the constant resistance principle.

DYNAMIC PROGRESSIVE RESISTANCE

This is perhaps the most popular form of exercise for rehabilitation of injuries. In this case the resistance increases progressively as you exercise. The best examples of progressive resistance are rubber bands, springs, and machines controlled by spring-loaded parts. The nice thing about such apparatus (not counting the latter) is that they are cheap and can be taken anywhere. Although of limited benefit for hardcore bodybuilders they provide a welcome relief to joints constantly subjected to the stress of free weights and machines.

DYNAMIC VARIABLE TRAINING

In a manner of speaking, this type of resistance picks up where constant training leaves off. Instead of a constant tension throughout the full range of a movement, the machine can be adapted to put less or more stress on a muscle depending on the muscles' varying strength points. We have to be honest in that even the machines designed with this concept strictly in mind don't always deliver.

Without sounding like an advertisement, the Strive line of equipment probably comes closest to the ideal. The machines are designed to allow the user to increase or decrease resistance at the beginning, middle, or end of an exercise. The end result is a tailor made movement that suits your muscle's idiosyncrasies.

ISOKINETIC RESISTANCE

With "iso" meaning the same, and "kinetic" meaning movement, this form of training involves keeping exercise speed the same during a set. Most machines based on this principle are hydraulically operated. The opposing forces mirror each other throughout the range of motion. Isokinetic exercises are among the safest available. Instead of building up momentum as with free weights, the joints are never subjected to sudden increases in resistance.

ISOMETRIC RESISTANCE

The best example of this type of training can be found in the back pages of millions of comic books. You know the old ad we mentioned earlier in the book about the guy getting sand kicked in his face, only to come back later and drop the guy with one punch. The originator was none other than Charles Atlas, and his exercise booklet was based heavily on isometric exercises. As the name implies the muscle neither lengthens nor shortens during the exercise. In other words the force of contraction equals the force of resistance. As an example put your hands together and push. Unless you are considerably stronger on one side of the body, no movement occurs, but we are sure you'll agree both arms are under tension. Likewise push against a stationary object such as a brick wall. Your chest,

Lee Priest

shoulders, and triceps are contracting very forcefully but no muscle lengthening or shortening takes place. If isometric training has a disadvantage, it's that the muscle only strengthens at the point of the contraction. To strengthen the muscle evenly you would have to perform numerous "sets" at the different points along the muscle's movement plane. Still, for rehab, or when you have no other means of training, isometric provides an alternative.

ISOTONIC TRAINING

Although similar to dynamic constant training, isotonic often doesn't involve a redirecting of the tension during a movement. Also complete immobility of the muscle throughout the movement is required. As you lift and lower the weight, the tension remains identical during both the positive and negative phase.

Henrik Thamasian

AND THE WINNER IS...

And now to answer that most basic question raised earlier. The best type of equipment to use for maximum development is all of them! We told you the answer would be simple and complex. No one form of resistance training will lead to maximum development. You can build a phenomenal physique with just free weights, but you will lack some of the detail that only specialized machines can bring out. Likewise, machine-only training will probably never give you the size and strength that some of the basic free weight exercises will provide.

Later in the book we will be looking at the routines of the sports top superstars. If there's one common denominator it's that they all use combinations of machines (all types) and free weights in their training.

INSTINCTIVE TRAINING

We could have left this concept until the very end of the book as it really ties everything together, training, diet, recovery, supplements, you name it. But as it falls under the category of advanced concepts, it fits in here quite nicely.

If there is one underlying principle in all of bodybuilding it's instinctive training. Like it or not humans are animals, and as such have built-in instincts. Most animals react out of instinct rather than conscious thought. It's possible some of the higher animals such as dolphins and monkeys may have limited thought processes, but for the most part animal behaviors are governed by pre-programming. Instincts are very powerful behavior modifiers. The lowly salmon may swim ten thousand miles back to the place of its birth, to do but two things; reproduce and die!

Mike Lackner

"I do two entirely different back workouts to achieve sufficient variety in my training. Once you get up to a certain level of experience, a workout program is really only a guideline, not a rule. You learn to train instinctively doing what feels right on any given day."

– Debbie Muggli, IFBB pro, commenting on the instinctive training principle.

Humans may have evolved well above the lower animals (although like the salmon, a few have been known to go thousands of miles for sex!), but we still retain some of our primitive instincts.

As it applies to bodybuilding, instinctive training means drawing on experience and listening to your body's signals. If the body tells you to take a day off you do so. If it says switch from light to heavy weight, then that's what you do. If you start get warning signals about a potential injury, you either cut back on the offending exercise or give it up entirely.

We should add that it generally takes a couple of years to master instinctive training. There is a very fine line between skipping a workout because of laziness and skipping because of genuine fatigue. Laziness means kicking yourself in the ass and hitting the gym. Fatigue means taking time off.

A couple of writers have criticized instinctive training saying it is too unorganized and will lead to haphazard training. This may be true for beginners and even some intermediates. At that level you need structured guidelines for safety and efficiency. But for advanced bodybuilders, rigid training can lead to stagnation. You have to experiment with different techniques and programs, not be a slave to conformity.

Once you master instinctive training, you will be in full control of your destiny. Think of the information in this book as the paint, and your are the master painter. Pick and choose your 'colors' to create that masterpiece – in this case your physique.

CHAPTER FOUR

Advanced Training Techniques

"Oh it's nothing to worry about. You are finished that's all."

– Krusty the clown giving Bart Simpson some advice after Bart's popularity disappears after his short-lived stint on the Krusty the Clown Show.

It's inevitable that sooner or later muscles will become stubborn and refuse to grow in response to normal training techniques. – Jean-Pierre Fux

"Have you ever noticed how so many guys come into the gym and do the same exercises every time? They always do the same exercises and the same sequence of exercises. They use the same amount of weight and the same number of reps and sets. And the funny thing is, they usually look the same too – year after year."

– Greg Zulak, *MuscleMag International* columnist commenting on some individuals who are a slave to conformity.

You can consider this chapter to be your initiation into hardcore training. The groundwork has been laid and now it's time to get down and dirty so to speak. The following techniques will shock your muscles into new growth. If you are like most bodybuilders the straight sets you've been following initially made great changes to your physique, but now you've plateaued. It's inevitable that sooner or later muscles will become stubborn and refuse to grow in response to normal training techniques. What happens is that they have accustomed themselves to the same routine day after day, month after month. To use a familiar drug term, they have built up tolerance to your program. Of course this is where we come in. What follows is the full spectrum of advanced training techniques that bodybuilding experts have evolved over the years. Some of them are very simple and most readers have no doubt already

Mike Francois

tried them. Others are alien and will take time to master. Our advice is to select a couple and work them into your training program. Please don't make the mistake of trying to do all of them during one workout. Such training is very taxing on the recovery system and you'd last about two weeks before nervous exhaustion set in. Try adding a few of them every week or so and then see your tailor about expanding your wardrobe size!

TIME OF DAY

Although ignored by many writers, sometimes the key to new growth is very simplistic. The body is a very peculiar machine, and it constantly adapts to repetitive routines. It "knows" that at 5:30 P.M. it will be doing nine sets of one muscle group or other. If your daily schedule allows (and the gym has good hours of operation), try coming in a few hours later, or even better before work or school in the morning. Numerous bodybuilders report that even though the rest of their program remained the same, a simple change in workout times kick-started their systems in the same manner that a total revamping would.

TYPES AND ORDER OF EXERCISES

Another simple technique is to change the exercises you perform for each muscle group. Odds are most of you have done this by now. Let's face it, performing the exact same exercises week in, week out, is the quickest way to stagnation. You'll see what we mean the first time you do it. Notice how sore your muscles are? That increased soreness is due to the muscles becoming accustomed to the same movements. Changing the exercises hits the muscle from a slightly different angle.

"Unless you've been in the iron game for 20 years we're willing to bet you haven't tried everything. Exhausting possibilities is important and no one's brain is powerful enough to think up alone every possible variation. In fact if you are anything like a typical bodybuilder you are probably long on desire and short on patience."

— *MuscleMag International* editors, commenting on the role variety plays in bodybuilding.

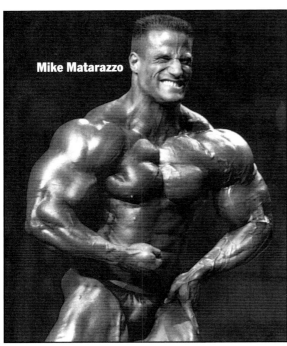

Mike Matarazzo

Sometimes it's not even necessary to change the exercises. Let's say you always start your chest training with flat barbell presses, and then finish with barbell or dumbell inclines. Try doing your inclines first and leaving barbell flats until the end. Chances are you'll notice the upper chest far sorer than ever before. Once again the chest muscles "know" that flats always come first and they are ready for it. But come into the gym and bang out inclines first in your routine and you catch the chest off guard.

We know both suggestions are not exactly the latest scientific breakthrough in bodybuilding, but does it really matter if they work? You know the old saying, the shortest distance between two points is a straight line. Sometimes you have to adopt the same philosophy to your bodybuilding.

CHANGING MUSCLE COMBINATIONS

Most bodybuilders quickly discover that some muscle groups go better with other muscle groups. Common combinations include chest and back, quads and hamstrings, and biceps and triceps. We should add that there is no "right" way to combine muscles, at least as a general statement. Try a number of groupings and see which feels most comfortable. This would then be the "right" combination for you. Now you could follow this pattern for the rest of your life (and a few bodybuilders have), but chances are the body would quickly adapt. It's now time to shift things around. If you normally train chest with back, try putting chest with shoulders. Likewise you could put triceps and biceps on different days. The choices are endless. The bottom line is that as soon as you feel the muscles adapting and getting stale, file the divorce papers and split them up! Here's a few sample muscle combinations.

Chest – Back – Biceps
Legs – Shoulders – Triceps
Legs – Arms
Chest – Back – Shoulders
Chest – Thighs – Triceps – Shoulders
Back – Hamstrings – Biceps
Chest – Shoulders – Triceps
Legs – Back – Biceps

"You can ensure variety by constantly changing your workout split. You should do this often because your body becomes accustomed to any established pattern. Introducing variety to retain some sense of sanity with an activity that can become repetitious by its very nature benefits the mental side of training."

– Charles Glass, top trainer and regular *MuscleMag International* columnist commenting on the need for variety in your training.

CHANGE REPS AND SETS

This is one of the easiest means of increasing the intensity of your workouts. Most bodybuilders start with 4 to 6 sets per muscle group, and then graduate to 8 to 12. A few genetically gifted or pharmacologically enhanced may even go up to 20 sets per muscle group. It seems bodybuilding comes under the "more is better" umbrella as well!

While a few authorities outright reject adding sets to training programs, the accepted practice is to increase workout volume as time goes on. As soon as the muscles adapt to the basic routine of two exercises of three sets, the norm is to add one or two exercises until 9 to 12 total sets per muscle group are being performed. In most cases this will stimulate the muscles to keep growing. Of course a point of diminishing returns is reached and adding extra sets may actually decrease results.

Charles Glass

Besides adding sets, another basic shocking technique is to change the rep range. You don't know what pain is until you perform a set of hi-rep squats or leg presses. Instead of loading the bar with huge poundages, drop it by 40 or 50 percent and blast out a set of 30 or 40 reps. We guarantee your thighs will be sore the next day. It's quite possible you won't be able to walk properly for a week. But it just goes to show you how stale the muscles had become. You can take this approach with every muscle group.

CHEAT REPS

Cheat reps are probably the first advanced technique bodybuilders learn. They are also one of the most abused. In a manner of speaking the term cheat rep is misleading as the technique is one of the most effective means to stimulate muscle growth, provided it's executed properly.

The concept behind cheating is simple. When you can no longer execute a given number of reps with a selected weight, you add just enough body momentum and assistance from other muscles to keep the weight moving. Now in theory this sounds straight forward, but it's the simplicity that leads many bodybuilders astray.

Let's say you are doing barbell curls for 10 reps. The first two sets go as planned and you manage to squeeze out 10 strict reps, but just barely. You know that there's no way you are getting 10 reps on the third set. You have three choices. You can drop the weight a few pounds and complete the set. You can have a training partner give you a spot on the last couple. Or, and this is where cheating comes in, you can leave the weight as is and commence the set knowing that you are probably going to fail at rep 7 or 8. This would still be a quality set, but you can improve on it and here's how. When you get the last strict rep using biceps and forearms alone, gently bend forward at the waist and add just enough body momentum to swing the weight up. Perform two or three reps in this manner and terminate the set. To really derive the greatest benefit from cheat reps, concentrate on lowering the weight as slowly as possible.

You would think that with such a simple concept, gyms would be filled with bodybuilders executing cheating properly, but such is not the case. In fact there's probably more who abuse the technique than use it properly. The problem you see is one of Sigmund Freud's novel concepts – the ego. Nothing sounds as impressive as being able to say you can "curl" 150 or 200 pounds. Next to bench pressing and squatting, curling is one of the status lifts in most gyms. You know, such and such has a 220-pound barbell curl. Yet when you observe such and such, you see he has more body contortions than the cast of Lord of the Dance. In fact his biceps are probably only con-tributing 20 to 25 percent of the strength needed to curl the bar. This we assure you is not productive use of the cheating principle. It may sound impressive to the less informed, but other than the flatter-ing the guy's ego, little benefit is being derived.

Proper cheating means per-forming about 75 to 80 percent of a set in strict style, and only then bringing in secondary muscles to assist in completing an additional two or three reps. It does not mean loading the bar or machine with so much weight that you have to cheat from the first rep. Just as supple-ments don't replace food, so too are cheat reps not meant to replace good form.

Before moving on to the next topic we should briefly discuss some of the exercises that lend themselves to cheating, and those that should never be performed in less that perfect style.

To really derive the greatest benefit from cheat reps, concentrate on lowering the weight as slowly as possible.
– Don Long

CHEAT EXERCISES

Barbell curls – This exercise is perfect for cheating on and we can almost bet that every reader has cheated on this one at some point in their lives. It only takes a slight bend at the waist and swing of the upper body to keep the weight moving. You shouldn't however, have to do partial bentover rows to lift the weight up. If it takes the thighs, lats, and entire bodyweight to complete the set, we really question what you are trying to do.

Lying leg curls – As the hamstrings are nothing more than leg biceps, you can use the hips and lower back to cheat up an additional few reps towards the end of a set. As a word of caution, however, excessive arching of the lower back puts tremendous pressure on the lower back ligaments and spinal column. If you have lower back problems you may want to give cheat reps a pass on this exercise.

Pulldowns – Most bodybuilders cheat on this exercise by swinging the torso back as they pull the bar downwards. Of course the key is to swing just enough to enable you to pull the bar to the collarbone. Some individuals will actually swing back until their torso is nearly parallel with the floor. We caution against this as the human spine was not meant to, excuse the expression, be "jerked around" like this.

Lying triceps extensions – Done strictly, this exercise isolates the triceps. But you can bring the chest and back into the movement by bringing the bar past the forehead and doing a sort of half pullover.

Lateral raises (front and side) – These are two other exercises that bodybuilders tend to abuse the cheating principle on. There should be little or no body sway as the dumbells are lifted upwards. At the end you can rock the body just enough to raise the dumbells and then concentrate on lowering them slowly.

Leg presses – Correct cheating on leg presses does not mean using your knees like elastic bands and bouncing off the chest. Such foolishness increases the pressure on the knees enormously. Instead gently push on your legs with your hands to complete a few extra reps.

Start

Finish

Chris Cormier demonstrates the leg press.

Done incorrectly, squats can put you in traction for six months. – Jean-Pierre Fux

DO NOT CHEAT EXERCISES

Squats – Hopefully we don't have to go into detail as to why you don't cheat on this one. Performed correctly, squats are probably the single best leg exercise. Done incorrectly they can put you in traction for six months. It's not worth destroying your lower back or knees for a few extra degrees of stimulation. Not to mention running the risk of collapsing under a bar loaded with a couple of hundred pounds of weight!

Deadlifts – As with squats, deadlifts are not conducive to cheat reps. The risk of tearing the lower back is too great.

Bench Presses – Bouncing the weight off the chest, or arching the lower back to squeeze out a few additional reps is dangerous to say the least. Yet this is what most bodybuilders do when benching. Contrary to popular belief, most shoulder injuries are not caused by shoulder training, but by chest training. And the bench press leads the pack when it comes to tearing the small shoulder rotator muscles. How many regular trainers in your gym have "bad shoulders?" Quite a few no doubt. In most cases it's from poor form on flat and incline barbell presses. When it comes to cheating on bench presses – DON'T!

Some of you may have noticed a common theme to the previous. It's easier (and safer) to cheat on exercises involving flexor muscles like biceps, hamstrings, and lats, than extensor muscles like chest, thighs, and triceps. We are not saying you can't cheat on the latter. In fact most bodybuilders probably do at one point in their lives. But from a safety and effectiveness point of view, flexors are the most conducive to cheat reps.

NEGATIVES

It only makes sense to follow cheat reps with negatives as both compliment each other. As discussed earlier, a rep has two phases, raising and lowering. Research has all but confirmed that both are equally important for muscular development. But go into any gym and you'll see guys lobbing up weight and then dropping it with little or no control. Not only are they losing 50 percent of the exercise's effectiveness, but they are setting themselves up down the road for a severe injury. The reason is the tremendous stress placed on the joints at the point the weight changes direction at the bottom of the movement.

Negatives are based on the fact that a muscle is capable of lowering more weight in a slow and controlled manner than raising it. You may be only able to curl 120 pounds for strict reps, but chances are you can lower 150 to 175 pounds in similar style. Some exercises like the previously discussed barbell curl are ideal for performing negatives as you can swing the weight up into the top position and then lower it in a slow manner. Likewise the lateral raise is a great movement for doing unassisted negatives. Other exercises, such as the bench press, or shoulder press, will necessitate the presence of a spotter. After you go to positive failure on the initial reps, have your partner assist in lifting the weight to the top position and then slowly lower it downwards. In most cases you will be able to perform 3 to 5 good, clean, controlled reps before you are unable to lower it in safe style.

Besides adding negatives to the end of a set, you can perform an entire set of negatives. Select a weight that is 25 to 50 percent heavier than what you can lift normally. With your partner ready to assist, lower the weight to the bottom position and then both of you return it to the top starting position. Repeat for the given number of repetitions. As a guide if you take 5 seconds to lower the weight, perform 10 to 12 reps. If you take 10 seconds to lower the weight, perform only 5 to 6 reps. Although it varies, a good rule of thumb is to keep the muscle under tension for 50 to 60 seconds.

As with cheat reps, there are a couple of exercises where negatives are potentially dangerous. For obvious reasons avoid negative squats. Most people find that muscles have a habit of "dying" or "giving out" without much warning. In other words you get a good rep and think there's one or two left, but as soon as you start lowering the weight you find you have no control. On a bench press your partner can grab the bar and together both of you can rack it. On squats, however, the amount of weight would be almost impossible to stop, even with a strong spotter behind you. This is especially true if you collapse without warning. If you want to do negatives for thighs, load up the leg press and have two spotters, one on either side of the machine. Between the three of you, you should have no trouble raising the weight to the starting position.

PARTIALS

Partials fall in the same category as cheat reps in that used properly they are terrific for increasing the intensity of a set. But unfortunately they can be easily abused and actually decrease the effectiveness of a set.

As the name implies, partials are reps that don't involve the muscles' full range of movement. Let's say you are doing a set of lying leg curls and you reach positive failure on the 10th rep. You have the option of stopping or you can raise the weight partial way up and then return to the starting position. The odds are you can squeeze out another 4 to 6 reps in this manner before you can even raise the weight from the starting position.

Start

Finish

Besides being an excellent way to finish off a set, partials have a role to play in overcoming sticking points. – Mike Lackner performing lying leg curls.

Finish

Because of the intensity of 21s, you will not be able to use your normal curling weight.
– Roland Kickinger

Start

Partials probably got their biggest boost from bodybuilding's first Mr. Olympia, Larry Scott. He called partials "burns" and attributes them to playing a major role in building his famous arms. Larry was particularly fond of doing partials on preacher curls (often referred to as the Scott bench in his honor).

Besides being an excellent way to finish off a set, partials have a role to play in overcoming sticking points. Most people find the weakest point in their bench press is about three-quarters of the way up. You can use partials to solve this by setting the pins in a power rack a couple of inches below your sticking point. Now load the bar with more weight than normal – 25 to 50 percent – and lower it down to within an inch or so of touching the pins and then return to the starting position. The advantage of doing partials is you can subject your muscle's sticking point to more weight than normal. Once you have the weak link strengthened then there should be no problem locking out on full range reps.

Most things have negative points and partials are no exception. Loading up a bar with more weight than you can handle for full reps is great for overcoming sticking points, but partials should not make up the bulk of your training. Partials only strengthen the muscle fibers associated with that part of the rep range. If you don't let the bar all the way down on barbell curls, then you will only be strengthening the biceps in the upper part of the rep. Your biceps will not be deriving much benefit towards the locked out position, i.e. when the arms are hanging straight down close to the thighs. Only use partials to finish off a set after 6 to 12 full reps have been executed, or on specific exercises to overcome sticking points.

21s

21s can be considered two partial rep sets rolled into one. Basically divide a set into two halves, bottom to mid point, and mid point to top. Let's use the barbell curl again as an example. Curl the bar from the bottom, arms locked out position, to the mid-point, arms roughly parallel with the floor. Perform 7 reps in this manner and then on the 7th rep curl the bar all the way up and then lower to the mid-point and do another seven reps in this manner. On the 7th rep (really rep 14) lower the bar all the way and attempt to perform 7 full reps. If you choose your weight correctly you should be able to complete 21 reps, made up of 14 partials and 7 full reps. Because of the intensity of the technique, you will not be able to use your normal curling weight. In fact you will probably need to drop it back to the 50 percent range.

Don't let your ego get in the way either. If someone comments about the "lightness" of the weight, politely ask them to try a set. We assure you they won't be so eager to comment next time.

As with many other advanced techniques, 21s work better with flexor muscles than extensors. It's easier to perform 21s with the biceps, hamstrings, and abs, than the chest, shoulders, and triceps; although the authors have witnessed the technique being used on triceps pushdowns and lower back extensions. In theory it will work with any exercise but in practice things are not that simple.

As with most shocking techniques, the body can quickly adapt so we suggest limiting 21s to once every two or three weeks. This way the body never adapts and you get the full benefit.

DOWN THE RACK OR STRIP SETS

After performing a given number of reps to positive failure you are faced with three options, have someone give you a spot, cheat the weight up and concentrate on negatives, or do a few partials (the fourth option is to put the weight down!). Well there is another method to keep the set going and it involves something very basic to weight lifting. If you can't lift a given weight, decrease it. Let's say you do 8 good reps on the lat pulldown and want to do a couple more.

Tho-mass Benagli and
Enzo Ferrari

Stop for a second and drop the pin two or three plates and then continue. Your lats and biceps may not be able to handle, say 200 pounds when fatigued, but they should be able to lift 170 for a couple of additional reps. You can even drop the weight a second time, down to say 120 and get 2 or 3 more reps. Dropping the weight on a machine, or taking a couple of plates off a bar is called "stripping." Of course you can perform the same technique using dumbells. In this case the phrase "down the rack" is applied. The next time you perform dumbell laterals, put two successively lighter sets on the floor in front of you. Perform the standard 6 to 12 reps to positive failure and then drop the first set and grab the next lightest set. Try to select the weight so that you can only perform 4 to 6 reps with the second set of dumbells and then grab the third, lightest set of dumbells. Carried to the extreme you could literally work your way down a dumbell rack, doing 4 to 6 to 8 drop sets.

Unlike many of the previous techniques where we cautioned against doing some exercises, strip sets can be performed on just about any resistance movement in a gym. Just make sure on exercises like squats and bench presses, that you have a spotter close by to keep an eye on you. At the very least it's embarrassing to be stuck under a barbell. At the worst it could drastically increase your health insurance payments!

SUPERSETS

Supersets are both a great way to save time and jazz up your workouts. Supersetting involves selecting two exercises and performing them back to back with as little rest as possible between them. There are two primary categories of supersets, those for the same muscle, and those for opposing muscles. Most bodybuilders perform supersets for opposing muscles.

Here are examples of both.

Supersets are both a great way to save time and jazz up your workouts. Superset upright rows with dumbell presses.
– Dennis Newman
Finish

SAME MUSCLE SUPERSETS

Quads –	Squats/Leg presses
	Leg presses/Leg extensions
	Hack squats/Leg presses
Hamstrings –	Lying leg curls/Stiff-leg deadlifts
Chest –	Bench presses/Dumbell flyes
	Incline barbell presses/Incline dumbell presses
Back –	Seated rows/Front pulldowns
	Chins/Barbell rows
Shoulders –	Front presses/Lateral raises
	Dumbell presses/Upright rows
Biceps –	Barbell curls/Seated incline curls
	Cable curls/Standing dumbell curls
Triceps –	Lying barbell extensions/Narrow presses
	Pushdowns/Bench dips
Abs –	Leg raises/Crunches
	Reverse crunches/Reverse crunches
Forearms –	Wrist curls/Reverse wrist curls
	Wrist curls/Standing reverse curls

Start

"Try to think the action into your lower pecs. Rest about a minute between supersets and aim for a good pump in the lower chest."

– Robert Kennedy, *MuscleMag International* publisher and editor commenting on the advanced training technique of supersets.

OPPOSING MUSCLE SUPERSETS

Chest and Back –	Flat bench presses/Front pulldowns
	Incline barbell presses/Barbell rows
Thighs and Hamstrings –	Squats/Lying leg curls
	Leg presses/Stiff-leg deadlifts
Biceps and Triceps –	Lying barbell extensions/Barbell curls
Incline dumbell curls –	Dumbell extensions
Abs and Spinal Erectors –	Crunches/Back extensions

Gunter Schlierkamp

You'll notice we left out shoulders. Unlike most of the body's other muscles, the shoulders don't really have an opposite muscle group – at least not in the same size range. Muscles evolved to work against gravity, and since the shoulders lift the arms upwards, there really wasn't a need to "evolve" an opposing muscle group to push downwards, as gravity does it for us. If something needs to be pushed down we can easily adapt other muscles to do the job for us. Now the evolutionary biologists among you are probably cringing at such a simplistic description, but for practical bodybuilding purposes, this is essentially how things work. Some bodybuilder's superset incline dumbell flyes and bent-over dumbell laterals as both movements are very similar. And in a manner of speaking the upper chest is opposing the rear delts. Remember the human body evolved long before humans started classifying and categorizing things!

TRISETS

From memories of school mathematics you know that the prefix "tri" means three. Trisets are one of the logical extensions of supersets. In this case select three exercises for a given muscle group and try to perform them with little rest in between. Going from the first to the second exercise should be straightforward, but going from the second to third may be difficult. In all probability you will need to drop the weight on the last two exercises.

Besides saving time, trisets offer the advantage of being able to hit the muscle from different angles. Where one exercise will activate so many muscle fibers, three will involve them all. Here are a few examples:

Thighs –	Leg presses/Leg extensions/Squats
Hamstrings –	Lying leg curls/Stiff-leg deadlifts/Back extensions
Chest –	Flat bench presses/Incline dumbell presses/Pec-dek
Back –	Chins/Front pulldowns/Dumbell pullovers
Shoulders –	Lateral raises/Dumbell presses/Reverse pec flyes
Biceps –	Cable curls/Dumbell curls/Narrow reverse chins
Triceps –	Pushdowns/Two-hand dumbell extensions/Bench dips
Abs –	Leg raises/Reverse crunches/Crunches
Forearms –	Wrist curls/Reverse wrist curls/Standing reverse curls

Markus Ruhl

GIANT SETS

If trisets severely "thrash" muscles, giant sets will kill them. Giant sets involve grouping four or more exercises together and performing them back to back. As with supersets and trisets the objective is to rest as little as possible between exercises, but by the time you get to the third and fourth, you may need to stop and catch your breath. If giant sets have one practical limitation it's they are difficult to perform in crowded gyms. You finish one exercise and just as you are ready to proceed to the next, someone jumps in front of you. Of course you have the option of doing all dumbell exercises but most prefer a mixture of free weights and machines. Our advice is to pick a slow time at your gym for giant sets. For most gyms this is usually late nights or mid mornings. Weekends are also a good time as most people spread their workouts out unlike weekdays where people live their lives around the common 9 to 5 schedule.

Here's a giant set for each major muscle group. We suggest doing no more than two revolutions (8 to 10 sets) for each muscle. And no more than once every week or two.

Thighs –	Squats/Leg presses/Leg extensions/Hack squats/Sissy squats
Hamstrings –	Lying leg curls/Stiff-leg deadlifts/Back extensions/High and wide leg presses
Chest –	Flat barbell presses/Incline dumbell presses/Pec-dek/Cable crossovers/Pushups
Back –	Chins/Seated rows/Front pulldowns/Dumbell pullovers
Shoulders –	Dumbell presses/Lateral raises/Reverse pec-dek/Upright rows
Biceps –	Barbell curls/Incline curls/Cable curls/Narrow reverse chins
Triceps –	Lying barbell extensions/Narrow presses/Pushdowns/Bench dips
Abdominals –	Leg raises/Crunches/Reverse crunches/Rope crunches
Forearms –	Wrist curls/Reverse wrist curls/Standing reverse curls/Wrist roller machine

REST PAUSE

The technique of rest pause is based on the fact that a muscle will regain much of its strength within a ten-second-time period. Here's how you employ it in your workouts. Select a weight and go to positive failure at a given number of reps. When you complete the last rep, stop, count to ten and then resume trying to squeeze out as many reps as possible, which for most people is somewhere between 4 and 6.

Rest pause is one of the most strenuous ways to train. We strongly suggest you limit such sets to the last set of a three set combination. Once a week is probably sufficient as any more may push you over the edge into the "overtraining" zone.

As with strip sets, rest pause can be performed on just about any exercise. Just make sure you have a spotter handy for those movements where safety becomes an issue.

Finish

Incline barbell presses – Greg Kovacs

Start

PRE-EXHAUSTION

Although others were probably doing pre-exhaustion before him, *MuscleMag International's* Robert Kennedy was the first major writer to discuss the technique in detail back in the late 1960s.

You have probably noticed that on some movements it's not the primary muscle that fails first but auxiliary muscles. For example the front shoulders and triceps usually give out before the chest on such exercises as flat and incline barbell presses. The way to get around this, however, is by pre-exhaustion. This means performing an isolation exercise first to tire out the primary muscle and then doing a compound movement where the smaller secondary muscles can assist the target muscle. Let's go back to chest training to illustrate. Start with a set of dumbell flyes to fatigue the chest. Then finish with a set of flat or incline barbell presses. Because the chest is already fatigued from the flyes, the triceps and front shoulders are now proportionally stronger and can be used to push the chest fibers past the normal fatigue point.

"The second pre-exhaust movement I'd suggest is the straight arm lat pushdown. This is another way to pre-exhaust the lats because the biceps are not involved at all."

– Greg Zulak, *MuscleMag International* columnist offering a tip on pre-exhausting the lats.

Another great combination is front barbell presses and dumbell lateral raises. By doing the laterals first the front delts and triceps can assist the side shoulders on an exercise like front barbell presses. The following are some other examples of pre-exhaustion combinations:

Thighs – Leg extensions/Squats or Leg presses
Chest – Flat (or incline) flyes/Flat (or incline) barbell presses
Back – Straight-arm pushdowns or pullover machine/Barbell rows
Shoulders – Dumbell lateral raises/Front barbell presses
Biceps – Incline dumbell curls/Standing barbell curls
Triceps – Lying barbell extensions/Narrow presses

Start

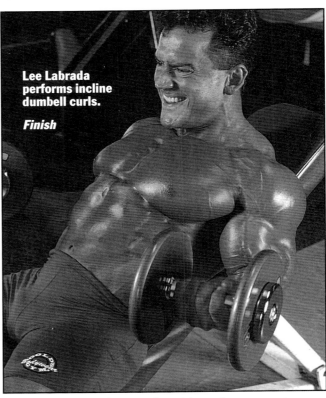

Lee Labrada performs incline dumbell curls.

Finish

PYRAMIDING

Pyramiding involves decreasing your reps as you increase the weight with each progressive set. Then after a couple of sets using your heaviest weight, you begin lowering the weight and increasing the reps. If you write things out on paper it looks like a "pyramid," hence the name. Here's an example using the bench press:

SETS	WEIGHT	REPS
1	135	15
2	185	12
3	225	10
4	275	8
5	275	8
6	225	10
7	185	12

Bruce Patterson

"Avoid going to muscular failure (the point at which you can no longer complete a rep correctly) until you reach your heaviest set. That way your energy reserves are not depleted nor is there any build up of waste products."

– John Parrillo, *MuscleMag International* columnist offering advice on the light warm-up sets performed before back-slope pyramids.

Pyramids fall into three categories, full, front slope, and back slope. Full pyramids involve increasing and decreasing the weights and reps as described in the previous paragraphs. Front slope pyramids involve increasing the weight and decreasing the reps, and then terminating the exercise. Back slope involves just the opposite, a decrease in weight and corresponding increase in reps. Here are examples of front and back slope pyramids:

Front slope pyramid for lat pulldowns

SETS	WEIGHT	REPS
1	80	15
2	140	12
3	200	12
4	240	8
5	240	8

Back slope pyramid for dumbell lateral raises

SETS	WEIGHT	REPS
1	45	6-8
2	45	6-8
3	35	10-12
4	20	12-15

We should add that "pure" back slope pyramids have an inherent safety issue. Starting with a heavy weight without a warm-up is potentially dangerous. In the previous example it would make far more sense to perform one or two light sets to get the blood into the muscle before launching straight into the 45s. Of course many readers may argue that by doing a few light sets you have now converted a back pyramid into a full pyramid! In a sense this is true but the difference is the intensity put into each set. For a full pyramid you go to positive failure on both the front and back slopes. In other words the lighter sets at the beginning are also playing a role in muscle stimulation. On the other hand the light sets conducted during the back slope pyramid are primarily for warm-up and not carried to failure.

STAGGERED SETS

Unless you are a genetic abnormality, you'll notice that some muscles respond better than others do. And more often than not, the lagging or stubborn muscles are the calves. Some people grow calves by looking at weights, other blast them mercilessly and they still won't grow. Staggered sets are one way to do extra work for a muscle group without necessitating spending extra time in the gym.

On most exercises you wait between a minute and a minute and a half between sets. This is more than enough time to do another set in between. A set of squats or bench presses is not practical as it would require too much energy and interfere with the primary muscle you are working. But a small muscle group like the calves doesn't take much energy expenditure. Sure, they may hurt like hell, but performing a set of calf raises should not interfere with the primary muscle you are training that day.

Jay Cutler blasts his calves between sets.

Besides calves there are a few other muscles that lend themselves to staggered sets. Dumbell side laterals don't require much energy and can be fitted in between sets for say legs or back. We wouldn't suggest doing them between chest exercises as your shoulders play a role in chest training and tiring them out would reduce your chest exercise poundages.

Another small muscle group is the abs and you can throw in a set of crunches or leg raises between most exercises. The only exception might be squats as the abs are used for stabilizing the torso. Tiring them out would put extra stress on the lower back, and this is the last thing you want.

Finally the forearms fall into the same category as the calves. They hurt like hell to train but don't really take much out of you while training. On leg days try inserting a few wrist curls between sets. We say leg-days as most upper body exercises require a strong grip and fatiguing the forearms would decrease the effectiveness of upper body training.

10 X 10

This is one of the oldest advanced training techniques but deserves a second look. With all the attention given to state-of-the-art machines and training, some of the sport's simplest yet most effective programs are being overlooked. Ten sets of ten reps or 10 X 10 as it's popularly called, goes back to the early days of Muscle Beach. In recent years it has become popular as a main ingredient in the German Volume style of training.

Many people find that it takes two or three sets of an exercise before the muscle is fully warmed up and they start getting anything out of the exercise. If you are following the traditional three sets per exercise routine, then the first exercise is often wasted on bringing the muscle up to peak efficiency. Ten sets of ten is one way to get around this. Instead of selecting three exercises and performing three sets each for a total of nine sets (not counting warmups) you pick one basic exercise and do ten straight sets.

Besides simplicity, ten sets of ten is a great way to increase your strength on a particular exercise. If for example your goal is a stronger bench press, three sets twice a week is probably not enough stimulation to produce maximum strength. From a bodybuilding perspective, three different exercises will probably build more muscle, but for increasing strength levels on one basic movement, ten sets of ten is superior.

You can perform ten sets of ten on any exercise in your routine. We suggest, however, utilizing the technique on basic, compound movements. The following are good candidates for ten sets of ten:

Squats
Leg presses
Barbell presses (flat and incline)
Front shoulder presses
Deadlifts
Barbell rows
Chins
Barbell curls
Narrow presses
Crunches
Standing calf raises

Squats are a good exercise to perform ten sets of ten. – Ronnie Coleman

Ronnie Coleman

BOOK TWO

THE BIG THREE: CHEST, BACK AND SHOULDERS

CHAPTER FIVE

Rock Hard Pecs

Jay Cutler

> **"The chest requires training with a variety of exercises to develop the upper and lower pectorals, the inside and outside pectorals and tie-ins to the deltoids."**
>
> – Curtis Schultz, *MuscleMag International* contributor offering advice on chest training.

It's safe to say that literally hundreds of thousands of bodybuilders first took up the sport upon spotting pictures of Arnold Schwarzenegger on the cover of old issues of *Muscle Builder Power*, the forerunner of today's *Muscle and Fitness* magazine. Arnold (with honorable mention to Sergio Oliva) was the first bodybuilder to combine massive size with shape and proportions. From those freaky calves to his baseball-sized biceps, the Oak's physique was the envy of millions. Although there's an argument to be made that Arnold's arms and calves were his best body parts, few could dispute the fact that his chest was one of a kind. Those two slabs of meat hung down like two plates of armor and struck terror into most of his fellow competitors back in the 1970s. Even by today's standards, few can turn sideways and duplicate Arnold's chest shots.

ANATOMY AND PHYSIOLOGY

The chest muscles can be subdivided into two parts, pectoralis major and pectoralis minor. While the pectoralis minor contribute to chest strength, it's the pectoralis major that bodybuilders focus on. The main reason for this is visibility, as the pecs minor are located below the pecs major and not seen in any bodybuilding pose. For the rest of this section, when we refer to the pecs or chest, we are talking about the pectorals major.

The two chest muscles are the large fan like structures located on the upper front torso, that extend laterally to the shoulders and upper arms, and originate on the sternum (breast bone). Their primary function is to draw the arms forward and downward at about a 45-degree angle. They also play a role in rotating the arms. For want of a better description, the chest muscles are the body's "hugging" muscles.

TRAINING THE CHEST

Despite the almost endless variety of chest exercises, most fall into three broad categories, all based on angles. When performed on a flat bench (horizontal to the floor) the exercise primarily hits the center and lower chest. When the bench is inclined (30 to 45 degrees with the floor) the movement primarily targets the upper chest. Finally declining the angle (30 to 45 degrees below parallel) puts most of the stress on the lower outer chest. For full chest development, a routine must include inclines and either flat or decline movements. Declines and flats are very similar and you probably don't need to perform both in the same workout. The primary benefit of declines is they put much less stress on the front shoulders. Many bodybuilders find it difficult to perform flat chest exercises after a shoulder injury. Declines allow the individual to give the chest a good workout without subjecting the shoulders to undue stress.

As discussed earlier, you have five main categories of equipment to work the chest. Most bodybuilders use barbells and dumbells as the primary strength and size builders, and then use machines and cables for refining. Of course the newer lines of equipment can be used as basic size builders as well. Like most things in life, experimentation is the key.

Chris Cormier and Nasser El Sonbaty

"The power rack is the best apparatus to use for breaking your sticking point and pushing through those stubborn lockouts on the bench. The many holes down the side columns of the rack make it especially useful."

– Curtis Schultz, *MuscleMag International* contributor commenting on one of the advantages of the power rack – breaking through sticking points on the bench press.

CHEST TRAINING EXERCISES

FLAT-BENCH BARBELL PRESSES

Execution – Position a barbell on the rack and lie down on the bench with your head between the two supports. With a slightly wider than shoulder-width grip grab the bar and lift it off the rack. Lower the bar down to the middle of the chest and then push straight up to just short of a locked out position. Repeat for the desired number of reps.

Muscles worked – The flat-bench barbell press primarily works the lower and center chest, but the front deltoids and triceps are also involved.

Comments – We are hesitant to say so but the flat-bench barbell press is probably the single best overall chest exercise. And since it also stresses the triceps and shoulders, it is one of the best overall upper body movements. The two big mistakes people make are arching the lower back and bouncing the weight off the chest. The former is dangerous as it could lead to a lower back injury, while the latter puts tremendous stress on the rib cage and shoulders.

Start

FLAT-BENCH DUMBELL PRESSES

Execution – Sit on the end of a flat bench and rest two dumbells on your thighs. As you lie back bring the dumbells to shoulder height with the elbows facing straight outwards. Push the dumbells up and inwards so that they just touch at the top. Lower the dumbells until the upper arms are a few degrees below parallel. Repeat for the desired number of reps

Muscles worked – Dumbell presses primarily work the lower and center chest but the triceps and shoulders also come into plays.

Comments – Many bodybuilders prefer dumbell presses over barbell presses as the dumbells can be lowered below chest level. Thus they give a greater range of motion. Also, unlike a barbell, which keeps the hands at the same distance, the dumbells allow the individual to push inwards at the top, giving the chest a few extra degrees of tension. The advantage of dumbells is also a disadvantage. Lowering the arms below chest level adds extra stress to the shoulder joint. Even though the option is there, you might want to lower the dumbells no lower than you would a barbell.

Jamo Nezzar blasts his chest with flat dumbell presses.

Finish

FLAT-BENCH DUMBELL FLYES

Execution – As with dumbell presses, sit on the edge of a bench and as you lie back bring the dumbells to shoulder height, this time with the hands facing inwards (i.e. the dumbells are parallel with the body). Instead of pushing the dumbells up and in, make a large circular hugging motion as you raise them. With the angle at the elbow locked, lower the dumbells down and outward. Repeat.

Muscles worked – By locking the arms the triceps are almost totally removed from the exercise. Also unlike presses, there is less front shoulder involvement. Flyes are as close to an isolation exercise as possible.

Comments – Flyes are great for those who find presses hard on the shoulder joints. They also add a few extra degrees of range of motion. As a word of caution, don't bounce the dumbells at the bottom. This is a great way to tear the pec-delt tie-in. If you are unsure how to perform dumbell flyes, check out Arnold in the documentary *Pumping Iron*.

FLAT-BENCH CABLE FLYES

Execution – Position a bench between two floor pulleys and either grab the handles yourself, or have a training partner pass them to you. Lie back and with the hands facing inwards squeeze the handles up and inwards in the same manner as two dumbells.

Start

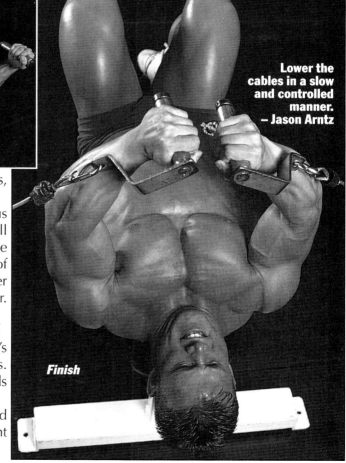

Lower the cables in a slow and controlled manner. – Jason Arntz

Muscles worked – As with dumbell flyes, cable flyes almost totally isolate the chest.

Comments – Cable flyes keep continuous tension on the chest throughout the full range of motion. Dumbells tend to lose some of their effectiveness near the top of the exercise. As with dumbell flyes, lower the cables in a slow and controlled manner.

FLAT-BENCH MACHINE PRESSES

Execution – Lie down on the machine's bench and grab the handle or handles. Push upwards, or upwards and inwards depending on the machine's peculiarities.

Muscles worked – Primarily lower and center chest, but the triceps and front shoulders also come into play.

Finish

Comments – Older model machines used a fixed one-piece handle that not only eliminated balance but also allowed the stronger side to do most of the work. The newer lines such as Hammer Strength and Atlantis have independent handles that not only force the weaker side to do its fair share of the work, but also go up and inwards, thus duplicating the chest muscles natural range of movement. While not a perfect substitute for dumbells and barbells, the newer machines come very close, and no less an authority than six-time Mr. Olympia, Dorian Yates makes heavy use of them in his workouts.

Milos Sarcev

FLAT-BENCH SMITH MACHINE PRESSES

Execution – Position a bench between the machine's vertical supports and lie back. Using a standard grip, lift the bar up and rotate slightly so the bar's hooks are free of the catches. Lower the bar to the center of the chest and push straight up to just short of locking out. Repeat.

Muscle Worked – As with flat barbell presses, Smith presses primarily work the lower and center chest, but the shoulders and triceps are also involved.

Comments – Smith presses fall in the same category as squats, you either love them or hate them. Charles Poliquin, one of the top writers and coaches in the world, states that Smith machine presses are totally useless and even dangerous. Supposedly he won't even allow them into gyms he designs. Our opinions are not as strong as Charles' are, but he has a point in that Smith presses by the machine's very design are not as effective as regular barbell presses. Despite looking like a barbell and having to put the weight plates on manually, the Smith machine is balanced. As with older designs, the Smith machine never allows the weaker side to lift its fair share of the weight. Also, the machine slides in one plane of motion (vertical or 90 degrees to the floor), which is not the chest muscle's range of motion, which is more of an arc. Our opinion is that the Smith machine makes a welcome change to barbells and dumbells, but not a pure substitute.

INCLINE BARBELL PRESSES

Execution – Position the bar on the rack supports and lie back. Grab the bar with a standard grip and raise it up and outwards. Lower the bar down just below the collarbone. Push upwards so the bar is directly above the bridge of the nose. Repeat.

Muscle worked – Done on an angled bench, barbell presses shift most of the stress to the upper chest. Because of the angle the front shoulders are stressed more than regular flat presses. The triceps are also stimulated.

Comments – Incline barbell presses are one of the best exercises for beefing up the upper chest. They are great for filling in the area around the collarbone. Those with shoulder problems will need to be cautious as the exercise does put additional stress on the shoulders, particularly the front deltoids.

INCLINE DUMBELL PRESSES

Execution – Set an adjustable bench at between 30 and 45 degrees. Hoist two dumbells to shoulder height and with the elbows pointing straight outwards push the dumbells up and inwards.

Muscles worked – Like the barbell version, incline dumbell presses primarily work the upper chest and front deltoids, but the triceps are also involved.

Comments – Some of you may find 30 to 45 degrees too steep and a shallower angle of 20 to 25 degrees may be needed to keep shoulder involvement to a minimum. Also, because of the distance the dumbells have to be initially raised, you may want to recruit one or two spotters to help you position the dumbells at the start.

Finish

Before starting incline dumbell presses, it is beneficial to have a spotter help you position the dumbells. – Jean-Pierre Fux

Start

INCLINE DUMBELL FLYES

Execution – Set an incline bench to 30 to 45 degrees and hoist two dumbells to shoulder height. With the hands facing inwards, lower the dumbells so your upper arm is just a tad below parallel with the floor. Push the dumbells up and inwards with a hugging type motion, trying to keep the elbows from bending.

Muscles worked – By not bending the elbows there is less triceps involvement than presses. Incline flyes primarily work the upper chest but the front shoulders are also involved but not to the same extent as incline dumbell presses.

Comments – As with incline dumbell presses you may want to experiment with angles to minimize shoulder involvement and maximize upper chest development. And like the flat version, avoid dropping the weight in an uncontrolled fashion. Your pec-delt tie-ins will thank you down the road!

INCLINE CABLE FLYES

Execution – Position a bench between two low pulleys and grab the handles yourself or have a partner pass them to you. From here push the cable handles up and inwards. Lower in the same manner as the dumbell version – a sort of hugging motion.

Muscles worked – Incline cable flyes work the upper chest but also bring the front shoulders into play. By keeping the elbows locked there is little or no triceps involvement.

Comments – Experiment with the bench's angle to isolate the upper chest. Also cables give you the option of crossing the handles in front of you. This will give you an extra 5 to10 degrees of motion. The drawback to this is safety. The authors have witnessed a couple of nasty knuckle gashes as a result of scrapping one hand against the other. Make sure the handles you are using are in good shape and have no sharp protrusions sticking out the bottom. You have to ask yourself whether you want to exchange stitches for a few extra degrees of motion.

Avoid dropping the weight in an uncontrolled fashion when doing incline dumbell flyes. – Lee Priest

INCLINE MACHINE PRESSES

Execution – Lie back on the machine's bench and grab the handle or handles. Push upwards or upwards and inwards depending on the machine's range of motion. Lower to the starting position.

Muscles worked – As with barbells and dumbells, incline machine presses primarily work the upper chest and front shoulders, with the triceps playing a secondary role.

Comments – Without repeating ourselves, if at all possible try to use a new model machine for this exercise. The older designs are balanced and use a one-piece handle that does a poor job of working both sides evenly. Also, if the option is there, try changing the bench's angle.

INCLINE SMITH PRESSES

Execution – Slide an incline bench over between the machine's vertical supports. From here perform the exercise like the flat version but lower the bar to the upper chest, just below the collarbone. Repeat.

Start

Muscles worked – Smith presses work the upper chest and deltoids, with the triceps playing a secondary role.

Comments – All the points raised earlier about the Smith machine apply here. This exercise is good for a change of pace, but is not as effective as barbells, dumbells, or some of the newer lines of equipment.

DECLINE BARBELL PRESSES

Execution – Lie back on the bench and grab the bar with a standard width grip. Lift the bar off the rack and lower it the lower ribcage. Push straight up to just short of locking out. Repeat.

Muscles worked – Decline presses put most of the stress on the lower and outer chest region. The angle removes most of the front shoulder involvement, but the triceps still play a role.

Finish

Comments – Declines are great for those with minor shoulder injuries that have trouble doing flat bench presses. They are also good for those who find their shoulders do most of the work during flats. Most decline racks have the bench's angle fixed, usually in the 25 to 30 degree range. If your gym has an adjustable bench, try experimenting with different angles to see which is the most effective.

If your gym has an adjustable bench, try experimenting with different angles to see which is the most effective when doing decline barbell presses. – Matt McLaughlin

DECLINE DUMBELL PRESSES

Execution – Set an adjustable bench at 25 to 30 degrees and hoist a couple of dumbells to your thighs. Lie back on the bench and bring the dumbells up to the shoulders so the elbows are pointing straight outwards. Push the dumbells up and inwards, and then lower until the upper arm is just slightly below parallel. Repeat.

Muscles worked – Decline dumbell presses work the lower and outer chest. There is some secondary triceps and front shoulder involvement.

Comments – The awkwardness of declines may necessitate having the dumbells passed to you by a training partner. Also, if your gym does not have an adjustable decline bench you can use a regular flat bench with one end propped up slightly on a board, couple of plates, etc.

DECLINE DUMBELL FLYES

Execution – Set yourself up in the same manner as dumbell presses but keep the hands facing inwards and press the dumbells upward with a circular hugging motion.

Muscles worked – Decline flyes work the lower and outer chest. There is some secondary front shoulder involvement, but little or no triceps.

Comments – Decline flyes almost totally isolate the lower and outer chest. As with all forms of flyes, avoid dropping the weights in a fast uncontrollable manner.

Flex Wheeler

DECLINE CABLE FLYES

Execution – Position a decline bench between two low pulleys and have a training partner pass you the handles. Push the handles up and inwards using the all-familiar circular hugging motion. Repeat.

Muscles worked – Decline cable flyes work the lower and outer chest with little or no triceps involvement. The front shoulders play a secondary role.

Comments – As with flat and incline flyes the option is there to cross the handles at the top of the movement.

DECLINE SMITH PRESSES

Execution – Position a decline bench between the machine's vertical supports and lie back. Lower the bar to the lower rib cage and return to the starting position.

Muscles worked – Decline Smith presses work the lower and outer chest, but the triceps and front shoulders also play a role.

Comments – All the disadvantages of the Smith machine apply here. If there is one advantage it's you can do the exercise in relative safety without a spotter. If you can't complete a rep, simply hook the bar's catches on a lower peg.

DECLINE MACHINE PRESSES

Execution – Lie back on the machine's bench and grab the handle or handles. Push up or up and inwards depending on the machine's range of motion.

Muscles worked – Decline machine presses work the lower and outer chest, with the triceps and front shoulders playing a secondary role.

Comments – To be honest, most gyms don't have decline press machines. If your gym has a flat machine press with a removable bench (such as the old Universal bench press station) you can perform declines by switching benches.

PEC-DEK

Execution – Sit in the machine's chair and either grab the handles with your hands, or place your elbows and forearms behind the vertical pads. Squeeze the handles or pads forward until they just touch in front of you. Slowly return to the starting position.

Muscles worked – Most Pec-dek machines primarily work the lower and outer chest, but the inner chest also comes into play as the handles or pad come together in front of the body. As the movement is similar to dumbell flyes, the triceps are virtually eliminated, although the front shoulders play a minor role.

Comments – Pec-deks are a great finishing exercise. Most designs have an advantage over other machines in that the handles are independent so the stronger side of the body cannot monopolize the lifting.

DUMBELL PULLOVERS

Execution – Grab a dumbell and lie across a flat bench so that the hips and shoulders are just below bench-height. Hold the dumbell vertical so that the palms are facing upwards. With the arms locked straight, lower the dumbell behind the head, and then return to the starting position so that the arms are vertical with the floor. Repeat.

Muscles worked – Dumbell pullovers work both the chest and back muscles. They also put secondary stress on the triceps.

Comments – Dumbell pullovers are one of those exercises that are hard to classify. Some individuals consider them a great chest exercise, while others feel nothing but lats. We should add that most pullover machines (described in the back training chapter) are marketed as back exercises. Our advice is to try them and make up your own mind. As a suggestion, if you are doing chest and back on the same day, do pullovers as a finishing chest exercise and warm-up for the back.

Jean-Pierre Fux pounds out one last rep of dumbell pullovers.

VERTICAL PRESS MACHINE

Execution – Sit in the machine and grab the handle or handles. Push out, or out and together depending on the machine's design. Return to the starting position.

Muscles worked – Vertical machine presses, despite the upright position, are equivalent to the flat version. That is, the stress is about 90 degrees to the body. This means they primarily work the lower and outer chest, but the triceps and front shoulders are also involved.

Comments – If your gym has a selection of machine presses, opt for the version that has independent handles that go towards the center as your arms extend. Such designs closely mimic the chest's natural movement.

If your bodyweight is not enough resistance, hold a dumbell between your legs. – Bruce Patterson

CABLE CROSSOVERS

Execution – Stand mid-way between two upright cable machines and grab the handles, one on either side. With your torso leaning slightly forward, knees and elbows slightly bent, bring the handles together at the front of the body about abdominal height. Slowly bring your arms back as if doing a dumbell fly.

Muscles worked – Cable crossovers primarily work the center chest, especially as the handles come together in front. The front shoulders also play a role, but the triceps are removed from the exercise, provided there is no bending at the elbow.

Comments – Cable crossovers play a major role in the precontest phase of training. Despite being as close to the purist chest exercise there is, cable crossovers are no where near as efficient as barbell or dumbell presses for building strength and size. Their main benefit is to shape and separate the chest muscles during pre-contest preparation. As mentioned earlier, you can cross the handles in front of you, thus obtaining a few extra degrees of motion. But make sure there's at least an inch or two of clearance between the hands. The authors have witnessed some nasty knuckle gashes from such movements.

PARALLEL BAR DIPS

Execution – Grab two parallel bars and hoist yourself up so that the arms are locked straight. With the chin resting on your chest, bend the elbows and lower down until your front shoulders are just in line with the bars. Return to the starting position by stopping just short of locking the arms out straight.

Muscles worked – One of the most basic chest exercises, dips are similar to declines in that the lower, outer chest receives most of the benefit. The front shoulders and triceps also are involved.

Comments – The late Vince Gironda considered dips the best chest exercise there is. To minimize the triceps involvement, lean slightly forward and keep the elbows flared out to the side. Also, dips require you to use your bodyweight, so they may have to be done at the first or last of your chest workout depending on your strength level. If your bodyweight is not enough resistance, even towards the end, you can either hold a dumbell between your legs, or use one of the specially designed chain apparatus that many gyms have for attaching extra weight around the waist.

Henrik Thamasian

PUSHUPS

Execution – Lie face down on a flat surface and with the feet shoulder width apart, hands pointing forward, push away from the floor until the arms are just short of being locked out.

Muscles worked – Pushups work the entire chest region as well as the front shoulders and triceps.

Comments – We thought it appropriate to end the chapter with the simplest and possibly most performed chest exercise (not counting bench presses). The mainstay of military discipline for decades, pushups can be done just about anywhere and by changing the angle you can target different parts of the chest. Elevate the legs and the lower chest takes most of the stress, while elevating the upper body brings the upper chest more into play. As with dips, pushups require the use of your body weight, which eventually may not be adequate. In this case you can have a willing partner sit on your back, or lay a plate or two between your shoulders.

ADVANCED CHEST ROUTINES

Now that you've seen the exercises it's time to assemble them into various pectoral building routines. The following routines are not meant to be followed for more than six to eight weeks. You use them to prioritize on your chest if it seems to be lagging. You'll notice we have mixed and matched to both hit the chest from different angles and vary the type of equipment used. Towards the end we will give examples of routines making use of only one type of equipment. Keep in mind the rep ranges listed are samples only. In most cases we suggest 6 to 8 reps on the first exercise as a strength and size builder and then a couple of exercises for 10 to 12 reps as the primary mass builders. As we said earlier, most people will obtain the most hypertrophy from reps in the 8 to 12 range. But since strength and size are interrelated, you should perform at least one basic power movement for 6 to 8 reps. Finally, we are convinced that anything more than 10 to 12 sets in total for a muscle group will quickly lead to overtraining. The occasional workout for more than 12 sets is fine, but don't make it a regular practice. In fact there are those who will overtrain on 12 sets.

MIXED EQUIPMENT ROUTINES

ROUTINE A	**Sets**	**Reps**
Flat barbell bench presses	3	6-8
Incline dumbell presses	3	10-12
Pec-dek flyes	2	10-12

ROUTINE B		
Incline barbell presses	3	6-8
Flat dumbell presses	3	10-12
Cable crossovers	2	10-12

ROUTINE C		
Flat smith presses	3	6-8
Incline machines	3	10-12
Flat dumbell flyes	3	10-12

ROUTINE D		
Flat barbell presses	3	6-8
Incline smith presses	3	10-12
Incline dumbell flyes	3	10-12
Pec-dek flyes	2	10-12

ROUTINE E		
Incline barbell presses	3	6-8
Flat machine presses	3	10-12
Incline dumbell flyes	3	10-12
Cable crossovers	2	10-12

ROUTINE F (Machines only)		
Flat machine presses	3	6-8
Incline smith presses	3	10-12
Pec-dek flyes	3	10-12
Cable crossovers (optional)	2-3	10-12

ROUTINE G (Free Weights Mixed)		
Flat barbell presses	3	6-8
Incline dumbell presses	3	10-12
Flat dumbell flyes	2-3	10-12

FREE WEIGHTS (Dumbells)		
Flat dumbell presses	3	6-8
Incline dumbell flyes	3	10-12
Flat dumbell flyes	3	10-12
Dumbell pullovers (optional)	2-3	10-12

Sherry Goggin-Giardina gets a lift.

THREE MONTH DOUBLE VARIABLE SWITCH

The following is one of the most effective routines for breaking out of a training plateau. Instead of changing one variable such as exercise order or rep number, you change both simultaneously. By changing the exercise order every month, it guarantees that you'll be able to start with your maximum weight on each exercise at least once. By changing the rep range you are assured of hitting both fast and slow twitch muscle fibers.

MONTH 1	Sets	Reps
Flat barbell presses	3	15-20
Incline dumbell presses	3	15-20
Pec-dek flyes	3	15-20

MONTH 2		
Incline dumbell presses	3	12-15
Pec-dek flyes	3	12-15
Flat barbell presses	3	12-15

MONTH 3		
Pec-dek flyes	3	6-8
Flat barbell presses	3	6-8
Incline dumbell presses	3	6-8

CHAPTER SIX

Back Training – Creating That Manta Ray Look

"Did you see that guy? He was built like a brick shit-house!"

How often have you heard such a comment? Or better still, been the subject of someone else's flattery. The phrase usually refers to someone who sports the classic V-shape. You know, the small, tight waist that flares out to wide, wide shoulders. While bone structure plays a role, the muscles that contribute the most to the much desired triangle shape are the two, fan-like latissimus dorsi muscles. Bodybuilders rarely call them by their full name and usually shorten it to "lats."

The great back of Roland Cziurlok

The lats cover most of the upper back of the torso and their primary function is to draw the arms downwards and backwards. In a manner of speaking, the lats work opposite in motion to the chest muscles. Where the chest muscles are the primary pushing muscles of the upper torso, the lats are the body's main pulling muscles. Such sports as rowing, kayaking, and judo, depend heavily on the lat muscles.

Lat training can generally be subdivided into two categories; pulling the arms about 90 degrees towards the torso, and pulling the arms horizontal to the torso. Exercises falling under the former category are usually referred to as rowing movements, while exercises in the latter consist of various chin-ups and pulldowns. Rowing exercises generally add the thick, meaty look to the back, while chins and pulldowns tend to hit the outer edges of the lats adding width. A well-rounded back routine should initially include an equal mix from both categories. As time goes on you can focus on one category more than the other depending on which areas need the most work.

BACK TRAINING EXERCISES

FRONT WIDE PULLDOWNS

Execution – Grab the overhead bar with a wide (6 to 8 inches wider than shoulder width on both sides) grip and sit down on

To insure maximum contraction in the back muscles, squeeze the shoulder blades together as you pull the bar down. – Aaron Baker

Start

the machine's chair. Lean back slightly and pull the bar to the upper chest, around the collarbone region. Extend the arms back overhead to just short of a locked out position.

Muscles worked – Front pull-downs primarily work the outer edges of the lats, but the rear delts, teres, rhomboids, and biceps also come into play.

Comments – As you pull the bar down, squeeze the shoulder blades together and arch the back slightly, i.e. stick the chest forward. This

Finish

will insure the maximum contraction in the back muscles. Another popular version of this exercise is to pull the bar behind the head. We caution against this as this places excessive stress on the shoulder joint, particularly the small group of tendons collectively known as the rotator cuff. We are not saying that pulling behind the head will definitely lead to shoulder problems, but the odds go way up. Our feeling is that unless you are deriving some extra muscular benefit from a particular variation (which in this case you're not) then why do it? We suggest sticking to the front version.

FRONT NARROW PULLDOWNS

Execution – Grab the overhead bar with a shoulder width or slightly less than shoulder width grip and sit down on the chair or seat. Pull the bar to the collarbone and then return to the starting position, with the arms just short of locking out.

Muscles worked – The narrow grip tends to shift the stress more towards the center of the back, i.e., close to the shoulder blades. The biceps, teres, and rhomboids also come into play.

Comments – From a kinesiology point of view narrow pulldowns put the back through a greater range of motion. Of course the narrow grip also stresses the biceps more, and you may find they give out before the lats. In this case, try experimenting with pre-exhaustion.

As with front pulldowns, try to squeeze the shoulder blades together and arch the chest.
– Jean-Pierre Fux

REVERSE PULLDOWNS

Execution – Grab an overhead bar with a shoulder width, palms facing you grip. Pull the bar to the middle chest, keeping the elbows as close to the sides as possible. Return to the starting position.

Muscles worked – Reverse pulldowns shift most of the stress from the upper outer lats, to the lower lats. They are a great way for stressing the area where the lat muscles attach to the lower torso. The reverse grip also puts more stress on the biceps than wide versions, so as mentioned previously you may need to pre-exhaust the lats first.

Comments – 10 or 20 years ago the "correct way" to do pulldowns was with a wide grip. But just as many bodybuilders opt for the reverse narrow grip as the wide version now days. Besides the better feel, most bodybuilders like the fact that they can lift more weight with a narrow reverse grip (due to the extra biceps involvement).

FRONT WIDE CHINS

Execution – Either jump up, or stand on a stool or bench and grab the overhead bar with a palms forward, wide grip. Pull yourself up until the bar just touches the upper chest around the collarbone region. Lower down to just short of a locked out position. Repeat.

Muscle worked – Front chins primarily work the outer, upper lats, but the biceps, teres, and rhomboids also come into play.

Comments – Chins fall into the same category as squats, and bench presses, in that they are among the best exercises to perform for strength and size. Virtually every top bodybuilder does chins in his or her workout. As with front pulldowns, try to squeeze the shoulder blades together and arch the chest at the top of the movement (i.e. as the bar approaches the collarbone).

Chins also fall into the same category as dips, in that you must lift your entire bodyweight. To get around this, many gyms have what are called assisted chin/dip machines that actually push you up slightly. These machines allow any size or strength person to perform chins.

REVERSE CHINS

Execution – Grab a chin up bar with a shoulder width reverse (palms facing towards you) grip. With the torso leaning slightly backward, pull yourself up until the bar is in line with your chin. Lower to just short of an arms-locked out position.

Muscles worked – Reverse chin-ups primarily hit the lower, outer lats, but the rear delts, biceps, teres, and rhomboids, also come into play.

Comments – As with reverse pulldowns, reverse chins are a great way to hit the lats down low on the torso. We should add that the exercise is probably as good a biceps movement as lat builder. In fact you may find the biceps are the weak link in the chain.

WIDE SEATED ROWS

Execution – Attach a standard wide pulldown bar to a seated row cable and sit down on the machine's pad. Grab the bar with a slightly wider than shoulder width grip and pull the bar to the upper chest. Return the bar to the starting position by stretching the torso forward.

Muscles worked – Wide seated rows to the collarbone hit the upper, center lats, as well as the traps. The biceps, spinal erectors, and rear delts play a secondary role.

Comments – For variety try the same exercise using the triceps pushdown rope. This will allow you to pull the elbows back further giving the traps and lats a few extra degrees of contraction. As a word of caution, seated rows are somewhat stressful on the lower back. If you have lower back problems you may want to avoid this exercise.

NARROW SEATED ROWS

Execution – Sit down on the machine's pad and grab the v-shaped attachment. As you lean back pull the hands in to the lower rib cage. At this point the torso should be between 90 and 100 degrees

Start

For those with lower back problems, you may want to avoid narrow seated rows.
– Aaron Baker

Finish

to the floor (i.e. vertical or just past vertical). Return to the starting position by stretching the arms forward.

Muscles worked – Narrow seated rows primarily work the lower and center lats. They also stress the traps, spinal erectors, and biceps.

Comments – Seated rows are one of the best exercises for thickening up the back. For variety try using a narrow reverse grip on a straight bar. As with wide seated rows, those with lower back problems may also want to avoid narrow seated rows.

TWO-ARM DUMBELL ROWS

Execution – Lie face down on an incline bench and grab two dumbells. With your elbows kept close to your sides pull the dumbells up as if you were sawing wood with a handsaw. Lower down and slightly forward to just short of a locked out position.

Muscles worked – Two arm rows primarily hit the lower and center lats, but the biceps, rear delts, and traps also come into play.

Comments – Keep the angle on the bench between 20 and 30 degrees. You'll find as you approach 45 degrees or more the traps take over and do most of the work. You can perform the exercise without the bench by just bending over and pulling the dumbells up. But many will find this too stressful on the lower back.

ONE-ARM DUMBELL ROWS

Execution – Place one knee and hand on a flat bench and pull a dumbell up in a sawing type motion. With the elbows close to the sides, lower the dumbell down and slightly forward. Repeat.

Muscles worked – One-arm rows primarily hit the lower outer lats. The biceps and rear delts also come into play.

Comments – Many people prefer one arm rows as it seems like a more natural movement. Two arm rows are somewhat constrictive. You can lift the dumbell straight up and down, but stretching forward at the bottom brings the lats through a few extra degrees of motion.

Many people prefer the one-arm row as it seems like a natural movement.
– Bruce Patterson

BARBELL ROWS

Execution – Grab a barbell with a slightly wider than shoulder width grip and with the torso bent almost parallel with the floor, pull the bar up to the lower rib cage. Lower slowly to just short of locking out.

Muscles worked – By very nature of the exercise and weight used barbell rows hit just about the entire back.

Comments – Barbell rows are one of the best overall back exercises and if chins can be considered the best width movement, barbell rows are probably the number one thickness movement. To get an extra stretch, try standing on a low step or block of wood. As with seated rows, those with lower back problems will have to be careful when performing this exercise.

REVERSE BARBELL ROWS

Execution – Grab a bar with a shoulder width, reverse grip. Pull the bar to the lower rib cage, keeping the torso just short of parallel with the floor. Slowly lower to the starting position.

Muscles worked – Reverse barbell rows shift most of the stress to the lower outer lats. The biceps and traps also come into play.

Comments – Six-time Mr. Olympia, Dorian Yates has done more to popularize this version of barbell rows than any one else. He also sports one of the most complete backs in the history of the sport. We should add that reverse barbell rows put extra stress on the biceps and numerous bodybuilders at all levels have torn biceps' tendons while performing this exercise. Don't yank or pull the bar with sudden, jerky movements. Keep everything slow and controlled. Finally, to lessen (but not eliminate) the stress on the lower back, always keep the knees slightly bent. Never do the exercise with the legs locked.

DUMBELL PULLOVERS

Execution – Lie across a bench and drop the shoulder and hips slightly below bench level. With the palms facing the ceiling, grab a dumbell on one end and lower it behind the head keeping the arms as straight as possible. Return to the starting position.

Muscles worked – Dumbell pullovers primarily work the outer lats, but the serratus, intercostals, and chest, also play a role.

Comments – We discussed this exercise earlier in the chest training chapter as bodybuilders are divided as to whether pullovers are primarily a back or chest exercise. Our opinion is that it depends on the individual's bone structure. So use your common sense and make up your own mind.

MACHINE PULLOVERS

Execution – Sit in the machine's chair and either grab the overhead bar, or place your elbows behind the two pads, depending on the machine's design. Pull or push downward as far as the machine's design will allow. Return to the overhead position.

Muscles worked – Machine pullovers work the upper, outer lats, as well as the intercostals, serratus, and chest.

Comments – Machine pullovers are one example where most bodybuilders actually

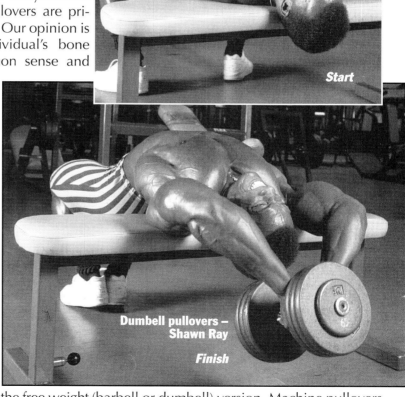

Start

Dumbell pullovers –
Shawn Ray

Finish

prefer the machine version over the free weight (barbell or dumbell) version. Machine pullovers provide a substantial increase in range of motion over free weights. The only way to duplicate this with a barbell or dumbell would be to hang upside down, something few bodybuilders are willing to do!

ONE-ARM CABLE ROWS

Execution – With your hand braced on a bench or other support, pull the handle connected to a low pulley, to the side of the lower rib cage. Stretch the handle forward until your arm is nearly locked out. Repeat.

Muscles worked – One-arm cable rows primarily work the lower, outer lats. The biceps and rear delts also come into play.

Comments – For variety you can try this exercise with two hands while lying face down on an incline bench.

T-BAR ROWS

Execution – Grab the machine's handle and pull up to the center chest.

Muscles worked – T-Bar rows hit virtually the whole back region. The traps and biceps also play a role.

Franco Santoriello

Comments – T-Bar rows place a close second to barbell rows as the number one lat-thickening exercise. As with barbell rows, always keep the knees slightly bent. Also, don't sway or yank with the torso just to lift a few extra pounds. If you can't lift in good style drop the weight.

STRAIGHT-ARM PUSHDOWNS

Execution – Stand in front of a cable pulldown machine and grab the bar with a shoulder width grip. With the arms locked straight and palms facing downwards, push the bar down to the thighs. Raise the bar up until the weight plates being lifted stop just short of resting back on the stack. Repeat.

Muscles worked – Straight-arm pushdowns primarily work the outer, upper lats. Although not a total isolation, few other muscles come into play.

Comments – Straight-arm pushdowns are one of the best isolation exercises you can do. There is no biceps involvement like most other exercises, and the traps play only a minor role. This exercise is similar to machine pullovers and makes a good substitute if your gym does not have such a pullover machine. As a final comment you will quickly realize that you can't lift near the weight you can on a regular pulldown exercise.

ADVANCED BACK ROUTINES

If your back begins lagging behind you'll need to start prioritizing and doing extra work for it. The following routines have been designed to hit that back from as many different angles as possible. Depending on the equipment available in your gym you may need to make substitutions (i.e. dumbell or barbell pullover in place of machine pullover).

MIXED ROUTINES

ROUTINE A	Sets	Reps
Front chins	3	6-8
Seated rows	3	10-12
One-arm rows	2-3	10-12

ROUTINE B		
Barbell rows	3	6-8
Front pulldowns	3	10-12
Straight-arm pushdowns	2-3	10-12

ROUTINE C		
T-Bar rows	3	6-8
Reverse pulldowns	3	10-12
One-arm cable rows	2-3	10-12

ROUTINE D		
Reverse barbell rows	3	6-8
Wide front pulldowns	3	10-12
Dumbell pullovers	2-3	10-12

ROUTINE E		
Front chins	3	6-8
Wide seated rows	3	10-12
Nautilus Pullover machine	2-3	10-12

ROUTINE F (Free-weight)		
Barbell rows	3	6-8
One-arm rows	3	10-12
Dumbell pullovers	2-3	10-12

ROUTINE G (Free Weights)		
Front chins	3	6-8
Reverse barbell rows	3	10-12
Two-arm rows	2-3	10-12

ROUTINE H	Sets	Reps
Chins	3	6-8
Barbell rows	3	10-12
Seated rows	3	10-12
Straight-arm pushdowns	2-3	10-12

ROUTINE I		
Front pulldowns	3	6-8
T-Bar rows	3	10-12
One-arm rows	3	10-12
Dumbell pullovers	3	10-12

ROUTINE J		
Barbell rows	3	6-8
Nautilus Pullovers	3	10-12
Two-arm rows	3	10-12
Wide seated rows	3	10-12

THREE MONTH TWO VARIABLE SWITCH ROUTINES

MONTH 1	Sets	Reps
Barbell rows	3	15-20
Front pulldowns	3	15-20
One-arm rows	3	15-20

MONTH 2		
Front pulldowns	3	10-12
One-arm rows	3	10-12
Barbell rows	3	10-12

MONTH 3		
One-arm rows	3	6-8
Barbell rows	3	6-8
Front pulldowns	3	6-8

SUBSTITUTES

T-bar rows for barbell rows
Chinups for front pulldowns *
Seated rows for one arm rows

* You may find that doing chins as the third or even second exercise in the routine is too difficult. If your gym has one you can use a Gravitron also called the assisted dip/chin machine. If not, stick with front pulldowns as the second or third exercise in the rotation.

Dave Palumbo

CHAPTER SEVEN

Building Yard-Wide Shoulders

"Come on, put your shoulder into it."

Sound familiar? Chances are those of you who played high school football or rugby heard the coach yell this a few times. While the biceps and chest may be the most trained muscles in gyms, the shoulders seem to get mentioned the most when brute strength is required. "Atlas held the world on his shoulders" or "shoulders, the mark of a man" or "shouldering a heavy burden." See what we mean? Wide powerful shoulders are a symbol of masculinity. They are also a must if you have competitive aspirations. Take a look at the shoulder development of Ronnie Coleman, Flex Wheeler, Kevin Levrone, and Paul Dillett. Now you see why some writers entitle their shoulder training articles "bowling ball-sized delts." The shoulders of some of the top bodybuilders are literally the size of ten-pin bowling balls.

Lee Priest

Gerard Dente

In reality the shoulders are not one but four distinct muscles. The deltoid complex consists of three parts commonly called "heads." The front deltoid elevates the arm to the front. The side deltoid raises the arms to the side. And the rear deltoid helps the traps and lats draw the arms toward the rear. Besides the three deltoid muscles, the shoulder region has two large triangle-shaped muscles located at the base of the neck called trapezius or traps for short. Technically the traps are part of the back, but the vast majority of body-builders train traps with the shoulders, so we are going to discuss them here. Finally, the shoulders also include a group of small muscles connected to the shoulder blades whose primary function is to stabilize and rotate the arms. Commonly called the rotator complex, these muscles are usually at the root of most shoulder injuries. The main reason is because of their invis-ibility. Bodybuilders tend to only focus on what they can see, after all this is what judges will be scoring. So while the large outer deltoid muscles continu-ously get stronger, the underlying rotators start lagging behind and eventu-ally become the weak link in the chain. Sooner or later they give out and the dreaded "shoulder problems" start. Despite their small size and unimportance to bodybuilding contests, you must strengthen them to help prevent injuries.

> **"Try training your shoulders once a week for four weeks, twice a week for four weeks, and three times a week for another four weeks. You're bound to see results after forcing your shoulders into going along with such a haphazard program."**
>
> – *MuscleMag International* editors, offering one suggestion for training shoulders or any other stubborn muscle group.

Shoulder training consists of four primary types of movements; presses which are primarily for the front shoulders, laterals for the side and rear shoulders, shrugs for the traps, and rotations for the rotator complex. For complete shoulder development your routine must contain at least one exercise from each category. As time goes on you can favor one category over the others depending on weaknesses.

SHOULDER EXERCISES

FRONT BARBELL PRESSES

Execution – Place a barbell on the shoulder press rack and sit down in the chair. Lift the bar up and outward so it's held just above the collarbone. Lower to the upper chest and then push straight up to just short of an arms locked out position. Repeat.

Start

Muscles worked – Front barbell presses primarily work the front shoulders, but the side shoulders, upper chest, and triceps can also benefit.

Comments – Another of the "best" strength and size exercises, front barbell presses evolved from the old standing presses performed by old-time circus strongmen. We suggest sitting down with your back braced against a vertical pad for support. As with lat pulldowns, you can lower the bar behind the head, but we caution against doing so. Behind the head presses subject the shoulder joint, in particular the rotator complex, to tremendous stress. There is a misconception that front presses work the front shoulder and behind the head presses work the side. Both exercises primarily stress the front deltoids. And since the behind the head version is potentially dangerous, we suggest avoiding it.

DUMBELL PRESSES

Execution – Sit down in a chair with a back support and hoist a set of dumbells to shoulder height with the palms facing forward. Press the dumbells upwards to just short of locking out. Lower down until the upper arm is slightly below parallel with the floor. Repeat.

Muscles worked – Dumbell presses mainly work the front delts, but the side delts, upper chest, and triceps get a workout as well.

Comments – Even though the movement is virtually identical, many bodybuilders find dumbells less stressful on the shoulders than barbell presses. They also offer the advantage of a few extra degrees of motion as the barbell has to stop at chest level, while the dumbells can be lowered below chest level.

SMITH PRESSES

Execution – Position a back-supported chair inside a Smith machine and grab the bar with a slightly wider than shoulder width grip. Lift upwards and rotate the bar so the hooks will clear the machine's catching pegs. Lower the bar to the collarbone and then push straight up to just short of locking out. Repeat.

Finish

Dumbell presses – Mike O'Hearn

Muscles worked – As with barbell presses, Smith machine presses primarily work the front delts, but the side delts, triceps, and upper chest feel the burn too.

Comments – Without repeating ourselves too much, Smith machine presses are a welcome change to barbell presses, but probably not an equivalent replacement. Because the machine is balanced, the stronger side of the body will always do most of the work. Also because the natural movement of the upper chest and front shoulders is a slight up and backward arc, the Smith machine actually goes against this by keeping you in one plane of motion. This is why some authorities, including highly respected writer and coach, Charles Poliquin, state that the Smith machine is not only limited in effectiveness but potentially dangerous. Our advice is to experiment and see how it feels.

MACHINE PRESSES

Execution – Sit down in the machine's chair and grab the handle or handles. Push up or up and inwards depending on the machine's range of motion. Repeat by lowering to the starting position.

Muscles worked – Machine presses chiefly work the front shoulders, but the side shoulders, triceps, and upper chest are worked too.

Finish

Don't use body momentum to sway the dumbells while doing dumbell laterals.
– Gerard Dente

Start

Comments – Most machine presses are balanced so the problem of one-sided development exists. The weaker side will never have to do its fair share of the load. We should add that some of the newer lines like Atlantis and Hammer Strength have independent arms so the stress is equally divided between both sides of the body. They also come closer to duplicating dumbells as they go up and inwards towards the top of the exercise.

DUMBELL LATERALS

Execution – Grab a set of dumbells and with the knees and elbows slightly bent, raise the dumbells to shoulder height. Lower the dumbells to just short of touching infront of the body around waist high. Repeat.

Muscles worked – Dumbell laterals are the primary side deltoid movement. There is some secondary trap and front delt involvement.

Comments – The first thing you will notice is that the side shoulders are nowhere as strong as the front shoulders. If you were pressing 60 to 80 pound dumbells, you will only use 20 to 30 pound dumbells for laterals. The big mistake people make on this exercise is to use body momentum to sway the dumbells up. This may do wonders for the ego – "I can do 60-pound lateral raises" – but it's really not doing much in the way of side shoulder development. If you find that no matter how hard you

Start

The advantage of cable laterals over dumbells is that there is continuous tension on the muscle at all times.

Finish

try, you still swing slightly, sit down in a chair with a vertical back brace. Yes, it may mean decreasing the weight, but we assure you your side delts will thank you for it.

FRONT DUMBELL RAISES

Execution – Grab a set of dumbells and with the knees and elbows slightly bent, raise the dumbells to the front and to shoulder height. Lower to the thighs and repeat.

Muscles worked – Raising the dumbells to the front shifts most of the stress to the front delts. The side shoulders, however, still play a role.

Comments – There are three versions to this exercise. The safest is to keep the palms facing inward so the ends of the dumbells are pointing up and down. This is pure front shoulder. Another variation is to turn the palms downward. This has the advantage of bringing in the side shoulders, but it also puts more stress on the shoulder joint. Finally you can grab one dumbell with both hands and raise upwards to the front. Although we feel the first version is the safest, try all three for variety.

CABLE LATERALS

Execution – With one hand grab a handle connected to a low pulley wheel and with the knees and elbows bent slightly, raise the handle to the side. Lower the handle so it's just in front of you. Repeat. You will need to grab a stationary upright with your free hand to stabilize the body.

Muscles worked – Cable laterals largely work the side shoulders but the traps and front delts also come into play.

Comments – The advantage of cable laterals over dumbells is that there is continuous tension on the muscle at all times. With dumbells, as soon as the arms start lining up with the direction of gravity (i.e. straight down or straight up) you begin to lose tension. A variation of this exercise is to grab a pulley handle with the opposite hand and perform two arm cable laterals. This is a difficult exercise to coordinate and it will take a couple workouts to get it right.

MACHINE SIDE LATERALS

Execution – Sit down in the machine's chair and either grab the handles or place the elbows behind the pads. Push out and up in the direction of the machine's range of motion. Slowly return to the starting position.

Muscles worked – Machine laterals are almost pure side delt. The traps and front delts play a secondary role.

Comments – There are many different versions of the lateral machine. You can either stand up or sit down. Some are two sided, while others require you to execute the exercise one arm at a time. Some machines use handles, while others use pads. From talking to bodybuilders, lateral machines fall into the "love 'em or hate 'em" category. Some individuals find they get a better feel out of the machines, while others are devoted to the dumbell version.

BENT OVER DUMBELL LATERALS

Execution – Grab a set of dumbells and sit on the end of a flat bench. With the torso bent forward about 45 degrees to the floor, raise the dumbells outwards and upwards to shoulder height. Lower so that the dumbells stop just short of touching in front of you. Repeat.

Muscles worked – Bent over laterals predominantly work the rear delts, but the traps, teres, rhomboids, and side shoulders also play a role.

Comments – There are two variations of this exercise. You

Finish

Matt McLaughlin works his delts with bent over dumbell laterals.

Start

can stand up and bend forward, or you can lie face down on a 30 to 45 degree incline bench. The latter placers the least amount of stress on the lower back but some bodybuilders find it restrictive and prefer the standing or seated versions.

BENT OVER CABLE LATERALS

Execution – Stand between a cable crossover machine and grab the handles with the opposite hands (i.e. the left handle in the right hand and the right handle in the left hand). Bend forward so that the torso is about 45 degrees to the floor. Raise the handles outwards and upwards to shoulder level. Lower them back so that they cross in front of the body. Repeat.

Muscles worked – Cable bent laterals first and foremost work the rear delts, but the side shoulders, traps, rhomboids, and teres also come out to play.

Comments – Bent over cable laterals have the same built in drawback as the standing version. It's going to take you a few workouts to get the coordination worked out. You also have to make sure the cable handles have no sharp protrusions as the risk of a serious cut is there when the cables cross in front.

REVERSE PEC FLYES

Execution – Sit facing the machine's back support and either grab the handles or place your elbows behind the pads. Draw the arms backwards until the hands are in line with the torso. Return to the starting position with the arms perpendicular to the torso.

Muscles worked – Reverse pec flyes particularly work the rear delts, but the traps, lats, teres, and rhomboids get some attention as well.

Comments – For those who have trouble performing bent over dumbell laterals because of lower back problems, reverse pec flyes are a good substitute. If you are using a machine with handles, try grabbing them both with the palms facing out and palms facing in.

UPRIGHT ROWS

Execution – Grab a short straight bar or EZ-curl bar with a 6 to 8 inch wide grip, palms facing towards you. Draw the bar straight up the center of the body and in towards the collarbone at the top of the movement. From the side the elbows make an upward and backward arc. Lower slowly until the bar is at thigh level (or just short of locking out). Repeat.

Muscles worked – Upright rows work the side delts and traps to a great degree, and the rear delts and rhomboids to a lesser degree.

Jean-Pierre Fux

Comments – Generally speaking, the wider the grip the more trap involvement, conversely the more narrow the grip the more side shoulder. If you find the barbell stressful on the wrists, try using two dumbells or a rope (the same one used for triceps pushdowns) connected to a low pulley wheel. Where the barbell locks the hands in one position, the dumbells or rope allow for some lateral movement as you lift thus placing less stress on the wrists.

ADVANCED SHOULDER ROUTINES

ROUTINE A (Mixed)	Sets	Reps
Dumbell presses	3	6-12
Side lateral raises	3	6-12
Bent over lateral raises	3	6-12
Barbell shrugs	3	6-12
ROUTINE B		
Smith presses	3	6-12
Cable lateral raises	3	6-12
Reverse pec flyes	3	6-12
Barbell upright rows	3	6-12
ROUTINE C (Free Weights)		
Front barbell presses	3	6-12
Side lateral raises	3	6-12
Bent over laterals	3	6-12
Barbell shrugs	3	6-12

ROUTINE D (Dumbells)

Front dumbell presses	3	6-12
Side lateral raises	3	6-12
Bent over lateral raises	3	6-12
Dumbell upright rows	3	6-12

ROUTINE E (Machines)

Machine front presses	3	6-12
Machine side lateral raises	3	6-12
Reverse pec flyes	3	6-12
Machine shrugs	3	6-12

THREE MONTH TWO VARIABLE SWITCH ROUTINE – DELTOIDS

MONTH 1	**Sets**	**Reps**
Barbell presses	3	15-20
Dumbell side lateral raises	3	15-20
Bent over lateral raises	3	15-20

MONTH 2		
Dumbell side lateral raises	3	10-12
Bent over lateral raises	3	10-12
Barbell presses	3	10-12

MONTH 3		
Bent over lateral raises	3	6-8
Barbell presses	3	6-8
Side lateral raises	3	6-8

THREE MONTH TWO VARIABLE SWITCH ROUTINE – TRAPS

MONTH 1	**Sets**	**Reps**
Barbell shrugs	3	15-20
Upright rows	3	15-20
Dumbell shrugs	3	15-20

MONTH 2		
Upright rows	3	10-12
Dumbell shrugs	3	10-12
Barbell shrugs	3	10-12

MONTH 3		
Dumbell shrugs	3	6-8
Barbell shrugs	3	6-8
Upright rows	3	6-8

These massive
pillars belong to
Roland Cziurlok

BOOK THREE

PILLARS OF POWER

CHAPTER EIGHT

Quads – Thunder From Down Under

Jean-Pierre Fux

"Squatting is a miracle exercise capable of extreme transformation. If ever you want to have legs bigger than a baby's arm, the squat is the best exercise to use. What's more the squat works the entire leg, not just the quads."

– Frank Shore, *MuscleMag International* contributor commenting on squats. Need we say more.

We are sure most readers have heard the old expression "a house is only as good as its foundation." Well, much the same can be said for a bodybuilding physique. Nothing looks as stupid (an ego shattering term but true nonetheless) as a set of twenty-inch arms and 50 inch chest teetering on stage on a set of 22-inch thighs! Yet go into any gym and you'll see bench press racks and preacher benches with line-ups, and squat racks gathering dust! We'll admit that a couple of bodybuilders are lacking in the leg area not from laziness but from being denied in the DNA department. But such individuals are in the minority. No, the reason so many bodybuilders have shaky foundations is from an unwillingness to bust ass at the squat rack. Leg training you see is nothing short of brutal. No matter how many sets of shoulder or bench presses, nothing separates the men from the boys like a quality set of squats.

Start

Tony Pearson performs the "King of leg exercises" – squats.

Finish

TRAINING THE QUADS

The quads, commonly called the thighs, are named as such because the muscle is composed of four distinct heads or "ceps." The prefix "quad" comes from geometry and means "four" as in quadri-lateral. As with biceps training, you can't totally isolate the heads, but changing the exercises can shift the stress more from one head to another. Despite the numerous exercises, leg training can be neatly divided into compound movements, such as squats and leg presses, and isolation movements such as leg extensions and sissy squats. You can think of it this way, compound movements build the cow, while isolation movements separate it into lean cuts of meat. For complete thigh development your training program must contain exercises from both categories.

THIGH EXERCISES

SQUATS

Execution – Position a barbell about shoulder height on a squat rack and step in under so that the bar rests at the base of the skull on top of the traps. Step back and position the feet just slightly wider than shoulder width, toes pointed slightly outwards (i.e. making a "V"). With the back kept straight, start descending by bending at the knees and hips until the thighs are at least parallel with the floor. Return to the starting position by straightening the legs.

Muscles worked – Squats stress just about every muscle below the waist! They even bring in many of the torso muscles for stability. The thighs and glutes do most of the work, but the hamstrings also play a major role. Even the calves come into play for stabilizing.

Comments – Considered king of leg exercises, squats are probably the best overall mass builder. Those with knee or lower back problems will have to make a judgement call as to whether they can perform squats. Form is essential on this exercise. The lower back must main-tain the natural curve (despite some writers saying the back should be kept "straight"). As well contrary to popular belief, not going all the way down to parallel or lower is as stressful on the knees as full squats. Sure you can lift more weight in a half or quarter depth squat, but you will never develop complete thigh size and strength unless you perform full range of motion.

FRONT SQUATS

Execution – As with regular squats, place a bar shoulder height on a rack and step in under, but this time rest it on the upper chest instead of behind the head. From here perform the exercise as described previously.

Muscles worked – Front squats primarily work the thighs, but the glutes, hamstrings, and calves come into play.

Comments – Some individuals find front squats less stressful on the lower back than regular back squats. Of course others find just the opposite as keeping the bar positioned on the upper chest necessitates leaning slightly backward, which may put more stress on the lower back! Front squats are more isolating than back squats as the role of the glutes is reduced. For this reason you won't be able to lift the same amount of weight as you could on back squats.

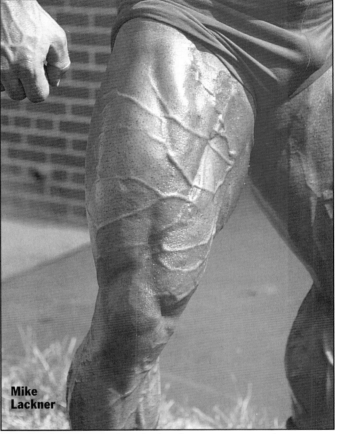

Mike Lackner

SMITH SQUATS

Execution – Step in under the bar so that it rests on the traps across the base of the neck. Place the feet slightly wider than shoulder width with the toes pointing slightly outward. Bend at the knees and hips and descend until the thighs are parallel with the floor. Return to the standing position.

Muscles worked – Smith squats primarily work the thighs and glutes but the hamstrings and calves also come into play.

Comments – Without repeating ourselves, Smith squats are not as productive as barbell squats as the machine has the balance component removed. Still, they offer one advantage in that you can position the feet forward or backward to target different parts of the thighs. Generally the farther forward, the more glute and inner thigh, while placed behind you more of the stress is placed on the outer thigh. If you decide to do the latter, keep in mind that there is also more stress placed on the knees.

DUMBELL SQUATS

Execution – Place two dumbells on either side of the body so that they run parallel with one another. Squat down and grab a dumbell with each hand, and with the back kept in good alignment, stand upright. Repeat as if doing regular barbell squats.

Muscles worked – Dumbell squats hit the thighs and glutes, as well as the hamstrings and calves.

Comments – Dumbell squats have one major limitation in that the legs will quickly outgrow the strength of the forearms. In other words you won't be able to hold heavy enough dumbells to adequately stimulate the thigh muscles. When this happens you have three choices. You can use a set of wrist straps to "tie" yourself on to the dumbells so to speak. Even then a point will be reached where it will become awkward trying to hold onto 100+ pound dumbells. A second option is to perform dumbell squats after doing one or two other thigh exercises first. This way the legs are already tired and you won't need to use as heavy a weight. The third option is to do the exercise as the second or third exercise in a superset or triset. Once again by having the legs pre-exhausted the lighter weight will still give them adequate stimulation.

HACK SQUATS

Execution – Position yourself against the machine's back brace and either grab the handles or place the pads on your shoulders. With the legs slightly wider than shoulder width and toes pointing slightly outward, squat down until the thighs are at least parallel with the floor. Return to the starting position.

Muscles worked – Hack squats primarily hit the thighs and glutes, but the hamstrings and calves also play a role.

Comments – The advantage of hack squats over regular squats is that you can position the feet forward or back to hit different parts of the thigh. Of course the disadvantage is the removal of the balance component. Like most machines, hack squats only require the lifting of the weight, not the balancing. Still, hack squats are invaluable as a second or third thigh exercise (after leg presses or regular squats) and during the precontest season.

Leg presses are great for the thighs and glutes. – Greg Kovacs

Finish

Start

LEG PRESSES

Execution – Sit in the machine's chair and place your feet on the pressing platform. With the feet slightly wider than shoulder width and toes pointing slightly outward, push the platform away from you, stopping just short of locking the legs out. Lower slowly until the thighs are parallel or just slightly below parallel. Repeat.

Muscles worked – With a standard stance, leg presses primarily hit the thighs and glutes, with the hamstrings and calves playing a secondary role.

Comments – If barbell squats are the best thigh exercise, leg presses place a close second. As with hack squats and Smith squats, you have the option of placing the feet high or low, wide or narrow. Generally, the higher and wider the more inner thigh, glute, and hamstring. Placing the feet low and narrow puts most of the stress on the outer thighs. We should add that the latter stance also places more stress on the knees, something to keep in mind if you have a pre-existing knee condition. There are four basic leg press designs. The most common is based on the old Universal design, that being sitting in an upright position and pushing straight outward. The evolution from this is the 45-degree leg press. In this case you lie back so you are pressing upwards at about a 45 degree angle. Many gyms also have horizontal leg presses where you lie completely flat on your back and instead of the legs moving away from the torso, the torso moves away from the legs. In a manner of speaking this is more of a hack squat than leg press, but most manufacturers market the machines as leg presses. We left the worst till last. Some of

Start

you may work out in gyms that have a vertical leg press where you lie back on the floor and push straight upwards. While some bodybuilders swear by the "feel," we caution against performing this exercise. Under normal circumstances leg exercises substantially increase blood pressure. Vertical leg presses literally put it through the roof. There have been bodybuilders (and other athletes we might add) who have suffered strokes from doing this exercise. Unless you don't have access to one of the other three designs, we strongly advise you to avoid the vertical leg press.

LUNGES

Execution – Place a barbell on a rack as if doing barbell squats. Step in under and rest the bar across the shoulders at the base of the neck. Step back and adopt a runner's stance with one leg forward and one behind. Slowly descend by bending the knees. The front knee will face upward, while the back knee will be facing downward. Return to the upright position.

Muscles worked – Lunges primarily work the thighs, but the glutes and hamstrings also play a major role.

Comments – In a manner of speaking the name lunge is misleading. You don't "lunge" forward. The knee on the front leg never goes past the toes. In other words there should not be less than a 90-degree angle between the upper and lower legs. Lunging forward puts tremendous stress on the knee cartilage and ligaments. There are two basic ways to perform lunges. You can maintain the same leg stance and perform a continuous set of reps, or you can alternate legs, one rep at a time. We suggest sticking with the former until you get the coordination down, and then if you want, try the alternating version.

Lunges work the thighs, but the glutes and hamstrings also play a major role. – Shawn Ray

Finish

SISSY SQUATS

Execution – Grab something upright with one hand and lean back slightly with the feet slightly wider than shoulder width, toes pointing slightly outward. Hold a weight plate to the chest with the free hand and squat down until the thighs are parallel or slightly below parallel. Return to the starting position.

Muscles worked – Sissy squats primarily work the thighs and glutes, the hamstrings and calves are worked to a lesser degree.

Comments – Few exercises are as mis-named as sissy squats. We assure you they are not for sissies! As with dumbell squats you will quickly reach the point where the thighs can lift much more than you can hold against the chest. Once again perform sissy squats at the end of your thigh workout, or as the second or third exercise of a superset or triset.

LEG EXTENSIONS

Execution – Sit down in the machine's chair and place the feet in behind the leg rollers. Extend the lower legs upward to parallel or just short of parallel with the floor. Lower down slowly to just short of having the moving plates touch the stationary plates. Repeat.

Muscles worked – Leg extensions primarily isolate the center and outer thighs. The inner thighs play a secondary role.

Comments – Leg extensions fall in the love 'em or hate 'em category. Some authorities suggest they are the best exercise to rehabilitate weak or injured knees, others say they are the primary cause of knee problems!

Our opinion is that leg extensions make a great second or third leg exercise but should never replace squats or leg presses as a primary power movement. Busting your ass at the squat rack will accomplish far more in the way of leg strength and size than leg extensions ever will. Use leg extensions as a finishing exercise.

Leg extensions are a great finishing exercise.
– Ronnie Coleman

ADVANCED THIGH ROUTINES

ROUTINE A

	Sets	Reps
Squats	3	6-8
Leg extensions	3	10-12
Hack squats	3	10-12

ROUTINE B

	Sets	Reps
Leg presses	3	6-8
Lunges	3	10-12
Sissy squats	3	10-12

ROUTINE C (Free weights)

	Sets	Reps
Squats	3	6-8
Lunges	3	10-12
Sissy squats	3	10-12

ROUTINE D (Machines)

	Sets	Reps
Leg presses	3	6-8
Hack squats	3	10-12
Leg extensions	3	10-12

ROUTINE E

	Sets	Reps
Squats	3	6-8
Leg presses	3	10-12
Leg extensions	3	10-12
Sissy squats	3	10-12

ROUTINE F

	Sets	Reps
Leg presses	3	6-8
Hack squats	3	10-12
Lunges	3	10-12
Sissy squats	3	10-12

THREE MONTH TWO VARIABLE
SWITCH ROUTINE

MONTH 1

	Sets	Reps
Squats	3	15-20
Leg presses	3	15-20
Leg extensions	3	15-20

MONTH 2

	Sets	Reps
Leg presses	3	10-12
Leg extensions	3	10-12
Squats	3	10-12

MONTH 3

	Sets	Reps
Leg extensions	3	6-8
Squats	3	6-8
Leg presses	3	6-8

Flex Wheeler

CHAPTER NINE

Steel Chord Hamstrings

Although the term "legs" usually refers to the thighs, a well-balanced set of legs also includes the leg biceps, commonly called the hamstrings. If you don't believe us take a look at Robby Robinson or Ronnie Coleman doing a side chest or triceps shot. Those my friend are hamstrings! And such poses would not create the same impact if the hamstrings were underdeveloped.

> **"Hamstrings are not as much fun to train as there are fewer exercises on the menu, and they are certainly not as glamorous. This practice leads to the common flaw of legs that look good from the front but horrible from the side."**
>
> – Ron Harris, *MuscleMag International* contributor commenting on why most bodybuilders have weak hamstring development.

It's not just bodybuilders who need great hamstring development either. Check out the top sprinters and quarterbacks in the world. Much of their great speed is due to the power generated by their hamstrings. In fact such is the stress placed on the hamstrings that hamstrings pulls are relatively common in such sports, not to mention hockey and basketball. Yet, how many readers devote 6, 8, 10 sets or more to thigh training, and finish off by doing three sets of lying leg curls? Do you really think your hamstrings are going to stay in proportion to the quads from such a half hearted approach. Sorry to burst your bubble, but no way! Look at it this way, would you perform three sets total for your arm biceps? Of course not. You blast the hell out of them. But the poor hamstrings get lost in the shuffle.

TRAINING THE HAMSTRINGS

If you are lucky enough to work out in a large, well-equipped gym, you'll have access to a wide variety of hamstring machines including lying, seated, and standing exercises. If your gym only has one machine – usually the lying version – you'll need to be more creative and include stiff-leg deadlifts and dumbell curls. In many respects the hamstrings are similar to the calves in that one rep range probably won't do the complete job. You'll need to alternate high rep, low weight days, with low rep, heavy weight days.

LYING LEG CURLS

Execution – Lie face down on the machine's bench with the heels placed underneath the rollers. Curl the feet upward, stopping a couple of inches from the butt. Lower to the starting position with moving plates stopping just short of touching the stationary weight stack. Repeat.

Muscles worked – Lying leg curls primarily work the hamstrings. The calves and glutes play a secondary role.

Comments – Resist the urge to "throw" the butt up into the air when doing lying leg curls. Yes, you can lift more weight this way, but the hamstrings won't receive the main benefit of the exercise.

SEATED LEG CURLS

Execution – Sit down in the chair with the heels resting on top of the leg rollers. Curl the legs backward and downward for the machine's full range of motion. Repeat.

Muscles worked – Seated leg curls predominantly work the hamstrings with the calves playing second fiddle. For variety, try the exercise one leg at a time.

Comments – For some individuals, lying leg curls are stressful on the lower back, whereas the seated version offers support. As with lying leg curls, you can perform the exercise one leg at a time.

STANDING LEG CURLS

Execution – Place the heel of the working leg behind the leg roller and grab the machine's handles for support. Curl the leg upward as if doing a dumbell concentration curl. Lower to just short of locking out.

Muscles worked – Standing leg curls work the hamstrings, calves and glutes .

Comments – From a kinesiology point of view there's little difference between standing and seated or lying leg curls. Still many bodybuilders find they get a better contraction while doing the standing version. If there's a disadvantage to standing leg curls it's that many gyms don't have this design in their inventory.

Many bodybuilders find they get a better contraction while doing standing leg curls.
– Mike Francois

Finish

Start

121

DUMBELL LEG CURLS

Execution – Lie down on a flat bench and have a partner position a dumbell between the feet. From here curl the lower legs upwards as if doing the machine version. Repeat.

Muscles worked – Dumbell leg curls principally work the hamstrings with the glutes and calves benefiting as well.

Comments – Although called a "poor man's" leg curl, dumbell curls are as effective as any machine version. They also offer the advantage of only requiring a flat bench and dumbell – something you rarely have to wait for in a well-equipped gym. Their only disadvantage is a point may be reached where you have trouble holding the dumbell between the feet.

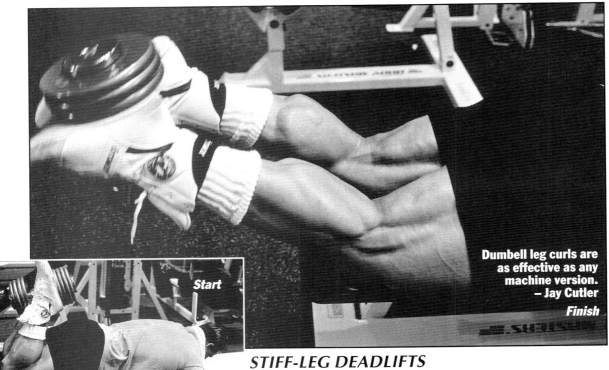

Start

Dumbell leg curls are as effective as any machine version. – Jay Cutler

Finish

STIFF-LEG DEADLIFTS

Execution – Bend over and grab a barbell with a shoulder width grip, and with the legs slightly bent, raise the torso so your are standing up straight. Lower slowly until the bar is a couple of inches from the floor. Repeat.

Muscles worked – Stiff-leg deadlifts largely work the hamstrings and spinal erectors, but the thighs, glutes, and forearms also get involved.

Comments – The name stiff-leg is misleading as you should never perform the exercise with the legs locked perfectly straight. Always keep a slight bend at the knees. For those used to performing regular powerlifting deadlifts, you'll notice that you won't be able to lift near the weight on the stiff-leg version. The main reason is that the thighs and glutes are reduced in role by keeping the legs relatively straight. If you are very flexible you may need to stand on a block of wood or low platform to get a full stretch at the bottom. Finally, some bodybuilders find that they get little or nothing out of stiff-leg deadlifts if they perform them first. Only by fatiguing the hamstrings with some sort of leg curl first do stiff-leg lifts seem to hit the hamstrings. For variety, try different orders with your hamstring exercises.

Start

Always keep a slight bend in your kness when performing stiff-leg deadlifts. – Jay Cutler

Finish

BACK EXTENSIONS

Execution – Position yourself in the back extension apparatus and bend downwards until the torso is just short of 90 degrees with the torso. Raise upwards until the torso is in alignment with the legs, or just slightly past the hips. Repeat.

Muscles worked – Back extensions especially hit the spinal erectors, but the hamstrings also come into play.

Comments – Although considered a lower back exercise, back extensions also hit the hamstrings especially if they've been first fatigued with leg curls or stiff-leg deadlifts. Some individuals hyperextend (the other common name for this exercise being hyperextensions) the torso, but we advise against this. Going a few degrees past vertical is fine but don't arch the back excessively.

Probably the main reason why so many individuals skimp on hamstring training is because their gym only has one piece of equipment – the lying leg curl. This excuse is unacceptable. Try the following routine and see what happens after a couple of months.

Lying leg curls	3 sets of 15-20 reps
Lying leg curl 21s	2 sets of 21 reps (3 X 7)
Dumbell curls	3 sets of 15-20 reps

ADVANCED HAMSTRING ROUTINES

If you have trouble feeling the hamstrings while doing lying leg curls, try this little technique recommended by well-known strength coach, Charles Poliquin. As you curl the weight up keep the feet dorsi-flexed, that is feet pointing towards the knees. Then as you lower down, plantar-flex the feet so they are pointing away from the body.

It doesn't sound like much, but there's a good kinesiology reason for doing so. When the feet are plantar flexed with the legs in a straight position, the involvement of the calf is greatly reduced forcing the hamstring to do most of the lifting. But the opposite is true when the legs start bending as you raise the weight. Dorsi-flexing the feet takes the calves out of the picture.

ROUTINE A	Sets	Reps
Lying leg curls	3	6-8
Stiff-leg deadlifts	3	15-20
Back extensions	3	15-20

ROUTINE B		
Seated leg curls	3	6-8
Lying dumbell leg curls	3	10-15
Stiff-leg deadlifts	3	15-20

ROUTINE C		
Standing leg curls	3	6-8
Lying leg curls	3	10-15
Back extensions	3	15-20

ROUTINE D (Machines)		
Lying leg curls	3	6-8
Standing leg curls	3	10-15
Seated leg curls	3	15-20

ROUTINE E (Free Weights)		
Lying dumbell curls	3	6-8
Stiff-leg deadlifts	3	10-15
Back extensions	3	15-20

Dave Palumbo

CHAPTER TEN

Those Stubborn Calves

Lee Labrada

> "In general they are the most difficult to work of all because there seems to be no foolproof establishment of result. For some people, working calves daily is the key to great development while others succeed by working them every other day."
>
> – Charles Glass, top trainer and *MuscleMag* columnist commenting on training the calves.

They probably hurt the most when you train them. They don't receive near the attention of such showy muscles as the biceps, chest, and shoulders. And after years of seemingly fruitless energy expenditure, the little suckers may have grown only an inch or two. Yet step up onstage with a large set and the audience gasps and judges trip over themselves in rewarding you points. We can only be talking about the calves of course. Those stubborn, little bastards located at back of the lower legs.

Calf training hurts like hell, and you have a limited number of exercises to choose from. But with a little ingenuity and a whole lot of perseverance, there's no reason why you can't build a decent set of calves.

STANDING CALF RAISES

Execution – Rest the machine's pad on your shoulders and step on to the platform. With the feet 6 to 8 inches apart and legs locked straight, stand up on your toes as high as possible. Stretch downward by dropping the heels below the platform. Repeat.

Muscles worked – Standing calf raises mostly work the large upper gastrocnemius section of the calf but the lower soleus is also given a good workout.

Comments – Calf raises are as much of a stretching exercise as a weight training exercise. Most ballerinas have large calves and they are only using their bodyweight. Go for the maximum range of motion as possible. Finally, unless you use extra padding, chances are you'll have a red rash on top of both shoulders the next day. This is the result of the pads resting on your shoulders as you lift up and down. While it's a tad distracting to look at, you have nothing to worry about health-wise.

Start

ONE-LEG CALF RAISES

Execution – Grab a dumbell with one hand and stand on a block of wood or platform. With one leg bent behind you stand up and down on your toes with the other.

Muscles worked – One-leg calf raises work the gastrocnemius, but the soleus also gets a bit of a blast.

Comments – The reason you do this exercise on one leg is because your calves will quickly outgrow the strength of your forearms. By doing the movement on one leg you double the resistance placed on the calf muscles. For support you will need to hold onto the side of a machine or other vertical structure.

TOE PRESSES

Execution – Sit in a leg press and place the toes on the edge of the pressing platform. Lock the legs out straight and flex back and forth at the ankles.

Muscles worked – Toe presses chiefly work the gastrocnemius, but the soleus will complain almost as loudly.

Comments – Some writers mistakenly believe that because you are sitting down, the soleus performs most of the work. But it's not the position of the body that counts but whether the legs are straight or bent. You can consider toe presses the seated equivalent of standing calf raises.

Finish

Calf raises are as much of a stretching exercise as a weight training exercise. – Claude Groulx

Start

SEATED CALF RAISES

Execution – Sit down on the machine's chair and rest the pads across the knees. With the toes resting on the edge of the foot-platform flex up and down at the ankle joint. Repeat.

Muscles worked – Seated calf raises work the soleus, but the gastrocnemius and tibias anterior also gets a jolt.

Comments – With the knees bent the gastrocnemius is reduced in role while the soleus does most of the work. As it's a smaller, weaker muscle, you won't be able to lift the same weight that you can on standing versions or toe presses.

DONKEY CALF RAISES

Execution – Find a willing partner and have them sit across your hips as you bend over and rest your forearms on a waist-high support. With the legs locked out straight and toes resting on a block of wood, flex up and down at the ankle joint. Repeat

Muscles worked – If you keep the legs locked the gastrocnemius does most of the work, while bending the knees brings shifts most of the stress onto the soleus.

Comments – Flip through old copies of *Muscle Builder Power* magazine and you'll see Arnold, Franco, and other greats from the seventies doing endless sets of donkey calf raises. There are some great shots of Arnold with two people across his back. This exercise is proof that you don't need fancy equipment to give a muscle a great workout. For obvious reasons donkeys may or may not be popular at your gym. Having patrons straddling one another is not an image some gyms want. Also, finding a willing partner may prove difficult. There may be talk you see. Try to find someone who's secure in his or her sexuality!

Aaron Baker concentrates hard while executing seated calf raises.

Finish

Bill Grant and Franco Columbu assist Arnold Schwarzenegger with donkey calf raises.

Flex Wheeler

BOOK FOUR

SMALL BUT DEADLY

CHAPTER ELEVEN

Building Matterhorn Peaks

Jamo Nezzar

"Probably the dumbell hammer curl. Hammer curls work the brachials, the forearms, the lower biceps, and – most people do not realize this – the outer head of the biceps."

– Robert Kennedy, *MuscleMag International* publisher and editor responding to a reader's question about the "best" biceps exercise.

No matter what the reason for taking up weight training, we doubt there are few readers who don't want bigger biceps. The front upper arm muscles can be considered the universal glamour muscles. As soon as people find out you lift weights they don't ask you to flex the calves, they ask you to roll up the sleeve and flex a biceps. Out of the hundreds, perhaps thousands of exercises that can be performed in gyms, odds are at any given time there are more people training biceps than any other muscle. Everyone whose ever picked up a barbell wants bigger, fuller, more peaked biceps. Much of Arnold's popularity was due to his monstrous upper arms. Take a look at the front cover of his book, *Arnold, The Education of a Bodybuilder.* See what we mean. To this day, no bodybuilder has been able to duplicate that single double biceps pose.

Aaron Maddron

TRAINING THE BICEPS

The biceps are named as such because the muscle is composed of two heads or "ceps." And while some writers suggest you can train the heads separately, the fact is all biceps exercises hit both heads. Changing the angle may stress one head slightly more than the other, but only marginally. Another misconception is that some exercises are mass builders and some are peaking movements. We hate to burst a few bubbles but all exercises are mass builders to one extent or another. Some are better because of the weight you can use (i.e. barbell curls); while others are more isolation movements and more suited to precontest training. But you can't change the shape of your biceps. That my dear friend is set for you the moment you were conceived. By this we mean genetics. Compare photos of bodybuilding superstars Sergio Oliva and Ronnie Coleman. Sergio's arms are among the largest ever seen on the Olympia stage, but despite their size, could never be considered "peaked." Full, yes. Large, incredibly so. But not high, sharp, or peaked. 1998 Mr. Olympia, Ronnie Coleman, on the other hand literally has a set of Swiss Alps protruding from his upper arms. Sergio's biceps were probably fuller, but they can't compare to Ronnie's in terms of peakness. Does this mean that Sergio neglected to perform peaking exercises? Certainly not. We assure you Mr. Oliva spent hundreds of hours doing concentration curls, cable curls, and just about every other so called "peaking" exercise there is. Conversely Ronnie Coleman does not do a proportionally higher amount of peaking exercises than other, less endowed bodybuilders do. Ronnie was simply blessed with the right genetics for building such guns. Of course he still had to spend thousands of hours busting his ass in the gym to bring out his unique biceps shape.

Ronnie Coleman

"I just do what I love, and I love to train biceps. I have my favorite exercises and I rarely mess with what has worked for me. It's worked so well that one time last year I had to sharply curtail my biceps workout and work arms only once a month. No one believes me but it's true!"

– Ronnie Coleman, 1998 Mr. Olympia commenting on a "problem" most bodybuilders would love to have, biceps that grow too fast!

Perhaps an even better example of genetics can be seen within the King himself, Arnold Schwarzenegger. Dig out an old copy of *Muscle Builder Power* magazine (the forerunner to today's *Muscle and Fitness* magazine) and take a look at one of Arnold's great double biceps poses and compare his arms. Notice how one is long and full much like Sergio's, and the other is high and peaked similar to Ronnie Coleman's. Do you think that Arnold planned it that way? Of course not. It just means that one arm had better genetics for peakness and the other for fullness.

A final myth about biceps training is that you can lengthen the biceps. In other words stretch the lower biceps so that they reach the elbow and fill in the gap between upper and lower arm. We hate to say it, but once again genetics dictates the length of the biceps. Some authorities say that by doing preacher curls you can lengthen the biceps, but this is just not the case. Biceps length is based on fiber length and where the biceps tendon attaches to the forearm bone – both of which are preset at conception. It is true that by doing preachers you can build up the lower biceps creating the illusion of length. But you have not changed a foot-long ruler into a yardstick!

Bodybuilders with great, long biceps include Sergio Oliva, Paul Dillett, and Kevin Lervone. Examples of greater shorter biceps include Franco Columbia, Dorian Yates, and Lee Haney. Notice that the last two names in the short list have won 14 Mr. Olympia's between them! Just because your biceps don't go right to the elbow doesn't mean your bodybuilding career is limited. Both Dorian and Lee made the best of what they had and combined with emphasizing their strong points (back, shoulders, triceps, etc.) and dominated the sport for the 1980s and 1990s.

BICEPS EXERCISES

BARBELL CURLS

Execution – Grab a barbell with a shoulder width grip and curl upwards until the forearms are about 45 degrees with the floor. Lower down until the bar is one or two inches from the thighs.

Muscles worked – Barbell curls not only work the biceps, but the front shoulders and forearms as well.

Comments – Another of bodybuilding's most basic exercises, barbell curls are to biceps what squats are to legs, and bench presses are to chest. If you need to swing the weight up using body momentum, you are using too much weight. It's as simple as that. Some bodybuilders find straight bars hard on the wrist and prefer the bent EZ-bar. Keep in mind that as soon as you start rotating the palms inward, the forearms start doing more of the work. If at all possible stick with the straight bar.

Preacher curls are probably the best exercise for filling in the space between the biceps and forearms. – Lee Priest

Finish

Start

"Boyer claims that even as a beginner he could split his biceps just by focusing on them with his mind, sort of the way some people can wiggle their ears! His incredible biceps peak is also a genetic gift. Boyer would have great peaks whether he did barbell curls or concentration curls."

– Greg Zulak, *MuscleMag* columnist commenting on the incredible biceps of bodybuilding legend, Boyer Coe.

PREACHER CURLS

Execution – Sit down on the bench and rest your forearms on the padded support. Grab a barbell and raise it until the forearms are vertical with the floor. Lower until the arms are just short of locked out. Repeat.

Muscles worked – Preachers stress the entire biceps, particularly the lower regions. By having the arms resting on a platform, the front shoulders play a smaller role than standing barbell curls. The forearms also play a significant role in this exercise.

Comments – Also called Scott curls in honor of the first Mr. Olympia, Larry Scott, preacher curls are the mainstay of most bodybuilder's arm routines. As a word of caution don't let the weight bounce at the bottom. Numerous individuals have torn biceps tendons in this manner. The only cure for this by the way is surgery. Finally, as discussed earlier, preacher curls will not lengthen the biceps. This is genetic. But they are probably the best exercise for filling in the space between the biceps and forearms.

SPYDER CURLS

Execution – If possible turn the preacher bench pad around so that the 45 degree side is facing you and the vertical side facing forward. From here perform the exercise as if you where doing normal preacher curls.

Muscles worked – Performing preacher curls on a 90-degree angle shifts more of the stress from the lower to the center and upper biceps.

Comments – Many bodybuilders find regular preacher curls stressful on the wrists or elbows. Spyder curls are one option. If the preacher bench in your gym cannot be set up in this manner, we have seen some bodybuilders use the back of the leg press chair. Others have wrapped a towel around a Smith machine bar and done them there. Odds are there's something in your gym that can be adapted for spyder curls.

STANDING DUMBELL CURLS

Execution – Grab a set of dumbells and curl them upwards until the forearm is about 45 degrees to the floor. Lower until the dumbells are in line with the thighs.

Muscles worked – Dumbell curls work the entire biceps, with the forearms and front shoulders playing a supporting role.

Comments – You can either keep the palms facing upwards at all times, or rotate from palms up at the top, to palms facing inward at the bottom. The latter is called supination and takes advantage of the fact the biceps not only elevate the forearm but also rotate it. Keep in mind that you can supinate a lot more weight than you can curl. This means that you will be obtaining a limited supination effect because of your weaker curling strength. As an example, if you can curl 45 pounds, you can probably rotate 100 pounds or more. Therefore supinating with 45 pounds is far below what you are capable of handling. Still, some bodybuilders, including Arnold "what's his name," swear by supination. Our advice is to give it a try and see how it feels.

Start

Standing dumbell curls
Finish

CABLE CURLS

Execution – Attach a medium length bar to a low pulley, with a shoulder width grip and the knees slightly bent, curl the bar upwards to just short of the shoulders. Lower until the bar is one or two inches from the thighs.

Muscles worked – Cable curls are very similar to barbell curls in that the biceps do most of the work, with the front shoulders and forearms playing a secondary role.

Frank Sepe

Comments – Cable curls have an advantage over barbell curls in that you can curl the bar higher than 45 degrees with the floor. With a barbell, once the forearms start approaching vertical, gravity starts losing its effect on the muscle. Instead of going against the muscle, it places the force down through the forearm bone. A cable on the other hand will provide continuous tension throughout the full range of motion. As with barbell and dumbell curls, don't swing the weight using body momentum. One or two cheat reps at the end is fine but don't swing on every rep!

INCLINE CURLS

Execution – Grab two dumbells and sit down on a 45-degree incline bench. Curl the dumbells upward until the forearm is about 45 degrees to the floor. Lower slowly until the dumbells are in line with your hips, or just before the arms lock out. Repeat.

Muscles worked – Incline curls work the entire biceps with special emphasis on the center and upper regions. The forearms and front shoulders also play a role.

Comments – The primary advantage of sitting in an incline chair is that you can't swing the weight up using body momentum. Also by leaning back on an incline, forearm involvement is reduced. As with standing dumbell curls you can try supinating the palms as you lift upwards.

**Ronnie Coleman
works his
biceps with
concentration
curls.**
Finish

Start

CONCENTRATION CURLS

Execution – Sit down on a bench and with the elbow resting on the inside of one knee curl a dumbell up to that by now familiar 45-degree angle. Lower the weight until the arms are just short of being locked out.

Muscles worked – Concentration curls work the entire biceps, with the forearms playing a secondary role. Bracing the arm on the knee removes most of the front shoulder involvement.

Comments – Some writers call this a great "peaking"exercise but hopefully by now you realize that peak is primarily due to genetics. Concentration curls are a great second or third exercise but because of the limited weight that can be handled, shouldn't replace barbell or preacher curls as a mass builder.

ONE-ARM PREACHER CURLS

Execution – Grab a dumbell and sit down on a preacher bench with the working arm rested on the pad. Lower until the arm is just short of locked out, and then curl it upwards until it's perpendicular with the floor. Repeat.

Muscles worked – One arm preacher curls are similar to the barbell version in that while the entire biceps is stressed, the lower part receives the most benefit. The forearms also play a minor role.

Comments – You can sort of consider this exercise as the concentration curl version of barbell preacher curls. They make a great second or third exercise, but probably won't build the same degree of strength and size as regular barbell preacher curls.

NARROW REVERSE CHINS

Execution – Grab a chin-up bar with a narrow, reverse grip. With the torso leaning slightly back, pull yourself up until the bar is about mid-chest. Lower slowly until the arms are just short of being locked out. Repeat

Muscles worked – Narrow reverse chin-ups stress the entire biceps, with the forearms and lats playing a major role as well.

Comments – Although considered a back exercise, narrow chins are about fifty percent biceps. This exercise makes a great second exercise in a superset. Do a set of standing barbell curls, and then jump up and grab the chin up bar and rep out. Many readers will no doubt be able to perform high reps on this exercise. In this case either do the previous superset, leave the exercise until last in your biceps routine, or hold a dumbell between you feet or thighs.

ADVANCED BICEPS ROUTINES

ROUTINE A

	Sets	Reps
Standing barbell curls	3	6-8
Incline dumbell curls	3	10-12
Concentration curls	2-3	10-12

ROUTINE B

Standing dumbell curls	3	6-8
Cable curls	3	10-12
One-arm preacher curls	2-3	10-12

ROUTINE C

Preacher curls	3	6-8
Standing dumbell curls	3	10-12
One-arm cable curls	2-3	10-12

ROUTINE D

Standing dumbell curls	3	6-8
Incline curls	3	10-12
Concentration curls	2-3	10-12

ROUTINE E

Standing barbell curls	3	6-8
Preacher curls	3	10-12
Spyder curls	2-3	10-12

ROUTINE F

Standing cable curls	3	6-8
Preacher curls	3	10-12
Narrow reverse chins	2-3	* 10-12

* If you can perform more than 10 to 12 reps either holding a weight between the knees or feet, or superset with preacher curls.

THREE MONTH TWO VARIABLE SWITCH ROUTINE

MONTH 1

	Sets	Reps
Standing barbell curls	3	15-20
Incline dumbell curls	3	15-20
Hammer curls	3	15-20

MONTH 2

Incline dumbell curls	3	10-12
Hammer curls	3	10-12
Standing barbell curls	3	10-12

MONTH 3

Hammer curls	3	6-8
Barbell curls	3	6-8
Incline dumbell curls	3	6-8

CHAPTER TWELVE

Triceps – Bodybuilding's Golden Horseshoes

Matt McLaughlin

"The triceps makes up almost two thirds of the arm's size if the arm is built proportionally. The triceps muscle is one third bigger than the biceps. The triceps has more muscle heads than the biceps. Hence the prefix tri meaning three compared to the prefix bi meaning two."

–The editors of *MuscleMag International*, commenting on the key to huge arms – the triceps!

Despite the amount of attention given to them, the biceps are not the arm's largest muscle. Located to the side and rear is a larger and more powerful three-headed muscle called the triceps. Not only do they make up 50 percent of the visual effect in a front double biceps pose, but also they are a major contributor on such basic exercises as bench presses and shoulder presses. The triceps are the "thighs" of the upper arm and you know how important the thighs are to the legs. If your goal is to step on stage sporting the largest guns possible, then triceps training is a must.

TRAINING THE TRICEPS

Triceps training generally falls into three categories, pushdowns, extensions, and narrow presses. As with biceps training you can't target one head individually, but you can shift the stress more from one to another. But keep in mind, all triceps exercises activate all three heads. Bodybuilders famous for their triceps include Dorian Yates, Aaron Baker, Flex Wheeler, Ernie Taylor, and Lee Priest.

TRICEPS EXERCISES

TWO-ARM PUSHDOWNS

Execution – Grab the pulley pushdown attachment with a palms facing down grip, about six to eight inches apart. With the elbows and upper arms locked to your sides, push the forearms downwards until the arm is locked out straight. Return to the starting position with the hands about chest high or forearms at about a 45-degree angle with the floor.

Muscles worked – Pushdowns work the entire triceps with the side and medial heads receiving the most benefit.

Comments – Pushdowns fall in the same category as leg extensions – bodybuilders either love 'em or hate 'em. This is one exercise where the "cheating" version may be more effective for some individuals. No doubt you have seen some bodybuilders performing this exercise by letting the elbows flare out to the side and almost pushing the weight down like a narrow press. In effect this is what they are doing – a reverse pressdown. USA National champion, Dennis Newman swears by this exercise. What attracts so many bodybuilders to this version is that you can lift considerable more weight, perhaps double what can be used on an elbows-in strict pushdown. So while the authors are sticklers for strict style, this is one case where cheating has a role to play.

Finally, most gyms have a wide assortment of triceps attachments including straight bars, bent bars, V-shaped bars, and ropes. One is no better than the other but most bodybuilders have their favorites so try them all.

Finish

Aaron Maddron works his triceps with one-arm pushdowns.

Start

ONE-ARM PUSHDOWNS

Execution – Grab a small, single grip handle and with the elbow kept close to the side, push downwards until the arm is locked out at the bottom. Raise upwards until your hand is about chest high.

Muscles worked – One-arm pushdowns work the entire triceps with the side head receiving the most benefit.

Comments – One-arm pushdowns are similar to one-arm concentration curls in that they are probably not as effective for building mass as the two-arm version. Instead they make a great second exercise or pre-contest exercise.

REVERSE PUSHDOWNS

Execution – Perform the two previous exercises using a supinated (palms facing up) grip.

Muscles worked – Reverse pushdowns work the rear, long head of the triceps.

Comments – The kinesiologists out there are probably questioning our sanity by now. Reverse pushdowns are an example of where anatomy and physiology dictate that changing the grip makes no difference, but bodybuilders find otherwise. Many bodybuilders find that by reversing the grip on one and two arm pushdowns allows them to get a better contraction in the rear head of the triceps. Whether it's biology or placebo, who knows. But bodybuilders swear by it. It's for this reason we discuss the two grips separately.

LYING BARBELL EXTENSIONS

Execution – Lay a barbell at the end of a bench and lie back with your head a couple of inches from the weight. Reach back and grab the bar with a palms up grip, about shoulder width apart. With the upper arm locked perpendicular with the floor, bend at the elbow and lower the bar to the forehead. Push back up until the arms are locked straight.

Muscles worked – Lying extensions target the whole triceps with special emphasis on the long rear head. The front shoulders and upper chest are worked as well.

Comments – Lying extensions are another of the so-called "basic" exercises. The biggest mistake people make is bringing the bar back behind the head in a pullover type manner. This defeats the purpose as the lats and chest end up doing most of the work. The upper arm must remain perpendicular with the floor. As soon as it starts moving back, you lose triceps' effectiveness. Finally you may want to experiment with an EZ-curl bar. Many individuals find the straight bar hard on the wrists. An EZ-curl allows you to rotate the palms inwards, which in most cases is less stressful on the wrists.

LYING DUMBELL EXTENSIONS

Execution – Hold a dumbell in each hand with the palms facing inwards. Lie back on a flat bench and lower the dumbells to the side of your head. Return to the starting position with the arms locked out straight.

Muscles worked – As with barbell extension, dumbell extensions target the whole triceps. The front shoulders and chest play a secondary role.

Comments – There are two advantages to using dumbells over a barbell. For starters they allow you to bring the weight lower, thus stressing the muscle with a greater range of motion. Second, they allow you some room for error. If something goes wrong with a barbell you have your face to worry about (the nickname for this exercise is skullcrushers!). Whereas losing control of a dumbell allows you to drop it to the side of the head.

NARROW PRESSES

Execution – Either set a barbell up on a bench press rack, or rest an EZ-curl bar behind you on the bench. Grab the bar with a shoulder or slightly less than shoulder width grip. From here the movement is identical to a regular bench press except you try to keep the elbows close to the body.

Muscles worked – Narrow bench presses work the entire triceps, but the front shoulders and chest also play a major role.

Comments – For variety try a false grip with the thumbs on the same side of the bar as the fingers. As with lying extensions some individuals may find the straight bar stressful on the wrist so try experimenting with an EZ-curl bar.

SEATED DUMBELL EXTENSIONS – ONE ARM

Execution – Sit down on the end of a flat bench and grab a dumbell so that palm is facing away from you and the heel of the hand is facing upward. With the upper arm locked perpendicular with the floor, Slowly lower the dumbell behind the head. Return to the starting position with the arm locked out straight.

Muscles worked – One-arm extensions work the long rear head of the triceps.

Comment – For extra support lay the free hand underneath the armpit or on top of the shoulder of the arm being exercised.

TWO ARM, TWO DUMBELL EXTENSIONS

Execution – Grab two dumbells with the heels of the hands facing forward and palms facing inwards. With the upper arm locked straight, lower the dumbells behind the head. Return to the locked out position.

Muscles worked – Two arm, two dumbell extensions primarily work the long rear head of the triceps.

Comments – Many bodybuilders prefer this version as it's more symmetrical. In other words, it's easier to keep your balance. As a word of caution don't bounce at the bottom as such movements place excessive stress on the elbows.

TWO ARM, ONE DUMBELL EXTENSIONS

Execution – Grab a dumbell with two hands so that the palms are facing upwards and thumbs pointing forward, in the same manner you would volley a volleyball. With the upper arms kept straight, lower the dumbell behind the head. Return to the locked out position.

Muscles worked – Two arm, one dumbell extensions primarily work the long rear head of the triceps.

Comments – Most bodybuilders find this the most comfortable of the three versions of dumbell extensions. You'll quickly discover that you can lift more than double the weight you'd use for single dumbell extensions.

Most bodybuilders find this the most comfortable version of dumbell extensions. Lee Priest

Finish

Start

FRENCH PRESSES

Execution – Lay an EZ-curl bar on your lap and sit down on the end of a bench. Raise the bar above your head with the hands holding the inner bend, palms facing upwards. Keeping the upper arm vertical, lower the bar behind the head. Return to the arms locked out position.

Muscles worked – French presses primarily work the long rear head of the triceps.

Comments – Although a great size and strength builder, many bodybuilders find French presses more stressful on the wrists and elbows than the similar dumbell extensions.

KICKBACKS

Execution – Bend forward and rest one hand and knee on a flat bench. Grab a dumbell so that the palm is facing inwards and upper arm locked parallel with the floor. With the upper arm kept stationary, extend the forearm back until the arm is locked straight out behind you. Return to the starting position with the forearm pointing towards the floor.

Muscles worked – Kickbacks work the entire triceps. The rear shoulders and lats also come into play as stabilizers.

Comments – Kickbacks fall in the same category as concentration curls and dumbell flyes. They make a great isolation exercise for finishing off your routine, but there are other exercises that are more effective for building size and strength. The biggest mistake people make on this one is to swing the weight up using the upper arm. In order to totally isolate the triceps you must keep the upper arm locked tight to the side. As soon as it starts moving the lats and rear delts take over.

BENCH DIPS

Execution – Set two benches four to five feet apart and rest the hands on one and heels of the feet on the other. With the knees kept slightly bent, bend the elbows and lower the body down between the benches. Return to the starting position with the arms locked straight at the top.

Muscles worked – Bench dips work the entire triceps with the front shoulders and chest also playing a major role.

Comments – You will need to experiment with hand and bench spacing to maximize triceps stimulation. Some spacings will put extra stress on the shoulders, while others will be hard on the lower back. If your bodyweight is not adequate have a partner lay a 45-pound plate or two across your lap. Or make the exercise the second or third movement in a superset or triset.

ADVANCED TRICEPS ROUTINES

ROUTINE A	Sets	Reps
Lying EZ-bar extensions	3	6-8
Narrow presses	3	10-12
Dumbell extensions	3	10-12

ROUTINE B		
French presses	3	6-8
Two-arm pushdowns	3	10-12
Bench dips	3	10-12

ROUTINE C		
Narrow presses	3	6-8
Kickbacks	3	10-12
One-arm pushdowns	3	10-12

ROUTINE D

Weighted bench dips	3	6-8
Behind-the-head rope extensions	3	10-12
One-arm dumbell extensions	3	10-12

ROUTINE E

Two-arm dumbell extensions	3	6-8
Pushdowns	3	10-12
Triceps machine extensions	3	10-12

ROUTINE F (Dumbells)

Lying dumbell extensions	3	6-8
Seated one-arm extensions	3	10-12
Kickbacks	3	10-12

ROUTINE G (Barbells)

Lying EZ-bar extensions	3	6-8
Narrow presses	3	10-12
French presses	3	10-12

In order to totally isolate the triceps you must keep the upper arm locked tight to your side.
— Aaron Maddron

Finish

THREE MONTH TWO VARIABLE SWITCH ROUTINE

MONTH 1

	Sets	Reps
Lying EZ-bar extensions	3	15-20
Pushdowns	3	15-20
Bench dips	3	15-20

MONTH 2

Pushdowns	3	10-12
Bench dips	3	10-12
Lying EZ-bar extensions	3	10-12

MONTH 3

Bench dips	3	6-8
Lying EZ-bar extensions	3	6-8
Pushdowns	3	6-8

Start

CHAPTER THIRTEEN

Formidable Forearms

"The answer is genetic ability. Many people are born with the capability to build large muscular forearms. Just as we've all seen guys who have never done calf raises in their lives but still have tremendous calf development, others are likewise blessed with naturally large well-developed forearms."

– Greg Zulak, *MuscleMag International* columnist commenting on the role genetics may play in muscle development, especially the calves and forearms.

Dan Freeman

Despite their diminutive size and overshadowing by the biceps and large torso muscles, the forearms are among the most important muscles in the body. Think about it, just about every single exercise you can perform requires you to grip something. Even such leg exercises as hamstring curls and leg extensions require the forearms for stability. If you don't believe us, just try leg extensions with your arms folded across the chest. Your workout poundages will drop by as much as 50 percent. Not because the thighs can't lift the weight, but because you can't hold yourself down in the chair. From the sailors of old having to hoist sails by hand, to modern wrestlers, judoists, and rugby players, all require tremendous forearm strength.

TRAINING THE FOREARMS

When we talk about the forearms we are really referring to three primary muscles groups. If you hold your hands palm up and curl them towards you, it's primarily the flexors that do most of the work. Conversely, face the palms downward and curl the knuckles up towards the forearm and the extensors do most of the work. Finally if you curl the entire forearm upwards as if doing a barbell curl but with the palms facing downward, you are mainly using the brachialus. This is the larger muscle located between the upper forearm and lower, upper arm.

"My suggestion is to begin by doing a couple of selected forearm exercises. Do them for a week and see what happens. Then try two new ones for a week. Before long you will be able to determine which exercises are most productive for you."

– Bill Starr, *MuscleMag International* contributor commenting on the role experimentation plays in training.

There are two schools of thought when it comes to forearm training. Some authorities suggest that the forearms get adequate stimulation from training the upper arms and torso muscles and don't require any additional exercise. Others believe the forearms are like any other muscle group and must be trained on a regular basis. By now you'll probably not be surprised to hear that our opinion is sort of a combination of both!

If you find that after six months to a year of training, your forearms are proportionally smaller, or weaker than your upper arms, then yes you need direct forearm training. This is especially true if your forearms give out first on such pulling movements as chins, front pulldowns, and various rows. But if you have a strong grip, and people keep calling you Popeye, then you probably don't need any additional forearm work. If you fall into the former group, then the following exercises are guaranteed to put some meat on your forearm bones.

FOREARM EXERCISES

WRIST CURLS

Execution – Grab a barbell with a four to six inch-wide grip, palms facing upwards. With the forearms resting on the end of a flat bench, lower the barbell by bending the hands downward. Let the bar roll to the tips of the fingers (or as far as you can without letting it go) and then curl the hands upwards so your knuckles are facing upwards. Repeat.

Muscles worked – Wrist curls work the flexors of the forearm.

Comments – For variety you can perform this exercise using one dumbell.

REVERSE WRIST CURLS

Execution – Sit down on the end of a bench and grab a barbell with the palms facing downward. With the forearms braced on the end of the bench bend at the wrist so the hands are pointing downward. Return to the starting position by drawing the hands up and backwards.

Muscles worked – Reverse wrist curls work the forearm extensors, but the brachialus also get a bit of a burn.

For variety, you can perform reverse wrist curls using one dumbell.
– Charlie Thomas

Comments – As with wrist curls you can use a dumbell in place of the barbell. In fact the dumbell may be more comfortable as the barbell prevents the hands from rotating slightly outward as they lift up. You can easily see this yourself by facing the palms downward and then lifting. Notice how the knuckles are facing slightly away from you? The barbell would prevent this from happening and put more stress on the wrist.

Hammer curls are a great way to fill the gap between the biceps and forearms.
– Joe Spinello

Finish

Start

REVERSE CURLS

Execution – Grab a barbell with the palms facing downward. From here curl the bar up as if doing regular biceps curls.

Muscles worked – Reverse barbell curls primarily work the brachialus, but the biceps and forearm extensors also come into play.

HAMMER CURLS

Execution – Grab a set of dumbells and curl them upwards keeping the palms facing inwards at all time. Slowly lower to just short of locking out.

Muscles worked – Hammer curls primarily work the brachialus, but the biceps and forearm extensors also come into play.

Comments – Hammer curls are an excellent way to finish the biceps and start the forearms. They also a great way to fill the gap between the biceps and forearms. As with regular dumbell biceps curls, you can stand up, or sit down in a straight or inclined bench.

ZOTTMAN CURLS

Execution – Grab a set of dumbells and curl them upward using the standard palms up grip. At the top rotate so the palms are facing downward and lower.

Muscles worked – Zottman curls work both upper and lower arms. Curling up primarily hits the biceps and forearm flexors, while lowering down primarily hits the forearm extensors and brachialus.

Comments – Although seldom seen in gyms, Zottman curls are one of the most complete arm exercises. If you are stuck for time and can only do one exercise for biceps and forearms, this is it. You can perform Zottman curls standing or seated.

ADVANCED FOREARM EXERCISES

ROUTINE A	Sets	Reps
Dumbell wrist curls	3	15-20
Dumbell reverse wrist curls	3	15-20

ROUTINE B		
Barbell wrist curls	3	15-20
Reverse barbell curls	3	15-20

ROUTINE C		
Barbell reverse wrist curls	3	15-20
Dumbell wrist curls	3	15-20

ROUTINE D		
Barbell wrist curls	3	15-20
Barbell reverse wrist curls	3	15-20
Barbell reverse curls	3	15-20

ROUTINE E		
Dumbell wrist curls	3	15-20
Dumbell reverse wrist curls	3	15-20
Barbell reverse curls	3	15-20

ROUTINE F		
Barbell reverse curls	3	15-20
Dumbell reverse wrist curls	3	15-20
Hammer curls	3	15-20

THREE MONTH TWO VARIABLE SWITCH

MONTH 1	Sets	Reps
Barbell wrist curls	3	15-20
Dumbell reverse wrist curls	3	15-20
Reverse curls	3	15-20

MONTH 2		
Dumbell reverse wrist curls	3	10-12
Reverse curls	3	10-12
Barbell wrist curls	3	10-12

MONTH 3		
Reverse curls	3	6-8
Barbell wrist curls	3	6-8
Dumbell reverse wrist curls	3	6-8

CHAPTER FOURTEEN

Absolute Abs

Whether you are a competitive bodybuilder or a weekend warrior, we are sure a small, tight waist is one of your goals. When we comment that someone is "putting on weight" it's usually the midsection we are referring to. Just about every pose you hit on stage involves the abs. As with the calves and shoulders, it's difficult to hide poor abs. Talk to any personal trainer and they'll tell you that nine out of ten clients list a smaller waist size as their primary goal. What's ironic is that the key to a smaller midsection is as dependent on what you do outside the gym as in it. What we are referring to here of course is diet. The greatest set of abs in the world are useless if covered by a layer of fat. Spending countless hours on the floor doing crunches won't get rid of the fat either. Only by burning more calories in the form of cardio exercise and reducing calorie intake (or rearranging the proportions of fat, carbohydrate, and protein) will accomplish this.

Mike O'Hearn

"When it comes to abdominal development, the old advice is still true. Do ab exercises to develop your rectus abdominal muscle and then burn away the fat with aerobics and diet to let them show."

—The editors of *MuscleMag International* commenting on the three variables for great abs — exercise, aerobics, and diet.

TRAINING THE ABS

One of the biggest misconceptions about ab training is that there are upper and lower abs. While the segmented appearance gives the impression of an upper and lower region, the fact remains that the abdominal muscle fibers run north and south, not east and west. This means they connect in under the rib cage and run down to the groin. It's one continuous length of muscle fiber. But, and here's the important point, despite kinesiologists saying otherwise, changing the exercises can shift the stress from upper to lower. As with other muscle groups it's not a total isolation, but you can prioritize nevertheless.

"Sharp, well built abdominals are worth a king's ransom. To my mind there is no more treasured possession."

– The late Vince Gironda, commenting on perhaps the hardest muscles to develop and see, the abdominals.

Darrem Charles

Abdominal training can be subdivided into two categories: having the legs move towards the stationary torso (leg raises), and having the torso move towards the stationary legs (crunches). Virtually all ab exercises fall into one of these two categories.

ABDOMINAL EXERCISES

CRUNCHES

Execution – Lie down on the floor so that the knees are bent and feet flat on the floor. With the hands behind the head, elbows pointing outwards, lift the torso upwards so that the shoulder blades only come four or five inches off the floor. Return to the starting position.

Muscles worked – Crunches work the entire abdominals with the hip flexors and intercostals also playing a role. Although kinesiologists say otherwise, crunches seem to place more stress on the upper abs than lower.

Comments – Crunches have replaced situps as the number one ab exercise. Lifting the torso only partways to the knees not only reduces hip flexor involvement, but also puts less stress on the lower back. With all-due-respect to military conditioners, situps are a mediocre ab exercise at best. Not to mention the fact that the human spine was not meant to curl up into a ball in this manner. The abs only move the torso by ten to twelve inches, the distance you move during a crunch. We suggest leaving situps to your drill sergeant!

REVERSE CRUNCHES

Execution – Lie face up on the floor and elevate your feet so your lower leg is parallel with the floor and thighs perpendicular with the floor. With the torso kept stationary, draw the knees back to chest level and then push forwards until the legs are just short of being locked out straight. Keep your feet off the ground at all times.

Muscles worked – Reverse crunches work the entire abdominals with the intercostals and hip flexors also playing a role. Unlike crunches, reverse crunches seem to place more stress on the lower abs than upper abs.

Comments – You can consider reverse crunches the opposite of regular crunches. Instead of the upper body moving towards the stationary lower body, the legs move towards the stationary upper body. Although some bodybuilders lock the legs out completely at the bottom, we caution against this as it places extra stress on the lower back.

LYING LEG RAISES

Execution – Lie back as if doing a reverse crunch. With the knees slightly bent, raise the legs until they form a 45-degree angle with the floor. Lower down until the feet are one or two inches from the floor. Repeat.

Muscles worked – Lying leg raises primarily work the lower abs but the intercostals, hip flexors, and upper abs also come into play.

Comments – Even with the legs bent, some individuals find this exercise too stressful on the lower back. At the first sign of lower back pain, stop the exercise. With other, safer exercises available it's just not worth the risk.

CHAIR LEG RAISES

Execution – Stand up on the machine's foot rests and place your elbows and forearms on the two pads. With the back placed firmly against the back support pad, bend the knees and raise the legs until your thighs are parallel or slightly higher than parallel with the floor. Lower the legs down to just short of locking out.

Muscles worked – Leg raises place more stress on the lower ab region, but the upper abs also come into play. Bending the legs will also activate the hip flexors.

Comments – Chair leg raises are an example of where the best version is not the recommended version. To totally isolate the abdominals the legs should be kept straight. But this places tremendous stress on the lower back ligaments. It's much safer to bend the knees and elevate the legs. Of course it's a trade-off since bending the knees brings the hip flexors into play.

HANGING LEG RAISES

Execution – Grab an overhead chinning bar and raise the legs by bending at the knees until the thighs are parallel with the floor. Lower slowly until the legs are just short of locked out.

Muscles worked – Hanging leg raises primarily work the lower abdominal region, but the upper abs and hip flexors also come into play.

Comments – This is an exercise where maintaining position is just as difficult as the exercise itself. Many individuals may find it difficult to support their entire body weight for extended periods of time with just their

forearm strength. In other words, the forearms may give out before the abs have been fatigued. If you fall into this category you can either leave the exercise until last when the abs are already fatigued and you won't need to do as many reps; or use a set of wrist straps to increase your grip strength. Finally, as with chair leg raises, raising the legs straight, while slightly more effective for the abs (because of less hip flexor involvement) places more stress on the lower back.

Although slightly more effective for the abs, raising the legs straight places more stress on the lower back.
– Lee Apperson

Perform rope crunches at
different points in your
routine and see how it feels.
– Abbas Katami

ROPE CRUNCHES

Execution – Grab the triceps pushdown rope and kneel down on the floor with the rope held
behind the head. With the elbows in close to the sides and rope resting on the shoulders, bend
forward (in effect downwards) into a crunch position. Only move the torso 10 to 12 inches in
range of motion.

Muscles worked – With the legs stationary, the upper abs do most of the work, but the lower
abs and hip flexors do play a supporting role.

Comments – This is an exercise where personal preference plays a major role. Some bodybuilders swear by it. Others find it useless. And finally a third group only derive some benefit
when the abs have been fatigued by some other exercise. Our advice is to perform rope
crunches at different points in your routine and see how it feels.

DECLINE HALF SITUPS

Execution – Lie back on the decline bench with the lower legs and feet locked in under the
upper and lower padded rollers. With the hands behind the head, elbows pointing outwards,
lie back until the torso is about 8 to 10 inches from the bench. Raise upwards until the torso is
just short of vertical with the floor.

Muscles worked – Decline half situps work the entire abdominal region with the hip flexors
also coming into play.

Comments – To execute this exercise properly you only move the torso through about a third of
the total range of motion. Going all the way down puts tremendous stress on the lower back,
while going all the way up is primarily a hip flexor movement. In effect you are performing the
middle third of the exercise. Finally, many individuals find this exercise very hard on the lower
back, even when performed in good style. At the first sign of lower back stress, stop the exercise
and stick with crunches or hanging leg raises.

Henrik Thamasian

ADVANCED ABDOMINAL ROUTINES

ROUTINE A

	Sets	Reps
Chair leg raises	3	15-20
Crunches	3	15-20
Reverse crunches	3	15-20

ROUTINE B

Hanging leg raises	3	15-20
Reverse crunches	3	15-20
Rope crunches	3	15-20

ROUTINE C

Chair leg raises	3	15-20
Crunches	3	15-20
Reverse crunches	3	15-20
Rope crunches	3	15-20

ROUTINE D

Crunches	2	15-20
Hanging leg raises	2	15-20
Reverse crunches	2	15-20
Rope crunches	2	15-20
Chair leg raises	2	15-20

If there's one muscle group you should experiment with in terms of rep ranges it's the abs. Traditionally the theory was to do high reps to "burn off" the excess fat around the midsection. But as we said earlier, fat must be burned with cardio (aerobic) exercise and a close attention to diet. While primarily composed of slow twitch muscle fiber and therefore probably more responsive to higher reps, nevertheless many bodybuilders are finding that by using extra resistance (i.e. a dumbell between the feet on leg raises) the abs will also respond. So even though we used 15 to 20 as a rep range in the previous routines, feel free to experiment from high reps (50 to 100) to low reps (6 to 12).

THREE MONTH TWO VARIABLE SWITCH ROUTINE

MONTH 1	Sets	Reps
Leg raises	3	20-30
Crunches	3	20-30
Reverse crunches	3	20-30

MONTH 2		
Crunches	3	15-20
Reverse crunches	3	15-20
Leg raises	3	15-20

MONTH 3 *		
Reverse crunches	3	8-10
Leg raises	3	8-10
Crunches	3	8-10

Most of you will find performing 8 to 10 reps for the abs very easy, especially after doing 15 to 30 during the two previous months. Even by slowing the speed down to ultra slow, 8 to 10 reps is not very taxing. It's almost a necessity to add extra weight to the exercises, either by holding a dumbell or plate to the chest on crunches, or by holding a dumbell between the feet on leg raises and reverse crunches. We don't, however, recommend using more than 15 or 20 pounds. Granted the abs don't have the same growth potential as the other torso muscles, but they are muscles just the same and using excessive weight could cause them to grow larger than you'd want. The trick is to use just enough weight to fatigue the muscles without stimulating excessive growth.

Jamo Nezzar

Mike and
Midajah O'Hearn

156

BOOK FIVE

THE HARDCORE JOURNEY CONTINUES

CHAPTER FIFTEEN

Stretching – Going to Great Lengths

"How would you like to add some size to your muscle? Add some polish? How about more posing grace and style? Everyone wants these results. But what if you could achieve such goals without iron? Is that possible? It is if you incorporate the fourth dimension – stretching – into your workout."

– Dwayne Hines II, Author and *MuscleMag International* contributor, commenting on the potential benefits of regular stretching.

Aaron Baker

Once thought to be primarily only for increasing flexibility, stretching is now recognized for the other benefits it conveys to athletes. Everything from increasing recovery and waste removal, to increasing a muscle's range of motion and stimulating muscle growth, is related to regular stretching. Let's take a closer look at why stretching should be part of any hardcore bodybuilder's program and not just the California fringe element!

INCREASED RANGE OF MOTION

While the old notion that weight training makes you muscle-bound is now considered part of bodybuilding mythology, nevertheless, it is true that constant muscle contracting (i.e. shortening) could decrease a muscle's range of motion over time. Further, any bodybuilder who fails to place equal emphasis on the negative (lowering) part of the rep is at special risk. Constantly shortening the muscles without a corresponding effort to lengthen (stretching) could result in the muscles adapting to the shorter length. Regular stretching counteracts this and helps keep the muscles at their pre-exercise length. Stretching also gives greater elasticity to the surrounding connective tissues. The more pliable the tendons, ligaments, and cartilage, the less chance of injury. And if this doesn't make an

Lee Priest

impression, how about the fact that the greater a muscle's range of motion during training, the bigger it will get? Stretching will optimize a muscle's range of motion.

LACTIC ACID ELIMINATION

You recognize it by the intense burning sensation that starts about half way through a set. Lactic acid is one of the primary breakdown products of anaerobic respiration, and is one of the main reasons why you have to terminate a set. Physiologically lactic acid build-up interferes with muscle contraction; while psychologically it damn well hurts! But a quality stretching program helps increase blood flow to the muscle which speeds lactic acid's removal. This means there's less present when you do the next set. And by stretching after your workout you help speed up the overall recovery process.

ENHANCED MUSCLE POTENTIAL

The outer covering surrounding your muscles is a dense fibrous sheath called fascial tissue. As its main purpose is to support and protect, the sheath is extremely strong. And while it does have some elastic properties, it can play a role in limiting muscle growth. The best example of what we are talking about is to put a balloon in a bottle and try blowing it up. Initially there's no problem but eventually a point is reached where the bottle's walls impede any further enlarging of the balloon. Many exercise physiologists propose that muscle growth may be limited in the same way by the tough outer fascial sheath. Regular stretching has been shown to loosen the sheath, making it more pliable and elastic. At least theoretically the greater expansion ability of the outer fascial covering may allow more room for muscle hypertrophy.

"For maximum muscle growth you have to stretch the fascia between sets. This is a protective sheath of connective tissue that envelops the muscle. By stretching the fascia you give the muscle underneath more room to grow."

– John Parrillo, *MuscleMag International* columnist, commenting on one of the least known benefits of stretching – increased muscle growth.

INCREASED MUSCLE RECOVERY

Hopefully by now most readers are aware that muscles don't grow in the gym during a workout. The growth phase takes place after you leave the gym. The time it takes the muscle to rebuild and the degree of rebuilding is called the "recovery ability," and is one of the most important variables in determining muscle growth. The popular athletic drugs, anabolic steroids, primarily work by speeding up an individual's recovery system. The faster your recovery system, the more exercise-induced stress your system can tolerate. The end result is larger and stronger muscles built in a shorter period of time.

Among the variables that determine recovery ability are the speed of nutrient delivery to the muscles and the corresponding rate of waste removal. The primary nutrient for muscle growth is protein, but carbohydrate and fat are also important. The primary waste products of muscle cell respiration are lactic acid and carbon dioxide. Stretching speeds up the rate of nutrient delivery to muscles and the rate of waste removal. More protein means faster muscle tissue repair, and additional carbohydrate and fat recharges the cells' energy systems for the next workout. Likewise getting rid of waste products faster allows the body to carry out the previous functions with more efficiency.

IGF-1 POWER

Back in the 1980s, insulin-like growth factor-1 (IGF-1) was unheard of in the athletic world. Unless you spent your days in a lab, IGF-1 wasn't an issue. But science is a very dynamic entity. Every month brings forth some new discovery, which has athletic implications.

IGF-1 is a peptide (protein) hormone that assists other hormones, particularly growth hormone, in their actions. On its own, IGF-1 doesn't seem to offer much in the way of performance enhancement. But when combined with steroids and growth hormones it seems to magnify the effects of the other two (called a synergistic effect). Two of IGF-1's primary effects are increasing amino acid uptake (the building blocks of protein) and promoting thermogenesis (stimulating fat loss by increasing temperature). Repeated stretching has been shown to elevate IGF-1 levels for up to several hours in some cases. Here's a perfect example of how stretching not only improves existing muscle tissue, but helps build new tissue.

HOW TO STRETCH

There are two broad categories of stretching; static and ballistic. Static stretching involves a slow, continuous movement that is held for an average of 15 to 20 seconds. Static stretching is the safest and most efficient way to stretch muscles.

Ballistic stretching involves rapid bouncing and jerking movements. With the possible exception of training for such sports as sprinting, basketball, etc, ballistic movements subject the muscles and connective tissues to tremendous stress. Instead of conditioning the body to help prevent injuries you may cause one.

Dave Fisher

WHEN TO STRETCH

BEFORE?

Many bodybuilders use light stretching as a form of warm-up. This is fine as long as you limit the intensity. But leave any vigorous stretching for later in the workout when the muscles are fully warmed up. A cold muscle has nowhere near the elasticity of a warm one. Try stretching an elastic band that has been kept in a freezer for a few hours. See what we mean. It doesn't take much to snap the band. Your muscles are the same.

DURING

Since you rest an average of 60 seconds between sets, this allows you plenty of time to stretch the muscle group you are working. Towards the end of the chapter we'll discuss individual stretching exercises. Suffice to say stretching a muscle between sets will make a big difference to your workouts. All the benefits we discussed earlier (speeding lactic acid removal, speeding recovery, etc.) apply. As stretching only takes 15 to 20 seconds and doesn't require much energy, it won't interfere with your weights, sets, or reps.

AFTER

By far the most popular time to stretch is after working out. By this time the muscles are fully warmed up, allowing for vigorous stretching without the risk of serious injury. Stretching at the end of a workout also serves as a cool-down period. Although by no means a necessity, it's easier on the system to gradually bring the heart rate back to normal rather than quit cold turkey. Another advantage to stretching at the end of a workout is the time factor. As this is probably the last activity you'll perform in the gym, there is less pressure on you to rush through and finish in a certain period.

SUGGESTED STRETCHING EXERCISES

The following are examples of some of the more common stretches. The list is far from complete. Stretching is a discipline all by itself and entire books and videos are available.

Thigh Stretch – Grab a stationary upright with one hand and bend the opposing leg so the foot points towards the butt. Hold the ankle with your free hand and maintain the position for 15 to 20 seconds. Lower the leg and repeat for the opposite side.

Hamstring Stretch – Place the heel of one foot on a waist-high support and gently bend the torso forward towards the elevated leg until you feel a gentle stretch in the hamstring. Hold, and then repeat for the other leg.

Calf Stretch – Stand in front of a wall and adopt a runner's stance with the rear leg straight and front leg bent. Place both hands on the wall for support and push the heel of the rear foot down on the floor. Try to keep the leg straight and foot flat on the floor. Repeat for the other side.

Chest Stretch – Grab a stationary upright with one hand and slowly turn away from the support trying to keep the arm as straight as possible. Hold for 15 to 20 seconds and then repeat for the other side.

Lat Stretch – Grab an overhead bar or machine with both hands. Bend the knees just enough to fully stretch the lats. Gently turn to one side, hold, and then turn to the other.

Shoulder stretch – Grab your left wrist with your right hand and gently pull the arm across the front of the body. Hold for 15 to 20 seconds and then repeat for the other side.

Triceps Stretch – Raise one arm above the head and bend the elbow so that it points toward the ceiling. Reach back and grab the wrist with the other hand, and gently pull downwards and backwards. Hold, and then repeat for the other side

CHAPTER SIXTEEN

Nutrition – Second to None

Jeramy Freeman

"You should be careful when reading books about health. Otherwise you might die of a misprint."

–Writer Mark Twain.

Diet can make or break a bodybuilder. The eternal struggle to gain mass is paradoxically done while fighting to drop body fat. The primary goal of any bodybuilder is to grow muscle, and keep it. In a society obsessed with looks, a significant proportion of our population is overweight, and that percentage is increasing every decade. Why?

Basically, the only guaranteed way to lose weight is to reduce your calorie intake and increase your calorie expenditure. But even then that simple process of dieting may cause you to lose both muscle and fat. What's the point? Fat or skinny, it reminds you of a presidential election. Your only thought is, are these my only choices? Fortunately, no. It is possible to lose body fat and build muscle at the same time. It's not complicated, but you need to be creative.

"We have met the enemy, and he is us."
– Pogo, from the comic strip of the same name.

Despite what you may or may not be taught in high school, depending on which state you live in, you can blame evolution (not low self-esteem, your inner child, or alien abductions, though we've both experienced the last one, but oddly enough only after consuming tequila) for being overweight. It is only in the last 100 years that many nations have managed to secure their food supply, and throughout the year food is normally available in abundance. If you've ever eaten wild meat (no, you Howard Stern-Wanna-Be, we're talking about venison) you'll notice how different it tastes. Venison has very little fat. You can eat pounds of the stuff and still be hungry. Our ancestors ate venison, berries, roots, bugs, and occasionally, each other.

"Like roast peacock."

A crusader from the middle ages, writing about the taste of human flesh. We'll take his word for it.

Greg Kovacs

In a lifestyle that was spent on the move, calories were burned quickly. Food was often scarce, and preserving food was technically challenging. So people pigged out, gorging themselves on the fats they craved. Those fat reserves could make the difference between death and survival. We've been programmed to binge. That midnight craving for cheesecake is an evolutionary echo from 10,000 years ago. You're not really hungry, but your body is preparing itself to face the next famine, which thanks to the Golden Arches, isn't coming. For some people the drive to consume fats is as strong or stronger, than their sex drive.

So now what? Is it all a lost cause? Shall we just surrender and head to a donut shop? Not at all. We know what causes the disease; the innate drive to consume fats. In this chapter, we present the cure.

THE CURE

How do you build muscle and lose fat at the same time? By frequently eating nutritious, high protein mini-meals that have a balanced mixture of fat, carbohydrate, and protein. Consuming small amounts throughout the day helps to maintain blood sugar-levels, so you don't develop serious hunger pangs. Eating small amounts at a time trains your digestive system to work with smaller amounts. Consuming smaller amounts reduces the calories you end up storing. Ingesting supplements such as creatine, multi-vitamins, and essential minerals ensure that your body's enzyme systems are ready to build muscles. And last but not least, burn those calories and stimulate overall muscle growth through strenuous workouts.

THE NUTRIENT GROUPS

Food can be subdivided into five broad nutrient categories: fats, carbohydrates, proteins, vitamins, and minerals. Some nutrients serve as the raw sources for building body tissue. Others are used as a fuel source. And still others are regulators and modulators. A diet that is deficient in any group will hinder your bodybuilding progress just as easily as overtraining or skipping workouts.

PROTEIN

Proteins make up about 12 percent of body mass. All proteins are composed primarily of amino acids, but the proportion in which the 22 amino acids are present differs greatly from one protein to another. Certain amino acids are essential to the diet (i.e. they cannot be synthesized by the body and are called essential amino acids). Unless the diet supplies proteins containing enough of these essential amino acids to meet minimum requirements, nutritional deficiencies will occur.

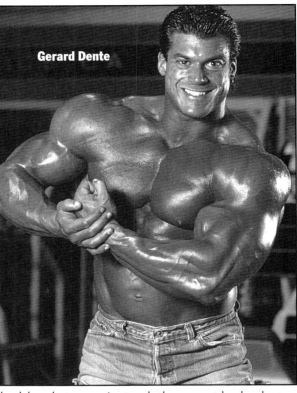

Gerard Dente

Nutritionally, the quality of a protein relates to its amino acid composition, and the digestibility of the protein. The essential amino acid requirements are the critical criteria for measuring protein quality. There are nine essential amino acids – histidine, isoleucine, leucine, lysine, methionine, phenylalanine, threonine, tryptophan and valine. The most abundant amino acid, glutamine, is considered conditionally essential. In times of stress demands may outstrip supplies.

Proteins are not absorbed directly into the blood stream. Instead, they must be broken down into peptides and amino acids, which are then absorbed and used by the body. Once the amino acids move out of the digestive tract they enter the blood stream and are transported to the liver and other organs and tissues. Most of the reassembling of the amino acids takes place in the liver. The cells of the various tissues form their own proteins from amino acids that diffuse from the blood into the interstitial fluid. The exact structure of a new protein is determined by the particular nucleic acid in the cell nucleus, responsible for its synthesis. While protein is used primarily for anabolic purposes, any surplus can be burned as fuel or stored as fat. This is why it is so important to include fats in the diet to provide for the body's energy needs, and to maintain regular exercise so that those fats are indeed burned.

HOW MUCH PROTEIN?

Few topics stir up the same debate as the amount of protein needed by athletes. For some, the old RDA (Recommended daily allowances) values are gospel and athletes need no more than the average person – about .3 grams per pound of body weight. At the other extreme are supplement manufacturers and pro bodybuilders who claim that nothing less than 1.5 to 2 grams per pound of body weight is needed. Inbetween we have the bulk of recent medical evidence that suggests athletes do need more, but not the 2 grams per pound of body weight frequently promoted in bodybuilding magazines. Something in the 1 gram per pound range seems to be sufficient.

The problem with the old RDA values was that they were calculated using sedentary individuals. Now in our opinion a fifty-year old couch potato is not comparable to a 220-pound competitive bodybuilder or wrestler. In addition the RDA values were based on mere survival, i.e. the minimum amount needed to keep an individual alive. The RDA's originated during the depression when starvation was unfortunately all too common. The U.S. government decided to come up with a series of minimums that would keep people alive. They certainly didn't have 280-pound Nasser El Sonbaty or 350-pound Greg Kovacs in mind when they worked out the mathematics!

Our advice is to consume about 1 gram of protein per pound of body weight. If you can get this amount in the diet, then you don't need to consume expensive protein supplements. But, and here's the key, most people find it difficult, if not impossible to take in this amount of quality protein in the form of food. Protein supplements do play a role. It takes all of two minutes to mix up a protein drink containing 30 to 50 grams of protein (for a closer look at protein supplements please see the chapter on Hardcore supplements).

PROTEIN SOURCES

Protein can generally be subdivided into two broad categories, plant and animal. From a long-term health point of view plant sources are better because they are much lower in fat. It's a fact that cultures around the world that have a low consumption of red meat have the highest life expectancy. But the problem with plant protein is that it's incomplete. That is it doesn't contain the full spectrum of amino acids. Strict vegetarians need to eat a wide variety of plant sources to get all the amino acids. On the other hand one good steak or

Torrie Wilson and Grant Henderson

chicken breast provides all the amino acids that the body needs for manufacturing protein. The down side to animal products is the fat content, especially beef, pork, and lamb. Poultry is better provided the excess fat and skin is removed before cooking. Fish is the best as it's very low in fat. Of course fish protein is lower on the evolutionary tree and as such the body needs to do more "reassembling" of the amino acids during digestion. So it's a trade off. Red meat is closest to human tissue, but has the highest fat content. Fish is less similar but has the lowest fat content. What's the solution? Eat a small to moderate amount of red meat, a moderate to high amount of poultry, and a high amount of fish.

FATS

Is there any nutrient group that has received the same degree of negativity as fats? With one or two notable exceptions, every diet plan that emerges these days basically preaches that fats are evil and must be avoided like the bubonic plague. Unfortunately, such a view tends to generalize and lump all fats into the same category. Thanks to the popularity of such books as *The Zone*, and others, fats are being looked at in a new light and bodybuilders should make a concentrated effort to consume adequate fats. This may fly in the face of everything you've heard over the years, but fats are just as important to muscle growth and recovery as carbohydrate and protein. Of course it all depends on the type of fat you are consuming.

Fats are generally divided into two categories: saturated or unsaturated. The former, are solid compounds at room temperature and considered unhealthy. Examples include margarine, shortening, and much of the white marble you find on animal meat. Unsaturated fatty acids are liquid at room temperature and include most of the common cooking and salad oils such as sunflower, peanut, and soybean. The terms saturated and unsaturated come from chemistry and refer to the presence or absence of double bonds. We have no intentions of boring you with first year university chemistry. Suffice to say most atoms like to have the full compliment of electrons surrounding their nucleus (the exact number being specific to each atom). In the case of organic compounds, which are based on carbon, the desired number is four. Atoms can still bond to one another without the full compliment of electrons but it means sharing. Bonds with the full complement are called saturated, while bonds with shared electrons are called unsaturated. Chemists use the symbol "−" to signify a saturated or full complement bond. If the desired number of electrons is not present the symbol "=" is used signifying a double bond. Now for the relevant part. From a health point of view, a diet high in saturated fats is linked to heart disease. The extra saturated fat builds up around the interiors of arteries and veins leading to reduced blood flow. This in turn means the heart has to pump harder to move the same volume of blood throughout the body. If the pressure builds too high, the old "weakest link in the chain" effect takes place. In many cases the weak link is a small blood vessel in the brain, the breaking of which causes a stroke. Another consequence of a high saturated fat diet is a partial or full blockage of the small arteries that supply the heart itself. In this case the end result is a heart attack. The solution to all this should be obvious; keep the intake of saturated fat to a minimum. When earlier we said to make an effort to consume fat, we were talking about unsaturated fat.

Mike Matarazzo

TRANS FATTY ACIDS – PRODUCTS OF THE MODERN AGE

If the terms saturated and unsaturated weren't enough, the food industry has thrown us another curve ball – cis and trans fatty acids. Earlier we mentioned how unsaturated fatty acids contain double bonds because of shared electrons. In a typical molecule the attached atoms may be on the same side of the molecule or arranged diagonal to one another. For simplicity let's use letters:

```
        CIS                    TRANS
  A           A          A           B
       C = C                  C = C
  B           B          B           A
```

Now you may wonder what the big deal is all about. Well it just so happens that most compounds exist in nature in the cis configuration. And as would be expected, our body's enzyme systems evolved to use cis molecules. But many modern food preparation techniques, especially hydrogenation, convert cis into trans molecules. All of a sudden we go from a fast ball to a curve ball. Our body's enzymes have difficulty handling the reconfigured compounds. The emergence of trans fatty acids (and other trans molecules) is believed to be one of the primary reasons for the drastic increase in heart disease. Just because a product contains unsaturated fatty acids

Mike Lackner

doesn't mean it's healthy. Check the label for such words as hydrogenation to see what you are getting.

FATS – OF WHAT USE?

Fats have numerous benefits. For starters they are essential for the production of various hormones and vitamin D. They are also an energy source and a way for the body to store energy reserves. Each gram of fat supplies nine calories, as compared to four calories each for protein and carbohydrate. Fat also serves as an insulator both for protection of the internal organs and as a way to conserve body temperature.

Just like amino acids there are essential fatty acids which must be supplied in the diet: linoleic acid which is an omega – 6 fatty acid and linolenic acid which is an omega – 3 fatty acid. Many deep-sea fish such as salmon, herring and cod, are rich in these important fatty acids and should be consumed regularly. If fish is a rarity in your area (or priced way out there) resort to good old flax oil. A couple of tablespoons of flax oil on your salad, in your shake, or straight down the hatch, will provide the daily recommendations for both fatty acids.

WHAT PERCENTAGE OF THE DIET?

One of the biggest debates in nutrition these days is of what percentage of the diet should fat make up? And the answer is, it depends. While the 30 to 40 percent recommended by some authorities is in our opinion too high, the less than ten percent preached by others is too conservative. If anecdotal evidence is any indication, those bodybuilders who increased their intake of unsaturated fat from ten to twenty percent of the diet, may be on to something.

Unsaturated fat not only increases muscle tissue synthesis but also contributes to fat loss. This sounds contradictory but hear us out. Increasing the consumption of unsaturated fat tricks the body into thinking fat levels are higher than needed, so the body responds by making stored fat more available as a fuel source. This is why bodybuilders who supplement with flax oil and fish oil are finding they actually lose body fat.

About the only reason we can think of for limiting fat intake to less than ten percent is the calorie issue. Fat contains 9 calories per gram, versus 4 grams each for protein and carbohydrate. If you are in the precontest phase of training, then reducing calorie intake is a concern. It's easier to cut calories by fat restriction than carbohydrate or protein restriction.

Chris Cormier

CARBOHYDRATES

It's a tossup as to which nutrient group receives the most bodybuilding press, carbohydrates or protein. And like protein, there's considerable debate as to how much carbohydrate body-builders need. The old view was 60 to 70 percent of the diet should be composed of carbohydrate. But in recent years this range has been lowered to 40 to 50 percent and protein and fat intake increased.

In simple terms, carbohydrates are chains of sugar molecules called saccharides. Think of saccharides as the amino acids of the sugar world. Just as amino acids can be combined to form larger units called polypeptide chains, so too can saccharides be linked to form larger chains. The simplest saccharides are called monosacchardides and cannot be broken down into smaller units. Some of the most common sugars are monosaccharides and include glucose, fructose, and ribose.

When monosaccharides are joined together we get more complex sugar molecules such as sucrose and lactose. Finally the most complex sugar molecules may be thousands of units long. The best example of this is the storage form of glucose called glycogen.

Carbohydrates are usually sub-divided into two categories, simple and complex. When we say sugar we are usually referring to simple carbohydrate and the best sources (we caution to use "best" here) are fruit, junk food, and soft drinks. Simple sugars are released into the blood stream very rapidly and cause an almost instant release in insulin. The problem with simple sugars is that unless they are immediately used as an energy source, they get stored as fat. This is why the high fruit diets that sometimes receive a lot of press are not such a great way to lose weight. Many fruits, especially the citrus variety, are loaded with simple sugar, and unless you run marathons all day, will make you fat!

Complex carbohydrates are released more slowly into the blood stream and as such produce less of an insulin spike and less fat storage. Such foods as pasta, breads, and beans are examples of complex carbohydrates. Besides their steady state release, one category of complex carbohydrates, fibrous carbs, help regulate the digestive system, and slow the digestion of starchy carbs.

GLYCEMIC INDEX

Besides complex and simple, biochemists use a scale called the glycemic index to rank carbs based on absorption rates. The slower the rate of absorption the lower the glycemic index. Conversely the faster the absorption, the higher the glycemic index rating. What does this mean for bodybuilders? Highly glycemic carbohydrates are best consumed during and after exercise. They enter the bloodstream quickly and are readily available for fueling exercising muscles. Low glycemic carbohydrates on the other hand enter the bloodstream slowly and are best eaten before exercise. They provide sustained longer-term energy, and help maintain stable blood sugar levels during extended exercise periods (greater than one hour).

The following table summarizes some common foods and their glycemic index.

Highly Glycemic	Moderately Glycemic	Low Glycemic
Glucose	Orange Juice	Apple
100	57	36
Baked Potato	White Rice	Pear
85	56	36
Corn Flakes	Popcorn	Skim Milk
84	55	32
Cheerios	Corn	Green Beans
74	55	30
Graham Crackers	Brown Rice	Lentils
74	55	29
Honey	Sweet Potato	Kidney Beans
73	54	27
Watermelon	(Ripe) Banana	Grapefruit
72	50	25
White Bread/Bagel	Orange	Barley
70-72	43	25
Table Sugar	Raisins	Raisins
65	64	64

We should add that the glycemic index is probably of more importance to athletes who compete in high endurance events, as it can help to determine which foods can benefit performance. Foods that have a high glycemic index such as bananas and raisins will give the athlete much needed carbohydrates when glycogen stores in the muscles start to be consumed, supplying the much needed energy midway through the event. However, it is important not to eat foods with too high a glycemic index (80-90 range), as too much insulin will be stimulated, causing sort of a yo-yo effect that will cause the blood-sugar levels to drop below normal after 3-4 hours. This could lead to fatigue and hunger towards the end of the competition or workout.

It would still be beneficial though for an athlete such as a long distance runner to eat foods with a high glycemic index for several days before a competition or event in tandem with training to increase glycogen stores in the muscles, as the body will use glycogen during strenuous workouts. Shredded wheat, which has a glycemic value of 97, would be a good choice for breakfast for several days before the event. It should be stressed that high glycemic

Darrem Charles

foods such as chips and candy bars should not be eaten, as they contain high amounts of saturated fats, poor levels of nutrients, and may contain other ingredients that are detrimental to performance and health.

GLYCOGEN – FOR A BETTER TOMMOROW

If everything goes according to plan, most excess sugar will not be stored as fat. Instead it is converted by the liver into a stored form called glycogen. Most glycogen is stored in the body's skeletal muscles and the process of converting glucose into glycogen is called glycogenesis. When the body's glucose levels drop, the process of glycogenolysis takes place and glycogen is broken down and back into glucose. The body doesn't alternate between glycogen storage and breakdown, instead both are occurring at the same time.

HOW MUCH?

Like most topics there's debate as to how much carbohydrate an individual should eat at the same time. Based on the numerous studies carried out, the best ingestion rate and amount is about 50 to 60 grams every two hours. For a bodybuilder who wants to consume 50 percent of his or her diet in the form of carbohydrate, the mathematics are as follows:

Total calories consumed – 3000
Percent carbohydrate – 50 percent or .5
3000 X .5 = 1500 calories
With 4 grams per calorie this equals 1500 divided by 4 = 375 grams of carbohydrate a day. If you eat six times a day then 375 divided by 6 gives you 62.5 grams of carbohydrate per meal.

CARBOHYDRATE AND INSULIN

As most people know, the body's primary hormone for sugar regulation is insulin. When there is a rapid rise in blood glucose the body secretes insulin from the pancreas to compensate. Insulin then lowers the level of blood glucose by shunting it into the liver and skeletal muscles.

Insulin controls excess blood sugar by storing carbs as fat to protect the body in case of future famine. Unfortunately, insulin not only stores carbs as fat, it tells the body not to release any stored fat. Therefore the body cannot easily use its own fat for energy. The startling conclusion is that not only do excess carbs cause obesity, they ensure the individual remains obese.

Brad Baker

    The best way to prevent this from happening is to primarily consume foods with a low glycemic index, which will decrease the rate of insulin secretion. Vegetables and fruits have a low glycemic index, whereas ice cream, bread, and candy all have a high glycemic index. By eating low glycemic foods not only do you not add more inches to your waistline, but also you release the fat stores from your body, allowing to you to lose the inches already there.

CARBOHYDRATE SUPPLEMENTS

Go into any health food store or flip through any athletic magazine and you are hit with a barrage of carbohydrate supplements. The usually include the words "energize," "power," or "carbo" in their titles. They are marketed as energy boosters and generally come in three forms, liquid, powder, and sports bars. Although most people assume the liquid form is better for quick energy, the fact is, studies show no difference in absorption rates between liquid (pre-mixed drinks and powdered) and solid (sports bars). If there is one word of caution it's that many carbohydrate supplements contain simple fructose as the primary ingredient. The reason is that fructose is very cheap and is very sweet. The sweetness helps sell the product, and the low cost keeps manufacturers' processing costs down. As we mentioned earlier, fructose is one of the easiest sugars to store as fat. You either use it or store it. Check the labels and try to find a product containing a good slow releasing carbohydrate like dextrin (made from rice).

VITAMINS AND MINERALS

The health of the digestive system is critical to the efficiency of nutrient digestion. As humans age, the amount of acids and enzymes in the gastric fluids decrease and protein is less effectively broken into its bioavailable amino acids. Besides producing indigestion and toxins in the bowel, inefficient digestion lowers the absorption of other nutrients, especially certain minerals like iron and calcium, since amino acids are required for their active transport absorption mechanism. Vitamins and minerals are the catalysts of the digestive system. They don't really start or stop biochemical reactions but speed up or slow down existing ones. Every metabolic activity that takes place in the human body relies on vitamins and minerals. With all the attention placed on protein and fat, vitamins and minerals often get over-looked. But a deficiency in any of them can lead to death!

VITAMINS – THE FORGOTTEN NUTRIENTS

It's ironic that many bodybuilders spend hundreds of dollars a month on such supplements as creatine, gluta-mine, and protein, and yet neglect to invest even a ten dollar bill towards one of the most important categories of ergogenic aids – vitamins.

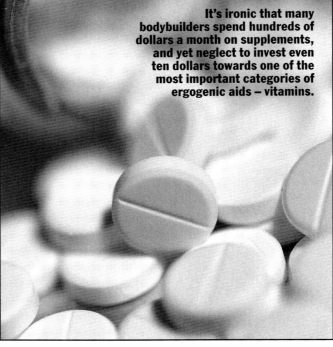

It's ironic that many bodybuilders spend hundreds of dollars a month on supplements, and yet neglect to invest even ten dollars towards one of the most important categories of ergogenic aids – vitamins.

Vitamins can be considered catalysts. That is they don't serve as the building blocks like protein, but instead modulate the various biochemical reactions that involve the other food nutrients.

Our knowledge of vitamins first started with Polish biochemist, Casimir Funk who studied the disease beriberi. Dr. Funk formulated an antiberiberi compound from rice. As the compound was both an amine (nitrogen containing) and "vital" to life, he put the two together and came up with the name vitalamine or "vitamin."

Vitamins can be subdivided into two categories, water soluble and fat-soluble. Water-soluble vitamins such as vitamin's B and C cannot be stored by the body and must be taken frequently. Of course the poor storage properties makes water-soluble vitamins the safer of the two categories and overdosing is extremely rare.

Fat-soluble vitamins on the other hand, such as vitamin's A, D, and E, can be stored by the body. This has both positive and negative outcomes. Storage means that in times of low intake, the body can draw on reserves to maintain normal metabolic functioning. On the other hand with the availability of today's high-potency vitamin supplements, it is possible for fat-soluble vitamins to reach toxic levels in the body. Vitamin D for example in high amounts has been linked to heart disease and kidney stones. The following is a description of the more common vitamins and their functions.

VITAMIN A

Vitamin A has a number of important functions, including anti-oxidant capabilities, supporting healthy skin and eye tissue, shortening the duration of diseases, and many more. Many experts have commented about the importance of vitamin A and beta-carotene, a derivative. For many, vitamin A, rather than beta-carotene, seems to be the most important with regards to immune function. But in large amounts, vitamin A can be toxic, which is why other biochemists favor beta-carotene, saying it is better than vitamin A because it's both an antioxidant and a vitamin A precursor. Beta-carotene can work independent of its vitamin A functions, whereas vitamin A is only vitamin A. The body converts beta-carotene into vitamin A when needed. If not needed, it simply excretes the excess.

Most beta-carotenes are synthetic. Our body has only processed natural forms of vitamins for thousands of years, so it knows how to deal with these forms. Synthetic forms, however, have molecular structures that differ from the structures of the natural forms. This makes all the difference in the world with what happens at the cellular level. In addition, our bodies need many carotenoids, not just one. The scientific community continues to recommend a diet high in natural fruits and vegetables – a diet that contains mixed carotenoids. Zeaxanthin, and lycopene are the most common carotenoids found in fruits and vegetables. Nutritional experts feel this broader spectrum of carotenoids assures you of a much more complete protection than if you were to get just vitamin A or beta-carotene alone.

VITAMIN B

Markus Ruhl

The B vitamins are associated with some of the body's most important duties. B1 helps fend off free radicals and supports healthy circulation. Riboflavin (B2) supports healthy cell growth and promotes eye health. Niacin and niacinamide, or vitamin B3, are powerful nervous system boosters. Pantothenic acid, also known as vitamin B5, helps support your body's production of adrenal hormones. A deficiency may also worsen arthritis symptoms, so it's important to get proper levels of B5. Pyridoxine (B6) promotes proper brain and immune functions. B12 promotes energy production. Senior adults and vegetarians are likely to lack enough of this vitamin.

Under many conditions, the liver is not able to properly phospholate the B vitamins, making the inexpensive HCL forms ineffective. In addition, the excessive use of the common HCL forms requiring transformation can be hard on the liver, as is the case with vitamin B6. For this reason, many supplement manufacturers use the considerably more expensive – but more effective – pyrodoxal-5-phosphate and riboflavin-5-phosphate forms of these vitamins. They are already in a form that can be used by the body. This is especially important for people with poor liver function. In order to make B12 more synergistic, many supplement manufacturers also add the co-enzymatic, or active form, dibencocide. One big benefit of dibencocide is that it provides better cellular oxygenation, which in turn promotes better energy production and helps reduce mental and physical fatigue.

VITAMIN C

No vitamin has received the amount of press coverage that vitamin C has. It plays a major role in the fight against infection by increasing the production of immune cells that help the body

Aaron Maddron

destroy unfriendly microorganisms. As an important antioxidant, it also neutralizes free radicals and helps repair skin tissue. Ascorbic acid is sometimes thought to be vitamin C because it is the most common form used and is one of the least expensive forms of vitamin C. However, because it is highly acidic, many find it upsets their stomachs, so they either don't take it or don't take enough of it. Ascorbic acid can also lead to copper deficiencies in the body. Moreover, ascorbic acid cannot stay in the body long – usually just two or three hours. As a result, many people that take vitamin C use it up so fast they remain unprotected after just a few hours.

All fruits and vegetables contain vitamin C, but it can be destroyed by cooking. Including clean, raw vegetables in your daily diet is a simple solution. A deficiency in vitamin C results in scurvy, a potentially fatal disease in which old scars open up and sudden exertions can result in heart failure. The Royal Navy lost over 1,000,000 sailors prior to the discovery of the source of the disease. Lemons and limes, able to stay fresh for long voyages, were made mandatory parts of the daily diet for the crews. Hence the source of the slang term in which the English are referred to as "Limeys."

Some authorities recommended taking up to 10,000 milligrams (10 grams) of vitamin C per day, but this is probably overkill. Unless your diet is extremely lacking in vitamin C, we suggest 500 to 2000 milligrams per day. As with most supplements, taking four 500 milligram doses will lead to better utilization than 2000 milligrams all at once. Some individuals will get stomach upset or diarrhea from large amounts of vitamin C.

VITAMIN D

Vitamin D is actually a family of related essential compounds, referred to as vitamins D-1, D-2, and D-3. Vitamin D is required for the proper regulation and absorption of the essential minerals calcium and phosphorus. Available primarily from animal sources, vitamin D is also commonly called the sunshine vitamin because of the body's unique ability to synthesize Vitamin-D from brief but regular exposure to sunlight. The light transforms an inert substance (ergosterol) in the skin into calciferol, or vitamin D2. Cod liver oil is a source of D3. Vitamin D is involved in the mobilizing of calcium (absorption, excretion and movement into bone). A deficiency can result in rickets, a disorder of bone formation. An excess can lead to kidney stones.

Adequate levels of vitamin D are required for the proper absorption of calcium and phosphorus in the small intestines. Because of this vital link, adequate intake of vitamin D is critically important for the proper mineralization of bones and teeth in developing children. Vitamin D also aids in the prevention and treatment of osteoporosis, osteomalacia, and hypocalcemia in adults.

Common food sources of vitamin-D include Fish liver oil, sardines, tuna, salmon, liver, and eggs. Vitamin D is also available in its supplement or food form, as vitamin D-2, called ergocalciferol, and as vitamin D-3, or cholecalciferol.

The current recommended daily allowance of vitamin D is 400 IU, or international units per day. Common current supplemental doses of vitamin D range from 400 to 1,000 IU per day, and are extremely safe at this level.

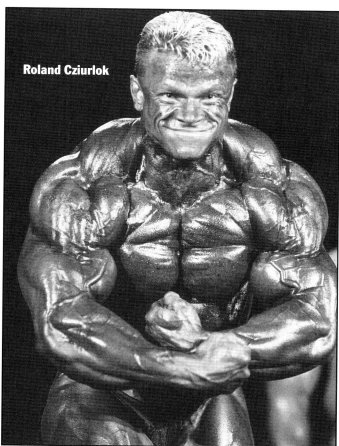

Roland Cziurlok

But high levels of vitamin D can be toxic. Children begin to show toxic effects when dosages exceed 1,800 IU per day. Adults can show toxic effects with dosages ranging from 10,000 to 20,000 IU per day over extended periods. Symptoms of vitamin D toxicity can include weakness, loss of appetite, unusual thirst, nausea, vomiting, high blood pressure, and elevated calcium levels in the blood. Toxic effects are easily corrected by simply cutting back on the daily intake of vitamin-D. Prolonged exposure to sunlight, while unsafe for other reasons, cannot lead to vitamin D toxicity.

VITAMIN E

Vitamin E is gaining popularity world-wide due to its antioxidant benefits, its benefits on the heart, and how it maintains proper blood flow. Vitamin E is involved in the manufacture of DNA and RNA, and red blood cells. It also assists many of the body's enzymes in carrying out their functions. The best sources of vitamin E are vegetable oils, green vegetables, and whole grain cereals and nuts. The RDA for vitamin E is 10 milligrams or 15 IU per day.

VITAMIN K

This vitamin is essential for the formation of the enzyme thrombin, which is necessary for blood clotting. Vitamin K is found in green vegetables and formed by intestinal bacteria. Deficiencies occur when there is a shortage of bile produced by the liver, which can happen if the liver is severely taxed or jaundiced. Without bile, vitamin K is poorly absorbed. Those on heavy steroid cycles should supplement vitamin K.

VITAMIN SUPPLEMENTATION

The supplementation of vitamins remains controversial. Most in the medical community adhere to the belief that an adequate diet is sufficient, as vitamins are inescapable in foods. Others point out that mass produced foods may be grown in soils lacking in the nutrients necessary to create enough vitamins, and that processing and cooking can further destroy the vitamins that are present. We agree with vitamin supplementation for bodybuilders as their bodies are under constant stress. But be careful when you purchase your vitamins. Adding vitamins to creatine or an energy bar does not justify an increase of 50 percent in the price. Vitamins are still the most affordable supplement on the market. It should cost you no more than ten bucks for a high-potency multi-vitamin supplement.

MINERALS

Minerals are as essential to long-term health as vitamins. They also have effects that cannot be duplicated by vitamins. Many minerals are called electrolytes and are lost in the sweat during exercise. Cramping is one of the symptoms of mineral loss.

Unlike vitamins, the body only needs very small amounts of minerals. In fact some minerals have the potential to be toxic in high dosages. Examples of minerals include: sodium, potassium, calcium, iron, phosphorous, iodine, selenium and chromium to name but a few. The later two minerals are of primary interest to athletes. Selenium works as an antioxidant by stimulating the enzyme glutathione peroxidase to prevent the conversion of potentially hazardous free radicals into carcinogens by oxidation. Chromium has a strong influence on metabolism. It has been linked to both fat loss and nutrient absorption (for more on chromium see the chapter on hardcore supplements).

Lee Priest

"He was the clear winner. All he had to do was make it through the stage door, start out as a man among boys for a little while and collect his title and the money. But even the best laid plans of giants... he cramped up."

– Editors of *MuscleMag International* commenting on Paul Dillett's experience at the 1994 Arnold Classic, due to a diuretic-induced loss of electrolytes.

CHELATION

While the body needs minerals, it cannot utilize them without other components from the diet. Amino acids, usually as hydrolyzed vegetable protein, are also used as chelating agents to aid in the absorption of minerals from the digestive tract. In the process of digestion, a considerable amount of vital trace elements can be rendered unavailable before they can be fully utilized by the body. Chelation is a chemical process where the mineral nutrient is protected until it is moved to or carried through the gut wall and can be used in nutritional pathways. The word chelate comes from the Greek "chels" meaning claw. Chelation can be visualized as surrounding the trace mineral and holding it in at least two places.

True chelates enter the blood as they are ingested. In the bloodstream, amino acids naturally migrate to particular organs and tissue groups according to the dominant amino acid configuration of the organ or tissue. Radioisotope studies have demonstrated the migration of minerals, chelated to specific amino acids, to specific body tissues. This means that one can build mineral chelates using purified amino acids in which the amino acid will carry the mineral ion to specific body sites. This enhanced specialization is the direction of present mineral supplement research.

The following is a brief description of some of the more common minerals.

Lou Ferrigno

Calcium

94 percent of all the calcium in the body is found in the bones and teeth. The rest is in the blood and soft tissues. Among its functions are regulating blood clotting, muscle contraction, nerve conduction, and enzyme activation. Calcium's most prominent role is serving as a precursor for bone and teeth formation. The RDA for calcium for adults is 800 milligrams per day. Good sources of calcium include milk and dairy products, sardines, and spinach.

Phosphorous

Like calcium, phosphorous is essential for bone and teeth formation. It also plays a role in energy storage and release. As a component of DNA and RNA, phosphorous is linked to cell replication. The RDA for phosphorous is 800 milligrams per day. Some good sources of phosphorous include dairy products, fish, peanuts, and green leafy vegetables.

Magnesium

Although the body has less than two ounces, magnesium is a vital mineral. It plays a major role in protein synthesis, muscle relaxation, and energy release. Most magnesium is stored in the body's bones. The RDA for magnesium is 350 milligrams per day. The best sources of magnesium are beans, granola, and green leafy vegetables.

Sodium

Sodium is comparable to cholesterol in that despite being essential to life, consciously trying to include it in the diet is not an issue. In fact trying to keep intake low is more of a concern. Without sodium, the body's water regulatory abilities would be impeded. Sodium also plays a role in nerve conduction and nutrient absorption.

Because of the link between sodium and hypertension, and the fact that most processed food is loaded with sodium as a preservative, most people take in far more than the RDA value of 500 milligrams per day. In fact the average daily intake is between 4000 and 5000 milligrams per day. Sodium deficiency is not an issue in modern Western society. The big problem is trying to cut back on its consumption. The best sources of sodium are fish, vegetables, and just about anything in a tin can!

Potassium

Another so-called electrolyte, potassium, plays an important role in maintaining water and acid-base balance. It also helps regulate nerve conduction, muscle contraction, and heart rate. Finally protein and carbohydrate metabolism is dependent on potassium levels. The RDA for potassium is 2000 to 3000 milligrams per day. The best sources include red meat, various beans, and fruits from the melon family.

Iodine

Iodine is one of the most well known minerals and most of the body's 25 milligrams are found in the thyroid gland. Indirectly, iodine helps regulate metabolism, body temperature, growth, and hormone production. The RDA for iodine is 150 mcg/day. As one teaspoon of iodized salt

Mike O'Hearn and Melissa Zee

contain 260 mcg, iodine deficiencies are extremely rare. The best sources are seafood, vegetable, grains, and some dairy products.

Iron

Iron is another staple of the supplement industry. The body contains 3 to 5 grams of iron, the vast majority of which is found in the blood's oxygen-carrying pigment, hemoglobin. Secondary roles of iron include enzyme formation, cholesterol metabolism, and immune system boosting. The RDA for iron is 10 milligrams per day for men and 15 milligrams per day for women. The higher value for women being due to the amount of iron lost during the monthly menstrual cycle. The best sources of iron are red meat, soybeans, grains, and potatoes.

Zinc

Most of the body's 2 to 3 grams of zinc are found within the bones. The rest of this trace mineral is found in the skin, nails and hair. In males the prostate gland contains more zinc than any other organ. Zinc contributes to more than 70 enzyme reactions, and plays a prominent role in nutrient metabolism. Zinc is also a vital component in insulin formation and testosterone production. The RDA for zinc is 15 milligrams per day for men, and 12 milligrams per day for women. The best sources of zinc are seafood such as oysters, meat, poultry, and beef liver.

Lee Apperson

MINERAL SUPPLEMENTS

Unless you are either following a lousy diet, or have been diagnosed with a specific mineral deficiency, the odds are you don't need mineral supplements. The only exception may be women who have heavy menstrual flows who need extra iron. As most vitamin preparations have minerals thrown in, few bodybuilders are deficient in any of the major minerals. We know this goes against what you read in the various magazines, some of whom have a "mineral of the month" article. But save your money for the supplements that do something for you like glutamine, creatine, and whey protein. Unlike vitamins, which may be destroyed in the food preparation process, minerals are very durable. Supplementation is rarely necessary.

Advanced Training Routines

Up to this point we've looked at the techniques and exercises that form the nucleus of hardcore bodybuilding. It's now time to combine them into advanced training routines. We have divided the chapter into four, five, and six-day split routines. By split we mean training different muscles on different days. Split routines are unquestionably the best method to pack on copious amounts of size and strength. Virtually every top amateur and pro bodybuilder follows some sort of split routine. We won't be discussing full body routines as these are mainly geared towards beginners. Suffice to say you perform one or two basic exercises for each muscle group during the one training session, take a day off, and then repeat. For a beginner, full body

Flex Wheeler

workouts are ideal as they don't tax the muscles too strenuously. Let's face it, beginners don't need a great deal of exercise volume to stimulate their muscles. In fact for those who have never worked out before, one exercise for two or three sets is often adequate. A beginner's recovery system is not sufficiently developed to handle an intense, multi-exercise split routine.

Before going into the routines in detail, a few points need to be clarified. Unless you work out in a large, well-equipped gym, the odds are you won't have access to some of the machines listed here. This is not the end of your bodybuilding career as you can substitute another machine in its place. If all else fails throw in an equivalent barbell or dumbell exercise. Every good weight training gym has these. If yours doesn't we strongly urge you to switch gyms.

When it comes to rep ranges we use the standard 6 to 12 range. We are sure there are readers who have discovered that higher or lower reps work best for them. But for most, 6 to 12 is the most productive. We would, however, suggest varying the reps periodically

Chris Cormier, Kevin Levrone, Flex Wheeler and Ronnie Coleman

to keep the muscles guessing so to speak. Even if your muscles respond best to 6 to 12, don't be afraid to throw in the occasional 15 to 20, or 4 to 6 rep-day. Variety is the spice of life even within bodybuilding!

Finally there are literally thousands of exercise and muscle group combinations. What we present is but a sample. As time goes on you'll discover exercise and muscle combinations that work best for you. Even then the odds are you won't keep responding indefinitely. You will periodically need to switch things around and re-tailor your routine. Enough said. Here are the routines that will transform that physique of yours.

FOUR DAY SPLITS

There are two basic ways to perform four day split routines. The first involves training the entire body in two halves on two consecutive days. You then take a day off and then repeat for two more days. In simple terms you alternate two days on with one day off. This type of schedule works great if you are flexible enough to get to the gym irregardless of what day of the week it is. But if you are like most individuals you live your life around the collection of seven days popularly called a week. There may be days when you can't get to the gym or simply don't want to. As the weekends are often two such days, many individuals modify the previous split by working out on Monday and Tuesday, taking Wednesday off, repeating the two halves on Thursday and Friday and then taking both weekend days off. Besides giving you more time to spend with family and friends, or devote to leisure activities, etc., this split gives you an extra day off for recovery. You are only exercising four days out of seven and you get three full days off.

ROUTINE A

Day 1		Sets	Reps
Legs	Leg presses	3	6-8
	Leg extensions	3	10-12
	Leg curls	3	6-8
	Stiff-leg deadlifts	3	10-12
	Standing calf raises	3	6-8
	Seated calf raises	3	15-20
Biceps	Standing barbell curls	3	6-8
	Incline curls	3	10-12
Triceps	Dumbell extensions	3	6-8
	Triceps pushdowns	3	10-12

Day 2		Sets	Reps
Chest	Flat barbell presses	3	6-8
	Incline dumbell presses	3	10-12
Back	Front pulldowns	3	6-8
	Seated rows	3	10-12
Shoulders	Front barbell presses	3	6-8
	Lateral raises	3	10-12
	Reverse pec-dek	3	10-12
Abs	Chair leg raises	3	15-20
	Crunches	3	15-20

Nasser El Sonbaty and
Kevin Levrone

Finish

Start

Aaron Maddron uses strict form when executing bench dips.

ROUTINE B

Day 1

Legs		Sets	Reps
	Squats	3	6-8
	Sissy Squats	3	10-12
	Lying leg curls	3	6-8
	Stiff-leg deadlifts	3	10-12
	Donkey calf raises	3	6-12
	Seated calf raises	3	10-12
Biceps	Preacher curls	3	6-8
	Concentration curls	3	10-12
Triceps	Lying EZ-curl bar extensions	3	6-8
	Bench dips	3	10-12

Day 2

Chest		Sets	Reps
	Incline barbell presses	3	6-8
	Flat dumbell flyes	3	10-12
Back	Front chins	3	6-8
	T-bar rows	3	10-12
Shoulders	Dumbell presses	3	6-8
	Cable lateral raises	3	10-12
	Bent over laterals	3	10-12
	Barbell shrugs	3	10-12
Abs	Reverse crunches	3	15-20
	Rope crunches	3	15-20

ROUTINE C

Day 1		Sets	Reps
Legs	Squats	3	6-8
	Hack squats	3	10-12
	Seated leg curls	3	6-8
	Stiff-leg deadlifts	3	10-12
	Toe press on leg presses	3	6-8
	Seated calf raises	3	15-20
Biceps	Cable curls	3	6-8
	One-arm preacher curls	3	10-12
Triceps	Lying dumbell extensions	3	6-8
	Narrow presses	3	10-12
Abs	Crunches	3	6-8
	Reverse crunches	3	10-12

Day 2		Sets	Reps
Chest	Flat Smith presses	3	6-8
	Incline dumbell presses	3	10-12
Back	Barbell rows	3	6-8
	Wide seated rows	3	10-12
Shoulders	Front machine presses	3	6-8
	Upright rows	3	10-12
	Bent-over cable raises	3	10-12
	Dumbell shrugs	3	*6-12

* alternate 6 to 8 reps with 10 to 12

Start

Don Long – Cable curls

Finish

ROUTINE D

Day 1

		Sets	Reps
Chest	Flat dumbell presses	3	6-8
	Incline dumbell flyes	3	10-12
Back	Barbell rows	3	6-8
	One arm rows	3	10-12
Biceps	Barbell curls	3	6-8
	One arm preacher curls	3	10-12

Day 2

Legs	Squats	3	6-8
	Leg extensions	3	10-12
	Leg curls	3	6-8
	Stiff-leg deadlifts	3	10-12
Shoulders	Smith presses	3	6-8
	Lateral raises	3	10-12
	Bent-over lateral raises	3	6-8
Triceps	Lying EZ-bar extensions	3	6-8
	One-arm dumbell extensions	3	10-12

Greg Kovacs belts out one last dumbell preacher curl.

ROUTINE E

Day 1

		Sets	Reps
Chest	Incline barbell presses	3	6-8
	Pec-dek flyes	3	10-12
Back	T-Bar rows	3	6-8
	Chins	3	10-12
Biceps	Cable curls	3	6-8
	Narrow chins	3	10-12

Day 2

		Sets	Reps
Legs	Squats	3	6-8
	Leg presses	3	10-12
	Standing leg curls	3	6-8
	Stiff-leg deadlifts	3	10-12
	Donkey calf raises	3	6-8
	Seated calf raises	3	15-20
Shoulders	Front barbell presses	3	6-8
	Dumbell upright rows	3	10-12
	Reverse pec flyes	3	10-12
Triceps	Dumbell extensions	3	6-8
	Kickbacks	3	10-12
Abs	Reverse crunches	3	15-20
	Rope crunches	3	15-20

Jamo Nezzar goes for the burn while performing pec-dek flyes. *Start*

Finish

ROUTINE F

Day 1

Chest		Sets	Reps
	Flat barbell presses	3	6-8
	Incline dumbell presses	3	10-12

Shoulders			
	Dumbell presses	3	6-8
	One-arm cable laterals	3	10-12
	Bent-over dumbell laterals	3	10-12

Thighs			
	Leg presses	3	6-8
	Hack squats	3	10-12

Triceps			
	Narrow presses	3	6-8
	Dumbell extensions	3	10-12

Day 2

Back		Sets	Reps
	Barbell rows	3	6-8
	Front pulldowns	3	10-12

Hamstrings			
	Lying leg curls	3	6-8
	Seated leg curls	3	10-12

Biceps			
	Preacher curls	3	6-8
	Concentration curls	3	10-12

Calves			
	Standing calf raises	3	6-8
	Seated calf raises	3	15-20

Abs			
	Reverse crunches	3	15-20
	Crunches	3	15-20

SIX DAY SPLITS

If four day splits have a disadvantage it's you need to train at least three muscle groups during the one session. And when one of those muscle groups is legs, let's face it, it's difficult to do justice to the last muscle group you train. One solution is to spread your entire body over three days instead of two. And more important put legs on a day all by themselves. Of course before you switch to a six-day split, we must give you the down side. Even though you are training different muscles, you are still placing a demand on the recovery system. By performing three different routines twice a week, it means you are in the gym, six out of seven days. This places a tremendous drain on your recuperative abilities. Even most top pros and amateurs, with their recovery systems heavily "modified" with various pharmaceuticals, only follow six-day splits for a limited time period – usually during the pre-contest system. Six-day splits are great for giving extra attention to lagging muscle groups, and for peaking during the contest season. But they should not be followed year round. Only a select few genetically gifted individuals could train year round on such a split. For most the energy drain is too taxing.

Chapter 17 – *Advanced Training Routines*

There are two ways you can divide a six-day split. The most common is to go three on, one off. But you could go six on, one off. The advantage of the former is that you are getting one days rest every four days, while the latter forces you to train six days straight before resting. Some bodybuilders take two days off but even then you are still training six days in a row. Most individuals will only be able to train intensely for the first three or four days, then fatigue sets in and you go through the motions. Our advice is to follow the former and give the body a chance to rest every four days.

ROUTINE A

Day 1

		Sets	Reps
Legs	Leg presses	3	6-8
	Leg extensions	3	10-12
	Lying leg curls	3	6-8
	Stiff-leg deadlifts	3	10-12
	Standing calf raises	3	6-8
	Seated calf raises	3	10-12
Abs	Crunches	3	15-20
	Leg raises	3	15-20
	Reverse crunches	3	15-20

Day 2

		Sets	Reps
Chest	Incline barbell curls	3	6-8
	Flat dumbell presses	3	10-12
	Pec-dek flyes	3	10-12
Back	Chins	3	6-8
	Barbell rows	3	6-8
	One-arm rows	3	10-12

Day 3

		Sets	Reps
Shoulders	Front barbell presses	3	6-8
	Lateral raises	3	6-8
	Bent over lateral raises	3	6-8
	Barbell shrugs	3	6-8
Biceps	Barbell curls	3	6-8
	One-arm preacher curls	3	6-8
Triceps	Lying dumbell extensions	3	6-8
	Bench dips	3	10-12

ROUTINE B

Day 1
Legs

		Sets	Reps
	Squats	3	6-8
	Hack squats	3	10-12
	Sissy squats	3	10-12
	Seated leg curls	3	6-8
	Standing leg curls	3	10-12
	Toe presses	3	6-8
	Seated calf raises	3	15-20

Day 2
Chest

		Sets	Reps
	Flat barbell presses	3	6-8
	Incline dumbell flyes	3	10-12
	Cable crossovers	3	10-12

Back

	T-bar rows	3	6-8
	Front pulldowns	3	10-12
	Straight arm pushdowns	3	10-12

Day 3
Shoulders

		Sets	Reps
	Dumbell presses	3	6-8
	Lateral raises	3	6-8
	Upright rows	3	6-8
	Reverse pec flyes	3	6-8
	Barbell shrugs	3	6-8

Biceps

	Cable curls	3	6-8
	Concentration curl	3	10-12

Triceps

	Lying EZ-curl bar extensions	3	6-8
	Narrow presses	3	10-12
	One arm pushdowns	3	10-12

ROUTINE C

Day 1		Sets	Reps
Thighs	Squats	3	6-8
	Leg presses	3	10-12
	Sissy Squats	3	10-12
Shoulders	Barbell presses	3	6-8
	Cable laterals	3	6-8
	Reverse pec flyes	3	6-8
	Dumbell shrugs	3	6-8

Day 2			
Chest	Flat Smith presses	3	6-8
	Incline barbell presses	3	10-12
	Flat flyes	3	10-12
Biceps	Barbell curls	3	6-8
	One-arm cable curls	3	10-12
Triceps	Pushdowns	3	6-8
	Two-arm dumbell extensions	3	10-12

Day 3			
Back	Wide seated rows	3	6-8
	Two-arm rows	3	10-12
	Narrow reverse pulldowns	3	10-12
Hamstring	Stiff-leg deadlifts	3	6-8
	Lying leg curls	3	10-12
Calves	Toe presses	3	6-8
	Donkey calf raises	3	10-12
	Seated calf raises	3	15-20

DOUBLE SPLIT ROUTINES

For those of you who can make it to the gym more than once a day, but only for short periods of time – say 45 minutes or less – the double split routine may be an option. Instead of splitting your training sessions into three groups, you subdivide into six, performing two per day. The most popular way to do this would be to train early in the morning (i.e. before school or work) and then add the second later in the day (after your other daily activities).

The advantage to splitting things this way is that you are in an out of the gym in about 30 to 45 minutes. As the body can only sustain high energy levels for about 60 minutes or so, you are assured that each and every workout is performed with maximum intensity. Of course by now you can probably see a disadvantage to such training. Six different workouts performed twice a week works out to twelve training sessions. A point will eventually be reached where the stress on the recovery system builds up and leaves you in a state of overtraining. For most this is usually between four and six weeks. As with standard six-day splits, most bodybuilders only follow double splits during the pre-contest season. The bottom line, however, is each individual's recovery abilities. By all means give double split training a try, and as long as you make progress and your motivation levels remain high, keep going.

FOUR DAY DOUBLE SPLIT ROUTINE
ROUTINE A

Day 1
Morning

		Sets	Reps
Thighs	Leg presses	3	6-8
	Leg extensions	3	10-12
Triceps	Dumbell extensions	3	6-8
	Bench dips	3	10-12
Evening			
Hamstrings	Leg curls	3	6-8
	Stiff-leg deadlifts	3	10-12
Shoulders	Front barbell presses	3	6-8
	Dumbell lateral raises	3	6-8
	Bent-over lateral raises	3	6-8
	Barbell shrugs	3	6-8

Day 2
Morning

Chest	Incline barbell presses	3	6-8
	Flat dumbell presses	3	10-12
Biceps	Barbell curls	3	6-8
	Incline dumbell curls	3	10-12
Abs	Chair leg raises	3	15-20
	Reverse crunches	3	15-20
Evening			
Back	T-Bar rows	3	6-8
	Front pulldowns	3	10-12
Calves	Standing calf raises	3	6-8
	Seated calf raises	3	15-20

ROUTINE B

Day 1 Morning		Sets	Reps
Legs	Squats	3	6-8
	Hack squats	3	10-12
	Seated leg curls	3	6-8
	Lying leg curls	3	10-12
	Donkey calf raises	3	6-8
	Seated calf raises	3	15-20
Evening **Triceps**	Lying EZ-curl bar extensions	3	6-8
	Pushdowns	3	10-12
Biceps	Preacher curls	3	6-8
	Concentration curls	3	10-12
Abs	Hanging leg raises	3	15-20
	Reverse crunches	3	15-20
Day 2 **Morning** **Chest**	Flat dumbell presses	3	6-8
	Incline dumbell presses	3	10-12
Back	Front chins	3	6-8
	Barbell rows	3	10-12
Evening **Shoulders**	Dumbell presses	3	6-8
	Upright rows	3	6-8
	Reverse pec flyes	3	6-8
	Barbell shrugs	3	6-8
	Dumbell shrugs	3	10-12

SIX DAY DOUBLE SPLIT ROUTINES
ROUTINE A

Day 1 Morning		Sets	Reps
Thighs	Squats	3	6-8
	Hack squats	3	10-12
	Leg extensions	3	10-12

Evening			
Chest	Flat barbell presses	3	6-8
	Incline dumbbell presses	3	10-12
	Pec-dek flyes	3	10-12

Day 2 Morning		Sets	Reps
Back	Front chins	3	6-8
	Barbell rows	3	10-12
	One-arm dumbell rows	3	10-12

Evening			
Triceps	Dumbell extensions	3	6-8
	Pushdowns	3	10-12
Calves	Toe presses	3	6-8
	Seated calf raises	3	15-20

Day 3 Morning			
Shoulders	Front dumbell raises	3	6-8
	Side lateral raises	3	6-8
	Bent-over lateral raises	3	6-8
	Barbell shrugs	3	6-8

Evening			
Biceps	Standing dumbell curls	3	6-8
	Cable curls	3	10-12
Abs	Leg raises	3	15-20
	Crunches	3	15-20
	Reverse crunches	3	15-20

ROUTINE B

Day 1 Morning		Sets	Reps
Chest	Flat barbell presses	3	6-8
	Incline machine presses	3	10-12
	Cable crossovers	3	10-12
Calves	Toe presses	3	6-8
	Seated calf raises	3	15-20
	Donkey calf raises	3	15-20
Evening			
Back	Seated rows	3	6-8
	Reverse pulldowns	3	10-12
	Straight-arm pushdowns	3	10-12
Day 2 Morning			
Shoulders	Dumbell presses	3	6-8
	Cable lateral raises	3	10-12
	Bent-over lateral raises	3	10-12
	Barbell shrugs	3	6-8
Evening			
Thighs	Leg presses	3	6-8
	Leg extensions	3	10-12
	Sissy squats	3	10-20
Day 3 Morning			
Biceps	Cable curls	3	6-8
	Incline dumbell curls	3	10-12
Triceps	Narrow presses	3	6-8
	Pushdowns	3	10-12
Evening			
Hamstrings	Lying leg curls	3	6-8
	Stiff-leg deadlifts	3	10-12
	Back extensions	3	15-20

FIVE DAY SPLITS

The five day split rotation is sort of halfway between the four and six day split routines; and we don't just mean numerically either. For some individuals hitting the same muscles every 72 hours (a four-day split) still doesn't give enough time for recovery. The six-day split increases the time between workouts for the same muscles, but it means training six out of eight days; for many, just too demanding on the entire recovery system. A good compromise is the five-day split, were you train on a two on, one off, one on, and one off schedule. It gives ample time between the same muscles, while at the same time means you get two days rest every five. Here are two sample routines.

ROUTINE A
Day 1

		Sets	Reps
Chest	Flat barbell presses	3	6-8
	Incline dumbell presses	3	10-12
	Dumbell pullovers	3	10-12
Biceps	Barbell curls	3	6-8
	Hammer curls	3	10-12

Day 2

		Sets	Reps
Quads	Barbell squats	3	6-8
	Leg extensions	3	10-12
	Deep dumbell squats	3	12-15
Hamstrings	Lying leg curls	3	6-8
	Stiff-leg deadlifts	3	12-15
* Calves	Standing calf raises	3	6-8
	Seated calf raises	3	6-8

*alternate high rep (15-20) with low rep (6-8) workouts.

Day 3 – OFF

Day 4

		Sets	Reps
Back	T-bar rows	3	6-8
	Front chins	3	10-12
	One-arm rows	3	10-12
Shoulders	Dumbell presses	3	6-8
	Lateral raises	3	6-8
	Reverse pec flyes	3	6-8
	Dumbell shrugs	3	6-8
Triceps	Lying extensions	3	6-8
	Narrow presses	3	10-12

Day 5 – OFF

ROUTINE B
DAY 1

Chest	Incline barbell presses	3	6-8
	Flat dumbell presses	3	10-12
	Pec flyes	3	10-12
Back	Barbell rows	3	6-8
	Front pulldowns	3	10-12
	Straight-arm pushdowns	3	10-12

Day 2

Quads	Leg presses	3	6-8
	Sissy squats	3	10-12
	Hack squats	3	10-12
Hamstrings	Seated leg curls	3	6-8
	Stiff-leg deadlifts	3	10-12
	Back extensions	3	15-20
* **Calves**	Donkey calf raises	3	6-8
	Seated calf raises	3	6-8

* alternate high rep (15-20) with low rep (6-8) workouts

Day 3 – OFF

Day 4

Shoulders	Flat barbell presses	3	6-8
	Cable laterals	3	6-8
	Bent-over laterals	3	6-8
	Upright rows	3	6-8
Biceps	Preacher curls	3	6-8
	Concentration curls	3	10-12
	Hammer curls	3	10-12
Triceps	Weighted bench dips	3	6-8
	Pushdowns	3	10-12
	One-arm extensions	3	10-12

Day 5 – OFF

Jeramy Freeman

Roland Cziurlok

BOOK SIX

THE CHAMPS' ROUTINES

CHAPTER EIGHTEEN

The Routines of the Stars

Lee Priest

Despite the great advice offered by writers, coaches, and a few media types, let's face it the one group that grabs the aspiring bodybuilder's attention the most are professional bodybuilders. It's one thing to talk about building great biceps, but when Ronnie Coleman or Flex Wheeler raise those great guns of theirs into the air – well you get the picture. And as the old saying goes a picture is worth a thousand words. It's safe to say the vast majority of bodybuilders no matter what their level, obtained most of their training routines from reading bodybuilding magazines. Other sources such as writers and coaches may offer more in the way of overall training advice, but when it gets down to specific body parts, most seek out those who have built the best. How many bodybuilders modified their leg training after reading Tom Platz's routine? How many bodybuilders follow Arnold's or Ronnie Coleman's biceps routines? Need a back, try Dorian Yates' program.

The following is a collection of body part routines from the sport's superstars. If there's one common theme you'll see here, it's variety. No two bodybuilders follow the exact same training program. What separates good from great is instinct. The top pros have modified their training to suit their needs and individual genetics. By trial and error they have discovered what works best for them. You

Thomas Zechmeister

must do the same. If a certain exercise program is not bringing you results – get rid of it! Just because a given collection of exercises built Arnold's biceps, it doesn't mean the same group will enlarge yours. And we assure you Arnold didn't follow the same training routine for his whole competitive career. He frequently modified and changed things around.

Our advice is to select a couple of the following programs and incorporate them into your training. If your chest is lagging behind, try Lee Apperson's program. Can't get the biceps to respond? Give Aaron Baker's routine a go. Keep in mind the champs frequently change their routines around and most switch exercises every 6 to 8 weeks. Of course there's the old saying "If it ain't broke, don't fix it!" This holds true for bodybuilding as well. Let's say you give one of the following routines a try and the body part in question starts making tremendous gains. As long as you keep getting results, stick with the program. You've discovered something that most bodybuilders only dream about, a program that keeps yielding progress. Why change it just because "you are supposed to" every 6 to 8 weeks. There's time enough for that later when things start slowing down. And we might add contrary to what we said earlier, a few bodybuilders have actually stuck with the same routine for years and continued to make progress.

Enough rhetoric. It's time to present to you the training programs of the world's greatest bodybuilders. And who knows, you may find one of your own routines here in a couple of years!

AARON BAKER'S BICEPS ROUTINE

He's big, cut, has few if any weaknesses, and commands undivided attention when he hits the posing dais. Yet California's Aaron Baker has never achieved the success that lesser physiques have. Some suggest he was blacklisted because of a brief foray into the now defunct WBF bodybuilding federation. Others suggest it's just bad luck. Whatever the reason, few can argue that Aaron doesn't sport one of the most massive physiques currently on the scene. And at the center of his great physique are two melon-sized biceps!

Finish

"**Connecting with your muscles sounds like a topic on the Mr. Rodgers show but it's the foundation upon which my physique is built. I design my workouts with this thought in mind, and I have a special way of getting inside my muscles before curling a bar.**"

—Aaron Baker, pro bodybuilder commenting on how there's more to training than just hoisting a bar.

Aaron is the first to admit he is not a slave to numbers when it comes to reps. He prefers to go by instinct. One workout may see sets of 12, the next it's only 6 or 8. For Aaron the most important thing is feeling each and every contraction. This means no bouncing or jerking the weight. Another thing, Aaron rarely does the same exercises two days in a row. He's a firm believer in variety. Of course he does have a set order to his biceps workouts. He usually starts with a basic power movement like barbell curls, followed by a fullness exercise like incline dumbell curls. To finish off his biceps workout Aaron employs concentration or hammer curls. We should add there are days when Aaron will switch things around just to keep the muscles guessing. Here's a sample biceps routine from one of bodybuilding's most underrated stars:

Start

Aaron Baker is a firm believer in variety. He rarely does the same exercise two days in a row. Here, Aaron incorporates barbell curls into his biceps routine.

	Sets	Reps
Standing barbell curls	2-3	6-12
Seated incline curls	2-3	6-12
Concentration curls	2-3	6-12

Start

To keep his muscles guessing, Lee Apperson likes to change his exercises around. Incline barbell presses are a part of his chest routine.

Finish

LEE APPERSON'S CHEST ROUTINE

Lee Apperson is another example of a bodybuilder who believes in basics. With all the attention given to fancy chrome-plated machines these days, Lee still believes that good old barbells and dumbells are the key to a great chest. Sure he'll throw in the odd machine exercise now and then, but for the most part barbell and dumbell exercises make up the nucleus of his pec training.

"Form is the tuner in chest development and weight is the amplifier. First you tune in by establishing proper form, and then you pump up the volume."

– Lee Apperson, American bodybuilding champion outlining his unique view on chest training.

No matter what exercise Lee starts with, he always does a good warm-up consisting of a couple of light sets. And he adds if it's cold outside and your body temperature is low to begin with, then your warm-up should reflect this: "Of all the injuries I have sustained, none has occurred during warm weather."

The following is a sample chest routine that Lee makes good use of during the off-season. For variety he frequently changes the exercises around to keep the chest muscles guessing.

	Sets	Reps
Flat dumbell presses	3-4	6-12
Incline barbell presses	3-4	6-12
Decline flyes	3-4	6-12
Cable crossovers	3-4	6-12

Standing preacher curls are a part of Gerard Dente's favorite biceps workout.

Start

Finish

GERARD DENTE'S BICEPS WORKOUT

Weighing close to 300 pounds in the off season, Gerard Dente is one of the sport's more imposing specimens. And with arms stretching close to 22 inches in contest condition, Gerard takes a backseat no one in the mass department.

Gerard attributes much of his muscle mass to his high school and college football training. But looking back he figures he was greatly overtraining his biceps; one of the common mistakes of aspiring bodybuilders. Nowadays Gerard does fewer sets utilizing higher reps usually in the 10 to 15 range. And instead of lifting weight just to flatter his ego, he now uses moderate poundages.

> **"When I was doing fewer reps and using heavier weight and doing more overall sets, I couldn't feel the contraction well enough. As a result I wasn't getting the outrageous pump I should have been getting based on my size and the capability of my muscles."**
>
> – Gerard Dente, Top amateur outlining his philosophy on the relationship between reps, weight, and muscle contraction.

Gerard's another bodybuilder who believes in keeping his total biceps routine to under 10 sets. He usually employs three exercises doing 6 to 8 sets total. Unlike some bodybuilders who constantly change exercises, Gerard sticks to the same ones, although he is not beyond rotating the order for variety. "I think a lot of bodybuilders make the mistake of trying new exercises all the time instead of quickly finding what actually works."

Another point to make concerns frequency. Gerard is not a slave to the old two to three a week per muscle group. After years of trial and error Gerard has found that once a week works best for him. But occasionally he'll alternate a heavy and light workout for biceps. The following is Gerard Dente's favorite biceps workout.

	Sets	Reps
Standing barbell curls	2-3	10-15
Standing preacher curls	2-3	10-15
Standing alternate curls	2-3	10-15

CHEST TRAINING WITH ARNOLD SCHWARZENEGGER

There's no reluctance on our part to say Arnold Schwarzenegger is bodybuilding's all-time greatest star. And while a few individuals have won more big titles than Arnold (Lee Haney, Vince Taylor), none have come close to transcending the sport like the Austrian Oak. From Mr. Olympia, to Mr. Hollywood, to perhaps Mr. President, Arnold has a knack for dominating every endeavor he chooses to engage in.

But we digress. Before Arnold was talked about as a possible future inhabitant of the Oval Office, he pranced around Venice Beach with the largest set of pecs ever to grace a human being. To this day Arnold's side chest shots make bodybuilders around the world go weak in the knees.

Arnold's chest training was a lesson in simplicity. Nothing fancy, just basic exercises performed for standard reps and sets. He usually started his chest routine with either flat or incline barbell presses. After a couple of warmup sets, Arnold performed five sets of 8 to 10 reps. After hitting his chest with 10 sets of barbell work, Arnold moved on to flat dumbell flyes. Again he blasted out five full sets. For those who want inspiration, take a look at Arnold's concentration on this exercise in the video *Pumping Iron*.

To finish his chest, Arnold usually added in five sets of cable crossovers. This was especially true around contest time when bringing out every striation was a necessity. Unlike the first three exercises, Arnold preferred higher reps on crossovers, usually in the 12 to 15 range.

Although the old Gold's Gym is long gone, and Arnold has traded in his posing trunks for various movie costumes, his presence is still felt at the major gyms in Santa Monica, California. Certainly anyone who picks up a barbell can't but help visualizing building a set of pecs like Arnold's. Let's face it if you are going to dream, dream big!

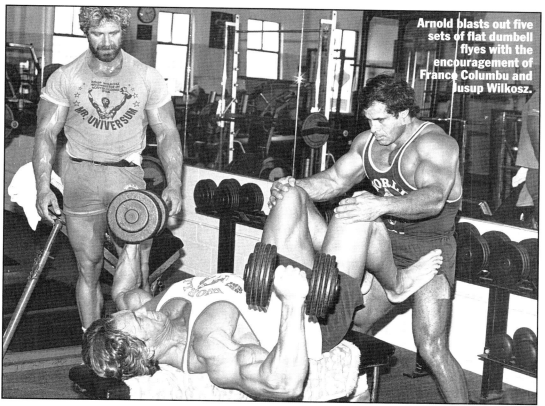

Arnold blasts out five sets of flat dumbell flyes with the encouragement of Franco Columbu and Jusup Wilkosz.

TRICEPS WITH EDGAR FLETCHER

Edgar Fletcher is one of those bodybuilders who many people assume is a pro because of his size and magazine coverage. Yet Edgar has yet to earn his pro card. The problem you see is Edgar has had to face some of the greatest names in the sport; Chris Cormier, Mike Francois, Dennis Newman, etc. With a second and three third places finishes to his credit at the U.S. Nationals, Edgar has established himself as one of the top amateurs on the scene. What's depressing is that while lesser bodybuilders can earn their pro card from winning their

Start

countries' thinly competitive national contests, Edgar is still battling in the amateur level despite sporting a physique that can stand next to anyone at the pro level.

If you like numbers, how about 220 sliced pounds at a height of just under 5'7"? Or how about 21-inch arms on the same frame grab you? Twenty years ago only men 6 foot or more sported such guns (with the possible exception of Sergio Oliva). For those who think Edgar's mass is the sole result of genetics alone, keep in mind it took him over ten years to add roughly 100 pounds to his frame. Now 100 pounds sounds impressive (and when displayed on Edgar it is), but 100 pounds over ten years works out to only ten pounds a year. This is the amount of muscle that the "average" individual can expect to gain after one year of solid training. Certainly not the 20 or 30 pounds that genetic freaks can expect to gain. No we can honestly say Edgar Fletcher's physique owes as much to consistency and hard work as superior muscle building genetics.

Like most bodybuilders these days, Edgar rarely sticks to the same routine for any length of time. He usually hits each muscle once a week; the only exceptions being twice a week for calves, and every day for abs. For those weight-at-any-cost readers out there, Edgar uses moderate weight for medium reps – usually in the neighborhood of 8 to 12 for torso and arms, and 15 to 20 for legs.

For most muscle groups, Edgar does between 9 and 12 sets total. This works out to three sets of three different exercises. As his arms seem to attract the most attention we will outline his approach to training triceps.

Edgar usually starts his triceps with either pushdowns or seated cable extensions. He starts with a light warmup set or two and then adds weight until he can just squeeze out 10 to

To finish off his triceps routine, Edgar Fletcher performs bench dips.

Finish

12 good strict reps. Next up is either one arm reverse pushdowns or one-arm seated dumbell extensions. While most people use a palms down grip on the pushdowns, Edgar prefers a reverse or palms up grip. He finds he can get a better contraction with this hand position.

To finish those great tris of his, Edgar does either bench dips or bent-forward cable extensions. Once again it's three sets of 10 to 12 reps. Here's Edgar Fletcher's triceps program in summary:

	Sets	Reps
Pushdowns or seated cable extensions	3	10-12
One-arm reverse pushdowns or dumbell extensions	3	10-12
Bench dips or bent-forward cable extensions	3	10-12

BICEPS WITH THOMAS ZECHMEISTER

Austria has never taken a backseat when it comes to turning out large muscular physiques. We need only point you in the direction of Roland Kickinger, the late Andreas Munzer, and strongman Manfred Hoeberl. And some guy named Arnold seems to have done very well for himself over the years. Now there's a new name to add to the list – Thomas Zechmeister.

Thomas first caught the attention of the bodybuilding press after placing third at the 1995 world championships held in Guam. Shortly after that he turned pro and entered the 1997 New York Night of Champions. Thomas has developed a reputation for having one of the most balanced physiques currently on the scene. And while he doesn't sport the overall mass of some of the larger pros, his biceps are second to none.

Thomas Zechmeister usually starts his biceps routine with his favorite exercise, EZ-bar curls.

Thomas usually starts his biceps routine with his favorite biceps exercise, standing EZ-bar curls. Although he's not immune to variety, Thomas tries to keep the reps between 4 and 12. After this basic mass exercise, Thomas moves on to single dumbell or cable concentration curls. To finish off his biceps he usually performs 2 or 3 heavy sets of hammer curls.

Like most top bodybuilders Thomas is a master of the instinctive principle of training and frequently changes his routine, "My training is all instinctive. It all depends on how I feel that day. When I don't feel well, I still try to train, but if the exercise doesn't seem to be working, or if I feel pain or an injury, I stop."

Thomas Zechmeister's Biceps Workout

	Sets	Reps
1) EZ-bar curls	2-3	6-12
2) Concentration curls	2-3	6-12
3) Hammer curls	2-3	6-12

22-INCH ARMS WITH DAN FREEMAN

"At the recent USA's, my arms were 22-inches. Even Chris Cormier came up to me afterwards and said "Man, what have you been doing for your arms lately? They really look thick and full."

252-pound Dan Freeman, first made his mark at the 1995 NPC California Championships where he placed second in the heavyweight class. A third at the NPC Junior Nationals and a fifth at the 1998 USA's cemented his reputation as one of the best amateurs in the country.

A native of Modesto, California, Dan was first introduced to weights while in grade seven. He is quick to point out that like most beginners he was grossly overtrained. He also made the classic mistake of doing "what you are supposed to do" and not what his body was telling him he should do. Since those early days, Dan has learned to rely heavily on instinctive training and experimentation. For example he found that higher rep ranges (12 to 15) quickly led to stagnation, and since switching to a 6 to 8 rep range he has made much more improvement. As Dan has two of the largest, most perfectly balanced arms in bodybuilding, we'll take a closer look at his biceps training philosophy.

Dan Freeman finds concentration curls excellent for mass.

Dan usually starts his biceps routine with that old standby, barbell curls. He doesn't jump right into the heavy weight but pyramids up, going from 135 to 185 to 225. Although it varies, generally speaking Dan rests 2 to 3 minutes between each set.

Dan's second biceps exercise is seated dumbell curls. He likes to run the rack on this exercise, starting with 35's and working up to a weight that limits him to 6 to 8 reps. Depending on how he feels, Dan will either stop at his heaviest weight, or start working back down the rack.

For his third exercise, Dan performs preacher curls. Once again variety is the key, and he'll alternate between a straight bar, EZ-curl bar, and the Strive preacher curl machine. Dan has a particular fondness for this machine as it allows the user to target different parts of the biceps by placing extra weights on three different levers.

Exercise four is the rope hammer curl, which Dan performs for both biceps peak and fullness, and to develop the brachialis that fills in the gap between the lower biceps and forearm.

To finish his biceps workout Dan performs either dumbell or overhead cable concentration curls. Unlike most bodybuilders who perform concentration curls for peak, Dan finds them excellent for mass.

From the previous you'll notice that Dan performs five different exercises during his biceps routine. For most bodybuilders this would be far too much. The biceps are a small muscle that can be easily overtrained especially since they contribute to back exercises. For beginner and intermediate bodybuilders two to three exercises would suffice. Even advanced bodybuilders shouldn't stay on such an intense routine year round.

Dan Freeman's Biceps Routine

	Sets	Reps
Standing barbell curls	5-6	6-10
Seated dumbell curls	5-6	6-10
Preacher curls	4-5	10-12
Rope hammer curls	4	12-15
Concentration curls	4	12-15

QUAD TRAINING WITH JASON ARNTZ

At 5'5", and weighing 198 pounds in contest condition, Jason Arntz is one of the new breed of bodybuilding champions. Where many previous bodybuilders ballooned to forty or fifty pounds over their competitive weights, Jason stays fairly lean year-round – say in the 215 to 220 range.

Start

> **"Go to failure, yes, but don't push beyond that. Once you fail, you fail. That's it. Just try to maximize every set."**
>
> – Jason Arntz, 1997 light heavyweight USA champion outlining the "do enough but not too much" principle of exercising.

Like many bodybuilders, Jason took up weight training to help another sport, in this case high school football. After three years and numerous muscular pounds of additional bodyweight, Jason decided to make the switch to bodybuilding. His rise through the ranks is more consistent than meteoric. From first place at the 1993 East Coast championships, to a number of seconds, thirds, and fourths, at the Junior Nationals, and finally his great 1997 light heavyweight win at the USA's. Most recently, Jason placed fifth at the 1999 Toronto Pro Invitational championships.

Jason Arntz prefers low to medium rep ranges using as much weight as he can handle.

Finish

With his idols being Dorian Yates, Mike Francois, and Arnold, it's not surprising that Jason has a liking for both mass and basic exercises. In fact both go together. Jason prefers low to medium rep ranges using as much weight as he can handle. Although he may occasionally throw in a "rep" set or two, most sets are performed for 6 to 12 reps.

Jason's thighs are among his best body parts and it's not surprising that he used to be a powerlifter, squatting 600 pounds for 4 reps (keep in mind this was at a body weight of under 200 pounds). At one time Jason's leg training consisted of just squats, leg presses, and stiff-leg deadlifts. In recent years Jason has been focusing on refinement and while he still does squats and leg presses, the weight is not as high as it once was. Here's a sample quad workout that helped Jason Arntz add the lightheavyweight USA crown to his titles.

	Sets	Reps
Leg extensions	3	12
Seated leg presses	4	12
45 degree leg presses	3	10-15
Hack squats	3	12
Sissy squats (pre-contest)	2-3	12-15

Finish

Recognizing that he could never match mass with with some of the pros today, Joe Spinello strives to develop a physique that is as close to symmetrical as possible.

POWERFUL PECS WITH JOE SPINELLO

Although he hasn't won a pro show, Joe was regarded as one of the top amateurs back in the mid to late 1980s. In short order he won both the Canadian and World championships, and has placed in the top ten in a couple of pro events. Recognizing that he could never match mass with the likes of some of the behemoths on the pro stage, Joe set out to develop a physique that is as close to symmetrical as possible. To many he has succeeded.

"I try to utilize all the tools at my disposal to create an individually great bodypart, no matter what I'm training. For the chest I often use different ranges of repetitions, heavier or lighter weight, different tempo/pace, varying rest periods, and I try to involve techniques like trisets, supersets and drop sets, depending upon how I feel on a particular day."

Joe Spinello, former Canadian and World amateur champion, commenting on how variety is the mainstay of his chest training.

Joe has two basic training styles when he trains chest. He may select four or five exercises and hit his chest just once a week, or he may train it twice using three different movements. If he performs the latter he uses the same three exercises but with varying rep tempos and ranges. Over the years he has found that he gets a better feel from dumbells and cables than barbells. Hence Joe's favorite three exercises are incline dumbell presses, incline dumbell flyes, and incline cable flyes. Some days he may perform the three exercises as straight sets, on others he combines them into a triset.

	Sets	Reps
Incline dumbell presses	3	6-12
Incline dumbell flyes	3	8-10
Seated incline cable flyes	3	10-12

Start

LEE PRIEST – BICEPS FROM DOWN UNDER

He stands just 5'4", yet the wonder from down under, Lee Priest, weighs from 210 to 220 in contest shape. He's also been known to go 280 in the off-season. Lee is proof positive that you don't need to stand six feet tall to carry proponderous amounts of muscle. If you want comparisons, Lee weighs thirty pounds more, 220 versus 190, than Frank Zane did when Frank won his three Mr. Olympia titles back in the late '70s. And keep in mind Frank is six inches taller.

Although he's packed head to toe with copious amounts of muscle, Lee's arms receive the most attention. Let's face it, how many 5'4" bodybuilders have 21-inch guns hanging by their sides? Not many, we assure you. In fact Lee is about the only bodybuilder who can perform Sergio Oliva's famous arms over the head pose and actually get away with it.

Lee is not a fan of the heavy-duty style of training. Instead he regularly blasts his biceps with 20 sets per workout. His first exercise is that old standby, barbell curls. He prefers the straight-bar to the EZ-bar, and is not afraid of expressing his opinion on the subject. "Everyone with big arms uses the straight bar. Everyone I've seen use the EZ-curl bar has arms that aren't very big. Maybe they can build OK arms but I'm talking freaky arms like Arnold's, or Sergio's, or Eddie Robinson's."

"When it comes to guns, this dude is a bad ass of muscle. He's packin' heat that Dirty Harry would never have ventured to carry."

Jason Mathas, *MuscleMag International* contributor commenting on bodybuilding's largest (proportional) competitor, Lee Priest.

Finish

Start

Although he's packed from head to toe with massive muscles, Lee Priest's arms receive most of the attention.

After barbell curls, Lee moves on to preacher curls. Once again Lee has his own view on preachers, preferring the standing version to the more popular seated version. He finds the seated version too stressful on the front delts.

Lee's third biceps exercise is seated dumbell curls, going from 60 to 70 pounds. Lee finds that by using lighter weight and momentarily stopping at the top he gets a better contraction.

To finish his biceps workout, Lee does standing Icarian curls. As this is his last exercise he prefers to do slightly higher reps, usually in the 10 to 15 range.

Even though he is only in his late twenties, Lee has the stage presence and muscle density of someone much older and more experienced. Here is Lee's favorite biceps workout.

	Sets	Reps
Standing barbell curls	6	6-8
Standing preacher curls	6	6-10
Seated dumbell curls	4	6-8
Standing Icarian curls	3	10-15

Start

MILOS SARCEV'S DAZZLING DELTS

He may not have the size of El Sonbaty, or the overall shape of Flex Wheeler, but few can argue that Milos Sarcev isn't passionate about the sport of bodybuilding. If you don't believe us, let's look at his competitive record. Most bodybuilders are content to compete once or twice a year. But not Milos. Try 70 shows in the span of six years or so! That works out to an average of between 11 and 12 contests a year. It's not surprising then that Milos had difficulty adding muscle to his frame during that time period. Let's face it, all that dieting and contest preparation leaves little room for building new muscle tissue. It was when he finally decided to cut back on the number of contests and concentrate on adding more mass to his frame that people began to take notice and ask, "What's Milos up to?"

> **"I know everyone gets sick of hearing me going on and on about mind/muscle connection and its role in bodybuilding training, but I can't stress it enough. It should be the cornerstone of everyone's training philosophy."**
>
> – Milos Sarcev, top pro giving his feelings on the mind/muscle link.

Utilizing such advanced training techniques as supersets, giant sets, and drop sets, Milos made his delts one of his best body parts.

Finish

What he was up to was re-examining his physique and tailoring his training to balance his proportions. Delt training was one area that needed extra work and Milos was up to the challenge. With a good deal of mass already laid down, Milos realized that the next order of business was refinement. Utilizing such advanced training techniques as supersets, giant sets, and drop sets, Milos made his delts one of his best body parts, and they are one reason he placed second at the 1999 Toronto Pro Invitational bodybuilding championships. Here's one of Milos' favorite shoulder routines:

	Sets	Reps
Seated dumbell presses	4	10
One-arm dumbell side laterals	3	8-10
Front dumbell raises/upright rows (superset)		
	3	8, 10, 12

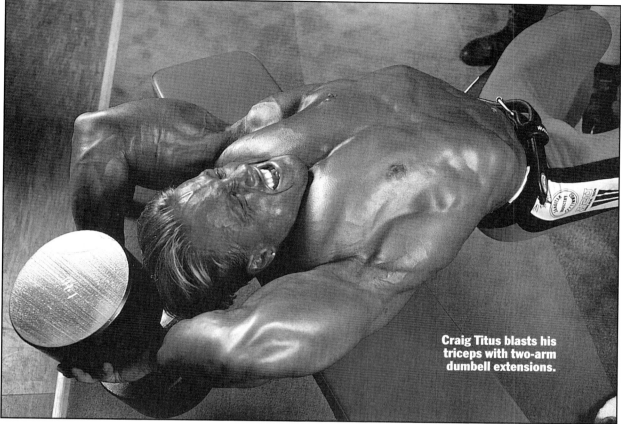

Craig Titus blasts his triceps with two-arm dumbell extensions.

TITUS-SIZED TRICEPS

Just when it seemed Craig Titus was ready to do battle with Wheeler, Coleman, and the other big boys on the IFBB circuit, the long arm of the law intervened. Craig was convicted of the now all too popular catch phrase "a conspiracy to sell steroids." We have no intentions of going into details. Suffice to say, Craig traded in his newly obtained IFBB pro card, for a pair of prison issues. For most, the switch would have meant the end of a promising career. But Titus is not the average bodybuilder. He worked long and hard for that coveted pro card. Unlike some, he paid his dues, and he wasn't about to let a few vertical bars stand in his way.

"I've got to say that being here in Lompoc has been a real blessing for my training believe it or not. When you have little to work with, you tend to create useful devices or practices out of nothing."

– Craig Titus, recently paroled IFBB pro commenting on one of the few positives attributes to being incarcerated.

When *MuscleMag International* interviewed Craig in 1998, we were surprised to see how positive he was. Granted it was only a few months from parole day, but nevertheless, Craig actually had good things to say about prison training. In fact he learned a few things while training in the prison courtyard. The first thing he did while walking through the gates was size up the weight training area. Obviously the days of Gold's and World Gyms were over. No machines, a few barbells, and an incomplete set of dumbells pretty much summed up the available equipment. Craig could have resigned himself to the fact that his physique would take a beating while incarcerated, but that's not his style. No, using the inventiveness that helped him win the Nationals, Craig set out to design an exercise program using the limited equipment available. As Craig is famous for his arms, in particular his triceps, let's show you what he came up with while wearing the black and white stripes.

"I remember I was holding the two dumbells up in the air during a shoulder workout and sort of staring off into space. Obviously they were light enough that I could space out in deep thought. When I finally lowered them, I felt a tremendous pump, both in my triceps and my delts."

Perhaps the biggest discovery Craig made was that you don't need heavy weight to fatigue a muscle. He found that by holding the weight stationary about three-quarters of the way up, it fatigued and pumped his triceps like never before. In fact he couldn't use heavier weight in this style even if he wanted to. Recognizing a good thing when he saw it, Craig employed the same principle to such other triceps exercises as one-arm extensions and kickbacks. In this manner Craig was able to hold on to about 90 to 95 percent of his muscle mass.

Of course when he has access to a full range of gym equipment, Craig follows a slightly different triceps program. He still does one arm dumbell extensions, but now incorporates cable extensions using both a rope and EZ-curl bar attachment. But Craig is quick to point out that he doesn't intend to abandon what he learned while in prison, and where possible incorporates the constant tension (isotension) training technique into his routine. Here are two of Craig's triceps routines:

	Sets	Reps
Two-arm dumbell extensions	3	8-10
One-arm extensions	3	8-10
Kickbacks	3	10-12
One-arm extensions	3	8-10
EZ-bar cable extensions	3	8-10
Rope cable extensions	3	8-10

GARRETT DOWNING'S CHEST ROUTINE

There was a time when a guy standing 5'6" would be expected to weigh 180-190 in contest shape. But don't tell that to Garrett Downing of Carlsbad, California. When he steps on stage, Garrett weighs an incredible 220 cut and chiseled pounds. Heck he goes up to nearly 250 in the off season.

Garrett took up bodybuilding after joining the marines at age 20. His first love was powerlifting, but soon the compliments started arriving about the physique he was developing. Like something out of a Hollywood script, Garrett won the heavyweight class of his first contest – the 1993 NPC IronMan. And this was while knowing little or nothing about diet, supplements, or precontest training. All this was to change, however, when Canadian pro bodybuilder, Sandra Blackie, offered to help him out in future contests. Sandra always had a reputation for coming in hard and tight. Further, she had established herself as a great personal trainer. She was just what Garrett needed.

The changes Sandra made to Garrett's diet started paying off as he won the heavyweight division at the 1995 California State championships, fourth at the 1995 NPC USA's, second at the 1997 North Americans, and third at the 1997 NPC Nationals. It was his placings at both the 1997 shows that established Garrett as one of the top amateurs in the country.

"People who lack chest size must learn how to put the overload on the pecs and not just use triceps and delts to get the weight up."

– Garrett Downing, top amateur bodybuilder offering advice to those who are pectorally-challenged.

Selecting a best body part on Garrett is difficult. Let's face it, he's sort of a cross between Flex Wheeler and Shawn Ray. That is, he's pretty much the complete package. As his chest enters a room a full second before the rest of him, lets see how he builds it.

It's not surprising given his powerlifting background, that Garrett prefers the good old, flat barbell bench press as his main chest exerise. He follows the standard pyramid style of training, going from 315 up to 405 for sets of 6 to 8 reps. Occasionally he will do something a tad strange however, in that he will jump back up to a heavier weight on his last set.

Garrett's second exercise is either incline barbell or incline dumbell presses. Once again he pyramids, this time going from 225 up to 315 for sets of 10 to 12 and 6 to 8 respectively.

After the two basic power movements, Garrett moves on to two isolation movements usually flat dumbell flyes and pec-dek flyes. With form utmost on his mind, Garrett keeps the weight moderate and squeezes out 10 to 12 ultra-strict reps.

As a final comment, Garrett doesn't alternate light and heavy days like most bodybuilders. Every day is a heavy day. Here's his favorite chest workout:

	Sets	Reps
Flat barbell presses	4	4-8
Flat dumbell flyes	4	10-12
Pec-dek flyes	4	15-20
Incline barbell or dumbell presses	4	6-8

Garrett Downing doesn't alternate light and heavy days like most bodybuilders. Every day is a heavy day.

BIGGER ARMS THE JOE DE ANGELIS WAY

IFBB pro, Joe De Angelis, is another bodybuilder who believes that many beginners get too carried away with how much weight they can lift and don't pay enough attention proper form. But he's the first to admit he did the same when he was just starting out and "getting the weight up was all that mattered and using any means necessary was OK."

Joe's philosophy took a turn after a chance meeting with Mr. America Rickie Barrette. Rickie taught Joe how to get the most out of the weight he was handling. As would be expected the more attention Joe began to pay to form, the less weight he could lift. "In lifting 60 pounds I was actually utilizing all 60 of these pounds. I think that's a connection many people forget to consider when choosing weight."

> **"Not that I practice stale training methods, but I just believe you can't reinvent the wheel when it comes to effective weight training. However there are definite right and wrong ways to executing those movements."**
>
> – Joe DeAngelis, IFBB pro commenting on his belief in getting back to basics.

Part of Joe De Angelis' arm training consists of preacher curls, paying more attention to form than poundage.

Another change Joe made was to take into consideration his back workouts when designing his biceps' routine. After all, an intense back workout gives the biceps a great workout as well. Joe trains biceps every two or three workouts, usually alternating four basic movements. He also maintains a supinated (palms up) grip on all his biceps exercises. He finds the extra stress placed on the wrist from rotating is just not worth it. Here are Joe's four primary biceps exercises.

	Sets	Reps
Alternate dumbell curls	3	8
Preacher curls	3	8
Concentration curls	3	8
Barbell curls	3	8

SHOULDERING THE BURDEN WITH DAVE PALUMBO

Dave Palumbo would probably be the first one to admit his physique will never win any aesthetic awards. But if it's pure mass you are looking for, then he's got it in spades. There have been few contests in his career where he was out-muscled by another competitor. And he wouldn't have it any other way. The audience wants muscle, so that's just what he gives them.

Dave Palumbo has developed a reputation over the years as a sort of, to quote *MuscleMag International* writer Lori Grannis, a "thinking man's bodybuilder." That's because in a manner similar to Mike Francois leaving the priesthood, Dave quit medical school just short of graduation. To quote Dave "I just saw that this was a really unhealthy way to live, what with 18-hour days, little food, and fierce bitterness and negativity." We have to admit this is kind of ironic given Dave's chosen career as a pro bodybuilder.

"I used to believe the more the better until those injuries really incapacitated me and left me with fewer options. I would do military presses with 315 pounds for 6 reps. It was insane, and very hard on such a fragile joint and soft tissue structure. Now I only use dumbells in a seated press that doesn't torque my shoulders backward into an unnatural position."

Dave Palumbo, top amateur commenting on an all too common problem among bodybuilders, shoulder injuries derived from years of heavy barbell presses.

Start

Finish

Dave works his shoulders with straight-arm barbell raises.

Whatever his reasons, Dave is still one of the most intelligent people around and has put that gift towards developing a set of the most prized delts on the bodybuilding scene.

When he trains shoulders (and most other muscles for that matter) Dave selects four or five exercises and performs only 2 sets for each. And like many bodybuilders these days, he only hits the muscle once every seven or eight days. Dave's also a great believer in advanced training techniques, and frequently adds drop sets, supersets, and negatives to his training program. Besides the variety, Dave likes the fact that advanced techniques force him to use less weight than straight sets. As alluded to earlier, Dave sustained a number of shoulder injuries from years of following the old philosophy of "the more weight lifted the bigger the muscle." He admits that early in a bodybuilder's career, lifting heavy on basic exercises is necessary, but he adds you have to know when to say enough is enough. The following is one of Dave's favorite shoulder routines:

	Sets	Reps
Dumbell or military presses	2	4-16
Dumbell side laterals	2	4-16
Straight-arm barbell raises	2	10-14
Upright barbell rows	2	4-16
High pulley reverse cable crossovers	2	8-10

ARM TRAINING WITH ROB RUSSO

1996 Junior National champion and second place finisher at the 1997 Nationals, Rob Russo, is one of the many bodybuilders who has made the switch from compound to isolation exercises. Once the basic mass has been built, it's time for refinement. Rob is also a great believer in focusing more on technique rather than how much weight he can lift. He's also one of the most consistent bodybuilders around "I don't take time off from training. I'm back in the gym right after a competition even if I'm disappointed with the results as I was last year (the 1998 Nationals where he placed third). I may contemplate a lay-off for a while, but I never actually do it."

Rob originally worked biceps and triceps on the same day, but since he started training them on alternate days, he's seen a big improvement. He's also taken a

Start

page from Dorian Yates' book and reduced his overall training volume. Instead of four sets per exercise per muscle group he cut it back to three.

Rob usually starts his biceps training with standing cable curls. Although some bodybuilders let the elbows hang loose, Rob keeps them locked into his side. After standing cables it's on to hammer curls. Rob feels this is one of the best exercises for filling in the gap between the lower biceps and forearms. For variety Rob may perform hammer curls straight up and down or towards the center of the body.

> **"Isolating the muscle is what I've determined is the key to building bigger arms, particularly when you've more or less exhausted the range of basic heavy exercises. They don't work when you've built your muscles to a certain point."**
>
> – 1996 Junior National Champion, Rob Russo, commenting on his approach to arm training.

Rob's final biceps movement is dumbell concentration curls. Once again Rob goes for variety, doing the exercise in the classic elbows against the knees version, and the elbows hanging loose style popularized by Arnold.

Triceps training is similar to biceps in that he performs three different isolation movements using as much variety as possible. His first triceps exercise is the standard triceps

Part of Rob Russo's triceps routine includes parallel bar dips. Rob finds he gets better triceps stimulation from the bar version over the bench dip.

Finish

pushdown on a cable machine. Rob alternates between standing straight up and leaning forward. He also alternates attachments, with the straight bar and rope being his favorites.

The second triceps exercise is overhead rope extensions. Rob performs this as both a triceps builder and as a means to give his triceps a good stretch.

Rob's final triceps movement is parallel bar dips. Rob finds he gets better triceps stimulation from the bar version over the bench dip. Every now and then Rob will superset rope extensions with bar dips – usually every fourth or fifth workout. Here are Rob's two primary biceps and triceps routines that have helped make him one of the top amateurs in the country.

Biceps	Sets	Reps
Standing cable curls	3	10-15
Hammer curls	4	8-10
Concentration curls	3	10

Triceps	Sets	Reps
Triceps pushdowns	3	8-15
Parallel bar dips	3	8-15
Rope extensions	3	8-10

MR. OLYMPIA'S BICEPS

What more needs to be said. The bodybuilding record shows that Ronnie Coleman was Mr. Olympia for 1998. For those who don't follow the sport closely, the decision may have come as a surprise as Flex Wheeler was "supposed" to win the whole shebang. But when you look at Ronnie's record over the past two years, the outcome on contest day was no surprise. While most of the other competitors made little or no improvement in their physiques over the last couple of years, Ronnie's went ballistic. From 225 to 230 mediocre pounds to 250 to 260 pounds of sliced and diced extreme muscle mass. In short, from nowhere to everywhere. What's even more amazing is that Ronnie accomplished all this while holding down a full time job as a police officer in Arlington, Texas.

To reach the pinnacle of the bodybuilding world, a physique must posses few weaknesses. There has to be symmetry, there has to be shape, and perhaps above all there has to be mass. Ronnie ranks supreme in all three categories. Some may argue that Flex has the edge in symmetry, and Nasser probably carries a few extra pounds of muscle, but when you look at the complete package, it's hard to argue that Ronnie Coleman is not a justifiable Mr. Olympia.

> **"I have my favorite exercises and I rarely mess with what has worked for me. It's worked so well that one time last year I had to sharply curtail my biceps workouts and work arms only once a month. No one believes me but it's true!"**
>
> Ronnie Coleman, 1998 Mr. Olympia commenting on one of his big problems, his biceps tend to grow too fast. If only we were all so lucky!

As would be expected, picking a "best" body part on a Mr. Olympia winner is not easy. From head to toe, Ronnie seems to be stacked. Still, what's probably going to make Ronnie such a popular Mr. Olympia is his arms, particularly his biceps. Not since Arnold-you-know-who strutted his stuff on Venice Beach has the sport witnessed such a huge set of cannons. It can't hurt Ronnie either that the two previous Olympia winners, Yates and Haney, while famous for the overall muscle mass, didn't blow the other competitors away with their arm size. But Ronnie does.

Many writers use the term "baseball-sized" when describing such monsters, but we think grapefruit-sized is more appropriate. They are that big.

Ronnie's favorite biceps exercise is surprisingly not heavy barbell or dumbell curls, but one-arm preacher curls. Placing second on his favorite's list is standing cable curls. Only after he does these two, will he grab a barbell and do barbell curls. And despite his size and strength, Ronnie prefers medium weight for 10 to 12 reps. You rarely see Mr. Olympia swinging up monstrous poundages for 4 to 6 reps. After all this is bodybuilding not powerlifting.

The following is Ronnie Coleman's primary biceps routine. Unlike other bodybuilders Ronnie doesn't change things around too often. He's a firm believer that once you discover a routine that works, and more important keeps working, it would be foolish to change it. Here's the program:

	Sets	Reps
One-arm preacher curls	3	12
Standing cable curls	3	12
Seated preacher curls	3	10

To reach the pinnacle of the bodybuilding world a physique must posses symmetry, shape and mass. Ronnie Coleman has them all.

Gerard Dente

BOOK SEVEN

THE HARDCORE EDGE

CHAPTER NINETEEN

The Plateau Busters

It's inevitable that sooner or later your progress will come to a halt. Those weekly increases in strength become monthly. Those monthly increases in muscular bodyweight stretch to a year. Bodybuilders use the term plateau to describe the condition where previously effective routines become ineffective. In a manner of speaking it's like getting a car stuck, with the wheels spinning out of control. No matter how hard you press on the accelerator, the car refuses to budge. In order to extract yourself from the predicament you must bring other resources to bear. You can place wood underneath the tires, recruit a few hardy individuals from the gym, or as a last resort call a tow truck. The bottom line is that simply sitting in the car with your foot on the accelerator is practically useless. You must adapt to the situation. Bodybuilding is no different. If your progress comes to a halt, you must adapt and employ strategies that will get you unstuck.

Bruce Patterson and Angelique Beltier

BREAK ON THROUGH TO THE OTHER SIDE

We're sure that the *Door's* great singer, Jim Morrison, didn't have bodybuilding plateaus in mind when he echoed the previous in the late sixties. But we have to admit, Jim was right on track and this is essentially what you must do to bust through a training plateau. The following are suggestions and tips to help you get back on track so to speak. We are by no means guaranteeing that you will "break on through." But we are convinced that it makes more sense to try one or more of the following than staying in an unproductive holding pattern.

REST

We are going to start with perhaps the simplest method of breaking a training plateau and that's ironically doing nothing. Bodybuilders are often their own worst enemies and most are in a state of overtraining. Although we'll touch on this in more detail in the chapter on injuries, suffice to say overtraining involves having exercise volume outstrip recovery ability. The end result is termination of growth – the dreaded training plateau. You may have noticed how taking an extra day off makes a tremendous difference to your training intensity. Your stamina is up, you get additional reps with the same weight, and most of all, your motivation levels are sky-high. All of this from an extra day's rest. What has happened is the body received an extra night's sleep and was given a chance to recharge its batteries so to speak. Sleep is as essential to bodybuilding success as training, nutrition, and supplements.

"Rest is the most important element in the cycle. When your body is at rest the muscles have adequate time to feed off the good nutrition you have ingested to promote muscle tissue growth and repair."

– Robert Kennedy, *MuscleMag International* publisher and editor commenting on the importance of rest.

For those about to dismiss this topic and skip to the next section, look at it this way, you spend approximately 25 to 30 percent of your life asleep (assuming an average of 6 to 8 hours per night). And this is not something you just decide to do, you need it. Try going more than 24 hours without hitting the sack and you'll see what we mean. The human body is not a static entity, it's very dynamic. By this we mean millions of chemical reactions are taking place simultaneously, whether you are sitting on the couch all day or busting your ass at the squat rack.

> Sleep is as essential to bodybuilding success as training, nutrition, and supplements.
> —Lee Priest

HOW MUCH REST?

According to medical types, the average sedentary individual needs a minimum of six hours of sleep per day. Noticed we used the word "minimum." For someone like yourself who regularly stresses the body with intense exercise, a minimum of eight hours is suggested. And for some, nine or ten hours is needed.

"You need to get a good eight hours of sleep a night. Your body secretes large amounts of human growth hormone when you sleep and this hormone acts as a messenger telling your muscle cells to get bigger while stimulating your fat cells to be burned."

– Frank Sepe, *MuscleMag International* columnist, and former top amateur bodybuilder commenting on the interrelationship between growth hormone, rest, and muscle growth and fat loss.

Lee Apperson

One of the convenient things about sleep is the body seems to function just as well on two, four-hour blocks as one eight hour stretch. This is why military personal can perform effectively despite their sometimes hectic sleeping patterns.

If there is a bottom line it's that it generally takes the body 60 to 90 minutes to reach what psychologists call deep sleep. This is the stage most productive for recuperation. It's also the stage needed for maximum growth hormone release – one of the most powerful anabolic hormones in the body. Given this, it means cramming six to eight hours sleep into an equal number of short sessions, is probably not as effective as fewer but longer sessions.

THE CASE FOR CONTINUOUS TIME OFF

Besides increasing your daily rest time in the form of extended sleep, you may also want to consider a couple of weeks of down time. No matter how strict your technique, you are still subjecting the body's joints and soft tissues to a tremendous amount of stress. Ten reps with 200 pounds on the bench press works out to 2000 pounds of force in under a minute. That folks is one ton of weight. Now do the same math for your entire workout. Sooner or later the body rebels against such intense pressure and one such form of rebellion is refusing to grow.

"Inadequate recuperation is probably the worst offender in the lot because it is the most insidious. You could be doing everything else perfectly but if you succumb to the popular notion that more is always better, you'll be asking for trouble in the long run."

– Brian Mongrauite, *MuscleMag International* contributor commenting on the importance of recuperation.

The solution to all this is taking a few weeks off from training. We don't mean reducing your weight or sets either. We mean avoiding the gym entirely. Don't even look at a barbell. Trust us, a couple of weeks won't cause you to lose all your size or strength. In fact if you are like many bodybuilders and in a state of overtraining, you may actually gain muscular weight during your time off. Further, the time off will allow any minor aches and pains to heal. Finally, your motivation levels will go through the roof. You'll be begging to hit the gym. But don't. Wait at least two to three weeks before hitting the weights.

CYCLING OR PERIODIZATION

As we said at the beginning of this chapter, the body quickly adapts to the same exercises day in and day out. That's why most bodybuilders change the exercises every couple of weeks. But even this may not be enough. Many of the world's top athletes follow a systematic routine that involves changing a number of different variables over an entire year. The technique goes by many different names but the most common are cycling and periodization.

> **"Stressing the body too much is counterproductive since it can't recover fully before the next workout. This scenario leads to overtraining and burnout both physically and mentally."**
>
> – Dr. Mauro Di Pasquale, *MuscleMag International* columnist warning against the dangers of year-round high intensity training.

Melvin Anthony

With a year being conveniently subdivided into 12 months, many athletes divided their training into cycles or phases of three or four months. A popular bodybuilding cycle would be to follow a heavy building phase for four months, a combination building/peaking routine for four months, and then a refining/peaking routine for the final four months. In rep form it would look like this:

First four months – Heavy weight 6 to 8 reps.
Middle four months – Medium weight 10 to 12 reps.
Final four months – Light weight 15 to 20 reps.

Another option is to divide the year into two halves, a building phase and peaking phase. Cycling plays many important roles. First, by reducing the weight every three or four months you give the joints and soft tissues a much deserved break. Few individuals can train heavy all year long without suffering some sort of stress injury. Another benefit to cycling is that the varied reps give the muscles a more thorough workout. As we saw earlier in the book, muscles are composed of both fast and slow twitch muscle fibers. No one knows for sure just what his or her ratios of each fiber type are. So it only makes sense to try and activate all of them over the course of a year.

Still another benefit to cycling is that the varied rep ranges and weights keep the muscles guessing. Cycling is one of the best ways to keep the dreaded training plateau at bay.

Finally, and we know there are exceptions to this, most bodybuilders, despite their love of training, find cycling a great way to alleviate boredom. Performing the exact same routine year after year is monotonous to most. Even die-hard types who love to train heavy find that backing off the weight and switching to a higher rep range is a welcome change of pace.

DIET

The late Vince Gironda is reputed to have said bodybuilding is 90 percent nutrition. Whether he said it or not, most will agree that nutrition is just as important as sets, reps, and exercises. Beginners may be able to eat haphazardly and get away with it, but sooner or later their gains come to a halt. As soon as you reach the intermediate and advanced stages of training the extra demands placed on the body's recovery system necessitate boosting nutrient intake as well. And this is what you'll see every day in gyms across North America. Bodybuilders who started out making great gains all of a sudden get stopped dead in their tracks. They made the mistake of keeping their nutrient intake the same while increasing their training volume. To use a simple analogy, if you increase the number of bricklayers at your construction site, it stands to reason you need to increase the supply of bricks. The same holds true for bodybuilding. If you up the training intensity, you must make a corresponding increase in the raw materials needed to build new muscle tissue. The key to breaking your training slump may not lie in the gym but your kitchen!

Nutrition is just as important as sets, reps and exercises.

SUPPLEMENTS

It only makes sense to follow the topic of nutrition with supplementing as the two are interrelated. And although we will be going into supplements in great detail later in the book, the topic needs discussing here as it relates to training plateaus.

There are two broad categories of supplements; nutrient supplements (indirect performance booster like protein, carbohydrate, and vitamins and minerals), and ergogenic aids (direct performance boosters like creatine, ephedrine, and glutamine). Athletes take the former to supplement their food intake. For a 200-pound bodybuilder trying to consume 200 grams of protein (the 1 gram per pound of body weight recommendation) it means eating a lot of high protein food. For some, time constraints or finances, make this all but impossible. But wiping up a 30 or 40 gram protein shake is easy and relatively inexpensive.

Jimmy Lee

Besides protein, it's almost a necessity to take extra vitamins and minerals. Even if you consume a good selection of food, the manufacturing process often destroys much of the vitamin and mineral content. For about $10 a month you can buy a multivitamin supplement that will meet most of your vitamin and mineral needs.

The other category of supplements, ergogenic aids, is the fastest growing area of the supplement industry. Instead of taking extra nutrients for the body to use at a fixed rate, you take substances that actually increase the utilization of other nutrients. For example the various pro-hormones on the market increase the level of testosterone and nandrolone deconate in the body. Both these anabolic agents increase the rate protein is converted in new muscle tissue. Often, training plateaus are due to the body's recovery system not being able to repair muscle tissue as fast as it's being broken down by advanced training techniques.

Despite the claims of a few individuals stuck in a time warp, the vast majority of athletes and coaches these days agree that supplementing is a must at the intermediate and advanced level of bodybuilding. Even those who increase their nutrient intake in the form of food will find supplementing makes a big difference to their recovery.

ASYMMETRIC TRAINING

One of the best ways to kick start stubborn muscles is to train them one side at a time. If you are like most bodybuilders, the bulk of your training is probably composed of bilateral exercises – two sides at the same time. Research, however, has shown that there may be a benefit to one-sided training. In activating two sides of the body at the same time, the brain has to split nerve impulses which according to some neurophysiologists may not be as efficient as sending one signal to one side of the body.

Besides physiology, there's a psychological benefit to one-sided training, that being concentration. It's difficult to concentrate on both biceps equally when doing barbell curls, but a set of one-arm dumbell curls allows for total focus on the biceps. In fact the name concentration curl comes from this.

The following are examples of muscles and exercises that you can weave into your workout to help bust through sticking points.

MUSCLE	EXERCISE
Biceps	Concentration curls
	One-arm dumbell preacher curls
	One-arm cable curls
Triceps	One-arm dumbell extensions
	One-arm pushdowns
	Kickbacks
Chest	One-arm pec-dek flyes
Shoulders	One-arm dumbell lateral raises
	One-arm dumbell front raises
	One-arm reverse pec-deks
	One-arm cable raises
Lats	One-arm dumbell rows
	One-arm cable rows
Thighs	One-leg, leg extensions
	One-leg, leg presses
	Cable or machine adductions
	Cable or machine abductions
Hamstrings	One-leg, leg curls
Calves	One-leg toe presses
	One-leg standing calf raises
	One-leg seated calf raises

Dan Freeman

Aaron Baker

You'll notice that some muscle groups lend themselves to one-sided training, while others are inconvenient to hit from one side. The chest is probably the best example. If you try to perform one-arm dumbell flyes or presses you'll quickly discover that it's virtually impossible to keep your balance. In fact it's dangerous to try and do so. About the only exercise that can be safely performed for the chest from one side is the pec-dek, as the machine allows you something to grab with the free hand for stability. We should also add that great care must be taken when doing one-legged leg presses. You will need to twist slightly to one side for stability. If you adopt the regular leg press stance and push with one leg you'll find it difficult to stay in the chair. Of course the downside to twisting is the extra pressure on the lower back. It's a trade-off between keeping balanced and not putting too much torque on the lower back.

THROUGH THE PLATEAU

Training plateaus are among the most frustrating problems you'll encounter during your bodybuilding career. And we'll be honest that solving them may take some time. You may have to employ more than one of the previous suggestions in order to make it over the hurdle. Even then you may be met with resistance. We are sure of one thing, however, few training plateaus go away on their own. By this we mean sticking points don't just disappear while keeping the same training program, diet, and rest intervals. If we go back to our stuck-car analogy, if five minutes spinning the wheels doesn't get you out, odds are another ten won't make any difference either. The same holds true for bodybuilding plateaus. The routine that put you in neutral, usually won't put you in drive. You have to change gears on your own.

CHAPTER TWENTY

Injuries

In the following chapter we are going to look at some common bodybuilding injuries and their potential causes. But a word of caution is needed. This chapter is not meant to be taken as a self-diagnostic manual! There is only one person, and one person alone who can make a proper evaluation of a potential injury, and that's a medical doctor. At the first sign of a major injury stop training and seek medical help. There's an old saying in law that someone who represents his or herself in court has a fool for a client. The same holds true for medicine. It takes from five to seven years to obtain those all-important MD initials after your name. Despite the authors' knowledge of the topic, there's no way this one chapter comes close to providing the same degree of advice and expertise that you can obtain in the physician's office.

"I hope you've had your knee checked out by a sports physician to see if there is any serious damage. You may need physical therapy to rehabilitate your knee."

– Greg Zulak, *MuscleMag International* columnist offering the best piece of advice when it comes to injuries – medical examination.

Even the most intense soreness should disappear within less than a week. If it doesn't you probably have incurred some sort of injury. – Joe Spinello

AM I INJURED?

By this stage in your training you've discovered that a really great workout is usually followed by a period of soreness. In fact most bodybuilders feel they've wasted time if they are not sore the day after. There's nothing like taking a wide grip on a bar to start a set of squats, and feeling that intense soreness from the previous day's chest workout. In a manner of speaking soreness is a form of injury but at the cellular or microscopic level. Over time bodybuilders learn to differentiate between the type of soreness that signals a great workout and soreness that suggests medical attention is warranted. Put another way, if you visit the medical clinic every time you get sore, you might as well cancel your gym membership and bring a sleeping bag to the doctor's office!

A CLOSER LOOK AT SORENESS

It is possible that many readers are experiencing muscle soreness above and beyond what you normally feel. The authors would like to take some credit for this. The advanced training techniques in this book have been designed to shock the muscles into new growth. After months, if not years, of staleness they have all of a sudden been hit with something new. And one of the indicators of success is soreness. You probably experienced this on a smaller scale just by switching one exercise for another. The next day the muscle in question is a tad tender and stiff.

There are four primary theories to explain muscle soreness. The first is the minor "damage" we alluded to earlier. When a muscle is subjected to a form of resistance, the various subcomponents (actin, myosin, etc.), break down. Over an average of 48 to 72 hours, they rebuild slightly larger and stronger, so that they can withstand slightly more stress the next time.

A second theory is that weightlifting stimulates the various nerve endings in and around the muscle fibers. The soreness you feel the next day is due to the nerves "recharging" their batteries so to speak. Like any form of muscle damage, the nervous system comes into play and once stimulated, produces varying degrees of soreness.

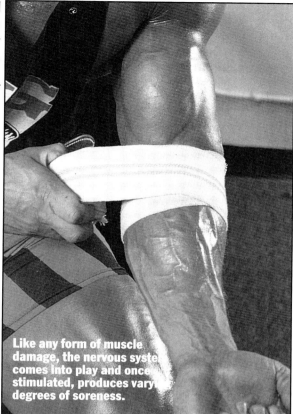

Like any form of muscle damage, the nervous system comes into play and once stimulated, produces varying degrees of soreness.

A third theory has to do with the buildup of waste products. Weightlifting falls into the category of anaerobic or "without" oxygen, exercise. This pathway is designed to provide high bursts of energy for short periods of time. This is opposite to the aerobic pathway which uses oxygen and provides medium amounts of energy for long periods of time. The chief waste product of anaerobic respiration is lactic acid. That intense burning sensation you feel while completing a set of squats or biceps curls is lactic acid building up. After you finish working out and leave the gym the soreness subsides. But 12 to 24 hours later it comes back in a lower intensity but longer duration form. Then within two to three days it gradually subsides. Of course, being the sadistic animal you are, you hit the gym again and inflict more "damage" on the muscles. Oh the joy of it all. The key point to the previous is the fact that even the most intense soreness (for example from a revamping of your entire exercise program) should disappear within less than a week. If it doesn't you have probably incurred some sort of injury.

A fourth theory is explained by what scientists call free radical and white blood cell intervention. As soon as a part of the body becomes injured or "damaged," the body sends in white blood cells to counter any infection. The body also sends more water to the area to dissolve waste products and remove them. Finally the level of free radicals (the dastardly little scavengers that roam around the body looking for oppositely charged particles to react with) increases.

The end result of all of the previous is an increase of pressure in and around the muscle fibers. Like any form of pressure, there will be associated tension placed on the surrounding nerves and muscle fibers; and the slight to moderate pain we feel, we call "soreness."

MEASURING SORENESS

Besides the different theories to explain how muscles get sore, there are four ways to measure the degree of soreness and associated muscle "damage." During intense exercise an enzyme called creatine kinase may leak out and can then be measured in the blood. The higher the levels the greater the degree of exercise induced damage.

A second technique is to use the visual approach. Under a powerful microscope it is possible to see the disruption at the cellular level. There is a direct correlation between observable damage and intensity of soreness.

The late Mohammad Benaziza

The third but least precise method is to measure a muscle before and after exercise. Post-exercise muscles are usually shorter than pre-exercise muscles. Of course keep in mind we are talking length in micrometers not inches or feet here.

Perhaps the easiest way to measure soreness is to use a "soreness scale." The most common scales range from 1 to 10, with 10 being most sore, and 1 indicating soreness that's barely perceivable.

If the last method has one advantage over the others is that ratings in the 8 to 10 range often signify the presence of an injury.

CRAMPING

Besides soreness, another painful condition that may be misinterpreted as an injury is cramping. Cramping can be defined as a sudden momentary freeze in the contracted position. The main causes of cramping are a reduced or interrupted blood flow to the muscle, dehydration and electrolyte imbalance. Even though every muscle is a candidate for cramping, those muscles involved in repetitive contracting (calves, forearms, and spinal erectors) are the most common sites.

Often the pain associated with a cramp leads the individual to assume an injury has occurred, but stretching of the muscle usually brings quick relief.

The best cure for cramping is prevention. That is, you adopt strategies to reduce the risk of developing a cramp. Always keep yourself well hydrated. Even if you don't feel thirsty, consume six to ten glasses of water a day, Conversely you may want to cut down on such diuretics as caffeine, tea, or ephedrine.

As electrolyte levels are also a primary cause of cramping, we suggest you focus on keeping their supply high as well. Green vegetables, fruits, and electrolyte-fortified sports drinks are three of the best sources. As with dehydration, diuretics can also deplete electrolyte levels. A couple of bodybuilding's most promising stars, Mohammad Benaziza and Hans Sallmeyer, have died from diuretic-induced electrolyte depletion.

As a final comment, while most causes of cramping are related to one of the previous causes and easily treated or prevented, continuous cramping could be symptomatic of something more severe. If you find the severity of cramping increasing, especially in the same muscle group, we strongly urge you to seek medical attention.

WHY OH WHY DID IT HAPPEN TO ME?

There is a whole spectrum of reasons to account for injuries. The following are the most common. No matter what the cause, the cure is to stop training and get it checked out. Training through a minor injury may lead to a major injury. And training with a major injury can be life threatening.

> **"As a trainer, I always instruct my clients to bend the knees ever so slightly during a straight leg deadlift because the bending protects your knee joint and lets you get a better stretch in the hamstrings. This style is also much better for the lower back."**
>
> – Charles Glass, top trainer and regular *MuscleMag International* columnist offering advice on good technique for the stiff-leg deadlift.

BAD TECHNIQUE

This is by far the most common cause of injuries. Despite what you read in some magazines and books about "all out, heavy as possible" training, strict style is king. Sacrificing style just to lift a few more pounds is only asking for trouble. Why do so many bodybuilders and power lifters have shoulder and rotator cuff problems? It's quite simple. In their attempt to impress others (or their ego) they put more weight on the bar than they could handle in a controlled manner and proceeded to bounce it off the chest. They rely more on physics than biology. In

Sacrificing style just to lift a few more pounds is only asking for trouble.
– Jimmy Lee

other words momentum takes precedent over actual muscle strength. The same reasoning can be applied to squatting. Dropping to the floor in a fast, uncontrolled manner, bouncing at the bottom, and then snapping to a legs-locked out manner, puts tremendous stress on the knees and lower back. The speed of the drop alone is increasing the resistance on the knees far above the actual weight on the bar.

How many bodybuilders have torn biceps tendons from performing preacher curls? It seems you are reading about someone new every month. At the bottom of the preacher curl movement, when you switch from lowering (negative) to raising (positive), the entire weight of the bar and forearm is placed on the biceps tendon. The switch from lowering to raising must be done in a slow and controlled manner. But go into any gym and you'll see most bodybuilders bouncing the weight at the bottom. The reason of course is they can lift more weight. But lift is not an appropriate word as they are really using (read abusing) physics and employing such principles as momentum and elasticity.

"The heavier the weight you use the more critical form becomes. Keep your back flat, your lifts in the groove, and never heave or jerk a weight."

– Ron Harris, *MuscleMag International* contributor outlining the relationship between heavy weight and strict form.

Most cases of bad technique are caused by trying to lift more than the muscle is capable of lifting.
– Melvin Anthony

Despite the common misconception about weightlifting, weight does not directly cause injuries; bad technique does. If you have the muscle strength, you can safely squat 300, 400, 500 pounds or more. Conversely you could end up in traction for three months using as little as 100 pounds if your style is out to lunch. Remember, you use the weight, don't let it use you.

TOO MUCH WEIGHT

It only makes sense to follow poor technique with the topic of too much weight, as the two are interrelated. Most cases of bad technique are caused by trying to lift more than the muscle is capable of lifting. In their attempt to emulate their favorite superstar, many bodybuilders forget the concept of "progressive overload" and jump right to "overload." Just because so-and-so uses 400 pounds in the shoulder press, doesn't mean you can do the same, at least not without building up to it. We assure you this individual did not start his bodybuilding career using such weight from day one (maybe in the case of Greg Kovacs, but scientists are not sure yet just which planet he came from). Even when performing the advanced training principles outlined earlier in the book, you must always use strict style. No exceptions.

"Perhaps you are trying to use too much weight and inadvertently bringing other muscle groups into play to help you lift the weight up as you do your presses or flyes."

– Robert Kennedy, *MuscleMag International* publisher and editor outlining the relationship between too much weight and exercise form.

TAKE A LESSON FROM YOUR CAR – WARM UP!

For those readers in northern climates you are probably aware that it's not a good idea to jump into your car on a cold winter's morning and take off without warming the car up. Machines work more efficiently and last longer when all the parts work smoothly. By this we mean they reach a steady state temperature that allows for proper oil circulation. The human body, like it or not, is a machine. Instead of metal parts we have bones and muscles. Instead of oil we have blood. And despite the presence of organic material, it follows the rules of thermodynamics. Going directly from work to car to 300-pound bench press, is only asking for trouble. The body must be conditioned to handle this weight.

> **"Injuries also happen as a result of insufficient warm-ups, or no warm-up at all. Warming up for the big weights may take a few minutes but that's better than missed days, weeks, or even years that a severe injury could keep you away from training."**
> – Ron Harris, *MuscleMag International* contributor commenting on the value of warming up prior to heavy training.

Jean-Pierre Fux

There are three categories of warming up. The first is cardiovascular. You may think that 300-pound bench press is only stimulating the muscles, but nothing could be further from the truth. It takes a tremendous amount of oxygen to generate the power to lift that weight. More oxygen necessitates an elevated cardiovascular system, i.e. the heart and lungs. Before heading to the squat, bench, or shoulder press rack, hop on a cardio machine for five or ten minutes. This is all it takes to get the cardiovascular system up and running at peak efficiency.

The next category of warming up is what could be termed "whole body" warming up. Even though you may be training chest, your arms, shoulders, back, even legs to an extent, play a role as stabilizers. Go over to your gym's stretching area and sit down on the floor and do some light stretching. You may even want to throw in a few pushups and crunches. Nothing strenuous mind you. Just enough to get the blood circulating throughout the major muscles of the body.

The final category of warming up is individual muscle warming. Let's use that 300-pound bench press as an example. Before putting your top weight on the bar, put a set of 45s on (135 total pounds) and do 10 to 12 smooth reps. Next add on another set of 45s and repeat. These two sets should be enough to get a good supply of blood to the chest, shoulders, and triceps. But you may even want to add on a set of 25's and do a few reps with 275 pounds.

Warming up takes a total of about ten minutes. The question you have to ask yourself is, is ten minutes too much time to take to prevent a lifetime worth of grief? We think not.

LACK OF CONCENTRATION

In this mad, mad world of ours, keeping your mind on one task can be difficult at the best of times. But this is what you must do when you hit the weights. Concentration can simply be defined as keeping your mind focused on the job at hand. In our case keeping focused on proper exercise technique. How long will you stay alive if you daydream while on the freeway? The same holds true in the gym. Raising and lowering a couple of hundred pounds on a particular exercise takes your undivided attention. Lose your concentration on a set of squats and it's off to the great training pit in the sky (or perhaps worse, spending the rest of your life in a wheelchair). And we think your ribs and internal organs will appreciate it if you keep your mind on what you're doing when bench pressing.

> **"For the best workouts we need to apply ourselves, concentrate, and get busy. Sometimes all the company we want is our own thoughts. This doesn't mean we can't share the odd remark with other gym members, but we don't want to get into long conversations either."**
>
> –The editors of *MuscleMag International*, commenting on the concentration and focus issue during training.

We know most readers have no problem staying focused while in the gym. But let's face it, everyone has days where the little things in life add up – the kid throws up in the car, the dog next door rips open your garbage, the boss gets on your case, that bastard in the BMW cut you off for the second time today. Odds are when you go to the gym you're in a foul mood. Which in itself is fine as long as you can convert that negative energy into a great workout. But as often happens, you can't get the day's frustrations out of your mind. When you should be thinking about pectoral contraction you're still back in traffic shaking your fist at the asshole in the BMW. Most days you'll get away with it. But chances are after having such a lousy day, you'll come in and skip your warm up as well. Now the old "adding of the ifs" takes place. And you can guess the rest – injury.

We know that there's no way to stay 100 percent focused at all times. But that's your goal. It only takes a momentary lack of concentration to turn a lousy day into a horrendous day.

It only takes a momentary lack of concentration to turn a lousy day into a horrendous day. Try to stay focused.

EQUIPMENT – SOMETIMES MORE FOE THAN FRIEND

If you happen to work out in a large, well-equipped commercial gym, chances are most of what we'll say in the next couple of paragraphs won't apply. But for those who inhabit smaller establishments, pay heed to what we are about to discuss.

There are two basic categories of exercise machines, commercially built and home built. Most large gyms buy the former as it looks nicer, in most cases has been designed by exercise kinesiologists, and above all is insurable. If a member injures themselves on such a machine the odds are good to excellent that it wasn't the machine's fault. More than likely the user screwed up somehow. But the same cannot be said for Pete's Gym down the street.

With the average cost of a strength training machine about $2500, it's not surprising that many small-time gym operators turn to a friend or brother-in-law to build the equipment.

Now this is fine if the individual has a decent knowledge about weight training. But in many cases while knowing their welding and materials, they lack even a basic understanding about human biomechanics. You can't just throw a few pieces of steel together and call it a lat pulldown machine. It must duplicate the body's natural plane of movement. And it's not just large machines either. One of the most popular candidates for home assembly is the T-Bar row. All, you need is one long and short bar, a hinge, and two pieces of wood for foot rests. It sounds simple enough. Make a T by welding the short bar across the long bar, bolt the hinge to the floor, and attach the long bar. Position the two blocks of wood on both sides towards the front, and away you go, right? Wrong!

Such a home built contraption has probably ruined more backs than any other. Everything from the length of the bar and position of the handle, to the location of the foot supports must be taken into consideration.

Besides basic biomechanics, there's also the issue of durability. The average person has no idea what kind of weight can be lifted on some exercises. Tell Joe welder that most beginners can easily use 300 or 400 pounds on a leg press and he'll laugh at you. Tell him that intermediates and advanced bodybuilders will use over a 1000 pounds on the same exercise and he'll question your sanity. But these are the facts. Now do you think such an individual takes this into account when they build the machines? Probably not. We are not trying to question the individual's skill as a tradesperson. He or she is probably very competent at what he or she does. But unfortunately in many cases they simply don't know the sport of bodybuilding.

If you notice that a particular machine seems to be producing more joint stress than muscle stress, we strongly urge you to give that item a pass.

We should add that some home-built exercise machines rival that of any major equipment manufacturer. In fact many of today's major lines got their start in someone's basement. The legendary Joe Gold supposedly had the original Gold's Gym outfitted with many of his creations. And we all know the quality of champions produced by that one gym.

Please don't go back to your gym and question every machine you see. But if your facility contains an assortment of home-built jobs, then a certain degree of caution is warranted. And if you notice that a particular machine seems to be producing more joint stress than muscle stress, we strongly urge you to give that item a pass.

POOR EXERCISE CHOICE

It won't take long before you'll notice that certain exercises just don't feel right, no matter how strict your training style. Even when you use light weight, the movement still hurts.

With the exception of identical twins, no two physiques are the same. A difference of a millimeter in tendon length or attachment can make a big difference in biomechanics. This means there will be exercises that are not suited to your individual bone and muscle structure, no matter how strict your technique. The good news is that there are alternative exercises. The bad news is that some of the culprits are the best exercises for mass and strength.

Let's start with squats. Squats are the best leg exercise, bar none. But for many people they are a shortcut to a set of wrecked knees or torn lower back ligaments. The one piece of good news is that it won't take years to discover if the exercise is not for you. Within a matter of weeks you'll be getting the warning signals that just won't go away. If this happens the first thing to do is have an experienced eye check your form. If your form is fine, then odds are you may be one of the unlucky few who have a legitimate excuse for not doing squats (as opposed to the many who skip squats out of sheer laziness.) You may be tempted to keep doing squats despite the pain, but we advise against this. You can build a great set of legs by using other leg exercises. It's not worth crippling yourself just because squats are a "must do" exercise. (later we'll see why other leg exercises may in fact be more dangerous than squats).

Surprisingly many abdominal exercises also put pressure on the lower back. A 1997 study in the *Journal of Medicine in Sports and Exercise* looked at twelve common abdominal movements and found six that contributed to lower back pain. The exercises in question were:
Lying straight-leg, leg raises
Lying bent-leg, leg raises
Cross-leg curl ups (twisting crunch)
Hanging bent-leg, leg raises
Hanging straight-leg, leg raises
Bent leg sit ups
In the same study the safest and most productive exercise was the bent leg crunch.[1] We should add that millions of bodybuilders over the years have performed the previous exercises without problem. But for those with a pre-existing lower back injury, you will need to constantly assess the cost/benefit ratio of each movement. As soon as the lower back starts talking – listen to it.

Another exercise that causes grief to many is the deadlift. As with squats many individuals find this exercise stressful on the lower back. Once again check your form and rule out bad technique first.
Other exercises that may cause problems are:
Dumbell flyes
Barbell rows
Upright rows
Preacher curls
Smith machine presses

MUSCLE IMBALANCE

One of the primary causes of sports related-injuries is muscle balance.

Jean-Pierre Fux

Muscle imbalance can be defined as having some muscles proportionately stronger than other muscles. It is especially true for paired muscle groups. How often do you hear about pulled quad muscles? Very rarely. But pulled hamstrings are a dime a dozen. Many top athletes have the quad muscles proportionally stronger than the hamstrings, and as the saying goes, the weak link in the chain usually gives out first.

One of the most common bodybuilding injuries is rotator cuff tears. The rotators are the collection of small muscles connected to the shoulder blades that assists in retracting and rotating the arms. Compared to the much larger deltoid muscles, the rotator muscles are relatively weak. What usually happens is that bodybuilders devote so much time and energy strengthening the deltoids that the rotators start falling way behind. Eventually one or more of the small muscles making up the rotator complex tears. The solution to this is quite simple. Regularly include rotation exercises in your workout to keep the rotators balanced and up to speed.

Include rotation exercises in your workout to keep the rotators balanced and up to speed.
– Milos Sarcev

A final example to illustrate muscle imbalance is the relationship between the chest and upper and lower back. Most bodybuilders tend to follow the "the more I see it the more I should train it" philosophy. As the chest muscles rank much higher on the most wanted scale, they tend to receive far more attention than the back, particularly the upper back. Over time the stronger front shoulders and chest muscles draw the shoulder girdle forward producing that familiar sunken upper chest look. This in turn changes the body's center of gravity and results in a tremendous increase in lower back stress.

The routines in this book have been designed to develop the body evenly. But should you notice one area of the body lagging behind, modify your program to address the situation.

OVERTRAINING

Overtraining is one of the most common mistakes of beginner and intermediate bodybuilders. In their quest to look like Ronnie Coleman they start training like Ronnie Coleman. The problem is that unless you naturally have an incredible recovery system or have things severely boosted with drugs, sooner or later your workouts will outstrip your body's ability to regenerate.

Nailing down a precise definition for overtraining is difficult. Generally speaking it means the chronic condition where there is an imbalance between training and recovery. In business terms, investments far outstrip dividends. Or simply put, you are not getting out of your workouts what you put into them. In bodybuilding terms it means that despite the intensity of your workouts, you make little or no progress. This is what exercise scientists refer to as staleness. In extreme cases the body actually loses strength and size.

> **"One of Bill's secrets to not missing workouts is flexibility in his training approach. He knows that not every workout can be an all out, ball-to-the-wall affair. Nobody can train at high intensity year in and year out. It's physically impossible."**
>
> – Mat Wilson, *MuscleMag International* contributor commenting on the training approach followed by bodybuilding great, Bill Pearl.

When the body is in a constant state of overtraining it can't recover fast enough between workouts, and progress comes to a halt.

Besides staleness, another common symptom is chronic fatigue. No matter how much carbohydrate, sleep, or over-the-counter stimulants, the individual feels lousy and has to kick him or herself through every workout. And even then, he or she merely goes through the motions.

Closely related to the previous is lack of motivation. Most bodybuilders love gyms. Even after they finish their workout they'll hang around talking shop. But chronically overtrained individuals have no desire to go to the gym. As a matter of fact just thinking about the next workout may make them physically ill. If you find this happening to you, odds are the body is telling you that you are physically drained.

The following are the most common symptoms of overtraining. It is possible to have one or more and still make progress. But if you find that you suffer from three or more of the following, chances are you are experiencing the overtraining syndrome and it's only a matter of time before your progress will come to a halt and you suffer that dreaded training plateau.

Chronic fatigue
Little or no training motivation
Problems sleeping
Elevated heart rate upon waking in the morning
Increased susceptibility to colds and infection
Increased anxiety
Increased irritability
Decreased sex drive
Increased frequency of training injuries
Little or no increase in exercise performance.

The last point is really the result of the first nine. That is, when the body is in a constant state of overtraining it can't recover fast enough between workouts, and progress comes to a halt.

BREAKING THE OVERTRAINING RUT

Breaking out of an overtraining rut is simple in theory but difficult in practice. Most body-builders reach a point where the gym is such an integral part of their lives that they are lost as soon as they have to give it up for any period of time. Even the one or two off-days become a form of psychological torture. Telling them that they should take a couple of weeks off and do nothing will only lead to hostility. But this is the primary cure for overtraining. To overcome overtraining you must undertrain. It's that simple. Continuously pounding away without giving your body a chance to catch its breath will not only keep you from improving, but it could also set you up for a major injury. Then you will have no choice but to take time off (perhaps permanently if it's a serious injury to the lower back, knees, or shoulders).

Breaking out of an overtraining rut is simple in theory but difficult in practice. – Thomas Zechmeister

> **"When I started bodybuilding I thought I had to train every bodypart twice a week doing a minimum of 20 sets for each. Now I spend less time in the gym and get more out of my training."**
> –Thomas Zechmeister, IFBB Pro commenting on the biggest mistake of many bodybuilders, overtraining.

How long you take off depends on the state of your recovery system. If you have been in a state of overtraining for months, then you may need three or four weeks to normalize your nervous and recovery systems. And some of you will hate to hear this, but if you have been chronically overtrained for a year or more, then it will probably take a couple of months to put the body back to rights. Of course you can ignore this advice and keep hitting the gym two hours a day, six days a week and making no progress. It all comes down to your primary goal, increasing size or strength, or satisfying your daily social needs.

In addition to taking a layoff, you should start taking a few immunity-boosting supplements. We know we discussed this earlier but it needs reiterating. Overtraining leads to a depression of the body's immunity system. Such supplements as whey protein and glutamine have been proven to boost the immunity system's pathogen-fighting abilities.

We can't tell you exactly when to resume training, but we can give you a general guide. After a few weeks off you'll start noticing that all those little aches and pains have cleared up. Your motivation levels will have returned, and you'll feel, for want of a better word, energized. These symptoms are a good sign that the body's recovery system is recharged and is capable of dealing with exercise. Don't make the mistake, however, of going into the gym and picking up where you left off. Not only are the muscles and tendons not ready for it, but more important, does it make sense to follow the same routine that led to your overtraining in the first place? To quote six-time Mr. Olympia, Dorian Yates, "Whatever routine you are following, cut it in half and see what happens." This means half the number of exercises and half the number of sets. You may also want to cut your training frequency back as well (i.e. from six to four, or from four to three times per week).

A CLOSER LOOK AT COMMON BODYBUILDING INJURIES

Although just about every muscle, tendon, ligament, and joint, is a potential site for injury, there are areas of the body that seem to go out of their way to cause you grief. The knees and shoulders, account for about 90 percent of all bodybuilding injuries and it's usually a combination of bad training and anatomy that sets up the injury in the first place. Let's take a look.

KNEE INJURIES

It's estimated that 20 to 30 percent of all sports related injuries involve the knee. To get a better understanding of why the knee region is so susceptible to injury we need to look at its anatomy.

The region we call the knee is actually the intersection of four bones and four ligaments. The bones consist of the lower leg tibia and fibula, the larger upper leg femur, and the small covering bone called the patella or kneecap. The four ligaments consist of the medial and lateral collateral ligaments, and the anterior and posterior cruciate ligaments.

The two collateral ligaments stabilize the knee in the side to side direction; while the cruciates help prevent forward and backward stress. Of the four ligaments, the anterior cruciate ligament (ACL) is the most common site for injury. Few injuries have ended as many promising careers as the dreaded ACL tear. ACL injuries are usually the result of a sudden blow to the shin, or hyper-extending the lower leg at the knee joint. Now you know why locking or snapping the legs out straight during squats and leg presses is a no-no.

> **"Squats per se are not bad for the knees. It depends on the style in which you perform them. If you lower down slowly under muscular control to parallel, or slightly below, do not bounce at the bottom, and drive up using the power of the legs, then squats are usually safe to do."**
>
> – Greg Zulak, *MuscleMag* columnist offering his view on the "squats are bad for the knees" debate.

MAY THE FORCE NOT BE WITH YOU!

Exercise kinesiologists have divided movements into a number of different forces. Two of the most applicable to bodybuilding are sheer and compression forces. Sheer forces occur when the ends of an object are rotated in opposite directions parallel to the surface the object lies on. Compression forces occur when two ends of an object are forced together. Now for the most important point. Most of the body's joints are designed to withstand compression forces better than sheer forces. To illustrate let's use the squat and leg extension as examples.

Grant Clemesha uses wraps to help alleviate stress on the joints.

Squats are called a close-chained exercise because both ends of the lever (the leg bones) are attached to something solid. In this case the hips and floor. As you contract the thighs and squat down you bend at both the knees and the hips. As the hamstrings are hip flexors they also contract but in the opposite direction. That is, instead of extending the lower leg forward they attempt to curl or flex it backward. This opposite force, besides helping you keep your balance and perform the exercise, provides stability at the knee joint. How? Well, if they didn't contract, the flexing thigh would put tremendous sheer forces on the ACL ligaments. As the thighs contract they extend the lower leg forward at the knee and literally try to pop the lower leg out of the knee socket! But the hamstrings offer a counter to this by helping stabilize the knee joint.

Leg extensions are called an open chain movement because one end of the lever is not attached to anything. Because there is no bending or flexing at the hips, the hamstrings are, to all intents and purposes, neutralized. Now from a balance point of view this is not important.

It's not surprising that rotator injuries are one of the most common problems associated with bodybuilding.

After all you are sitting in a chair. But it's the stability aspect that could lead to an injury. No hamstrings means no opposing force which means no counter to the contracting thighs at the knee joint. The end result is the ACL ligament has to absorb all the sheer force by itself. Despite being popular at one time for rehabilitation purposes, most physiotherapists now recognize that leg extensions are not the ideal movement for strengthening the knee region. Instead squats and leg presses (also a closed chain movement) are now becoming the exercises of choice.

ROTATOR CUFF INJURIES

Located on top of the shoulder blade are a collection of small muscles that assist the deltoids in lifting and rotating the arms. These muscles, including the infraspinitis and supraspinitis, combine to form a single tendon that kinesiologists call the rotator cuff. The name is rather appropriate as the tendon covers or "cuffs" the ball and socket joint of the shoulder.

Rotator problems are common in sports that require a lot of over overhead lifting and throwing. Given the volume of pressing movements that most bodybuilders perform, it's not surprising that rotator injuries are one of the most common problems associated with the sport. The reason rotator injuries are common is because of where the structure lies; trapped between the above clavicle and below ball of the humerus. Every time you lift the arm, the rotator cuff rubs against one or both of these bony surfaces and begins to chafe. Eventually the area becomes inflamed leading to the condition called bursitis. Continued friction may wear a small hole in the tendon. Finally, the cuff may tear away completely.

As would be expected, the symptoms of bursitis are intense pain, stiffness and soreness when performing pressing movements particularly overhead exercises. Treatment consists of

Garrett Downing

avoiding any movement that puts pressure on the shoulder, and in extreme cases the use of anti-inflammatory drugs like cortisone.

In the case of a rotator tear, not only will there be pain and stiffness, but in all like-lihood a reduction in range of movement as well. Rotator tears can be considered mechanical in nature and will not heal themselves. The only option for full recovery is surgery. Given this, it only makes sense that you do everything possible to prevent rotator problems in the first place. Here are a few suggestions.

ROTATOR STRENGTHENING EXERCISES

In a way it's not surprising that most bodybuilders ignore direct rotator training. After all you can't see them. The judges won't give you points for a well-developed set. The audience won't be yelling out "flex those rotators," like they do for other muscle groups. Out of sight out of mind right? Wrong! Fail to keep the rotators healthy and they'll derail your bodybuilding career just as effectively as weak calves or a poor back. In fact a weak back can be brought up over time with diligent training, but a rotator tear could terminate any thoughts of future competitive bodybuilding.

The following four exercises are among the most effective for strengthening the rotator muscles and tendons. A couple of sets of each will only take ten to fifteen minutes, and unlike the larger muscles, they don't require that much energy. As a matter of fact you can do these exercises on an off-day and not have to worry about interfering with your recovery from your heavy workouts. So let's get to it!

THE EXERCISES

Note – Perform all four exercises for 2 sets of 15 to 20 reps.

90 degree vertical to horizontal rotation – Hold a plate or dumbell in one hand with the upper arm held straight out, parallel to the floor and the forearm facing the ceiling (as if you were doing a single biceps pose). With the palm facing forward (as opposed to facing inward on the biceps pose) lower the forearm forward until it's horizontal to the floor. Return to the starting position with the knuckles once again pointing at the ceiling. Repeat for the other arm.

Cable pulls front to side – Stand in front of a cable machine, preferably one with the pulley wheel about waist height. Grab the handle with one hand so that the forearm is held 90 degrees to the body (i.e. pointing away from you). Rotate the arm backward until it's straight out from the side. Return to the front position.

Cable pulls side to front – This is really the opposite of the previous exercise. Grab a handle with the forearm held straight out from the side. Rotate forward until the forearm is pointing directly away from you at the front. Return to the side.

Dumbell hoists – Hold a dumbell in each hand so that the thumbs are pointing downward and palms facing backward. Slowly raise the dumbells to the side. With the palms facing backward rather than downward as with lateral raises, there is less side deltoid involvement. Repeat for the opposite side.

INJURY TREATMENT

At the first sign of an injury stop training and seek medical help. For those of you familiar with First Aid, the R.I.C.E. principle is a good guide to follow.

    R – Rest
    I – Ice
    C – Compression
    E – Elevation

Rest – The first step in first aid is rest or in bodybuilding terms, stop training. It may sound tough and manly to "work through" the pain, but you only run the risk of doing more damage. It doesn't take much extra stress to turn a mild injury that could be healed in a week, into a major injury that could take months. Or worse turn a major injury into a life-threatening one (as in continuing to bench press after breaking a rib).

Ice – To help reduce swelling and pain, apply ice as soon as possible. If you don't have the genuine article most gyms have ice packs in their first aid kits. An ice pack is really making use of high school chemistry. Two chemicals that separately just sit there, when combined form a reaction that turns intensely cold. Simply break the internal seal (follow the directions on the bag) and wrap it around the injured area.

Compression – This step really only applies to injuries involving major cuts. To stop bleeding apply pressure to the wounded area using a bandage or other sterile material. As cuts are rare in gyms, we are going to modify the step and relate it to sprains, strains, and breaks. Instead of applying pressure try to immobilize the area. If it's an injury to an arm, tie the arm against the chest using a sling. If you don't have an athletic bandage, you can make do with a towel or T-shirt. The best way to immobilize a leg is to tie it to the other leg. Once again use a bandage, towel, or T-shirt.

Elevation – Once again this applies more to preventing blood loss injuries than sprains or strains. But you can cut down on swelling by slightly elevating the injured area, particularly if it's a limb. Keep in mind, however, that under no circumstances should you move a limb that you suspect has a fracture. Doing so could cause you to sever an artery or increase the damage to the bone. Immobilize the area and get medical help to the victim, or get the victim to medical help.

REFERENCES

1) *Medical Science in Sports and Exercise,* 29, 804-810, 1997

CHAPTER TWENTY-ONE

Staying Motivated

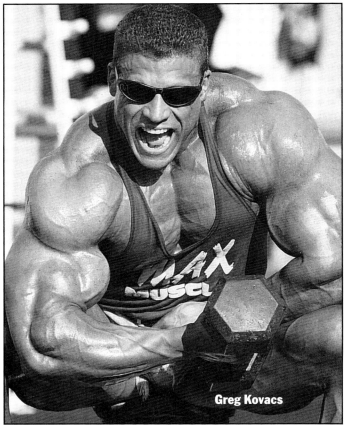

Greg Kovacs

THE KEY TO SUCCESSFUL BODYBUILDING

There are those that scoff at motivational tapes and books (an annual billion-dollar business), just a lot of psychobabble designed to separate losers from their money, say the skeptics. Let us provide a simple example of the power of motivation. What if we told you that some of the best, biggest, and strongest bodybuilders don't use supplements or steroids, only have access to old free weights, and are limited to three square meals a day? What could possibly motivate a person to train, and progress, under those conditions? A simple word: survival. Some of the ultimate physiques can be found in America's federal prisons. In the over-crowded, gang-ridden hell of one of the world's largest penal systems, only the strong survive. To fight-off gang-rapes, enslavement by other prisoners, and violent attacks, convicts lift weights to develop the one weapon permitted, their bodies. Every day, week after week, month after month, year after year, they train their bodies as if their lives depended on it; and let's face it, in many cases it does!

"People are often greater than they dare to believe."
– Old Irish saying.

Why do some people succeed, and others fail? How is it possible that in an age of easily accessible and high quality supplements, advanced training techniques, and scientifically engineered equipment, that so many bodybuilders drop their gym memberships after only a few months? Why are others able to persevere, and produce bodies that glorify the human physique? For the same reason that so many others succeed or fail in business, school, and love – motivation. A single word that encapsulates so many meanings: drive, hunger, ambition and determination. Motivation can carry you through the most difficult trials that life has to offer. And it is the only thing that will bring you the goals that your heart desires. In this chapter we explore how people can tap their inner resources, change their lives, and develop the focus that only motivation can provide.

> **"My mom asked me if I was gay! She'd seen how much time I was spending looking through bodybuilding magazines, and the pictures of the top bodybuilders I had up on the walls of my bedroom and in the basement where I worked out. She figured that I must be gay since I spent so much time looking at guys. I explained to her that I had those pictures and magazines for inspiration. I want to look like those guys. I don't want to be with those guys. There's a big difference,"**
>
> – Canadian Provincial (and decidedly straight) Champion, observing how sources of motivation can be misinterpreted.

SELF-ESTEEM

The Vikings, a group that make the modern Hell's Angels look like Girl Guides, followed a Norse Mythology that revolved around a central concept: the Gods don't care so you're on your own. Therefore they believed in themselves. Their self-confidence made them expert mariners, able to cross the North Atlantic in simple long boats. Unfortunately, they also believed in theft, arson, rape and murder. The point is that you have to believe in yourself, in your own capabilities and potential, if you are to succeed in bodybuilding or anything else in life. A common strategy among competitive bodybuilders is to "psych-out" the competition. The most effective way is to undermine someone's self-confidence. Constructive criticism is one thing, verbal abuse is another. Avoid those who would derail your dreams.

> **"Our lives improve only when we take chances — and the first and most difficult risk we can take is to be honest with ourselves."**
>
> –Walter Anderson

Laurie Donnelly, Mike O'Hearn and Mia Finnegan

MOTIVATE THROUGH MEASUREMENT

How do you measure success? How do you measure anything? By setting an arbitrary reference point, and using that as the standard to which you will compare something. The same approach works in bodybuilding. Begin by measuring your waist, legs, chest and biceps. Record your weight and bodyfat percentage. Get a picture of yourself in a bathing suit (it doesn't matter if you don't look great, it's going to be the before picture you'll use as a reference point). Now each month from when you start working out, you will repeat these measurements and take a new picture. You will notice subtle changes. Every month, provided you stick to the diets and workout routines explained in this book, you will be able to measure the resulting physical changes. Measurable success is perhaps the most powerful motivation.

Measurable success is perhaps the most powerful motivation. – Lee Priest

"Take away the right to say "fuck" and you take away the right to say "fuck the government."

– Comedian, Lenny Bruce, offering his views on censorship.

SET APPROPRIATE GOALS

"...Hey guys, this isn't Masterpiece Theater!"

– Actress, Pamela Anderson Lee, stating the obvious about her days on *BayWatch*.

We blame this one on the supplement ads (of course, not the ones we write). Many bodybuilders operate on the idea that big muscles = more sex. And when you're not getting any to begin with, that becomes even more motivating. Men think that in no time at all women will kill to be with them. Women think that with a build like Xena, men will swarm around them like flies. Is it true? We believe the following quote answers this question best:

"Surprise! Surprise!"

– Gomer Pyle (Actor Jim Nabors), from the TV show of the same name.

Regrettably life rarely works that way. Look who Pamela ended up with. The guy is a refugee from an '80s hair-band who looks like Pee Wee Herman with an attitude! And while guys love fit women, steroid-induced muscle-babes tend to turn off most guys. If you're extremely muscular you can be extremely intimidating. This will put off a lot of potential mates. Successful marriages among the pros are a rarity. With the amount of effort you have to spend developing yourself, there is often very little room for someone else. It can be done, and we discuss how to maintain that balance later in this chapter. But if your only motivation is to get laid, then drop bodybuilding. There are easier ways.

> **"If life were fair, Dan Quayle would be making a living asking 'Do you want fries with that?'"**
> – British comedian, John Cleese.

SET REALISTIC GOALS

The best way to achieve success is to avoid disappointment. And you can do that by setting realistic goals. Gaining 100 pounds of pure muscle in one year may be possible for one or two people on this planet. But given the fact that there are now over six billion people alive today, the odds aren't that likely that it's you. You won't be a 300-pound monster overnight. Muscular development takes time, plus good genetics. A gain of 10 pounds of pure muscle over 12 months, that's possible. If you've been at the same plateau for the last 10 years, it's going to be difficult, but it can be done.

The best way to achieve success is to avoid disappointment.
– Joe Spinello

> **"I am running for the Republican Party Nomination, to become the Republican Candidate for the office of the President of the United States..."**
> – Dan Quayle, Former Vice President.

You can dream about the Olympia, but most of us stop there. If you're into competition, then by all means enter the local contests. A win here, a placing there, a write up in the local paper, not to mention all the back-slapping at the gym afterward, are often reward enough. But to compete at the higher levels requires serious cash (Many bodybuilders have been known to spend more on drugs to get ready for a competition then they can receive in actual prize money. And for the drug-free crowd, there are still supplements, hotel rooms, meals and flights). The only way to get that kind of green is through a sponsor, usually a supplement company, or a sugar-daddy. These rich men provide everything for the bodybuilders (male and female), in exchange for sexual favors. We call it prostitution. And nothing, not even bodybuilding, is worth that. Unless you can find a legitimate sponsor, don't bother. Besides, if a sponsor wants you, then you know you have good potential because the sponsor is not out to lose money by backing a loser. One realistic goal, however, might be professional wrestling.

"...these wrestlers showed up, and one was the villain. We were all yelling, since we were all kids. Anyway the bad guy started walking past the fans, and this real old guy must have gotten caught up in the scene. Because he picked up his folded, metal chair, and hit the villain over the head with it! Knocked him out cold..."

—Adam MacIsaac, wrestling fan describing a memorable bout in Cornwall, Prince Edward Island.

Make the commitment and stick to it. – Lee Priest

This is the one that always seems to hit the gyms in the fall. Someone whispers conspiratorially, "I hear Hollywood is looking for another Schwarzenegger, and they're scouting the gyms." Hollywood isn't looking for another Schwarzenegger, they've still got the original. And even after heart-surgery he can still kick your ass!

A new opportunity that can provide money and media exposure is professional wrestling. If you're big, athletic and in good health, then you can enter local competitions. These "entertainment" bouts are geared for small towns and generally attract small fans (kids), but also a hardcore group of adults. However, depending on your charisma and acting ability, you can develop a following and a shot at the big time. The big advantage over competitive bodybuilding is that you don't have to diet down (fans like their heroes and their villains big). And depending on the take at the door, you'll get paid. And if you are looking to meet someone who is attracted to muscle, you can mix with the adult fans both during and after the show.

SET LONG TERM GOALS

Great, now you're huge. People turn and stare when you walk into a restaurant. That's fun for the first 15 minutes. Now what? What's the game plan? Have you any career goals? Thought about starting a family? Opening a business? Put away money for your retirement? Or are you living from paycheck to paycheck, barely keeping up with your tab at the supplement store? Your body will only last so long. The odds of making it as a professional bodybuilder are probably slimmer than being selected as a mission specialist for the next shuttle mission. Bodybuilding as a fitness lifestyle is great for augmenting your life, but don't let it take over your existence. Get an education. Develop marketable skills. Take up the arts. There is a broad stereotype of bodybuilders being big and dumb. Well, in some cases they are. But imagine the impression you'll make at the next family wedding or company party when you demonstrate a skillful, passionate tango with a gorgeous babe you met at dance school. Try acting lessons and join the community theatre. Try getting your own program on local cable TV. The possibilities are endless. But plan for the future, because it's coming, and you'd better be ready for it.

COMMIT YOURSELF TO A ROUTINE

I'm too tired. It's too late. It's too early. I'm not in the mood. Any excuse. If this sounds like your marriage then you've probably got a date with the Jerry Springer Show. If this sounds like you skipping another workout, then expect to get whipped at the conversation/brawl on said show.

"You will never find time for anything. If you want time you must make it."
– Charles Buxton

Treat bodybuilding as a second job. Imagine calling your boss and trying these excuses. Bet she'd laugh. You're expected to show up at the office or plant for a specific shift. We all manage to do it. There's no reason why you can't do the same with your workouts. Get a calendar, and plan out your workouts. Set times for when you'll be there. Socialize while you're there, but don't forget to lift some weights while you're being a social butterfly. Make the commitment and stick to it.

SEEK ADVICE

You can go into the gym with the best of intentions, but without knowing what to do you can expend a lot of energy doing things wrong. Ask people for advice, but be careful. Speak to other bodybuilders, physiotherapists, and professional trainers. Local athletes are a great source of information. And since info doesn't come cheap, hit the bookstore and subscribe to some bodybuilding publications. There's a lot to learn, and only an idiot thinks he knows it all.

"A man who has committed a mistake and doesn't correct it, is committing another mistake."
– Chinese philosopher, Confucius

Flex Wheeler

GET A TRAINING PARTNER

Sometimes we need someone to motivate us. A favorite teacher might inspire a life-long love of chemistry. A spouse might inspire us to work harder. But to train regularly, intensively, and with fire, sometimes the best choice is a buddy. Don't pick your significant other, it won't help your relationship if you're screaming "Go for the burn you maggot!" By having to meet someone else, support someone else, and guide someone else; you get the same in return. Your own private cheering squad and/or drill sergeant from hell.

"It was about this time that my parents realized that I was possessed by Michalik. They despised him for turning me into a living, eating, breathing, training machine. They tried to keep me away but it was too late. Once I realized that these long, hard training sessions were the key to my progress, there was nothing on earth that could have kept me away from the gym. Ah, the gym. Michalik's gym. No aerobics classes . . . no cardio equipment . . . no sauna, steam, or pool . . . no racquetball! Just big heavy black steel machines and benches with red padding to remind you of the old torture chambers. When you came to Mr. America's Gym to train, there was only one way, one speed — very hard and very fast! The facade and grounds to the front door were hosed down several times a day to wash away lost breakfasts and lunches. This was the hardcore Mecca of bodybuilding, a shrine to gut wrenching, ball busting workouts. No Tony Little exercise tapes found in these premises! If you didn't train hard, you were shown, or should I say thrown through the back door! Medals were won by how many brutal workouts you could endure and you were only as "bad" as your last workout. You were respected not so much by how you looked but how hard you could train!... It was much more important to be on time for the workout than it was to be on time for work. If someone trained with us and they ended up in the hospital, which was the case several times, we didn't even visit them but instead passed them off as mentally and physically weak. And as I sit here and think about the past, I have one thing to add to that Friedrich Nietzsche quote . . . "That which will not kill you . . . will only only make you stronger, and if it does kill you . . . You shouldn't have been training with us to begin with!"

– From the online article *Intensity Or Insanity?* by John DeFendis, writing about a training partner.

KEEP A LOG BOOK

This is probably the most important thing you can do. People routinely carry planners, electronic and otherwise, to juggle work and family obligations. Ever forget how many sets of laterals you did? Left out calves? Once again, how do you measure success? The best advice for bodybuilding is the same for tax time, keep detailed records. Record your reps, sets, exercises, and pounds lifted. If you have a computer at home, transfer those records to your hard drive. Graphics packages make it easy to build graphs, allowing you to see the progress you've made. The point here is that the best workouts are organized warfare. Follow your plan of attack. If you go in blind, expect to be ambushed. Injuries, lack of progress and frustration are common among those who fail to appreciate this basic fact.

Milos Sarcev and
Cory Nadine

"Documentation is like sex:
when it is good, it is very, very good;
and when it is bad,
it is better than nothing."

– Dick Brandon

PAYOFFS!

No, we're not talking about the mob (and we never will, we saw *The Untouchables*, we know what can happen). We're talking about what you get from bodybuilding. How about a better self-image? A tight waist and buns of steel can do a lot for your self-esteem. Your old clothes won't fit anymore, so you'll just have to go out and buy a new wardrobe. Isn't it amazing how much younger you look when you lose that potbelly? People treat you differently just because you look good. That's not fair, it's just the way it is. That's just one example. Watch your bad cholesterol levels drop while your energy levels go up. Your doctor will like you, your HMO will love you! Your spouse or significant other may become "more aggressive" in the bedroom. This is a win-win situation. You don't have to wait until you win a contest to get a pay-off from bodybuilding. It's yours for the taking, you just have to recognize it.

REWARD YOURSELF

Often bodybuilders become so addicted to conformity that they forget how to let loose and have fun. Here are a few suggestions to add some variety to your life.

- Once a week hit the junk food palace of your choice. But don't overdo it. Do you really want the part of "Fat Bastard" in the next *Austin Powers* movie?
- Plan a trip to Venice Beach. Work out in front of the tourists. Charge them to have their picture taken with you. Buy some tequila. Send it to our mailing address on the inside cover (we don't get out much).
- Buy an excellent bodybuilding book, preferably a *MuscleMag* publication. (Okay, okay, but we had to slip that one in.)
- Hit the dance clubs with your buddies (But remember, if you're on the juice, stay off the sauce).
- Go skiing. Try skydiving. Try something different. Attend a classical music performance, or just go to your local aquarium with a boom box, and serenade the seals with Killer Whale songs. Works for us!

HAVE MORE THAN ONE GOAL

Why just be the biggest bodybuilder? Greg Kovacs has wrapped up that title. But others are up for grabs. If you don't have the genetics for size, what about definition? You could try for most ripped in your own gym. Just watch the jaws drop when you take off your shirt and flex the coiled snakes that make up your upper body! How about most flexible? Combine bodybuilding with yoga. You'll find yourself in demand for guest appearances at local contests. And there's that old standby, you can try for the strongest. Strongman competitions go back to ancient history. Modern bodybuilding champions are so dehydrated they can barely walk on stage, let alone exert themselves. Perhaps, thanks to genetics, you're a freak of nature. Tom Platz couldn't develop the symmetry to sweep body-building contests, because his legs

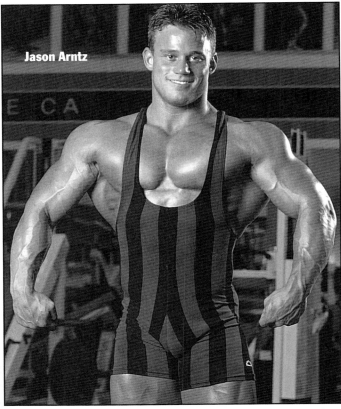

Jason Arntz

were so massive. Did he let that stop him? No! Just like thousands of Las Vegas showgirls, he used his legs to make his fortune. Everyone wants legs like Tom, and he's still a popular guest speaker. He turned his bodybuilding career into a lucrative business, and now he's able to enjoy that success. If it's distinctive, it's probably marketable.

"If you wish your merit to be known, acknowledge that of other people."
– Oriental Proverb

MAINTAIN A BALANCE

The body regulates its processes by establishing an internal balance called homeostasis. When that balance is thrown, things go wrong and we get sick. Our mental health is no different. We all have basic cravings: food, water and sex. We need shelter. We define ourselves by the work we do. We seek the companionship of others. The ultimate punishment in a Federal Prison is to be put in solitary. Most prisoners would rather risk assault and death than be separated from others. You can all too easily isolate yourself from others. When was the last time you socialized with people from work? Have you missed social events like weddings because you couldn't miss a workout? Have you refused a promotion, or chosen a lower paying job simply to afford you the time to workout? When was the last time you went on a date? Have you explored your spiritual beliefs? Personal development, social relationships, and family bonds combine together to form the whole person. Without other people in our lives a part of us ceases to grow. The reason Arnold has been such a success has been because his personal life is balanced. It is not enough to build your body, you must develop your ability to communicate emotionally with others and with yourself. Failure to maintain your mental health can put you at risk for getting ill. One in five North Americans will be treated for a mental illness. People eat healthy to avoid heart disease. They stop smoking to prevent cancer. Prevent mental illness by avoiding self-destructive behavior, maintaining healthy relationships, and develop all the facets that make you a vital, balanced bodybuilder.

"Not everyone is going to love you, so concentrate on the ones who do."

The best piece of advice Richard Simmons (*Sweatin' to the Oldies*) ever got from his mother.

MEDITATE

You refuel your body with food and supplements. But what about energizing your mind? If there's a way to detoxify your system, is there a way to clear your consciousness of the stresses caused by daily life? Meditation is the answer. Find a quiet place where you can be alone. You should sit comfortably. Close your eyes and focus on one thing. Some choose the spiritual.

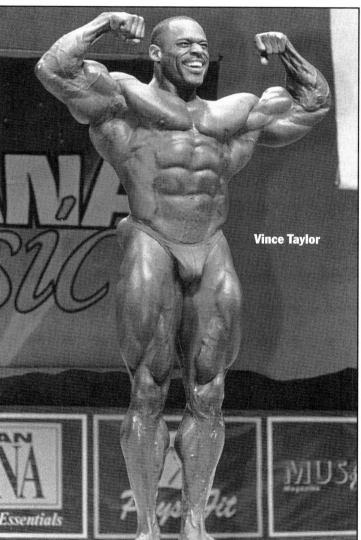

Vince Taylor

"I focus on God. Only on God. Not on material things. Only the spiritual."

Raghu Kumar Tirukkovaluri, Computer Consultant and practitioner of meditation.

Others visualize a jungle valley, or a calm lake. A very simple approach is to focus on breathing through the nose. Or mentally repeat a neutral word over and over so that it has no meaning. After doing this a few times you will find it a refreshing experience. Some people report the sensation of flying, but as this can lead to exorcisms, we recommend you keep this to yourself.

ENTHUSIASM IS KEY

Network marketing organizations have known about this for a long time. They regularly get their marketers together at huge conventions where prizes are given out for top sellers and the lavish lifestyles of those at the top are celebrated. The organizers know that enthusiasm is infectious. The mood is set with good food, plentiful drink, and friendly surroundings. Talented speakers reach out from the podium while company officials mingle and work the crowd. After a weekend like that, people return to the daily grind of selling with an energy that knows no bounds. Enthusiasm is one of the last legal highs. You can stay enthusiastic about bodybuilding by focusing on the positive. Then you are better able to deal with and put in perspective the failures and frustrations that are a natural part of training. Too many let a series of setbacks completely derail their bodybuilding goals. By keeping it fun, telling yourself that you like training, and remembering to laugh while you lift, you control your mood. That may sound strange, but we actually have the ability to create a positive mood. Capture the mood, and then you can move the weights. Remember, we're all mortal.

"You can get everything you want in life — if you just help enough other people get what they want."

– Zig Ziglar

Roland Cziurlok

Life is short. Well, okay Methuselah did pretty good, and Lazarus got a second chance, but for the rest of us, it's a short deal. There is so much to be done, to be seen and experienced. And those are things that should be shared. Get out and meet people, do volunteer work and become a part of your community. Develop the whole person, which means having a life. Share yourself with others. We don't have to go through it alone (we don't have to go through it skinny either). Make friends in the gym. That's half the fun. Now that you're big, you're ready to meet the world.

"It's not that I'm afraid to die, I just don't want to be there when it happens."

– Woody Allen

Gerard Dente and Debee Halo

BOOK EIGHT

HARDCORE DRUGS AND SUPPLEMENTS

CHAPTER TWENTY-TWO

Hardcore Drugs

"The drug issue is real. It is an issue that threatens to derail our sport and destroy our heroes. I am not referring to steroids here. Anabolic steroids are not going to kill anyone in the short term, and the long-term verdict has yet to be decided."

—Tony Monchinski, *MuscleMag International* contributor adding his voice to the drug debate.

The downside to oral steroids is that these drugs also tend to be the most toxic with more side effects.

DRUGS

Drugs, in a bodybuilding book? Imagine that! Well, if you're hardcore then you're not surprised. This chapter covers the main drugs that are popular with the pros and top amateurs. While there are details here that you won't find in our other books, for a more comprehensive list we strongly urge you to consult *Anabolic Primer* and *Anabolic Edge.* If you've read any of our other books, then you know we don't skirt the issue. We talk about the drugs, what dosages, stacks and cycles. What we don't do is tell you how to make your own, how to smuggle them in to the country, how to buy them on the Internet, or how to spot fakes. We've always been up front in our belief that anabolic steroids as a class of drugs are safe, provided they are used by individuals past their early 20s, obtained from a pharmacy, and used under medical supervision. In the US and Canada, anabolic steroids are legally a controlled class of drugs, and personal use and possession for physical performance (or cosmetic improvement, take your pick) is illegal. Even though we may disagree with a law, that does not give us the right to disobey a law that applies equally to all citizens. In a democratic society, it is the responsibility of the individual, through intellectual debate and the power of thoughtful persuasion, to bring about legislative change. If you want to use these drugs in a safe manner, then write your legislators and educate your family, your neighbors, your co-workers, and your fellow bodybuilders. The following is information that we hope one day can be used openly in a doctor's office. Until then read, learn, think, but don't use.

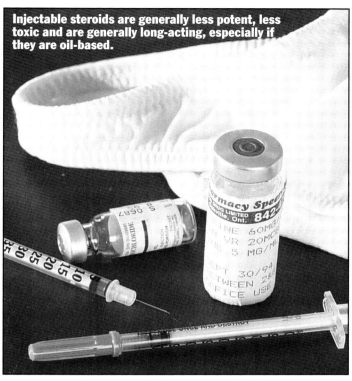

Injectable steroids are generally less potent, less toxic and are generally long-acting, especially if they are oil-based.

"God forbid he fails to win at his natural contest because then you have to hear endlessly how the people who beat him were on drugs. If he has a poor bodypart or is weak on an exercise it's because he's "natural." His pessimism can sometimes get you down – so much so that you want to hang out with the guys on drugs just to piss him off."

– Ron Harris, *MuscleMag International* contributor commenting on the "natural crusader" types who take the anti-drug stance to the opposite extreme.

ANABOLIC STEROIDS

It only makes sense to start this chapter with the most famous of all athletic drugs, anabolic steroids. Anabolic steroids are analogues of the male hormone testosterone. This class of drugs has a core 17-carbon steroid chemical structure that gives them anabolic (protein building) and androgenic (masculinizing) properties. Pharmacologists have attempted to separate the anabolic from the androgenic effects, with mixed results. The main androgenic effects of testosterone are the development of the male reproductive system and the secondary sexual characteristics.

The anabolic effects include growth and closure of the epiphyses of the long bones during puberty, enlargement of the larynges and vocal cords (causing a deepening of the voice), increase in red blood cell count, reduced body fat, and improved muscle mass.

Anabolic steroids are administered sub-lingually (under the tongue), sub-cutaneously (in the form of a pellet implanted under the skin), as a nasal spray, ingested (oral) and injected. Oral steroids are highly potent and are excreted rapidly from the body due to short metabolic half-lives (usually within weeks). Thus oral steroids are the first choice for athletes who want to rapidly improve their performance and escape from the drug tests. The downside is that these drugs also tend to be the most toxic with more side effects. Injectable steroids are generally less potent, less toxic and are generally long-acting, especially if they are oil-based.

Here's a brief description of some of the more popular anabolic steroids.

ANABOLICUM VISTER

Anabolicum vister is a very weak androgenic oral steroid. It is either taken as a capsule or in drops. Clinically it is used primarily in treating of the elderly, in particular women after menopause, and for the treatment of geriatric conditions. It does not aromatize and causes low retention of water and salt. Female bodybuilders, older bodybuilders, and steroid novices may gain some advantages while the more advanced will be disappointed by its effect. Men usually need very high doses in the range of 80 to 120 milligrams per day to feel anything at all, while some women react with a small muscle gain and a nice strength gain by taking only 30 to 40 milligrams per day.

Generic Name: Oxymetholone
Brand Names: Anadrol-50, Hemogenin, Anapolon 50, Oxitosona 50

Syntex is the world producer of this drug, and markets it under a few different brand names in other areas. Because of this drug's extremely poor affinity for receptor sites, it is only effective as a 50 milligram tablet. As it often causes gastric distress, it should always be taken with food. Oxymetholone is used medically to treat anemia (low red blood cell count); to control breast cancer in women; to improve weight loss due to severe illness (AIDS), and to treat osteoporosis (bone loss). There can be serious interactions with other drugs, especially: blood thinners, warfarin or any oral medications for diabetes.

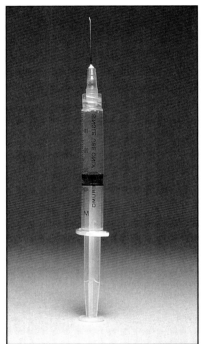

"To tell you the truth, I never tried Anadrol... I never got my hands on any! And my biker friend who was using it complained incessantly of stomach upset while on it. I knew he was using the real stuff, too, as it came from a guy who stole from a central pharmacology warehouse."

—A bodybuilder nicknamed Mailbox, talking to testosterone.net editor TC Luoma.

Anadrol will produce extremely dramatic weight and strength gains in its user. Almost all of this weight gain will be due to the drug's heavy water retention, which can cause high blood pressure. Therefore those with kidney problems should avoid this drug. Users of Anadrol report severe crashes when stopping usage. Aside from the water, Anadrol will pack on the mass like no other steroid. A four to six week cycle of Anadrol could account for a gain of over 20 pounds in many users, sometimes more.

This drug's anabolic and androgenic properties are very high, thus while the side effects may be tolerable in men it should be avoided by women. Unlike Dianabol (another 17-alpha alkylated oral) which is effective in doses of as little as 15 milligrams, Anadrol users generally start with 50 milligrams per day and often lead up to 150 milligrams per day. So when a user takes three Anadrol tablets, his liver is processing roughly the equivalent of 30 Dianabol tablets. Liver enzymes should be checked regularly. The therapeutic dose is one to five milligrams per kilogram of bodyweight per day, making the usual dosage for androgen replacement in males 1/2 to 2 tablets every day.

SAMPLE CYCLE
Week 1   (100 mg) Deca, (25 mg/day) Anadrol-50
Week 2   (200 mg) Deca, (50 mg/day) Anadrol-50, (20 mg/day) Nolvadex
Week 3   (300 mg) Deca, (75 mg/day) Anadrol-50, (10 mg/day) Nolvadex
Week 4   (300 mg) Deca, (50 mg/day) Anadrol-50, (10 mg/day) Nolvadex
Week 5   (200 mg) Deca, (25 mg/day) Anadrol-50, (10 mg/day) Nolvadex
Week 6   (100 mg) Deca, (5 mg/day) Nolvadex
Week 7   (2500 units) HCG
Week 8   (2500 units) HCG

THE NANDROLONES

Please note, if you expect to be drug-tested forget about this class of anabolic steroids. Even up to 18 months from last use, the metabolites can be detected.

Generic Name: nandrolone hexyloxyphenyipropionate
Brand Names: Anador, Anadur, Anadurin

Nandrolone hexyloxyphenyipropionate (NH) is one of many steroids which contains the compound nandrolone. NH is the longest lasting nandrolone. After only one injection the substance remains active in the body for four weeks. NH, above all, has an anabolic effect, which stimulates the protein synthesis and, as with all nandrolones, requires a high protein intake. Although almost everyone knows that during the intake of steroids more protein is needed, the effect of nandrolone depends on this requirement more than any other steroid. NH is not a steroid to be used to achieve rapid gains in weight and strength but is a classic, basic anabolic steroid which can be stored in the body, allowing a slow but solid muscle gain and an even strength gain. Bodybuilders using NH report less water retention than with Deca. For this reason some bodybuilders prefer NH when preparing for a competition. It must be observed, however, that in this phase usage of NH should be combined with stronger androgenic steroids such as Parabolan or Testosterone propionate, since the androgenic effect of NH is too low to protect against the loss of muscle from overtraining during a diet.

For steroid users who have often felt like walking pincushions, NH is a popular injectable as it does not have to be used daily or weekly.

Because of its slow, even, and compatible effect it is mostly used during steroid treatments which last for several months. For the most part, progress made during this period usually remains after discontinuing the product. NH is also a suitable compound for steroid novices and female athletes. When taking 50 to 100 milligrams every 10 days women normally show no virilization symptoms and they like to combine NH with Winstrol tablets, Primobolan 5-tablets, or Oxandrolone. Men do not have to take antiestrogens since NH hardly aromatizes at all.

The side effects of NH are hardly noticeable. It is not toxic to the liver and androgenic effects rarely occur, making it popular among women. High blood pressure is occasionally seen. The use of testosterone-stimulating compounds such as HCG is not necessary since NH influences the hypothalamohypophysial testicular axis only slightly so that the endogenous testosterone production is not significantly reduced and the risk of spermatogenetic inhibition is minimal. The typical gym dose is 200 milligrams every 10 days. For steroid users who have often felt like walking pincushions, this is a popular injectable as it does not have to be used daily or weekly.

Generic Name: Nandrolone decanoate
Brand Name: Deca Durabolin, Norandren 50, Extraboline, Retabolil

Nandrolone decanoate (ND) is one of the most popular injectable steroids. This is because ND has significant anabolic effects with minimal androgenic side effects. ND is most commonly injected once per week at a dosage of 200 to 400 milligrams. With this amount, estrogen conversion is slight so side effects are not a problem. At higher dosages, side effects may become increasingly more frequent, but this is still a very well tolerated drug. ND is known to boost the immune system and aid in the rehabilitation of joint or tendon injuries and inflammation (tendonitis). ND is used in both mass and cutting cycles. It's off-limits to the drug-tested set, as it can be detected even a year after last use.

SAMPLE CYCLE
Week 1   Norandren 50 (100 mg), Dianabol (20 mg/day)
Week 2   Norandren 50 (200 mg), Dianabol (30 mg/day)
Week 3   Norandren 50 (300 mg), Dianabol (40 mg/day)
Week 4   Norandren 50 (400 mg), Dianabol (50 mg/day)
Week 5   Norandren 50 (400 mg), Dianabol (50 mg/day)
Week 6   Norandren 50 (300 mg), Dianabol (40 mg/day)
Week 7   Norandren 50 (200 mg), Dianabol (30 mg/day)
Week 8   Norandren 50 (100 mg), Dianabol (20 mg/day)
Week 9   Norandren 50 (200 mg), 2500iu HCG/week
Week 10   Norandren 50 (200 mg), 2500iu HCG/week

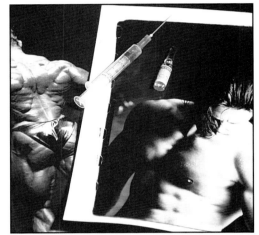

Generic Name: Nandrolone laurate
Brand Names: Fortabol, Fortadex, Laurabolin, Laurabolin V, Laurabolin 50

ND is known to boost the immune system and aid in the rehabilitation of joint or tendon injuries and inflammation.

Nandrolone laurate (NL) is basically a long acting nandrolone, staying active for up to a month in the body. Bodybuilders inject 200 to 400 milligrams of this drug on a weekly basis. Being a nandrolone, NL will exhibit noticeable anabolic effects with weaker androgenic side effects. Androgenic effects can appear in women who use the nandrolones, especially if blood levels build up too high with such a long acting drug like NL.

SAMPLE CYCLE
Week 1   Laurabolin (100 mg), Dianabol (20 mg/day)
Week 2   Laurabolin (200 mg), Dianabol (30 mg/day)
Week 3   Laurabolin (300 mg), Dianabol (40 mg/day)
Week 4   Laurabolin (400 mg), Dianabol (50 mg/day)
Week 5   Laurabolin (400 mg), Dianabol (50 mg/day)
Week 6   Laurabolin (300 mg), Dianabol (40 mg/day)
Week 7   Laurabolin (200 mg), Dianabol (30 mg/day)
Week 8   Laurabolin (100 mg), Dianabol (20 mg/day)
Week 9   Laurabolin (200 mg), 2500iu HCG/week
Week 10   Laurabolin (200 mg), 2500iu HCG/week

Generic Name: Nandrolone undecanoate
Brand Name: Dynabolon

This drug is claimed to be the most potent of the nandrolones. Bodybuilders inject an ampoule twice weekly. Each ampoule contains 80.5 milligrams of the drug, in 1 millilitre. It has a shorter life in the body than other nandrolones. Bodybuilders find this to be a very good training drug and excellent for recovering from muscle injuries.

Generic Name: dihydrotestosterone
Brand Name: Anapolon

This oral steroid is known as an instant gratification drug among users. Dihydrotestosterone is used clinically to treat anemia. Strength and weight increases are obtained in a short period of time, primarily due to water retention. It also has harsh androgenic effects and being 17-alpha alykylated, toxic to the liver. Water retention renders it useless as a precompetition drug, as muscle definition is lost. Many veteran bodybuilders choose to add this drug to their stack as chronic joint problems are often cured or relieved due to this side effect's subsequent lubricating quality. Because dihydrotestosterone increases the number of red blood cells, the muscles have access to more oxygen. Thus the muscle is able to endure more physical stress. This in turn leads to longer and more intense workouts. But there is a cost. The increase in blood volume can cause a side effect known as the "pump" effect. The muscles being trained can become so swollen and painful that the exercise must be abandoned. Still it remains popular because dihydrotestosterone and its derivatives do not aromatize, thus sparing the user of unwanted estrogenic effects.

Generic Name: dihydrotestosterone
Brand Name: Androstanolone

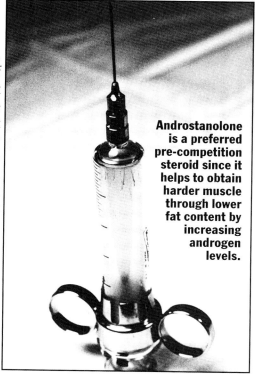

Androstanolone is a synthetic dihydrotestosterone. This drug is highly androgenic and being a form of dihydrotestosterone, cannot be converted into estrogen. It doesn't do much anabolically, so novices tend to be disappointed. It is a preferred pre-competition steroid since it helps to obtain harder muscle through lower fat content by increasing androgen levels. It is a favorite among the drug-tested set because the steroid remains in the body for only a short time and the testosterone/epitestosterone value is not influenced. The injectable version is popular because it is not liver-toxic. Due to scarcity, most users have switched to Masteron.

Androstanolone is a preferred pre-competition steroid since it helps to obtain harder muscle through lower fat content by increasing androgen levels.

Generic Name: drostanolone propionate
(a derivative of dihydrotestosterone)
Brand Name: Masteron

Drostanolone propionate (DP) is a popular injectable among competitive bodybuilders generally used for contest preparation. It does not aromatize into estrogen, thus estrogenic side effects are not an issue. This drug does not cause the water retention seen among other steroids. The strong androgenic effect of this steroid can cause a noticeable improvement in muscle density and hardness, which can help the bodybuilder obtain the "ripped" look if his bodyfat percentage is low enough. The androgenic effect is also crucial because it provides the drive for intense training when a bodybuilder is dieting down. This drug is fast-acting and quickly broken down thus allowing it to be used up to ten days before a drug test.

The average dosage of DP is 100 milligrams injected every other day. It is best to inject DP every 2 or 3 days because it has a short duration of effect.

SAMPLE CYCLE

Week 1   Deca (100 mg/week), Parabolan (76 mg/week), Clenbuterol (80 mcg/day)
Week 2   Deca (200 mg/week), Parabolan (152 mg/week), Clenbuterol (100 mcg/day)
Week 3   Deca (300 mg/week), Parabolan (152 mg/week), Clenbuterol (120 mcg/day)
Week 4   Deca (400 mg/week), Parabolan (152 mg/week), Clenbuterol (120 mcg/day)
Week 5   Primobolan (50 mg/day), Parabolan (152 mg/week), Clenbuterol (120 mcg/day)
Week 6   Primobolan (75 mg/day), Parabolan (152 mg/week), Clenbuterol (120 mcg/day)
Week 7   Primobolan (100 mg/day), Masteron (300 mg/week), Clenbuterol (120 mcg/day)
Week 8   Primobolan (75 mg/day), Masteron (300 mg/week), Clenbuterol (120 mcg/day)
Week 9   Deca (400 mg/week), Primobolan (50 mg/day), Masteron (300 mg/week),
              Clenbuterol (120 mcg/day), Cytomel (25 mcg/day)
Week 10   Deca (300 mg/week), Masteron (300 mg/week), Clenbuterol (120 mcg/day),
              Cytomel (50 mcg/day)
Week 11   Deca (200 mg/week), Masteron (300 mg/week), Clenbuterol (120 mcg/day),
              Cytomel (75 mcg/day)
Week 12   Deca (100 mg/week), Masteron (300 mg/week),Clenbuterol (120 mcg/day),
              Cytomel (100 mcg/day)

Generic Name: testosterone undecanoate
Brand Names: Andriol, Androxon, Panteston, Restandol, Undestor, Virigen

According to Oragnon, which makes Andriol (this drug is oil-based, sealed in a capsule and taken orally), this form of manufacture bypasses the liver and enters the body as a fat through the lymphatic system. Nice theory, but everyone doubts it works. No matter who the manufacturer is, it's a weak steroid. At doses of less than 240 milligrams per day, nothing much happens. Above that dosage, not much more occurs. It's possible it might do something when combined with other steroids in a stack. But we doubt it.

Generic Name: Testosterone
Brand Name: Android

Androderm is a transdermal patch, designed to release testosterone over a 24-hour period, in a natural pattern resembling that of a health young man. Legally, a natural product is not patentable. Because natural testosterone is not a patentable product the company which sells the Androderm patch, has a patent and FDA approval for its delivery system. This product is being used primarily by older men who have reached an age in which there body no longer produces sufficient amounts of testosterone (a still controversial condition called the male

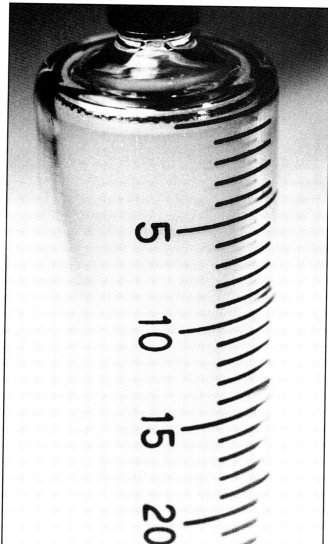

climacteric, male menopause or Andropause). Each patch contains 12.2 gm of testosterone, but only about 2.5 milligrams is dispersed in each 24-hour application. Two patches are most commonly used, and are applied to the abdomen, back, thigh or upper arm. If you have normal testosterone levels, you'd have to coat yourself from head-to-toe in these things to get any anabolic effect. This is strictly for therapeutic uses only.

Generic Name: methandrostenolone
Brand Names: Anabolene, Dianabol, Pronabol, Reforvit

Methandrostenolone (M) was at one time the most popular anabolic steroid available. It's known as the Beginner's Choice and an instant gratification drug. A dose of 20 to 25 milligrams (4 or 5 tablets) a day is enough to give almost anybody dramatic results. M has both strong anabolic and androgenic effects. It is a 17-alpha alkylated steroid and therefore high in liver toxicity. M aromatizes to estrogen, so anti-estrogens should be used with this drug. Much of the increase in mass is due to water retention. The increase in blood pressure may account for the mild headaches experienced at the beginning of the cycle. Even though it is available as an injectable, the oral form is just as effective and therefore more popular. The only oral steroid that can produce better size and weight gains in the same time period is Anadrol-50.

SAMPLE CYCLE

Week 1   Dianabol 10 mg/day, Testosterone Cypionate 200 mg/week
Week 2   Dianabol 15 mg/day, Testosterone Cypionate 300 mg/week
Week 3   Dianabol 20 mg/day, Testosterone Cypionate 400 mg/week
Week 4   Dianabol 15 mg/day, Testosterone Cypionate 300 mg/week
Week 5   Dianabol 10 mg/day, Testosterone Cypionate 200 mg/week
Week 6   Dianabol 5 mg/day
Week 7   HCG (5000 I.U./week)
Week 8   HCG (5000 I.U./week)

Generic Name: boldenone undecylenate
Brand Names: Equipoise, Ganabol

This popular injectable is strongly anabolic and only moderately androgenic. Alone this drug will provide steady gains in mass and strength. Boldenone undecylenate (BU) is highly effective for contest preparation since it aromatizes very poorly. Bodybuilders use doses of 200 to 400 milligrams per week, one injection every second day. Since Equipoise is only available in a 25 or 50 milligrams per milliliter version, the volume being injected may cause discomfort. If large volumes are repeatedly injected at the same site, an oil abscess may form. This should dissipate on its own, but in extreme instances, a doctor will need to drain it. To prevent this bodybuilders should rotate injection sites. But the best results are achieved when Equipoise is combined with other steroids. For mass, Equipoise stacks exceptionally well with Oxymetholone, methandrostenolone, or an injectable testosterone like Sustanon 250. Muscle hardness and density can be greatly improved when BU is combined with trenbolone hexahydrobencylcarbonate, fluoxymesterone, or stanozolol.

SAMPLE CYCLE

Week 1   300 mg/Decadurabolin, 200 mg/Equipoise, 10 mg/Dianabol 2Xday
Week 2   300 mg/Decadurabolin, 200 mg/Equipoise, 10 mg/Dianabol 2Xday
Week 3   400 mg/Decadurabolin, 300 mg/Equipoise, 15 mg/Dianabol 2Xday
Week 4   400 mg/Decadurabolin, 300 mg/Equipoise, 15 mg/Dianabol 2Xday
Week 5   400 mg/Decadurabolin, 200 mg/Equipoise, 15 mg/Dianabol 2Xday
Week 6   300 mg/Decadurabolin, 200 mg/Equipoise, 10 mg/Dianabol 2Xday
Week 7   200 mg/Decadurabolin, 100 mg/Equipoise, 10 mg/Dianabol 2Xday
Week 8   100 mg/Decadurabolin, 100 mg/Equipoise, 5 mg/Dianabol 2Xday
Week 9   2500 iu HCG/week
Week 10 2500 iu HCG/week

Generic Name: formebolone
Brand Names: Esiclene, Hubernol

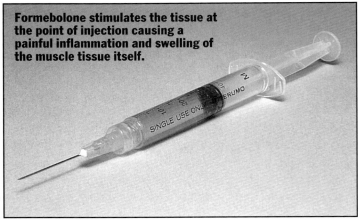

Formebolone stimulates the tissue at the point of injection causing a painful inflammation and swelling of the muscle tissue itself.

This is strictly a cosmetic drug, and acts like a gigantic mosquito bite. Formebolone stimulates the tissue at the point of injection causing a painful inflammation and swelling of the muscle tissue itself. Thus any muscle will increase in size within a very short period of time. To help control pain each formebolone ampoule contains 20 milligrams of lidocaine, a mild painkiller. The swelling only lasts for about four to five days making this a popular right-before-competition (or photo-shoot) drug to help pump-up the under developed muscle groups. Formebolone is often injected daily to make up for the decrease in swelling. This drug only promises temporary gains of around 1 to 1.5 inches on arms and calves from daily injections of around 1milliliter the first day and 2 milliliters (one per muscle) on the days following. Formebolone is a water-based steroid making it good for getting hard muscles and because it has no real side effects. Despite the recent popularity of Pump 'n Pose (also known as Synthol), the pros continue to use Esiclene, as it is not nearly as painful as Synthol. Further, as many bodybuilders have or know someone who has had an oil-based abscess, repeatedly injecting an oil into the same muscle on a daily basis is not an attractive prospect.

> Generic Name: This drug is a blend of testosterone propionate, testosterone phenylpropionate, testosterone isocaproate and estradiol.
> Brand Names: Ambosex, Estandron

The testosterone composition of this injectable is similar to that found in Sustanon but does not contain testosterone decanoate. Estandron is known as an instant gratification drug because it produces a rapid build-up of strength and muscle mass. It is very anabolic yet is almost completely free of androgenic side effects, thanks to the addition of estradiol. It is clinically used to treat menopause and osteoporosis. Estradiol is included to neutralize the androgenic effect of the three testosterone esters, eliminating the androgenic symptoms in women.

Female bodybuilders are able to enjoy the anabolic effects of Estandron and avoid the androgenic effects so tragically common with other steroids. As small amounts of estrogens are also anabolic and

Estandron is known as an instant gratification drug because it produces a rapid build up of strength and muscle mass.

in particular stimulate blood circulation, this could also be one of the reasons why this drug gives its users an enormous pump and a considerable increase in mass.

Another positive aspect is also the fact that estrogens reinforce the storage of calcium in bones. These estrogens have the negative effect of putting male bodybuilders at risk of developing gynocomastia. Both sexes run the risk of fat gain, water retention, and high blood pressure. Male bodybuilders should consider adding HCG toward the end of their cycles as natural testosterone production is normally low.

The gym dose for male bodybuilders usually lies between three to five milliliters per week. In order to minimize androgenic side effects, bodybuilders combine Estandron with milder anabolic steroids. An example might be an intake of three milliliters Estandron/week and 200 milligrams Primobolan Depot/week or 200 milligrams Deca-Durabolin/week. If rapid gains in mass are your only objective, than try taking 5 milliliters Estandron/week, 200 milligrams Deca-Durabolin/week, and 30 milligrams Dianabol/day. The gym dose for female bodybuilders is one or two milliliters Estandron/ week. Most female bodybuilders achieve good gains without enduring significant androgenic side effects on 20 milligram Winstrol tablets/day and one or two Estandron/week.

Generic Name: trenbolone acetate
Brand Names: Finaject,
Finajet, Finaplix, Revalor

Finaject and Finajet are not made anymore. What's out there is either fake or out of date. Clinically it was a veterinary drug used to increase muscle mass in livestock. Concerns about drug residues affecting human consumers led to it being discontinued. Trenbolone acetate (TA) had a very strong androgenic/anabolic effect. Bodybuilders reported rapid strength gains without excessive weight gain. Since TA did not aromatize or cause water retention, it became almost legendary among power-lifters who had to stay within a certain weight class. This drug's strength gains are comparable to Anapolon 50 and Dianabol. Pros used TA as a pre- competition drug because of its fat-burning properties. Nothing's perfect and TA is no exception. It's a short-acting drug, requiring frequent injections. Bodybuilders inject one to two milliliters (30 to 60 milligrams) every second day. Bodybuilders obtained good strength gains with 30 milligrams TA every one or two days and 50 milligrams Winstrol Depot every one or two days. No other stack gives the bodybuilder such an incredible hardness and such a defined muscle gain. TA is extremely toxic to the kidneys and use may cause pain and damage. The first symptom of possible kidney damage manifests itself in blood in the urine. TA cannot be taken in high dosages over a prolonged period of time. Fluid intake must be increased to at least one gallon (4 liters) per day so that the kidneys are well flushed while taking TA. The androgenic side effects are severe. Female bodybuilders should avoid this drug at all costs. In both sexes TA also causes mood swings, particularly aggression. Our advice is to avoid derivatives of this drug.

"Someone on Finajet is no fun to be with."

– Daniel Duchaine in his *Underground Steroid Handbook*

Finaplix and Revalor are veterinary drugs that come in pellet form. Animals are shot with Finaplix using an implant pistol. Bodybuilders follow a series of chemical procedures to produce an injectable form (very unhygienic and dangerous) and a transdermal form (absorbed through the skin). Finaplix was recently discontinued and its successor, Revalor, also contains estradiol.

Generic Name: fluoxymesterone
Brand Names: Halotestin, Ora-testryl tabs, Stenox, Ultandren

This oral is 17 alpha-alkylated, making it toxic to the liver. Fluoxymesterone is highly androgenic with only a slight anabolic effect. Bodybuilders make good strength increases with little body weight gain. For this reason it is generally used by powerlifters or those who need to stay in a certain weight class. One of this drug's most interesting side effects is that the user can get by with little sleep. This allows a bodybuilder to work all day and train most of the night. Others find that this insomnia inhibits growth, and can't deal with the headaches that can be caused by this drug. Fluoxymesterone does not readily convert to estrogen, making this one of the few highly androgenic steroids favored for contest preparation. There are those who believe that this anabolic steroid should be avoided because it completely shuts down the production of endogenous testosterone and has long lasting and enduring negative effects upon the endocrine system. One should not use this drug for extended periods of time. The normal dosage follows a ski-slope pattern, starting around 250 milligrams the first week and decreasing to 140 milligrams by the third.

SAMPLE CYCLE

Week 1   (350 mg) Stromba, (700 mg) Deca-Durabolin, (1,050 mg) Oxymetholone, (1,000mg) Omnadren
Week 2   (280 mg) Stromba, (500 mg) Deca-Durabolin, (700 mg) Oxymetholone, (750mg) Omnadren
Week 3   (280 mg) Stromba, (300 mg) Deca-Durabolin, (700 mg) Oxymetholone, (500mg) Omnadren
Week 4   All drugs stopped
Week 5   (700 mg) Anabol, (400 mg) Durabolin, (280 mg) Halotestin, (2,000 mg) Sustanon
Week 6   (525 mg) Anabol, (300 mg) Durabolin, (210 mg) Halotestin, (1,500 mg) Sustanon
Week 7   (350 mg) Anabol, (300 mg) Durabolin, (140 mg) Halotestin, (1,000 mg) Sustanon
Week 8   All drugs stopped
Week 9   (700 mg) Anabol, (400 mg) Primobolan, (280 mg) Halotestin, (700 mg) Masterone
Week 10 (525 mg) Anabol, (300 mg) Primobolan, (210 mg) Halotestin, (500 mg) Masterone
Week 11 (350 mg) Anabol, (300 mg) Primobolan, (140 mg) Halotestin, (300 mg) Masterone
Week 12 All drugs stopped
Week 13 (532 mg) Parabolan, (400 mg) Primobolan, (420 mg) Oxandrolone, (700 mg) Masterone
Week 14 (380 mg) Parabolan, (300 mg) Primobolan, (315 mg) Oxandrolone, (500 mg) Masterone
Week 15 (304 mg) Parabolan, (300 mg) Primobolan, (210 mg) Oxandrolone, (300 mg) Masterone
Week 16 All drugs stopped
Week 17 (1,000 mg) Propionate, (350 mg) Winstrol, (420 mg) Oxandrolone, (700 mg) Masterone
Week 18 (750 mg) Propionate, (300 mg) Winstrol, (315 mg) Oxandrolone, (500 mg) Masterone
Week 19 (500 mg) Propionate, (250 mg) Winstrol, (210 mg) Oxandrolone, (300 mg) Masterone
Week 20 All drugs stopped

Generic Name: drostanolone propionate
Brand Names: Drolban, Masterid, Masteril, Masteron, Permastril

It is commonly used in contest preparation. This drug is a derivative of DHT (dihydrotestosterone), thus it will not aromatize into estrogen. Therefore feminizing side effects in males are not a problem. The androgenic effects of DP causes an improvement in muscle density and hardness, as well as being effective at burning off body fat. This drug is fast acting and quickly broken down, making it popular among the drug tested set as it can be used up to ten days before a drug test. The androgenic effect is of this drug is crucial because it helps to provide sufficient "drive" for intense training when on a restricted diet. But anecdotal reports indicate that testosterone propionate makes a more effective substitute in a stack. The gym dose is 100 milligrams injected every other day. It is recommended to inject DP every two or three days because it has a short duration of effect. DP is often stacked with trenbolone hexahydrobencylcarbonate, stanozolol and Oxandrolone.

Generic Name: Closlebol acetate
Brand Name: Megagrisevit
The drug contains the following:
    clostebole acetate
    vitamins B6 and B12

Drolban is fast acting and quickly broken down, making it popular among the drug tested set as it can be used up to ten days before a drug test.

This drug is used clinically to stimulate protein synthesis and restore a positive nitrogen balance. It has a mild anabolic effect and an even weaker androgenic effect. The vitamin component comes separately and can be discarded. This cuts down on injection volume, even though B6 and B12 can increase the appetite and improve the mood. The drug is water-based, has a short half-life, does not aromatize, does not retain water, and is non-toxic. Bodybuilders report that it is a precompetition steroid. The gym dose is two 1.5 milliliter vials per day, which can be combined into one large three milliliter injection, equal to a daily intake of 20 milligrams of clostebole acetate. Female bodybuilders achieve remarkable results and inject the same amount every second day.

A powerful stack is produced when Megagrisevit is combined with stronger androgenic steroids such as Parabolan, Masteron, or Testosterone propionate. Megagrisevit is not liver-toxic and in these dosages rarely has side effects. This makes it a favorite among female pros

Generic Name: methylandrostenediol dipropionate
Brand Names: Andris, Arbolic, Crestabolic, Drive, Durandrol, Filbiol Forte, Geldabol, Hybolin, Methyldiol, Metylandrostendiol Novandrol, Spectriol

Methylandrostenediol Dipropionate (M.D.) is a form of the water-dissolved methandriol but it remains effective for a longer period of time. It comes in both an oil-based medium and in tablet form. M.D. has both strong anabolic and androgenic effects, making it ideal for building

The bodybuilders using this drug report good strength gains, a solid muscle gain, and low water retention.

strength and muscle mass. The effect can be compared to a cross between Deca-Durabolin and Testosterone enanthate. Like testosterone enanthate it contributes to a gain in both strength and muscle but does not retain more water than Deca-Durabolin. M.D. is best taken with another steroid as M.D. is able to magnify the effects of other steroid compounds. It does this by increasingly sensitizing the androgenic receptors of the muscle cell, allowing a higher amount of the steroid molecules of the additionally taken steroids to react with the receptors. This also explains why injectable M.D. is only available today as a combination compound with an additional steroid substance. If MD is taken alone it should be combined with an injectable steroid. The usual dosage for bodybuilders is 100 milligrams every two or three days. The normal daily dose is 40 to 60 milligrams and is usually taken in two or three individual doses spread over the day. The tablets are usually taken for only four to six weeks since the effect decreases quickly, thus requiring higher dosages. They are also 17-alpha alkylated so even a low dosage and a short intake can be toxic to the liver. Because of its androgenic effect women rarely use M.D. The bodybuilders using this drug report good strength gains, a solid muscle gain, and low water retention. The combination steroids aromatize only slightly, but when taking only M.D the use of antiestrogens is recommended.

Generic Name: methyltestosterone:
Brand Names: Afro, Agoviron, Android, Androral, Arcosterone, Hormobin, Longivo, Mediatric, Mesteron, Metandren, Oreton Methyl, T. lingvalete, Teston, Testormon, Testovis, Testred, Virilon

This drug is very androgenic with slight anabolic effects. Methyltestosterone (M) is generally used to stimulate aggression among power lifters and those looking to boost up their workouts. M tabs are sublingual (to be placed under the tongue) for faster absorption. Two tablets placed under the tongue before a visit to the gym will make for an aggressive workout. It will also put your Clearasil bill through the roof. Stay away from this one.

Brand Name: Omnadren 250
This drug is a blend of the following:
        30 milligrams testosterone propionate
        60 milligrams testosterone phenylpropionate
        60 milligrams testosterone isohexanoate
        100 milligrams testosterone hexanoate

This drug is an oil-based injectable. Because it contains four different testosterones, it is commonly compared to Sustanon. Omnadren does contain testosterone propionate and testosterone phenylpropionate in the same strength as Sustanon; however, testosterone isohexanoate and testosterone hexanoate replace the testosterone isocaproate and testosterone decanoate in Sustanon. As a result, Omnadren has a very different effect than Sustanon. Omnadren users experience heavy water retention. This drug gives rapid gains in size and strength, but also causes the muscles to look very smooth. Unlike Sustanon, Omnadren readily converts to estrogen, which may cause gynocomastia. The estrogen-linked side effects can be reduced or prevented with the simultaneous use of tamoxifen citrate and mesterolone.

Omnadren readily converts to estrogen, which may cause gynocomastia.

"The Polish Omnadren made me very puffy and irritable, yet I don't have the same problem with Sustanon."

– ES, Italian Professional Bodybuilder, in an interview with writer TC Luoma.

Omnadren gym doses range from 250 milligrams every second week up to 1000 milligrams or more per day. An effective dosage is 250 to 1000 milligrams per week. Omnadren is active in the body for a few weeks, but an injection should be taken at least once a week. Many athletes like to combine Omnadren with a strong anabolic like nandrolone decanoate or boldenone undecylenate. For a dramatic gain in mass and strength stack Omnadren with heavy orals such as Oxymetholone and methandrostenolone.

Generic Name: Oxandrolone
Brand Names: Anatrophil, Anavar, Lonavar, Vasoprome, Oxandrin

Oxandrolone has a reputation of being one of the safest oral anabolics available. Women and children are often given this drug with little or no adverse side effects. For athletes, it is a mild anabolic exerting more strength than muscle mass increases. It is normally stacked with Masteron and stanozolol. The normal dosage ranges from over 400 milligrams to just over 100 milligrams in a ski-slope pattern over a three-week period inside a cycle. Perhaps the most amazing effect this drug has is as a diet pill. Both of the authors met with a user and the dealer who supplied him. The user was over 400 pounds, and desperate to lose weight. He bought a bottle of Oxandrolone, used two tablets a day and within three months lost 95 pounds without dieting! Even after he finished the Oxandrolone, the effect continued. Alarmed that something might be wrong, he sought advice from his doctor. His doctor explained the situation this way, "Imagine driving down the highway with your foot to the floor. Even after you take your foot off the accelerator, it's going to take some time for the engine to rev down..." Which is exactly what happened. The weight loss stopped shortly after the visit. The only side effects the user noticed were sleep disturbances and nightmares. Yet he found this quite tolerable as he had never been able to lose weight before, and he was amazed by the energy he had while on Oxandrolone. With many in our society suffering from chronic obesity that leads to heart disease and expensive medical care, it is shocking to think that an effective treatment that would only cost around $6.50 at the pharmacy is not legally available for this purpose. This drug is 17-alpha alkylated so toxicity to the liver is a concern.

Generic Name: trenbolone
Brand Name: Parabolan

This injectable steroid has strong anabolic and androgenic qualities and does not readily aromatize to estrogen (no gynocomastia!). Trenbolone is an advanced user's drug, too strong and harsh to recommend to a beginner or non-competitive bodybuilder. For competition purposes, it produces a very hard and vascular look. When trenbolone is combined with Stanozolol and Sustanon 250, this stack produces excellent mass gains. Bodybuilders normally use a cliff hanger pattern of one weekly injection of one ampoule (76 milligrams per 1.5 milliliters) the first week, followed by two ampoules injected once a week for the rest of the cycle. Others recommend that only one millilitre be injected per week, following a Straight-Arrow pattern.

Generic Name: methenolone enanthate
Brand Name: Primobolan Depot

This injectable steroid is a long acting drug with mild anabolic and androgenic properties. Primobolan is most commonly used during cutting cycles (when combined with stanozolol or Oxandrolone) although some users do stack it with stronger drugs like testosterone and methandrolone for mass cycles. This drug is most commonly injected on a weekly basis and dosages range between 100 to 200 milligrams, normally following a Pyramid pattern. This dosage should not interfere with natural testosterone levels. Female bodybuilders should not exceed 1/3 of this dosage. More experienced bodybuilders will inject doses higher than 200 milligrams for a stronger anabolic effect. This drug comes in an oil-based injectable form (100 and 50 milligrams/cc) or as an oral (50 and five milligrams tabs).

SAMPLE CYCLE
Week 1   Primobolan Depot (50 mg), Dianabol (20 mg/day)
Week 2   Primobolan Depot (100 mg), Dianabol (30 mg/day)
Week 3   Primobolan Depot (1500 mg), Dianabol (40 mg/day)
Week 4   Primobolan Depot (200 mg), Dianabol (50 mg/day)
Week 5   Primobolan Depot (200 mg), Dianabol (50 mg/day)
Week 6   Primobolan Depot (150 mg), Dianabol (40 mg/day)
Week 7   Primobolan Depot (100 mg), Dianabol (30 mg/day)
Week 8   Primobolan Depot (50 mg), Dianabol (20 mg/day)
Week 9   Primobolan Depot (100 mg), 2500 iu HCG/week
Week 10 Primobolan Depot (100 mg), 2500 iu HCG/week

Brand Name: Sustanon 250
The drug contains:
>   30 milligrams testosterone propionate
>   60 milligrams testosterone phenylpropionate
>   60 milligrams testosterone isocaproate
>   100 milligrams testosterone decanoate

This is an oil-based injectable containing four different testosterone compounds. The mixture of the testosterones are time-released to provide an immediate effect while still remaining active in the body for up to a month. Bodybuilders use Sustanon to put on mass and size while increasing strength. Unlike testosterone cypionate and testosterone enanthate, the use of Sustanon leads to less water retention and estrogenic side effects. Gym doses range from 250 milligrams every second week, up to 2000 milligrams or more per week. An effective dosage ranges from 250 milligrams to 1000 milligrams per week. Although Sustanon remains active for up to a month, injections should be taken at least once a week to keep testosterone levels stable.

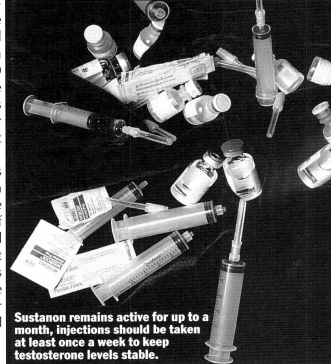

Sustanon remains active for up to a month, injections should be taken at least once a week to keep testosterone levels stable.

With dosages exceeding 1000 milligrams a week, use an antiestrogen such as tamoxifen citrate or Proviron. Sustanon 250 can reduce natural testosterone production, so the use of HCG or clomiphene citrate should be added toward the end of a cycle. Bodybuilders find that Sustanon 250 stacks extremely well with orals such as Oxymetholone and methandrostenolone if the goal is a rapid gain in size and strength. For a precompetition cycle, Sustanon is combined with Parabolan, Masteron and stanozolol.

SAMPLE CYCLE

Week 1   Dianabol (15mg/day), Deca-durabolin (200 mg/week)
Week 2   Dianabol (20mg/day), Deca-durabolin (200 mg/week)
Week 3   Dianabol (25mg/day), Deca-durabolin (250 mg/week)
Week 4   Dianabol (30mg/day), Deca-durabolin (250 mg/week)
Week 5   Dianabol (25mg/day), Deca-durabolin (300 mg/week)
Week 6   Dianabol (20mg/day), Deca-durabolin (300 mg/week)
Week 7   Dianabol (15mg/day), Deca-durabolin (350 mg/week), HCG (5000 I.U./week)
Week 8   Deca-durabolin (350mg/week), Sustanon 250 (500mg/week),
          HCG (5000 I.U./week)
Week 9   Deca-durabolin (300 mg/week), Sustanon 250 (500mg/week)
Week 10   Deca-durabolin (300 mg/week), Sustanon 250 (500 mg/week)
Week 11   Deca-durabolin (250 mg/week), Sustanon 250 (250 mg/week)
Week 12   Deca-durabolin (250 mg/week), Sustanon 250 (250 mg/week)
Week 13   Deca-durabolin (200 mg/week), HCG (5000 I.U./week)
Week 14   Deca-durabolin (200 mg/week), HCG (5000 I.U./week)

Brand Name: Sten
This drug contains the following:
        25 milligrams testosterone propionate
        75 milligrams testosterone cypionate
        20 milligrams DHEA.

This drug is a low dose testosterone blend. Each two milliliters ampoule contains (not counting the DHEA) 50 milligrams of testosterone per milliliter. The gym dose is 600 to 800 milligrams per week. This adds up to six to eight milliliters per week, which is a large and painful volume. Thus Sten is the testosterone of last choice. This drug is used for gaining mass.

> Generic Name: Testosterone propionate
> Brand Name: Synovex
> > Each eight-pellet implant contains the following:
> > 200 milligrams testosterone propionate
> > 20 Estradiol Benzoate

This drug is a veterinary implant used to build mass in livestock. The estradiol is used to improve carcass quality. Bodybuilders will grind up these pellets and chemically prepare them for transdermal or injectable use (very unhygienic and dangerous). This drug has severe estrogenic side effects. You'd have to be stupid and desperate to use this stuff.

> Generic Name: testosterone cypionate
> Brand Name: Testoprim-D
> This drug contains the following:
> > 50 milligrams of testosterone propionate
> > 200 milligrams testosterone enanthate

This drug is an oil-based injectable. It is a mass building drug. It is a long acting ester of testosterone, which is slightly stronger than enanthate. The gym dose is 200 to 600 milligrams (though 2000 milligrams per week has been reported).

SAMPLE CYCLE

Week 1   Anadrol (50 milligrams per day)
Week 2   Anadrol (100 milligrams per day)
Week 3   Anadrol (150 milligrams per day), Test Cypionate (200 milligrams per week)
Week 4   Test Cypionate (300 milligrams per week)
Week 5   Test Cypionate (400 milligrams per week) Dianabol (20 milligrams per day)
Week 6   Dianabol (25 milligrams per day)
Week 7   Dianabol (30 milligrams per day) Deca (300 milligrams per week)
Week 8   Deca (200 milligrams per week)
Week 9   Deca (200 milligrams per week), HCG (5000 I.U./week)
Week 10   HCG (5000 I.U./week), Clenbuterol (80 mcg/week)
Week 11   HCG (5000 I.U./week), Clenbuterol (100 mcg/week
Week 12   Clenbuterol(120 mcg/week)

> Generic Name: testosterone enanthate
> Brand Names: Testoviron, Testoviron depot

This injectable is a long acting testosterone with very strong anabolic/androgenic effects. Gym dose is 250 to 500 milligrams per week. Water retention is very common.

Generic Name: Testosterone Heptylate
Brand Name: Theramax
This is a long acting, oil-based injectable that has strong anabolic/androgenic effects. The gym dose is 250 to 500 milligrams per week. Bodybuilders report testosterone heptylate has fewer side effects than enanthate due to it's slightly shorter action.

Generic Name: testosterone propionate
Brand Names: Agoviron inj, Androfort-Richt, Androlan, Ara Test, Neo-Hombreol, T. Jenapharm, T. propionicum, T. Streuli, T. Vitis, T. Berco Supp, T. prop. Eifel fango, T. prop Disp, Testex, Testex Leo, Testoaterone Prop, Testogan, Testorona 50, Testosteron, Testovis depo, Triolandren, Virormone

This drug is an oil-based injectable testosterone with powerful anabolic properties. Its androgenic properties are not as severe as testosterone cypionate and testosterone enanthate. The gym dose is 250 milligrams every three days to keep blood levels steady. For strength and muscle mass gains, this drug is very effective. With propionate, androgenic side effects seem somewhat less pronounced than with the other testosterones, probably due to the fact that blood levels do not build up as high. On the down side, have lots of painkillers handy. Injections result in swelling and pain that will last for a few days.

A very effective mass building stack combines testosterone propionate at 250 milligrams every three days, eight Oxandrolone per day, and 200 milligrams of Primobolan a week for twelve weeks in a row.

Generic Name: testosterone suspension
Brand Names: Agoviron-depot, Androlan Aqueous, Androlin, Andronaq-50, Histerone inj, Malogen, Malotrone, Testolin

This drug is a water-based injectable containing unesterfied testosterone. Very anabolic/androgenic and fast acting, testosterone suspension will sustain elevated testosterone levels for only two or three days. Due to water retention it cannot be used as precontest drug. Tamoxifen citrate should be used with testosterone suspension as it aromatizes easily. The gym dose is 50 to 100 milligrams per day. Although this drug requires frequent injections, it will pass through a needle as fine as a 27 gague insulin. This allows users to hit smaller muscles such as delts for injections.

Generic Name: stanozolol
Brand Names: Winstrol, Winstrol V, Winstrol Depot, Stromba, Strombaject

Stanozolol was made famous by Canadian sprinter, Ben Johnson, at the 1988 Olympic games. It is a 17-alpha alkylated steroid that comes in both oral and injectable forms. This drug is a moderate but reliable anabolic with mild androgenic side effects. It is very effective as a recovery drug, and speeds healing of muscle injuries. Stanozolol is supplied in two milligram tabs and 50 milligram water-based injectable ampoules. This drug is used for for androgen replacement, the usual dosage is 50 to 400 milligrams every two to four weeks. The gym dosage for size and strength increases is 150 to 300 milligrams every week Winstrol Depot, 50 to 100 milligrams three times a week Winstrol), or 6 to 15 tabs everyday.

Others recommend dosages of 10 to 25 milligrams per day orally and 25 to 50 milligrams daily injected. While a few users are able to obtain impressive gains on stanozolol alone, they are the exception to the rule. Combined with other steroids, stanozolol is an effective component of cutting and mass cycles. Primobolan and Winstrol are both claimed to work well together as a cutting cycle. Parabolan, Sustanon 250, and Winstrol Depot is claimed to be one of the best cycles for gaining mass. Stanozolol is often used as a replacement for dbol in steroid stacks. The dosage of stanozolol must be increased by 50 percent to do this.

SAMPLE CYCLE

Week 1 Primobolan Depot (100 milligrams per week), Deca (100 milligrams per week)
Week 2 Primobolan Depot (100 milligrams per week), Deca (150 milligrams per week)
Week 3 Primobolan Depot (150 milligrams per week), Deca (200 milligrams per week), Winstrol (100 milligrams per week)
Week 4 Primobolan Depot (150 milligrams per week), Deca (200 milligrams per week), Winstrol (150 milligrams per week)
Week 5 Primobolan Depot (200 milligrams per week), Deca (200 milligrams per week), Winstrol (150 milligrams per week)
Week 6 Primobolan Depot (200 milligrams per week), Deca (200 milligrams per week), Winstrol (200 milligrams per week)
Week 7 Primobolan Depot (150 milligrams per week), Deca (200 milligrams per week), Winstrol (200 milligrams per week)
Week 8 Primobolan Depot (150 milligrams per week), Deca (150 milligrams per week), Winstrol (150 milligrams per week)
Week 9 Primobolan Depot (150 milligrams per week), Deca (100 milligrams per week), Winstrol (150 milligrams per week)
Week 10 Primobolan Depot (100 milligrams per week), Deca (50 milligrams per week), Winstrol (100 milligrams per week)
Week 11 HCG (5000 I.U./week)
Week 12 HCG (5000 I.U./week)

OTHER DRUGS

Generic Name: Catapress
Brand Names: Catanidin, Catapresan, Clonidin, Clonidine, Clonidine HCL, Clonisin, Clonistada, Combipress, Dixarit, Mirfat, Paracefan

Catapres, an antihypertensive drug is used to treat high blood pressure. Bodybuilders became interested in this drug because Catapres stimulates the endogenous production of the growth hormones. It is taken before going to sleep at night and in the morning immediately after getting up. The gym dose is one 0.3 milligram tablet at night and a 0.15 milligram tablet on an empty stomach immediately after waking up in the morning. The nightly dose increases the concentration of growth hormones for several hours, which then again can be increased by taking the morning dose. As a result Catapres has a profound anabolic effect. Despite it's proven efficacy, its side effects (lethargy, fatigue, dry mouth, erectile dysfunction, and vertigo) are so unpleasant as to make training next to impossible for most bodybuilders. Those who have a low blood pressure and a low heart rate should avoid it altogether.

CLENBUTEROL

Generic Name : Clenbuterol
Brand Names: Cesbron, Clenasma, Contrapasmina, Contrasmina, Monores, Novegam, Pharmachim, Spiropent, Spriopent mite, Ventipulmin, Ventolase, Spasmo, Mucosolvan

The side effects of Catapress are so unpleasant, they make training next to impossible for most bodybuilders.

Clenbuterol is a beta-2 agonist used in Europe as a broncodilator for the treatment of asthma. Similar to adrenaline, clenbuterol acts as a CNS stimulant and users quite commonly report side effects such as shaky hands, insomnia, sweating, increased blood pressure and nausea. These side effects generally subside quickly once the user becomes accustomed to the drug. Athletes find clenbuterol attractive for it's pronounced thermogenic effects as well as mild anabolic properties. Dosage varies depending on the user's tolerance and desired effect. Users will usually tailor their dosage individually, depending on results and side effects, but somewhere in the range of two to eight tablets per day is most common. The anabolic effect will cease after two weeks. Clenbuterol generally come is 20 mcg tablets, although it is also available in syrup and injectable form. For fat loss, clenbuterol seems to stay effective for three to six weeks, then it's thermogenic properties seem to subside (normally after 18 days).This is noticed when the body temperature drops back to normal. During a steroid cycle clenbuterol is taken to keep fat burning at a maximum. The usual dosage for this purpose is five tablets a day, two days on, one day off. Clenbuterol is often combined with Cytomel towards the end of a cycle. The two drugs work synergistically to burn fat even more efficiently.

LEUTINIZING HORMONE STIMULATOR

Generic Name: clomiphene citrate
Brand Names: Clomid, Ardomon, Clom, Clomifene, Clomipheni citras, Clomipheni citrate, Clomivid, Clostillbegyt, C-ratioph, Dufine, Dyneric, Gravosan, Indovar, Klomifen, Kyliformon, Omifin, Pergotimine, Pioner, Prolifen, Serofene, Serophene, Serapafar, Tokormon

This drug is typically prescribed for women to aid in ovulation. In men it causes an elevation of follicle stimulating hormone and luteinizing hormone; which in turn causes an increase in natural testosterone production. Clomiphene citrate is a logical addition at the end of a steroid cycle when endogenous testosterone levels are low. Bodybuilders find that a daily intake of 50 to 100 milligrams of clomiphene citrate over a two-to-three week period will bring endogenous testosterone production back to an acceptable level. The drug will gradually raise testosterone levels over its period of intake. Since an immediate boost in testosterone is often desirable, bodybuilders will commonly use HCG (human chorionic gonadotropin) for a couple of weeks. If you don't have access to clomiphene citrate, it is suggested that you increase your HCG dosage to 2500 i.u. per injection to compensate. If you don't have access to HCG, keep your clomiphene citrate dosage at 100 milligrams per day. This drug is also effective as an anti-estrogen (admittedly, not as effective as Nolvadex or Provirion). The biggest problem commonly experienced by steroid users is an elevated estrogen level at the conclusion of a cycle. This can cause a net loss of muscle mass and estrogenic side effects. Clomiphene citrate has the dual effect of blocking out some of the effects of estrogen, while increasing endogenous testosterone production. This drug is quite safe, and the side effects include hot flashes and temporary blurred vision.

Generic Name: Cyclofenil
Brand Names: Fertodur,Neoclym, Ondogyne, Rehibin, Sexovid

Cyclofenil is another non-steroidal ancillary drug used by athletes, similar to HCG and Clomid in action. This drug is most commonly used to increase endogenous testosterone levels after a cycle in an attempt to avoid a hard crash while waiting for your hormone levels to naturally balance. Anecdotally however, cyclofenil does have the reputation of being the weakest of the three. Like Clomid, cyclofenil may also act as an anti-estrogen, binding to estrogen receptor sites and blocking out other estrogens. This is especially helpful when natural testosterone levels are suppressed and an excess of estrogen may be present upon steroid termination. It has no anabolic effect if used alone.

THYROID DRUGS

Generic Name : tricodide thyronine (LT-3)
Brand Names: Cynomel, Cytomel

Cynomel is a synthetic form of the natural thyroid hormone 3, 5, 3' triodothyronine. Cytomel is used to treat hypothyroidism (thyroid deficiency), obesity, metabolic disorders, and fatigue. Thyroid hormones exert many of their actions through the control of protein synthesis. Moderate amounts of thyroid hormones can increase the synthesis of RNA and protein, which is then followed by an increased basal metabolic rate and stimulation of the oxidative enzyme systems. This causes the release of free fatty acids from adipose tissue and increases the intestinal absorption and utilization of glucose.

Bodybuilders often use this hormone several weeks prior to competition, to maintain extremely low body-fat levels, without the extremes of a starvation diet. This drug is very popular with female bodybuilders and fitness athletes, due to the fact that women generally have slower metabolisms than men do. Provided the bodybuilder continues taking steroids and stays on a high-calorie, high protein diet, there will be no loss of muscle mass.

Under normal circumstances, the thyroid usually produces two hormones, L-T4 and L-T3. This drug closely resembles the latter hormone and is much stronger and more effective of the two and approximately 4 times as potent as L-T4 by weight. When administered orally 95 percent of the dose is absorbed within 4 hours from the gastrointestinal tract. The biological half-life of LT-3 is two and a half days, with the maximum pharmacological response occurring within 2 or 3 days. This drug has a host of side effects, including: heart palpitation, trembling, irregular heartbeat, heart oppression, agitation, shortness of breath, excretion of sugar through the urine, excessive perspiration, diarrhea, weight loss, psychic disorders and hypersensitivity. These negative side effects can often be eliminated by temporarily reducing the daily dosage. But it must also be pointed out that this drug is EXTREMELY dangerous, and should never be used without medical supervision. That's not just to keep our own lawyers happy, that's reality. It's no surprise that many bodybuilders refuse to use this drug.

If you are stupid enough to try thyroid drugs, begin with a low dosage, increasing it slowly and evenly over the course of several days. Begin by taking one 25 mcg tablet per day and increasing this dosage every three to four days by one tablet. A dose should never exceed 100 mcg/ day. The daily dose must be broken down into three smaller individual doses so that they become more effective. LT-3 can not be taken for more than six weeks. This must be followed by a minimum of two months off the drug.

Thyroid medications are very tricky to use, and can quickly lead to life-long thyroid problems. As a result, most bodybuilders prefer to use clenbuterol and ephedrine to burn off body fat. Many report that the synergistic effect of these two drugs is more effective than L-T3.

ANTI-GYNOCOMASTIA

Generic Name: Danacrine
Brand Names: Danatrol, Winobanin,
Anargil, Mastodanatrol

This drug is an antigonadotropin with no anabolic effect and a slight androgenic effect. It is used to treat hormone-related disorders such as gynocomastia. Side effects include high blood pressure, increased libido, increased perspiration and hot flashes. Bodybuilders use it to self-medicate steroid-induced gynocomastia and to correct hormone-related erectile dysfunction. The daily dose is 400 milligrams per day.

HUMAN CHORIONIC GONADOTROPIN – HCG

Generic Name: human chorionic gonadtrophin (HCG)
Brand Names: APL, Biogonadyl, Brumegon,
HCG Lepori, Pregnyl, Profasi, Rochoric

HCG (an injectable drug) is a hormonal preparation derived from the urine of pregnant women. Clinically HCG is used in the treatment of undescended testicles in very young boys, hypogonadism (underproduction of testosterone) and as a fertility drug used to induce ovulation in women. Bodybuilders use HCG to stimulate natural testosterone production during or after a steroid cycle. Stopping a steroid cycle abruptly, before natural testosterone levels have had a chance to return to normal, can cause both depression and loss of muscle mass. HCG use prevents this "crash." Female bodybuilders may require only one dose a week. Male bodybuilders may inject 2 to 3 times a week, for 2 or 3 weeks. The gym dose is 1500 IU or 2500 IU per injection. An alternative is to shoot 1500 IU of HCG every two days for a 10-day off period

HUMAN GROWTH HORMONE

Generic Name: Human Growth Hormone (hGH)
Brand Names: Humatrope, Protropin

Commercially available human growth hormone is bioengineered and produced in vats of genetically altered bacteria. Clinically, this drug is used to treat growth deficiency in children and teenagers, and is being tested as anti-aging drug. It is the most expensive drug used by the pros, and for most is probably a complete waste of money. For example, Serostim human growth hormone (hGH) at a full six milligrams per day dose, costs over 100 times more than nandrolone, but it delivered only a little over half as much lean body mass over 12 weeks.[1] Even low doses of other steroids appear to do as well as or better than hGH for anabolic activity for much less cost. Growth hormone itself is very delicate and is best stored at cool temperatures and used quickly. In our opinion this drug's black market price cannot be justified given it's generally low to moderate anabolic effects. For a pro trying to break through a plateau, the cost may be justified, but not for a weekend warrior!

INSULIN

Generic Name: insulin
Brand Name: Humulin R

Insulin is a hormone produced by the Islands of Langerhans in the pancreas to regulate glucose levels in the body. Medically, it is used to treat diabetes. Recently, insulin has become quite popular among bodybuilders due to the anabolic effect it can offer. With well-timed

injections, insulin will help to bring glycogen and other nutrients to the muscles. It is true that insulin seems to increase the rate of creatine absorption. If you take any of the glucose/creatine mixtures available, you'll load the muscles with creatine much more quickly.

"Everyone says my skin has taken on a different look. I was mixing insulin with GH and it really fucked me up. My pancreas took a wicked beating and I was even hospitalized. As a result, I have to really control my calcium intake right now. As soon as my calcium values go up, my pancreas hurts terribly."

– Mailbox, a bodybuilder interviewed by testosterone.net editor, TC Luoma.

Of all the different brands, Humulin R is the safest because it takes effect quickly and has the shortest duration of activity. The other insulin preparations stay active longer and can put the user in an unexpected state of hypoglycemia (low blood glucose levels). This is a potentially fatal reaction experienced by insulin users. Before a bodybuilder begins taking insulin, it is critical that he understands the symptoms of hypoglycemia: hunger, drowsiness, blurred vision, depressive mood, dizziness, sweating, palpitation, tremor, restlessness, tingling in the hands, feet, lips, or tongue, lightheadedness, inability to concentrate, headache, sleep disturbances, anxiety, slurred speech, irritability, abnormal behavior, unsteady movement, and personality changes. If any of these warning signs occur, the bodybuilder should immediately consume food or drink containing sugar such as a candy bar or carbohydrate drink. This will treat mild to moderate hypoglycemia and prevent a severe state of hypoglycemia. Severe hypoglycemia is a serious condition whose symptoms include: disorientation, seizure, and unconsciousness. Whether mild or severe, seek medical attention right away. Ensure that someone you train with is aware of your insulin use and these symptoms. Wear a medic alert bracelet and carry a piece of paper in your pocket detailing the doses you have taken that day. This can provide vital information to paramedics.

Bodybuilders generally choose to use it immediately after a workout. Gym doses are usually 1 IU per 10 to 20 pounds of lean bodyweight. First-time users should start at a low dosage and gradually work up, beginning with 2 IU and then increase the dosage by 1 IU every consecutive workout. Insulin doses vary significantly among bodybuilders and are dependent upon insulin sensitivity and the use of such hGH and thyroid, which lead to higher insulin requirements, and therefore, will be able to handle higher dosages.

Insulin should be refrigerated, but it is all right to keep it in a gym bag as long as it is kept away from excessive heat. Immediately after a workout, the athlete will inject his dosage of insulin. Within the next fifteen minutes, he should have a carbohydrate drink. The athlete should consume at least 10 grams of carbohydrates for every 1 IU of insulin injected. Bodybuilders will also take creatine monohydrate with their carbohydrate drink since the insulin will help to force the creatine into the muscles. An hour or so after injecting insulin, bodybuilders will eat a meal or have a protein shake. The carbohydrate drink and meal/protein shake are necessary. Without them, blood sugar levels will drop dangerously low and the athlete will most likely go into a state of hypoglycemia. Nutritional factors may also play a part in effectiveness. A deficiency in vitamin E might interfere with creatine absorption by failing to maximize the insulin response. It is also necessary to add fats to your diet to help stabilize blood glucose levels.

Injecting insulin can make the user sleepy. This may be a symptom of hypoglycemia, and an athlete should probably consume more carbs. Avoid the temptation to go to bed since the insulin may take its peak effect during sleep and significantly drop glucose levels. Humulin R usually remains active for only four hours with a peak at about two hours after injecting. The bodybuilder must stay awake for four hours after injecting.

Insulin use can not be detected during a drug test. For this reason, along with the fact that it is cheap and readily available, insulin has become a popular drug among pro bodybuilders. On the down side, one mistake in insulin dosage or diet can be fatal. Our advice is to leave insulin to the pros. The risks far outweigh the benefits.

ANTI-ESTROGEN

Generic Name: tamoxifan citrate
Brand Names: Ceadon, Crioxifeno, Defarol, Dignotamoxi, Emblon, Farmo, Jenoxifen, Kessar, Ledertam, Mandofen, Mastofen, Noltam, Nolvadex, Nolvadex D, Nolvadex Forte, Noncarcinon, Nourytam, Oxeprax, Riboxifen, Tadex, Tafoxen, Tamax, Tamaxin, Tamcal, Tamexin, Tamifen, Tamofen, Tamofene, Tamoplex, Tamox, Tamox Al, Tamoxan, Tamox-GRY, Tamoxifen, Tamoxifen Ebene, Tamoxifen Funk, Tamoxifen Hexal, Tamoxifen Lederle, Tamoxifen Leivas, Tamoxifen medac, Tamoxifen mp, Tamoxifen NM, Tamoxifeno, Tamoxifeno Septa, Tamoxifeno Tablets Hs, Tamoxifenum, Tamoxifenum gF, Tamoxifenum pch, Tamoxigenat, Tamox-Puren, Tamoxusta, Taxus, T. cell pharm, T. citrate, T.dumex, T. Farmitalia, T. Fermenta, T. Heumann, T. Hexal, T.Lachema, T. Onkalon, T. Pan Medica, T. Pharbita, T. Ratiopharm, T. Sopharma, T. Wassermann, Teenofen, Tesamone, Zemide, Zitazonium

Tamoxifen citrate (TC) is a potent antiestrogenic drug. Clinically it is used to treat breast cancer because of its ability to compete with estrogen for binding sites in target tissues such as in the breast. Male bodybuilders use this drug to prevent gynocomastia. Many anabolic steroids "aromatize" into estrogens. TC competes for and occupies estrogen receptors, preventing the estrogens from binding and causing estrogenic side effects. This drug also seems to slightly reduce gains made during a steroid cycle. It is possible that estrogen plays a role in keeping androgen receptors open. It is known that TC decreases the GH and IGF-1 production, while part of the gains made, are a direct result of the anabolic / androgen increasing the GH and IGF-1 production. Thus TC use would reduce gains in both strength and size.

There is a real struggle between using TC (to prevent side effects) and anabolic activity, causing a decrease in optimum muscle growth. Rather than start taking TC right away, bodybuilders often wait until they experience itching, soreness, or excessive sensitivity in the nipples. Bodybuilders will then take 40 milligrams per day of TC for one week, then decrease the dosage to 10 milligrams per day, for the rest of the duration of the cycle. Regardless of this effect Nolvadex is the most popular anti-estrogen used by bodybuilders.

Generic Name: Mesterolone
Brand Name: Proviron

This drug is a popular antiestrogen used by bodybuilders. It acts as an antiaromatase, which means it prevents the aromatization of steroids into estrogen. Bodybuilders on heavy cycles of steroids use Proviron to prevent gynocomastia. Also a lower estrogen level corresponds with increased muscle hardness and lower water retention. The gym dose is 25 to 50 milligrams per day. Proviron can also be combined with tamoxifen citrate if needed. Side effects are extremely rare with dosages under 100 milligrams per day.

One major problem with Proviron is that it tends to reduce the gains made from a cycle. Proviron has a negative affect on the GH and IGF-1 production that is much lower than that of Nolvadex. Also Proviron is an androgen and therefore binds to androgen receptor sites within the body. With Proviron binding to androgen receptor sites, the other steroids present in the body (androgens) are blocked out and unable to take effect. Pros use Proviron for its high toning capabilities when stacked with both a high anabolic – high androgenic steroid and reducing water retention normally associated with androgenic steroids.

DIURETICS

If you want to kill a bodybuilder, put him into a contest and load him up with diuretics before he goes on stage. These drugs are used to dehydrate the body, to better reveal muscle striations beneath paper-thin skin. The stupidity of this practice is mind-boggling. Our ancestors evolved in the ocean. Even today, our blood has the same salt content as seawater. We are internally marine creatures, who survive on land thanks to a suit of skin and an adequate internal ocean that is routinely replenished by eating and drinking. Want to screw up your internal eco-system and kill everything in the pond? Drain the water and add salt. That's the effect of using diuretics on healthy people. Diuretics have no place in bodybuilding, but that doesn't stop people from using them. Many herbal ingredients in supplements are diuretics, and we discuss them in the diet chapter. Stay away from them. A trophy isn't worth your life. Remember what happened to Mohammed Benaziza? He turned into a piece of iron and died in his hotel room after winning the 1993 Belgium Grand Prix.
Here's some of the more popular diuretics bodybuilders use:

ALDACTONE

Aldactone is a diuretic and belongs to the subgroup of potassium-sparing diuretics. Aldactone is an aldosterone antagonist. It influences the body's own hormone, aldosterone, which accelerates the excretion of potassium and reduces the excretion of sodium and water. Simplified, aldosterone regulates the endogenous water household. The higher the aldosterone level, the more water is stored in the body. The use of Aldactone results in a significant reduction in the aldosterone level so that an increased excretion of sodium and water occurs while, at the same time, potassium is reabsorbed. This also explains why Aldactone is called a potassium-sparing diuretic since it does not cause a loss of potassium like thiazides and furosemides. The side effects of potassium-saving diuretics are relatively low compared to thiazides and furosemides. The main problems in men consist of gynocomastia and possible impotence. Other side effects can be low blood pressure, muscle spasms, dizziness, gastrointestinal pain, vomiting, irregular pulse rate, and fatigue. It is important to note that there is a significant increase in the serum potassium level . Bodybuilders on Aldactone cannot ingest additional potassium in their diets since this would cause a life-threatening increase in the serum potassium level. Potassium sparing diuretics have relatively low diuretic effects. Aldactone is also an antiandrogen since it reduces androgen levels. Female bodybuilders take advantage of this by using Aldosterone to minimize the virilization side effects from steroid use. For this purpose Aldactone is normally taken daily for 10 to 14 days, usually at a dose of 50 milligrams per day. In male bodybuilders this causes problems as estrogen levels rise. Bodybuilders use Aldactone almost exclusively during the last week before a competition. Since this causes neither a dramatic nor an immediate noticeable draining effect, it is usually taken over 5 or 6 days in a dosage of 2 tablets of 50 milligrams daily.

LASIX

Lasix is a saluretic (or loop) diuretic. Its effect consists of distinctly increased excretion of sodium, chloride, potassium, and water. Clinically Lasix is used for treatment of edemas and high blood pressure. It is very important to monitor the reabsorption of potassium ions, sodium ions, and chloride ions. This causes a considerable disturbance of the electrolyte threshold. Bodybuilders use Lasix shortly before a competition to excrete subcutaneous water so that they appear hard and defined. The effect of the tablets begins within an hour and continues for three or four hours. This can cause a considerable weight loss within a very short time. For this reason, powerlifters often use Lasix to qualify for a lower weight class. While most prefer the oral form of the compound, the pros occasionally use the injectable and intravenous version the morning of the competition. In order to compensate for the potassium loss bodybuilders may take potassium chloride tablets. This is risky since an overdose of potassium can cause cardiac arrest. Lasix is normally taken orally for the two days before a competition. The gum dosage varies and depends on the individual. Bodybuilders begin with 20 to 40 milligrams and observe the effect. The dose may be repeated after a few hours as needed. Side effects of Lasix include: circulatory disturbances, dizziness, dehydration, muscle cramps, vomiting, circulatory collapse, diarrhea, and fainting, and in extreme cases cardiac arrest.

SOURCES

1) HYPERLINK *www.testosterone.net* online magazine

REFERENCES

1) Mooney, Michael, Cost Comparison Of Anabolic Agents Available In The United States: Weight Gained Versus Time versus Cost Per Month, *Medibolics*, 7, October, 1998, updated July, 1999.

Hardcore Supplements

Tho-mass Benagli and Enzo Ferrari

"The bad news is that more and more low-life slimeballs are coming out of the woodwork and seeing the money that can be made in supplements."

–Will Brink, author and regular *MuscleMag International* columnist commenting on the number of shady characters getting involved in the supplement business these days.

Few bodybuilding issues have undergone the same degree of evolution as supplements. After forty years bodybuilders are still doing bench presses, flyes, and curls in their routines, but when it comes to ergogenesis, today's trainer has at his or her disposal substances that bear no resemblance to the concoctions of yesteryear.

Ergogenesis can be defined as the art of improving athletic performance by supplementation. At one time there was a clear line separating drugs from natural supplements, but this is no longer the case. Modern biochemistry has created a huge gray area that overlaps both categories.

Supplements can boost performance by direct and indirect means. Direct boosters include creatine, glutamine, and ephedrine. Examples of indirect boosters include protein, vitamins, and minerals. Indirect supplements can only boost performance if the individual's levels are low to begin with. For example the body needs a certain amount of the various minerals and vitamins to carry out its various metabolic functions. If these amounts are met by the diet, then taking extra in supplement form will not boost performance, no matter what the advertisers say. On the other hand such supplements as creatine and glutamine have a huge volume of medical evidence behind them to show that taking more than is naturally found in the body will lead to increases in athletic performance.

"Congress cannot construct legislation for stupidity or laziness. If the inability of the consumer to think arises from a lack of available information, then act rationally. Don't buy the product."

– Pete Ingraham, *MuscleMag International* guest editorialist voicing his concern over the United States Government's continued efforts to place health food supplements under stricter legislation.

In the following chapter we are going to look at examples from both categories. Keep in mind there's no way we can cover the full spectrum of supplements in one chapter. For those wishing additional information, please refer to either of our ergogenesis books, *Anabolic Primer* and *Anabolic Edge*, or *Bill Phillips Supplement Review Guide*.

WATER – THE ULTIMATE ERGOGENIC AID

Humans have existed for millions of years without creatine, protein, and glutamine supplements, but try going a couple of days without water. Now before many of you start questioning our sanity for including water in a chapter on hardcore supplements, keep in mind the human body is over 90 percent water. We may have "left" the oceans hundreds of millions of years ago but we are still dependent on this simple, life-giving substance. The reason the earth is the only planet known to support life is because of water. You can go many days without food, but not much more than 24 hours without water. Water is so important to survival that the body has evolved numerous systems for conserving it. If we haven't convinced you yet, how about the fact that water demands go up with the more protein consumed? Or the fact that you can lose five to ten pounds of water through evaporation on a hot day?

Think of your body as an internal combustion engine. Just as your car's engine must be kept cool, so too does the human body need a form of thermoregulation. And here's something to ponder, the more muscle you carry, the more heat produced. After all, muscle is living, highly metabolic tissue. Maintaining it produces waste in the form of heat.

You can lose five to ten pounds of water through evaporation on a hot day.

Although body size and environment play a role, generally speaking the average male needs six to eight glasses of H2O per day. Instead of gulping a couple of glasses in quick succession, try sipping it throughout the day. The nice thing about water is it's cheap, readily available, and easy to use. No mixing required! Failure to consume adequate amounts of water can derail your bodybuilding success just as easily as a vitamin deficiency or inadequate protein intake.

CREATINE

Anyone who has followed the supplement industry knows that most athletic supplements fall far short of what the advertisers claim. Creatine was probably the first supplement that had good scientific evidence to establish its credibility. Since its introduction in the early 1990s, there have been dozens of studies confirming that creatine does in fact boost athletic performance.[1,2,3]

As far as bodybuilding is concerned, since the development of steroids the greatest product to come on the scene has been creatine. Why the buzz? Because after buying lots of supplements and wading through enough advertising-fertilizer to grow a garden in the Sahara, bodybuilders have a product that actually works! A few people get nothing from Creatine, but they are the exception to the rule

For those new to bodybuilding, a short history lesson is in order. Creatine is a naturally occurring substance derived from the three amino acids: arginine, methionine, and glycine. The primary sites for creatine synthesis in the human body are the kidneys, pancreas, and liver. Once synthesized, creatine is transported to the brain, heart, and skeletal muscles for use as an energy source. Although it varies, the average male's body contains about 2 grams of creatine.

Besides internal synthesis, creatine can be obtained in the diet with the best sources being such animal products as fish, beef, and pork. As plant material is low in creatine vegetarians have to be very creative to get sufficient creatine. In fact strict vegetarians rely almost entirely on internal synthesis for their creatine supplies.

Creatine supplementing boosts strength in virtually everyone who uses the product.

Bodybuilders and other athletes take creatine for a number of reasons. For starters creatine serves as a back-up energy source when ATP levels fall. In fact creatine plays a prominent role in ATP regeneration. Without conjuring up too many memories of high school biology, ATP or adenosine triphosphate is the body's primary energy source for short-term muscular contraction. During exercise, ATP is broken down into ADP (adenosine diphosphate) and a single phosphate group. The following equation simplifies the reaction:

$$ATP \quad (ADP + P + energy)$$

It is the breaking of the bond between the phosphate and adenosine groups that releases the energy used in muscular contraction. Unfortunately there is a limited amount of ATP available but this is where creatine plays a major role. Creatine combines with the single phosphate group to form phosphocreatine. When ATP levels drop the phosphate group in phosphocreatine is "donated" back to ADP to reform ATP. It stands to reason that the more creatine available (and hence more phosphocreatine) the greater the stored energy reserves available for rebuilding ATP. And this is what virtually every creatine user reports – much improved stamina during intense workouts.

Besides energy, bodybuilders use creatine for a second reason – increased size. Creatine causes what is called "cell volumizing." Basically the more creatine stored in muscles the more water the muscles will hold. This increased water causes the muscles to swell and in effect get larger and firmer. What's great about the whole thing is that it doesn't take weeks either. Usually after the loading phase (more on this later) which lasts about a week, the individual will have gained anywhere from five to tens pounds of additional body weight. Granted this is transitory and will disappear when creatine is discontinued, but for someone stuck at the same weight for months or even years, the extra few pounds makes a big difference to their self esteem.

A third benefit to creatine usage is increased strength. This is probably the least understood of the three variables, but just as welcome. Most creatine users report their strength levels increase anywhere from 15 to 25 percent (the numbers most often quoted) after just a few weeks of creatine supplementing. A number of theories have been put forward to explain the strength increases.

The first is that the extra size of creatine loaded muscles somehow changes the body's levers. In the same way that longer crowbars allow you to lift heavier loads, so too may larger muscles (albeit from water retention) produce greater strength. No doubt many kinesiologists are saying lever strength is primarily genetic (and in some respects they are correct), but many of these same individuals say that over-the-counter supplements are totally useless – something millions of athletes have disproved.

A second theory for increased strength relates to stamina. The more energy individuals have, the harder they can train. This is exactly the stimulus needed to increase muscle strength. So in a manner of speaking the extra strength is a "side effect' of the primary effect – increased stamina.

A final theory suggests some unknown variable is behind the increased strength. Whether it's increased mitochondria levels (the energy producing organelles of cells) or increased cross-bridges (the connections between muscle cell filaments), no one really knows for sure. The bottom line is that creatine supplementing boosts strength in virtually everyone who uses the product.

For best results, mix your creatine with lukewarm water.

USING CREATINE

If you decide to give creatine a try (and we recommend that you do), a few words of advice on using are in order.

You'll obtain the best results by following what is commonly called the loading/maintenance cycle. Basically take 20 to 30 grams of creatine a day for five to seven days, and then switch to five to ten grams per day. The loading (20 to 30 grams) phase supersaturates the muscles with creatine. It is during this phase that you will see the most rapid weight gain (remember the water retention we talked about earlier). Loading forces as much creatine as possible into the muscles for use as ATP regeneration. The maintenance phase then keeps the levels high. While anti-supplement groups proclaim the loading phase as a waste of time and a ploy by manufacturers to get you to use more, the volume of anecdotal evidence suggests otherwise. Taking only five to ten grams a day without first loading is not as effective as first loading for five to seven days with 20 to 30 grams.

A second piece of advice concerns temperature. Even though most creatine products are carefully prepared some of the creatine may come out of solution if mixed with cold water. To keep everything dissolved, try warming the mixture. Don't bring it to a boil, however, as the temperature can denature many of the ingredients. For want of a better phrase try lukewarm.

The final piece of advice concerns quality. When you go into your favorite supplement store you'll notice an endless supply of brand names. You'll also notice a tremendous difference in prices. Please don't fall for "Tom's bargain brand creatine." It sounds great to buy 2000 grams of creatine for $30 but in short you're being ripped off. It costs big bucks to manufacture a good quality supplement and as would be expected, much of the cost gets passed on to you, the consumer. Please stick with a quality brand like, Formula One, EAS, or TwinLab. Yes they are more expensive but at least you know you are getting what you paid for. The same cannot be said for "Danny's discount creatine."

PROTEIN – THE STUFF OF CHAMPIONS

Proteins are complex molecules consisting of sub units called amino acids. There are approximately 22 amino acids in nature; although it often depends on who's doing the naming. Some biochemists say there are only 20, while others vouch for 24. In any case all the proteins in your body are made from combinations of only 20 to 24 amino acids. Protein is essential because it not only makes up the various tissues of the body but also helps form other substances that help the body function properly. As an example many of the body's hormones and enzymes are proteins (called peptide hormones and enzymes) in nature.

HOW MUCH PROTEIN?

Most biochemists agree on the definition for protein, but there is heated debate as to how much protein individuals should consume. The general recommendation is based on RDA values, which suggest about .4 grams per pound of bodyweight. The problem with the RDA values is that they were calculated using sedentary (read – couch potato!) individuals. There's no way you can compare a hard training bodybuilder to the inactive TV watcher. Most bodybuilding experts these days suggest 1 to 1.5 grams of protein per pound of bodyweight. As an example for a 200-pound male this works out to 200 to 300 grams of protein.

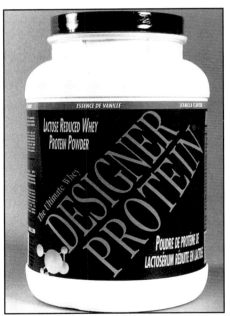

Another way to calculate protein intake is to base it on your total calorie intake. A good rule of thumb is that approximately 40 percent of your calories should be derived from protein. Based on a 2000-calorie diet this works out to 800 calories, which is 200 grams of protein (each gram of protein has 4 calories).

Although there are a few who argue otherwise, the vast majority in the supplement industry consider whey protein as the ultimate protein source. Whey is just the liquid that remains after milk has coagulated. At this stage it is about 94 percent water and only 1 percent protein. A

Protein is essential because it not only makes up the various tissues of the body but also helps form other substances that help the body function properly.

series of refining and processing techniques removes the water, fat, and other substances to produce a substance that is about 90 percent protein and 1 percent fat. The protein is then hydrolyzed which is very important because it breaks the protein down into smaller chains of amino acids called peptides. Studies have shown whey protein has the best biological (BV) value of any protein source (4,5).

The BV scale was devised to compare protein sources based on the amount of protein retained versus the amount absorbed. When first devised all foods scored lower than whole egg, which was, assigned the value 100. New technology has led to protein scoring higher than egg and some new whey sources score up to 159 on the scale.

What makes whey protein superior to other protein sources is its versatility. Lets start with immune boosting. Whey protein has this ability because of its high concentration of the amino acid glutamine. Although called a nonessential amino acid (because the body can manufacture it from other sources) glutamine is essential under certain conditions, one of which being exercise-induced stress. Glutamine has an excellent scientific record for counter-acting such stress and the associated detrimental effects to the immunity system. It does this by increasing levels of glutathione – one of the primary precursors needed for the formation of lymphocytes and antibodies.[6]

Closely related to the previous are whey's antioxidant abilities. For those not familiar with the term, antioxidants are substances that reduce the damage brought on by free radicals. Free radicals are electrically charged molecules and atoms that are produced during cellular respiration or oxidation. In the atomic world charged atoms and molecules go around looking for other charged substances to react with. Unfortunately such reactions can occur with body tissues. The end result is the build up of damage that is commonly called "aging." Antioxidants give free radicals something to react with before they attack body cells. In doing so they reduce the buildup of oxidative damage. While other protein sources (i.e. egg and soy) provide some defense against oxidation, whey protein is far superior.

Besides Glutamine, whey protein is proportionally higher in branched chain amino acids (BCAAs) than other protein sources. BCAAs are named as such because of the methyl groups branching off from the central amino acid nucleus. BCAAs are also essential as the body lacks the ability to manufacture them.

BCAAs first came to the attention of athletic nutritionists, from studies done on monkeys which showed supplementing the diet with BCAAs reduced muscle wasting associated with intense exercise and reduced calorie intake. In fact such results prompted cancer and AIDS researchers to start using BCAAs in the fight against these wasting diseases.

What makes BCAAs so important to athletes is that these aminos can be used as a fuel source. One of the reasons marathon runners are so drawn and stringy in appearance is their energy expenditures far exceed their calorie intake. After burning all the stored fat and carbo-hydrate, their bodies start using amino acids (in the form of muscle tissue) as a fuel source. Now bodybuilders are not in the same category as marathon runners, but anyone following the trad-itional style of training (i.e. 20 sets per body part) is at great risk. If at any time your sweat or workout clothes start smelling like ammonia (the classical telltale signs of amino acids being used as an energy source), reduce your training volume and increase your whey protein intake.

With whey protein, you needn't worry about any digestive problems.

Before leaving BCAAs we should add that besides serving as a back-up energy source, BCAAs also facilitate the absorption of other amino acids by muscles. This property has led some manufacturers to call BCAAs anabolic substances. While by some definitions BCAAs are creating an anabolic environment, the term "anabolic" is really an advertising ploy to make them sound like anabolic steroids. As beneficial as they are, BCCAs are nowhere near as anabolic as anabolic steroids.

OTHER BENEFITS OF WHEY

One of the problems with milk and egg or soy protein supplements is their poor mixing properties. Now things have come a long way since the days of Muscle Beach, but even the best milk and egg or soy proteins still need a blender to mix properly. Not so with whey protein. Put a couple of tablespoons in a glass and mix with milk, water or juice. A couple of stirs with a spoon and mixing is complete. No more clumping or nauseating mixtures. Just a nice, evenly blended protein shake, worthy of any ice-cream parlor. The only difference is that most whey protein powders contains 24 to 30 grams of protein per serving with only 2 grams of fat (less than 20 calories).

As for the digestive problems discussed earlier, no worries with whey. The high quality of whey protein, combined with the lack of air bubbles often produced by blenders, gives you a mixture that is very easy on the digestive system. No more gas, bloating, or social embarrassment!

GLUTAMINE

Glutamine is one of the most abundant non-essential amino acids in the human body. It makes up over fifty percent of the amino acids found in muscle cells. But please don't let the word non-essential mislead you. Even though the body can manufacture glutamine from other sources (thus meeting the definition of non-essential), in times of stress – of which exercise is one – glutamine levels may drop dangerously low. The end result is the aspiring bodybuilder's worst nightmare – negative nitrogen balance leading to muscle wasting! High levels of glutamine counteract this by keeping the body in positive nitrogen balance – the necessary environment for laying down new muscle tissue.

Besides its role in preventing muscle wasting, glutamine stimulates the activity of immunocyctes – small cells that can be called the garbage collectors of the body. Among their functions are the tracking down and removal of the waste products of metabolism. The faster the waste products are removed, the faster muscle recovery takes place.

Not convinced yet? There's more. Depending on glycogen levels, glutamine can be converted into glutamate and then into the amino acid alanine. Big deal you say. Well it just so happens that the liver can convert alanine into glucose, which is then returned to the muscles to be used as an energy source. The process is just one example of what biochemists call

gluconeogenesis – the production of glucose from nonglucose sources.
Other important functions of glutamine are:
stimulation of the immunity system
structural integrity of various organs
fuel source for red and white blood cells
role in the molecular process of transcription

Finally glutamine supplementation helps muscle cells maintain maximum volume by preserving their most abundant amino acids, taurine and glutamine. Clinical studies have consistently demonstrated the role of these amino acids in muscle growth, protein synthesis, and anti-proteolysis (inhibition of protein catabolism. If glutamine and taurine levels drop below a certain point, protein synthesis stops, which means zero progress and no muscle growth!

HOW MUCH?

Although the scientific literature is lacking in this area, the volume of anecdotal evidence from bodybuilders suggests ten to twenty grams of glutamine per day. And like creatine, it probably makes more sense to take four, five-gram dosages over the day, rather than taking the full twenty grams at once. Not only does this insure better absorption, but also for many people the higher dosage may be hard on the gastrointestinal tract.

GAMMA-HYDROXYBUTYRATE (GHB)

GHB is a naturally occurring metabolite and precursor to GABA (gamma-aminobutyrate). GHB was a widely available over-the-counter supplement until it was banned by the FDA in 1990. Bodybuilders use GHB because it can cause a sixteen-fold increase in growth hormone levels. Unfortunately, this increase is also accompanied by an increase in prolactin levels. This counteracts many of the positive effects of an elevated GH level, resulting in a very small amount (if any) of muscle growth. Some bodybuilders report an increase in lean body mass and strength while on GHB.

There is no general gym dosage for GHB. To determine correct dosage of GHB, take a gram or two on an empty stomach. With an empty stomach, the GHB should take effect within twenty minutes. If no effect is felt in twenty minutes, ingest another gram. Continue in this process until a desirable dosage is reached. Some bodybuilders notice effects after 1 gram while others can go up to 10. There really is no danger of overdosing in this way, provided GHB is not taken with other drugs such as alcohol or other CNS depressants. A slight overdose of GHB will cause a person to fall asleep, but if a person takes more than the desirable dosage and/or takes it with alcohol, he may get dizzy and then vomit, even while asleep. A full stomach can delay the onset of GHB. This can lead to an overdose because the bodybuilder may not feel any effects after a half an hour, and incorrectly assumed he needed to take more. Some bodybuilders have claimed that GHB has a thermogenic effect. Due to the use of stimulants as part of thermogenic stacks, sleep cycles can be disrupted. GHB is an effective sleep aid, and is often used for this purpose. Unlike other sleep aids, it is not habit forming nor does the user experience nightmares (rem-rebound) after discontinuing use. It was also effective in treating the symptoms of alcohol-withdrawal. This drug can cause euphoria, allowing it to became a favorite party drug in the early '90s. This drug also aids erectile function, intensifies orgasms and enhances tactile sensations. Bottom line, it's an amazing aphrodisiac. Naturally, someone had to ruin the party. When dissolved in alcohol it is colorless and tasteless, but it also causes loss of control and memory loss. It became a date-rape drug.

Others chose to consume it willingly, but the combination proved deadly and people have died of overdoses. This led to the FDA banning this drug. Many have resorted to home manufacture. This is both illegal and downright dangerous.

EPHEDRINE

Trade Names of Popular Tablets : Ceepa, Central, Dymetadrine 25, Efedrin, Efedrin DAK, Ephedrina Level, Ephedrine HCL, Ephedrine HCl-Antos, Ephedrin Spofa, Ephedrini HCL, Ephedrinium HCL, Ephedroides, Lardet Expectorant, Mudrane GG, Perspiran N, Pyrralan Expectorant, Quadrinal,

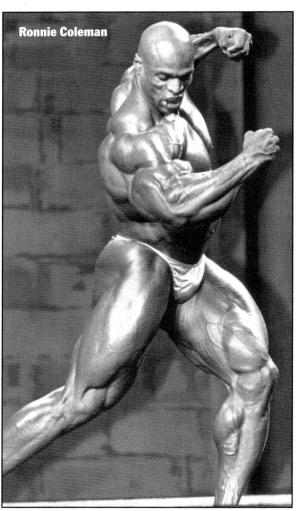

Ronnie Coleman

Ephedrine is one of those substances that despite the bad press it occasionally receives, is one of the most effective over-the-counter fat loss supplements available.

Ephedrine falls into the pharmacological category of beta agonist. This means it stimulates the sympathetic nervous system. The increased heart and respiratory rate associated with dangerous situations is an example of the sympathetic nervous system preparing the body for "fight or flight."

Bodybuilders and other athletes use ephedrine for two reasons, fat loss and stimulation. Let's look at both.

Besides increasing heart and respiratory rate, sympathetic stimulation also produces thermo-genesis. Thermogenesis is the increase in body temperature that makes fat deposits more readily available for burning. This drug also stimulates the thyroid gland to transform the weaker LT-4 (L-thyroxine) into the stronger LT-3 (liothyronine), thus accelerating the metabolism and increasing fat loss.

Although a crude analogy, the process is similar to turning up the heat underneath a frying pan. The higher the temperature the faster butter will melt. We apologize to the thermodynamicists out there, but this is essentially how ephedrine works; it cranks up the body's internal furnace.

Bodybuilders also take ephedrine for its direct stimulant properties. Being a sympathetic nervous system stimulant, ephedrine can give you quite the energy boost. There's also a volume of anecdotal evidence to suggest this extra energy translates into increased strength – up to 20 percent by some reports. Whether the effect is physiological (an actual increase in muscle contractile power) or psychological (the good old placebo effect) the fact remains that most bodybuilders can perform extra reps with the same weight, or increased weight for the same reps, after taking a couple of ephedrine tablets.

EPHEDRINE – A KILLER?

We would be remiss if we left the topic of ephedrine without commenting on the media's bashing of ephedrine over the last couple of years. If you go by the headlines, ephedrine falls into the same category as radioactive plutonium – it's a bonafide killer that should be sealed in a lead container and buried two miles below the surface! Unfortunately this is typical overreacting by the media. Basically what happened was a few teens decided to use ephedrine as a party drug and mixed it with alcohol. As is often the case, the individuals died of the combination. The problem was the media downplayed the alcohol factor and the dosages (hundreds of milligrams) of ephedrine involved. Readers were left with the impression that the victims died after consuming a few tablets of ephedrine. For those who use ephedrine or are contemplating doing so, unless you have a pre-existing heart or nervous system condition, ephedrine is relatively safe. We say relatively because there will always be a small percentage of the population who have adverse reactions to a given drug. But for the vast majority of the normal healthy population, when used intelligently, ephedrine is safe.

Most ephedrine supplements come in 12.5 or 25 milligrams capsules or tablets. The standard dosage for stimulation is one to two tablets about an hour before a workout. Of course with time individuals will build a tolerance to the drug. The temptation is to increase the dosage but this is where use becomes abuse. It's far safer to go off the drug for a couple of weeks. Then when you resume the lower dosage will once again be effective. Another option is to only take it on your heavy workout days; which should be no more than two or three workouts a week.

For fat loss the standard dosage is 25 milligrams taken three to four times a day. Keep in mind that for some individuals this amount of ephedrine will be too high a dosage. Our advice is to slowly work up the dosage and see how your system responds. You may find one or two 25 milligrams dosages is the maximum your system can tolerate in a given day without such side effects as insomnia, jitters, and an elevated heart rate occurring.

HYDROXY CITRIC ACID – HCA

Hydroxy citric acid or HCA is a substance obtained from the rinds of the Garcinia fruit of South Asia. HCA's primary role in athletics is fat loss. But unlike caffeine and ephedrine, which speed up the removal of existing fat deposits, HCA works by preventing new fat from forming. It does this by interfering with the enzyme citrate lyase. This enzyme converts excess carbohydrate into fat if it is not burned as a fuel source.

HCA also plays an indirect role in fat loss. As the body "thinks" it has enough fuel available the sensation of hunger is greatly reduced. And as most people eat when they feel hungry, the suppressing of appetite leads to fewer calories ingested, ultimately leading to reduced weight.

CONJUGATED LINOLEIC ACID –CLA

Conjugated Linoleic Acid or CLA is an ironic supplement in that despite being a fat itself, actually speeds up the removal of stored body fat.

Studies have shown that subjects supplementing with CLA's lose much more bodyfat than non-using control groups (the fact that the same groups also gained lean muscle tissue should not be overlooked either).

The exact mechanism of action is unknown but the general consensus is that the high levels of CLA's "trick" the body into thinking it has more fat than it needs so it is less likely to hold on to fat stores. In addition, many biochemists suggest that CLA's may have anti-catabolic properties that can counteract the loss of muscle mass associated with illness or overtraining.

Although found in animal meat, milk, and cheese, to get the two to four grams of CLA per day that most biochemists recommend, supplementing is the best alternative. Two of the best sources of CLA's are flax oil and fish oils.

TRIBULUS TERRESTRIS

Tribulus terrestris is an herb that has a long history in traditional medicine as an aphrodisiac. Its primary method of action is to stimulate the pituitary to release increased levels of leutinizing hormone (LH). LH is the primary hormone responsible for telling the testes to increase testosterone production. What separates tribulus from other so-called aphrodisiacs is that it has good science to back it up. Laboratory studies have found increased sperm production and motility, and elevated testosterone levels after administration. The recommended daily dosage of tribulus is 500 to 750 milligrams.

ANDROSTENEDIONE

Kevin
Levrone

Andro got its first big "break" from research carried out in the former East Germany. With success in athletics being part of the communist statement, athletic researchers were always on the lookout for substances that could boost performance but not be detected in a drug test. According to declassified reports from the East German doping program, many of the athletes were using an andro nasal spray that would boost testosterone levels for a few hours – enough to increase performance, but not enough to fail a drug test. We'll never know just how effective such supplements were, but the science of testosterone precursors had begun.

> **"Whether you decide to take 4-androstenedione or any other substance for that matter, remember that the only constant in bodybuilding is regular, serious training. No amount of hype can substitute for sweat."**
>
> – Will Brink, *MuscleMag* columnist and author commenting on the real key to bodybuilding success – hard and consistent training.

If the East Germans can be credited with introducing andro to the athletic world, then baseball player Mark McGuire holds the honor of bringing andro to the masses. Although banned by most sport's federations, andro is perfectly legal in professional baseball. As soon as a snooping reporter spotted it in McGuire's locker, the media went into a frenzy. So called "experts" came out of the woodwork to denounce McGuire for using anabolic steroids. The fact that andro is not an anabolic steroid seemed to be conveniently omitted. The genie was out of the bottle and supplement companies made a fortune. Which was ironic as andro was on it's way out in bodybuilding circles. It had one or two good years, the results were less than expected, and it slowly began to disappear. But along came McGuire and andro rose to the top of the charts like the latest Teen Sensation's CD. Ah the power of the media!

Biochemically, androstenedione is an intermediate precursor to testosterone. In fact it's only one enzyme and step away. Now in theory this sounds great but there's a host of variables that must occur for andro to be converted into the desired hormone. Even when it does, it's not all it's cracked up to be. Most andro marketers say it "increases testosterone levels" and leave it at that. What they don't tell you is only a small amount (five to ten percent is the range most commonly quoted) makes the journey from andro to testosterone. Another point to consider is that andro only stays active in the system for a short period of time, say a few hours. From a biochemical point of view andro has a short half-life. This is the time needed for half the substance to degrade or be converted into another substance. We also must point out that there's little research to suggest, slightly elevated testosterone levels can make much of an impact on athletic performance. Unless you were to continuously consume andro every couple of hours, a few capsules a day is probably not going to lead to any meaningful muscle growth.

Another consideration is that testosterone is only one of the end products of andro metabolism. Andro can also be converted into estrogen. Now even though there's limited evidence that estrogen can stimulate testosterone levels, there's more evidence to show that higher estrogen levels lead to increased fat storage (one of the primary reasons why women on average have higher fat levels than men).

Andro is not in the same category as some of the harsher anabolic steroids when it comes to producing unwanted side effects (Anadrol-50 for example), but there are still risks. In many users andro can increase facial and torso acne. Remember testosterone and its derivatives also have androgenic effects (development of the secondary sex characteristics, hair growth etc). The reason acne is common in the teenage years and especially in males is because of high levels of testosterone. If you had severe or even moderate acne as a teenager then taking andro puts you at risk.

If there's one side effect that may offer an athletic edge it's elevated aggression levels. It's long been known that elevated testosterone levels and aggression are related. Numerous studies with prisoners have confirmed this (of course there's many more variables that lead to incarceration) For athletes in a sport requiring a certain aggressive mentality (i.e. football, rugby etc), andro might offer a slight edge.

A less common but potentially more severe side effect concerns andro's effects on the prostate gland. This small organ located in the lower groin region of males is very susceptible to high androgen levels. In fact many men (twenty to twenty five percent by some accounts) will naturally have prostate problems later in life. Taking any substance that's biochemically similar (or into the case of andro possibly converted to) testosterone increases the risk of prostate problems including cancer.

Finally assuming andro actually does get converted to testosterone, then you have the problem of feedback interference to consider. Most of the body's hormones including testosterone are regulated by a biofeedback mechanism. In effect the body increases or decreases levels depending on how much of the hormone is circulating. As soon as you bring in an outside source, you are disrupting the body's natural hormonal axis.

The "accepted" dosage for androstenedione is 100 to 200 milligrams per day – preferably spread over three or four smaller dosages. This is probably enough to slightly elevate testosterone levels (but as we said earlier how relevant this is we don't know) without producing the unwanted side effects. The bottom line, however, depends on the individual. If you have a history of hair loss, prostate problems, or acne in your family, then we strongly advise against using andro products.

19-NOR-4-ANDROSTENEDIONE (19-NOR)

Like androstenedione, 19-Nor is another example of a group of substances called prohormones. They work in one of two primary ways. They either convert to testosterone, or they convert to another anabolic hormone. 19-Nor is an example of the latter. It is converted by the liver into nandrolone. Now the name nandrolone might not ring any gym bells, but perhaps nandrolone deconate will. Nandrolone is the active ingredient in the very effective anabolic steroid deca-durabolin also called deca for short. Deca has a cult following among bodybuilders because it is very anabolic, but low in androgenic properties. It also has a reputation as being one of the safest anabolic steroids ever created.

Taking 19-Nor gives you the option of naturally creating nandrolone without having to worry about legal issues. Now we are not about to say nor-19 is as powerful as deca. But for a natural trainer who has never used steroids, 19-Nor will make a significant difference.

As a final comment on nor-19 and other nandrolone derivatives, they are among the easiest to detect in a drug test. The 1999 Pan American Games in Winnipeg, Canada, turned up numerous positive tests for nandrolone. Most of the athletes claimed they never took injectable nandrolone products, but many admitted to taking over the counter nor-19. Now for those athletes telling the truth, the positive tests help confirm what many considered hype by the supplement manufacturers, that nor-19 could in fact convert to nandrolone. Well not only does nor-19 convert to nandrolone, but it converts at a rate high enough to be picked up by a drug test. And for those of you who have stopped taking nandrolone and its relatives, you are not out of the woodwork just yet. Nandrolone can be detected as far back as 18 months after its last usage. It may take your body nearly two years to clear the product from your system. Please keep this in mind if you plan on competing in a sport that has a reputable drug testing policy.

7-KETO-DIHYDROXYEPIANDROSTENEDIONE

Dihydroxyepiandrostenedione is a derivative of the popular supplement DHEA. DHEA is produced by the adrenal glands and is one of the most dominant hormones in the body. In a manner of speaking DHEA is a sort of a "mother" hormone as it can give birth to a host of other hormones depending on what's needed. What's so exciting about DHEA is that studies show supplementing can increase circulating testosterone levels. Other studies show that DHEA users gain more muscle mass and lose more bodyfat than non-users. Once again DHEA is not an anabolic steroid replacer, but, depending on the individual, may increase circulating levels of testosterone.

We must add that most studies on DHEA and its efficacy have focused on the elderly or DHEA deficient individuals. Long-term studies using bodybuilders or other healthy athletic subjects are few and far between. True, there is a mountain of positive anecdotal evidence to suggest DHEA may help promote muscle size and fat loss. But the scientific backing is limited at best.

5- ANDROSTENEDIOL (DIOL-5)

Diol-5 is a close cousin of nor-19, which is also reported to be converted to nandrolone in the liver. It is sold in many countries as methandriol. According to manufacturers of the substance, diol-5 produces three main effects in the body. First, it's supposedly anticatabolic. This means it suppresses cortisol and other stress hormones released by intense training. Cortisol by way of review causes protein to be leeched from muscle tissue, leading to muscle wasting. The higher cortisol levels the harder it is for the body to recover from exercise.

Another proposed property of andriol-5 is its ability to bind to estrogen receptors. The more estrogen receptors "blocked" the fewer effects this feminizing hormone can have. Closely related to this, diol-5 also has the ability to prevent the conversion of testosterone to estrogen (called aromatization).

A final benefit of diol-5 is that like glutamine, it can strengthen the immune system by increasing the activation of lymphocytes.[17] As many bodybuilders will admit, a couple of months of intense training often leaves them in a drained state and open to every flu or bug that comes along. Diol-5 may boost the immunity system, helping to ward off such stress-induced ailments.

As with most pro hormones, precise dosages have never been worked out for andriol-5. The anecdotal evidence suggests 50 to 100 milligrams of diol-5 per day.

Lee Priest

4-ANDROSTENEDIOL

4-AD is the brainchild of chemist Patrick Arnold and his company LPJ. 4-AD is promoted as being the best of the current generation of precursors because it converts to testosterone at three times the rate of other precursors like androstenedione.[15] In one study presented at a major conference in Finland in late 1998, 100 milligrams of 4-Ad was found to raise testosterone 42.5 percent as compared to only 10.9 percent for an equal amount of androstenedione.[16]

4-AD is found in several tissues of the body including the adrenal cortex, hypothalamus, and testes. Besides raising testosterone levels higher than other precursors, 4-AD may have another advantage – it doesn't seem to aromatize to estrogen like many other precursors. Without insulting the biochemists among you, suffice to say 4-AD is missing a side group (in this case a ketone) that most of the others have. Of course the extra testosterone produced by 4-AD can and will aromatize somewhat, but that's the price you pay for playing chemist with your hormone levels.

ONE FINAL COMMENT ON PROHORMONES

As of this writing, prohormones are probably second only to creatine in terms of popularity. And a flip through any muscle magazine will see just how much money is invested in ads for prohormone promotion. The two primary questions relating to prohormones are, are they effective, and what are the long-term dangers? The answer to the first question is, while not in the same category of anabolic steroids, prohormones will give most natural bodybuilders an increase in size and strength beyond what they'd gain without the substances. Of course this raises the question, what is natural? Is not taking a substance that converts to an anabolic steroid molecule, not in the same category as injecting the compound directly? As we said earlier there is a huge gray area when it comes to many modern supplements, and prohormones lead to the most debate.

The second question concerning long-term side effects is more difficult if not impossible to answer right now. Prohormones have only become a major player in athletics in the last five years or so (not counting the East German use of androstenedione back in the seventies and eighties). Such recent usage means there are no long-term studies. Who knows what will happen in ten or twenty years. The fact that most prohormones are naturally found in the body suggests there should be no side effects. But then again they are not usually found in the dosages routinely taken by bodybuilders. To use a common analogy, small amounts of alcohol are not dangerous and in some cases actually beneficial. But heavy alcohol use leads to a whole host of problems. Could the same be true for prohormones? Only time will tell.

INSULIN MIMICKERS AND ABSORPTION BOOSTERS

From research carried out in the field of diabetes comes an assortment of amazing substances that increase insulin effectiveness – either by assisting or mimicking the hormone. Now those new to the sport may be wondering what insulin and supplements have in common. Well it just so happens that insulin does more than increase sugar removal from the blood. It also speeds removal of many other nutrients from the blood stream into the skeletal muscles. It stands to reason that anything that can increase insulin's properties can also boost nutrient absorption. The following are some of the popular supplements that bodybuilders use to increase creatine and other nutrient absorption.

ALPHA-LIPOIC ACID

Alpha Lipoic acid, also called thioctic acid, has been used in Europe for years as both an antioxidant and antidiabetic agent. Alpha lipoic acid has an excellent record in the scientific community for its ability to cleanse the liver especially when it comes to chemical poisons. Many internal and external stressers can elevate liver enzymes to the point that the liver's detoxifying abilities are diminished. If the condition persists, liver degeneration occurs, often leading to death. The best example of this is cirrhosis brought on by years of alcohol abuse. Numerous studies have found that lipoic acid enhances the production of glutathione, the main antioxidant within cells.[10] Glutathione plays a major role in mopping up and neutralizing various toxins and free radicals. Other evidence suggests lipoic acid may slow the progression of HIV-infection in AIDS patients.[11]

Now while the previous is important, it's lipoic acid's second role that makes it such a popular ingredient in many creatine supplements. Research carried out in Europe has shown lipoic acid to be an excellent insulin modulator. That is it helps insulin transport glucose and other nutrients out of the bloodstream. It also reduces insulin resistance thus making the body more receptive to this all-important hormone.[12,13]

CHROMIUM PICOLINATE

Chromium is a trace mineral that despite being needed in small amounts plays a major role in glucose regulation. In one study involving 180 patients with diabetes, those receiving either 200 mcgs or 1000 mcgs of chromium had lower levels of glycerated hemoglobin (a hemoglobin molecule linked to a sugar molecule). Glycerated hemoglobin is a good predictor of diabetes control with lower levels indicating better management of the disease.

Besides glucose regulation there's mounting evidence that chromium may increase fat oxidation. One study published in *Current Therapeutic Research* found that those taking chromium supplementation lost over six pounds of bodyfat as compared to a control group who only lost 3.4 pounds.[14] The exact mechanism of action for chromium is unknown but researchers theorize that the element increases the efficiency of insulin by making the hormone bind stronger to receptors. The recommended dosage is 200 to 400 mcg per day.

VANADYL SULFATE

Unlike lipoic acid and chromium, which assist insulin in carrying out its functions, vanadyl sulfate actually mimics the hormone's effects. Vanadyl sulfate is the "salt" version of the trace element vanadium. In its natural state vanadium is toxic, but when combined with other compounds such as sulfate, it is quite safe.

Studies with mice have found vanadyl sulfate produces its effects in the liver and peripheral tissues by mimicking insulin. Test subjects using vanadyl had more efficient glucose regulation than non-using groups.[15,16]

The recommended dosage of vanadyl is 40 to 50 milligrams per day.

MOMORDICA CHARANTIA

Momordica charantia or bitter melon is a member of the Chinese cucumber family that has been used for thousands of years in traditional medicine. This simple vegetable contains numerous compounds that make it another ideal ingredient in creatine and other supplements.

Like glutamine, bitter melon seems to play a role in boosting the immunity system. Studies with AIDS patients show bitter melon has the ability to inhibit growth of HIV-infected cells. In fact an AIDS intervention team in Los Angeles has begun collecting anecdotal evidence from people using bitter melon to treat AIDS. Among the reports are increased energy, clearing of skin rashes, and a more positive mental outlook.[17]

Momordica's second property is what's causing biochemists and bodybuilders alike to sit up and take notice. Scientists have extracted a protein from bitter melon called gourdin,

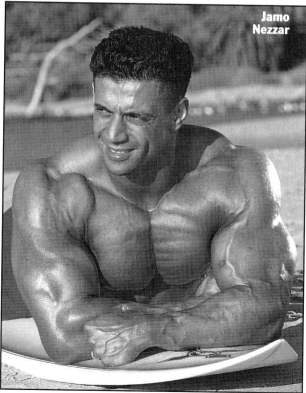
Jamo Nezzar

which shows great promise in the treatment of diabetes. Researchers gave 150 milligram doses of gourdin to various categories of diabetes patients (juvenile, maturity onset, old age, etc). In *all* groups, sugar levels decreased to the point that many of the patients could cease regular insulin administration.[18]

By now the words insulin and diabetes should be very familiar to you at least as they apply to supplementing. As with chromium and vanadyl sulfate, bitter melon increases the removal of glucose from the blood stream. But it's not specific for glucose alone. Other nutrients such as creatine also get carried along in the shuffle. The recommended dosage is 200 to 400 milligrams per day.

BERGAMOTTIN

Bergamottin is a member of a group of compounds called furanocoumarins.[19] Bergamottin seems to have the ability to inactivate an enzyme in the liver and small intestine called cytochrome P-450. This enzyme is one of the pharmaceutical industry's biggest challenges as it deactivates up to 60 percent of all known drugs.[20] As an example, nisoldipine, a calcium channel blocker, has a bioability of only 5 percent because of metabolic deactivation in the gut.[21] But bergamottin blocks the activity of the enzyme thus allowing more of the drug to escape deactivation.[22,23]

Bergamottin was first discovered when researchers evaluating the effects of alcohol on a new blood pressure medication found those subjects taking the drug with grapefruit juice had blood levels of the drug much higher than those using just the alcohol.

Studies with grapefruit juice and red wine (another great source of furanocoumarins) showed enzyme activity impeded by up to 90 percent for the grapefruit juice and 84 percent for the red wine.[24] In fact so powerful and conclusive is the evidence that medical boards have issued warnings to physicians about patients overdosing on medications mixed with grapefruit juice. And it's not just short-term concerns either as the evidence suggests the anti-enzyme effects of bergamottin can last up to 24 hours.[25] This stuff is so powerful it could turn life-saving drugs into killers.

To quote Dr. Kenneth Lown of the University of Michigan Medical Center, "If you regularly drink grapefruit juice, don't change. If you are on those drugs and don't normally take them with grapefruit juice, you may need to consult your physician before adding grapefruit juice to your diet."

Of course we are talking about medications here, and most warnings are aimed at the elderly. Many physicians are now recommending patients take their drugs with grapefruit juice to increase absorption, especially those with pre-existing absorption problems.

PIPERINE

Piperine is a compound isolated from the fruit of the black pepper plant. Unlike bergamottin, which increases absorption by interfering with a degradation enzyme, piperine exerts its effects on the intestinal wall, causing it to become more permeable to nutrients and drugs. There's also evidence to suggest that it can form bonds with nutrients (called apolar complexes) allowing them to cross membrane barriers more easily.[26] Studies conducted in the United States have shown that piperine increases the absorption of such nutrients as Beta-carotene, vitamins B-6 and B-1, and the mineral selenium.[27, 28]

BODYBUILDING HERBS

Unless you've been in a coma for the last ten years, you've probably noticed some changes in supplements. In an effort to separate bodybuilders from their hard-earned dollars, manufacturers have begun adding exotic ingredients to their products. Notably herbs. Some work, some don't.

David Palumbo and Barbara Moran

Jean-Pierre Fux

How do you tell the difference? This section covers many of the herbals found in the market, and a few that industry sources have told us that are due for release. And since some bodybuilders have discovered benefits from using herbs while on a cycle, we felt it important to give these substances a proper review. But before using any herbal supplements, check with your doctor, your pharmacist, and a naturopath if you can find one. Read up on the ingredients if you don't recognize them. And don't expect the same results every time you use an herbal. Growing conditions, time of harvest, length of storage and production techniques can affect the concentration of active compounds in an herb. Basically, welcome to the world of hit and miss. Few products are standardized (that makes them less consistent, and also more expensive). When it comes to herbals, remember the Latin phrase, "Caveat Emptor," buyer beware.

> **"... and mega-dosages (of anabolic steroids) did not affect my liver enzymes much when I took the right hepato-protectants... I take this herb which I think is called Syllimarin – two capsules after every meal. It is sold in France under the name Legalon... I also take an anti-oxidant formula that contains glutathione. With these products, my liver enzymes were normal, even at dosages as high as 3,000 to 4,000 milligrams a week of various anabolics."**
>
> – Mailbox, a bodybuilder interviewed by Testosterone.net editor, TC Luoma.

What are the possible benefits of using herbs? A big problem for many bodybuilders is indigestion. As teenagers, people are able to consume vast quantities of food, but as we age we can develop hiatal hernias, reflux indigestion and a host of other problems that affect our ability to maximize our food intake and absorb the nutrients. In the past we have taken a negative stance toward playing with supplements that are designed to enhance nutrient uptake. But for those who are experiencing problems, the following herbs might be their best chance of overcoming a dietary problem that has thrown up a road block on their path to bodybuilding success.

We have long taken a hard stand against the use of diuretics in our sport. Herbal diuretics are generally not as potent as the pharmaceutical kind. If you must resort to this before a competition, then try a small amount of an herbal diuretic. You're just less likely to die.

Some herbs have anabolic properties. More likely they appear anabolic but the growth is the result of better digestion. Either way, certain herbs have gained a reputation of being growth enhancers.

Perhaps the greatest benefit to be derived from herbs is from their rejuvenating properties. Bodybuilding puts tremendous stress on the body, causing wear and tear to the muscles and joints, and forcing the body to maximize performance on reduced calories. If one does not ensure adequate sleep, proper nutrition, and correct training, the overall stress can impede the immune system and negatively impact on your progress. Herbals can help restore this balance.

SOME COMMON HERBS

Alfalfa (Medicago sativa)
Alfalfa was called the "father of all foods" by the Arabs, who first discovered it. The name comes from the Iranian word "aspasti," which means horsefodder. It is the highest source of chlorophyll in the plant kingdom. It is very rich in minerals and nutrients, including calcium, magnesium and potassium and is high in beta-carotene. It also contains natural fluoride thus helping to prevent tooth decay, and is used as a folk remedy for arthritis, as a laxative, and as an overall tonic. Perhaps most important for bodybuilders, alfalfa contains the digestive enzyme betaine. This substance aids digestion, and is traditionally consumed for this purpose as a mint/alfalfa tea.

Daily Dosage:
Dried : 6 to 12 gm
Fresh: 1/4 to 1/2 cup

Aloe Leaf (Aloe spp.)
Aloe is derived from the Arabic word, "alloeh," which means bitter and shiny substance. It has been used since ancient times to treat skin and digestive disorders. Cleopatra reportedly used it daily as part of her beauty regimen. In more recent times, the Japanese used it to treat radiation burn victims after the bombings of Hiroshima and Nagasaki, and found it to be an effective treatment. It is not uncommon to find people growing their own aloe plants. Snap off a leaf, break it open, and you have fresh aloe juice to apply to your skin. Aloe makes an excellent acne treatment, and should be part of any bodybuilder's precontest preparations. It can also be taken internally to treat the digestive tract, but the taste leaves something to be desired.

Daily Dosage:
Internal: one tablespoon of fresh leaves
External: Apply as needed

Althea Root (Althea officinalis)
Known since ancient times, althea was considered a delicacy in roman times. This herb aids digestion and is also used as a diuretic.

Daily Dosage:
Dried root: 2 to 5 gm
Fresh root: 1/8 to 1/3 cup

Asparagus (Asparagus officinale)
This popular vegetable is well known to most readers. While the stems are commonly eaten, it is the root that holds particular interest for us. This herb has diuretic and laxative properties.

Daily Dosage:
Dried Root: 1 tablespoon
Fresh Root: 1.5 gm

Astragalus (Astragalus membranaceus)

Oriental herbalists have used astragalus for many centuries for ailments including diabetes, heart disease and high blood pressure. It is traditionally used to help activate the immune system thus enhancing the body's natural ability to fight disease. Of interest to bodybuilders, it has been used to regulate blood sugar. Given the common use of insulin among bodybuilders, this herb is a far safer alternative. Astralagus is said to rejuvenate the digestive organs.

Daily Dosage:
Dried Root: 3 to 6 gm
Fresh Root: 2 to 4 tablespoons

Bayberry (Myrica cerifera)

This Native American plant was often prescribed by 19th century physicians to nutritionally support the improvement of all kinds of vascular problems. It was also recommended to support the body's fight against colds, coughs and flus as well as an effective gargle for sore throats. An immune system enhancer, this herb is a must for any bodybuilder coming off a drug cycle. It is also an effective digestive aid.

Daily Dosage:
Dried Bark: 1.5 to 3 gm
Fresh Bark: 1 to 3 tablespoons

Bilberry (Vaccinium myrtillus)

Bilberry causes improvements in circulation, enzyme activity, night vision and its ability to fight blurred vision, eyestrain and nearsightedness have been confirmed. During WWII British pilots consumed Bilberry prior to night missions to improve their night vision. It has rejuvenating effects, and is believed to be helpful in controlling diabetes and joint problems. Many bodybuilders have been forced to give up the sport because of arthritis and other connective tissue problems. This may help in their recovery.

Daily Dosage:
Dried Fruit: 1/2 to 1 cup
Fresh Fruit: 12 to 24 gm

Black Cohosh (Cimifuga racemosa)

Native Americans used this herb in the treatment of arthritis and as a traditional remedy for inducing menstruation, relieving cramps and facilitating labor and delivery. It is a source of natural estrogen, which can induce the production of testosterone receptors in bodybuilders. Bodybuilders on a steroid cycle should avoid this herb, as gynocomastia is always a risk when on steroids.

Daily Dosage:
Dried Bark: 1.5 to 3 gm
Fresh Bark: 1 to 3 tablespoons

Black Walnut (Juglans nigra)

Black Walnut is especially useful in the treatment of yeast infections. That's good news for female bodybuilders. It works as a digestive aid, and bodybuilders who have used thyroid medications can use this herb to treat thyroid deficiency.

Daily Dosage:
Dried Hulls: 1 to 1.5gm
Fresh Hulls: 2 to 3 teaspoons

Blessed Thistle (Cnicus benedictus)

The name comes from the Latin "benedictus," meaning blessed. It's curative properties were believed to be a gift from God. It has been used to treat everything from the Black Plague (didn't work) to regulating the menstrual cycle, and treating liver disorders. It is used as a digestive aid and for treating arthritis.

Daily Dosage:
Dried Plant: 3 to 6 gm
Fresh Plant: 2 to 4 tablespoons

Boneset (Eupatorium perfolium)

Native Americans used this herb in the treatment of broken bones, hence the common name. This herb is used as an aid in structural repair, an anti-inflammatory, and has flavonoids that may have anti-cancer properties.

Daily Dosage:
Dried Plant: 1 to 2 gm
Fresh Plant: 2 to 4 teaspoons

Burdock Root (Arctium Lappa)

This is a common weed used for arthritis and applied externally for skin problems. Burdock is used as a diuretic, a digestive aid and to treat acne and psoriasis.

Daily Dosage:
Dried Root: 6 to 12 gm
Fresh Root: 1/4 to 1/2 cup

Butchers Broom (Ruscus aculeatus)

European doctors have used this herb for centuries to relieve excess water retention and to treat the discomfort and pain caused by poor circulation in the legs. Also used to treat arthritis.

Daily Dosage:
Dried Root: 1.5 to 3 gm
Fresh Root: 1 to 2 tablespoons

Cascara Sagrada (Rhammus purshiana)

Also called Buckthorn, this herb is a great remedy for chronic constipation as it is not habit forming. It will benefit the entire digestive system, and has also been used for gallstones and liver ailments. It is said to be helpful in treating liver problems.

Daily Dosage:
Dried Bark: 1 to 3 gm
Fresh Bark: Don't even think about it! USP standards require that the bark be aged for one year before use. It's far too potent to be used fresh.

Catnip (Nepeta cataria)

Catnip is a mild sedative when brewed as a tea, and is claimed to have similar effects to marijuana when smoked. It is used as a digestive aid. If nothing else, if the cable goes you can give it to your cat and watch him freak out.

Daily Dosage (Human, forget about the cat already):
Dried Plant: 0.5 to 1 gm
Fresh Plant: 1 to 2 teaspoons

Chamomile Flower (Anthemis noblis)

The Ancient Egyptians dedicated chamomile to the gods because of its curative powers. Europeans have used chamomile as a cure for insomnia, back pain, rheumatism and the relief of menstrual cramps since the middle ages. As a side note, chamomile will enhance the highlights of blond hair, and is commonly used as a tea. It is used as a digestive aid.

DailyDosage:
Dried Flowers: 3 to 6 gm
Fresh Flowers: 2 to 4 tablespoons

Chickweed (Stellaria media)

Chickweed has been traditionally used as an external remedy for cuts, and especially for itching and irritation. Considered to be an excellent blood purifier as it can help carry away toxins. It is rich in calcium, potassium, magnesium, and vitamin C. It may decrease plaque in the bloodstream. Can be used as a diuretic.

Daily Dosage:
Dried Plant: 6 to 12 gm
Fresh Plant: 1/4 to 1/2 cup

Comfrey Leaf

Comfrey leaves are traditionally eaten as a cure for poor circulation and as a blood strengthener and cleanser. It is also useful in healing ulcers. It is beneficial to the stomach, kidneys, bowel, and lungs. Bodybuilders use it as a digestive aid.

Daily Dosage:
Dried Leaf: 6 to 12 gm
Fresh Leaf: 1/4 to 1/2 cup

Damiana (Turnera diffusa)

Damiana comes from Mexico, and Aztec legends claim that this herb is a powerful aphrodisiac. Herbalists also recommend it as a laxative and as a general tonic for overall good health. It can be used as a diuretic.

Daily Dosage:
Dried Leaf: 0.5 gm
Fresh Leaf: 1 teaspoon

Devil's Claw (Harpagophytum procumbens)

This herb has been popular in Africa and in Europe for more than two hundred years. It is primarily used as an anti-inflammatory and pain reliever against arthritis and rheumatism, and acts to reduce cholesterol. Used to boost the immune system.

Daily Dosage:
Dried Root: 0.5 to 1 gm
Fresh Root: 1 to2 teaspoons

Dong Quai (Angelica sinensis)

Dong Quai is considered by the Chinese to be a wonderful herb for female disorders. It may help maintain a proper balance of female hormones and regulate monthly cycles. It is also said to calm the nerves and aid in Vitamin E deficiency. An excellent herb for female bodybuilders as it has an estrogenic component. It can also be used as a diuretic.

Daily Dosage:
Dried Root: 2 to 4 gm
Fresh Root: 1 to 3 tablespoon

Echinacea

Native Americans used this plant for snakebites and other skin wounds. It was also used to treat strep throat and is popular in Europe for its positive effect on the immune system.
Daily Dosage:
Dried Root: 3 gm
Fresh Root: 1 to 2 tablespoons

Ephedra (Ephedra sinica)

Known as Ma Huang in China, this herb has a history of over four thousand years as a treatment for asthma and respiratory infections. It contains two alkaloids, ephedrine and pseudoephedrine which are used in many cold and allergy medicines. American ephedra is known as Morman Tea, Squaw Tea, and Desert Tea, and shares the same properties, though, to a lesser degree.
Daily Dosage:
Dried Herb: 3 to 6 gm
Fresh Herb: 2 to 4 tablespoons

Eyebright (Euphasia officinalis)

Eyebright has been used since the middle ages as a tonic and as an astringent. It is said to be especially useful for weak eyesight, eye inflammations and other eye ailments, and to bring relief to sore, runny eyes due to allergies or colds. Eyebright is also used to treat hay fever as it shrinks swollen sinuses. Bodybuilders can use this herb as a digestive and circulatory aid.
Daily Dosage:
Dried Plant: 6 to 12 gm
Fresh Plant: 1/4 to 1/2 cup

Fennel Seed (Foeniculum vulagare)

For centuries, this herb has been used to promote appetite and relieve gas. Used externally, the oil is a folk remedy for inflammation, rheumatism, and arthritis. Calming for coughs and colds, it will also increase lactation in nursing mothers. An excellent choice for female bodybuilders who are looking for a digestive aid or a diuretic.
Daily Dosage:
Dried Seed: 1 to 3 gm
Fresh Seed: 2 to 6 teaspoons

Fenugreek (Trigonella foenum-gracum)

One of the oldest known medical plants, Fenugreek was used by Hippocrates "The father of medicine", for sore throats and colds. It is also reputed to be an aphrodisiac, and to be useful for allergies, coughs, digestion, headaches and ulcers. Bodybuilders may be interested in this herb because it can be used as an oral hypoglycemic agent as it lowers blood glucose.
Daily Dosage:
Dried Seed: 6 to 12 gm
Fresh Seed: 1/4 to 1/2 cup

Garlic (Allium sativum)

Ancient Egyptians considered garlic the wonder drug of the herbal world, using it for everything from treating ear infections to tuberculosis. It is said to help prevent heart disease and cancer. Albert Schweitzer used garlic to treat cholera, typhus and dysentery. Garlic is also said to be good for indigestion. Garlic is claimed to be able to do the following:

> Strengthen your immune system
> Lower cholesterol levels
> Protect cells from toxins and aging
> Improve entire cardiovascular system
> Fight viral, fungal and bacterial infections

Daily Dosage:
Dried bulb: 6 to 12 gm
Fresh bulb: 1/4 to 1/2 cup

Ginger Root (Zingiber officinale)

Ginger is a time-proven remedy for cramps, indigestion and upset stomach. It has also been used for stimulating the circulatory system, easing cold symptoms and sore throats, and helping to cleanse the kidneys and bowels. Ginger is also effective for motion sickness and morning sickness. It is an anti-inflammatory and an analgesic.

Daily Dosage:
Dried Root: 2 to 4 gm
Fresh Root: 2 to 4 tablespoon

Ginkgo (Gingko biloba)

For five thousand years, Chinese herbalists have used this herb to treat coughs, asthma, and allergies. Today, Ginkgo is widely prescribed in Europe for improving circulation, improving mental functioning and for slowing aging and preventing cancer. This herb increases blood flow to the brain and improves peripheral blood circulation. When used in combination with the caffeine/ephedra/aspirin stack, has a powerful stimulant effect.

Daily Dosage:
Dried Leaf: 2 to 3 gm
Fresh Leaf: 1 to 2 tablespoons

Ginseng (Panax ginseng)

Ginseng is considered by many to be the King of Herbs, and is used in China as a cure-all. It is used to increase physical and mental endurance, increase energy, normalize body functions, reduce cholesterol, and prevent cancer. Traditionally, it has been used to enhance sexual desire. It supports the natural balance of your body to combat fatigue and strengthen and protect your nervous system. For bodybuilders its reputation for boosting energy, strength and endurance and promotion of sex hormone production should be reason enough to use this herb.

Daily Dosage:
Dried Root: 1 to 2 gm
Fresh Root: 1 tablespoon

Golden Seal Root (Hydrastis canadensis)

Discovered by Australian aborigines, it has traditionally been used as a natural antibiotic for the treatment of colds and flus, as well as congestion. Used externally, it is considered an excellent antiseptic. It will stimulate mucous membrane secretions and is helpful in gastritis, ulcers and allergies.

Daily Dosage:
Dried Root: 1.5 to 3 gm
Fresh Root: 1 to 2 tablespoons

Gotu Kola (Centella asiatica)

Known as the "memory" herb, Gotu Kola stimulates the circulatory system and is considered a nerve tonic. Bodybuilders can use it as a diuretic.

Daily Dosage:
Dried leaf: 6 gm
Fresh leaf: 1/4 cup

Hawthorne Berries (Crataegus oxycantha)

Hawthorne has long been used for insomnia and digestive problems, and in the late 1800s, European healers discovered its benefits to the heart. It is useful in regulating blood pressure and strengthening and regulating the heart. It can also be used as a diuretic.

Daily Dosage:
Dried Berries: 1 to 3 gm
Fresh Berries: 2 to 6 teaspoons

Hops Flowers (Humulus lupulus)

Hops has traditionally been valuable in treating insomnia. It has a calming effect on the body and is used to relieve cramps and gas. It can be used as a diuretic.

Daily Dosage:
Dried Flowers: 1 to 3 gm
Fresh Flowers: 2 to 6 teaspoons

Hydrangea Root (Hydrangea arborescens)

Hydrangea's greatest use is in the treatment of inflamed or enlarged prostate glands. It may also be used for bladder problems and urinary tract infections. It aids the kidneys, particularly when combined with parsley and bearberry and is considered an excellent herb for rheumatism. It can be used as a diuretic.

Daily Dosage:
Dried Root: 1.5 gm
Fresh Root: 1 tablespoon

Juniper Berries (Juniperus communis)

For centuries, Juniper Berries have been a folk remedy for urinary tract problems and gallstones. It can be used as a diuretic.

Daily Dosage:
Dried Berries: 0.5 to 1 gm
Fresh Berries: 1 teaspoon

Kelp (Fucus vesiculosis)

Due to its iodine building ability in the thyroid gland, Kelp is considered to be a radiation antagonist. Iodine is known to help the body fight infection. Kelp is also an excellent source of calcium, magnesium and potassium, and other trace minerals. It is a valuable digestive aid.

Daily Dosage:
Dried Seed: 2 to 4 teaspoons, 1 to 3 gm
Fresh Seed: 2 to 6 teaspoons

Lobelia

This herb is a powerful relaxing agent, as well as being beneficial for allergies, coughs, colds and headaches. It has a powerful effect on numerous other ailments and is considered one of the most valuable herbs due to the holistic combination of stimulation and relaxation.

Ma Huang – aka – Ephedra

Family: Ephedraceae; other members include broom and horsetail
Genus and Species: Ephedra sinica, E. vulgaris, E. nevadensis, E. antisyphilitica,
and other species
Also known as: Ephedra, Mormon tea, whorehouse tea.
Parts Used: Stems, branches
Ma Huang is a powerful bronchial decongestant, and is known as one of the world's oldest medicines. Pseudoephedrine is the herb's laboratory analog which has been used in modern over-the-counter products since the 1920s.

Ma Huang and Mormon Tea

The use of ma huang has loosely been traced to around 3000 BC where Chinese physicians began prescribing ephedra tea for colds, asthma, and hay fever. This Chinese variety is known as ma huang.

When the Mormons arrived in Utah in 1847, the native Indians introduced them to the native American variety of ephedra, a piney-tasting tonic beverage. The Mormons used it as a substitute for coffee and tea, and therefore the name arose – Mormon Tea. Herbalists recommend ephedra today, as it has been for centuries, to treat asthma, hay fever, and the nasal and chest congestion of colds and flu.

Healing With Ephedra

Ephedra's active ingredients (ephedrine, pseudoephedrine, and norpseudoephedrine) are strong central nervous system stimulants, but less potent than amphetamine. Ephedrine opens the bronchial passages, stimulates the heart, and increases blood pressure, metabolic rate, and perspiration and urine production. It reduces the secretion of both saliva and stomach acids. Chinese ephedra (ma huang) contains significant amounts of ephedrine, while the American species is richer in norpseudoephedrine.

Be very careful when you buy these products – Mormon Tea is not ma huang and there have been problems reported from the use of ma huang due the high concentration of ephedrine.

As A Decongestant

From the late 1920s through the 1940s, ephedrine was used in various products as a decongestant and broncodilator. Ephedrine was generally effective and safe, but it was also known to produce potentially damaging side effects – i.e. increased blood pressure, and heart palpitations. It was replaced with a chemical substitute – pseudoephedrine which scientists considered equally effective but with reduced side effects. This is the active ingredient in many over-the-counter products – like Sudafed.

Weight Loss

As a central nervous system stimulant, the ephedrine in ma huang increases basal metabolic rate (BMR), meaning it spurs the body to burn calories faster the performance of ma huang. When ma huang is taken with caffeine, they cause insomnia, nervousness, irritability, and "speediness." The weight loss effects of ma huang may not be permanent. Real weight loss is a combination of reduced caloric intake, high fiber intake, and aerobic exercise.

Smoking Cessation

One study shows ephedrine helps smokers quit by decreasing cigarette cravings. You might want to try this.

Women's Health

Ephedrine causes uterine contractions. Pregnant women should absolutely not use it.

Rx for Ephedra

Use a decoction or tincture to take advantage of ephedra's potent healing benefits as a decongestant or weight-loss aid, to help quit smoking, or to initiate menstruation.

For a decoction, mix 1 teaspoon of dried ma huang per cup of water, bring to a boil, and then simmer for 10 to 15 minutes. Drink up to 2 cups a day.

In a tincture, take 1/4 to 1 teaspoon up to three times a day. If you are using a commercial preparation, follow the package directions. Ephedra should not be given to children under age 2. For older children and adults under 65 begin with a low-strength preparation and increase strength if necessary.

The Safety Factor

Mainstream medical researchers insist pseudoephedrine, the related chemical used in commercial cold preparations, is safer than ephedrine. Herbalists will agree with that, but they insist that the whole ephedra plant is safer than either ephedrine or pseudoephedrine. In *Herbal Medicine for Everyone*, British herbalist Michael McIntyre writes that pure ephedrine "markedly raises blood pressure....but the whole (ephedra) plant actually reduces blood pressure." German medical herbalist Rudolph Fritz Weiss, M.D., maintains that the whole plant " has certain advantages (over pseudoephedrine). Above all, it is better tolerated, causing fewer heart symptoms such as palpitations."

The ephedra/pseudoephedrine issue remains unresolved. Anyone who has high blood pressure should consult his physician before using this herb. Also, he should invest in a home blood pressure device to self-monitor his condition. If you have one, you can check ephedra's effects. If the herb lowers your blood pressure, your physician will probably give you the go-ahead to use it. If it raises your blood pressure, don't use it. Anyone with heart disease, diabetes, glaucoma, or an overactive thyroid gland (hyperthyroidism) should exercise caution and not use ephedra.

Ephedra often causes insomnia. People with sleep problems should not take it late in the day. Finally, ephedra causes dry mouth. Increase, your nonalcoholic fluid intake when you use it.

The Food and Drug Administration considers ephedra an herb of "undefined safety." For otherwise healthy nonpregnant, nonnursing adults who do not have high blood pressure, heart disease, glaucoma, or overactive thyroid, and who are not taking other medications that raise blood pressure or cause anxiety or insomnia, ephedra is considered relatively safe when used cautiously for short periods of time.

Ephedra should be used in medicinal amounts only in consultation with your doctor. If ephedra causes insomnia, nervousness, or stomach upset, use less or stop using it. Let your doctor know if you experience any unpleasant effects or if the symptoms for which the herb is being used do not improve significantly in two weeks.

Marshmallow Root

Charlemagne ordered this herb planted throughout his kingdom to ensure a plentiful supply. It is an old-time remedy for gastrointestinal disorders, and is recommended for raw throats and chests, due to coughs and bronchitis.

Milk Thistle

Milk Thistle is extremely popular in Europe, being used as a tonic for the liver. Numerous studies show this herb enhances liver function and stimulates production of new cells. It is also said to work as a protectant from chemicals, thus preventing damage from free radicals. This herb contains a flavonoid called silymarin, which has a powerful effect on liver cells and may offer many other health benefits. Research documents that milk thistle can help support liver healing, protect the liver from toxins, combat hardening of the liver, and improve skin problems related to poor liver function.

Muira Puama

Often used as a steroid replacer, Muira Puama is also highly regarded by Brazilians as a stimulant and stomach tonic. It is used to treat rheumatism and is reputed to be an aphrodisiac.

Mulein Leaf

This herb is an old time remedy for bronchitis and coughs. A good expectorant, it is high in iron, potassium and magnesium. It may strengthen the sinuses and has been used successfully to treat swollen joints. The oil is used for earaches, and as a pain reliever and antibacterial.

Myrrh Gum

Used since biblical times, the resin of the Myrrh plant has been used as a mouthwash for sores in the mouth and throat. It cleans the colon and aids the digestive system. It is often called an herbal breath freshener and may help with sinus problems.

Nettle

Rich in iron and vitamin C, Nettles can help prevent anemia. It is a well-known folk remedy said to be good for fevers and colds, hayfever and allergies. Traditionally, it has also been used to lower blood sugar, and is an excellent supplement due to its high content of calcium and chlorophyll.

Oatstraw for fiber

This herb is used in external preparations in baths, for hemorrhoids, and for foot baths. May also bring relief to irritating skin conditions. Very good for children. It is strengthening and nourishing to the nervous system.

Oregon Grape Root

Historically, this herb has been used to cleanse the blood by removing toxins. It may also be very useful in treating rheumatism and arthritis, chronic liver problems, and is beneficial for skin conditions such as herpes, acne and eczema.

Osha

Western American Indians originally used this herb for colds, flus and respiratory infections. Osha is also said to aid the immune system and help the body fight infection. It is useful for sore throats, smoking and helps to relieve dry membranes.

Papaya Leaf

Papaya contains a digestive enzyme called papain that helps digest protein. Considered a safe and natural digestive aid, if you suffer from heartburn, try this herb for relief without the side effects of antacid tablets. Also good for constipation.

Passion Flower

This herb is one of nature's best tranquilizers, used to relieve muscle tension and anxiety. Passion flower is a safe natural alternative to promote a restful sleep and is recommended by herbalists for times of emotional upset. It has also been used for asthma and seizures.

Pau D'Arco

The bark of this Brazilian tree has many historical health benefits, including a remedy for Candida, athlete's foot, and other fungal infections. It is reputed to be effective in nutritionally supporting the body's fight against some forms of cancer, and to be good for the digestion. This herb is also used to support red blood cell count. Great herb that can help provide natural antibiotic, antiviral and antifungal benefits and inhibit yeast infections.

Peach Leaf

The leaves of this tree provide soothing relief for the digestive tract in conditions such as gastritis. Traditionally used in relieving coughs and bronchitis. It is also excellent for bladder and uterine problems.

Peppermint Leaf

This wonderful mint is one of the oldest known home remedies for indigestion. It relaxes the stomach muscles, relieves gas, and is also good for nausea and vomiting. A delicious tea, it is also used to treat headaches. Peppermint has the ability to normalize the entire system.

Psyllium Husk

For decades, herbalists have known that Psyllium is one of the highest sources of dietary fiber. One of the best colon cleansers, it swells 30 to 50 times its original size to bind to and to remove toxins from the intestines. It has been used to treat ulcers, colitis and constipation, and help clear away excess cholesterol.

Red Clover

This wonderful herb has long been considered one of the very best blood purifiers. It contains small amounts of silica, choline, calcium and lecithin, which promote normal body function. A muscle relaxant and expectorant, red clover is also combined with other herbs to fight cancers and tumors.

Rosehips

Rosehips provide one of the best natural sources of vitamin C, which is considered an infection fighter. Rosehips will help against the development of colds and makes an excellent tonic for exhaustion. Herbalists also use them for constipation and problems of the kidneys and bladder.

Safflower

The flowers of this plant are used as a laxative for adults and also have many uses in treating children's ailments, including measles, fevers and skin complaints. It is also used as a digestive aid, and can help relieve arthritis, rheumatism and gout. Safflower is widely used in China for coronary disease and menstrual disturbances.

Sage

Sage is a classic remedy for inflammation of the mouth, throat and tonsils, its volatile oils being very soothing to the mucous membranes. It is also used to increase circulation and is considered an excellent remedy for poor digestion and stomach problems.

Sarsaparilla Root

Brought to Europe from the New World by the Spanish in the 1600s, this herb is known as a tonic for male sexual potency. Herbalists say its steroid-like compounds actually contain testosterone. It is also used as an anti-inflammatory for arthritis and as a treatment for urinary tract disorders. Native Americans used this herb as a rejuvenating tonic.

Sassafras

Primarily used in skin problems such as eczema, Sassafras may also be used to treat rheumatism and gout. It is a blood purifier, which, in part, explains its effectiveness on the skin. May also be beneficial to the liver, which it stimulates to help expel toxins.

Saw Palmetto

This herb is used to tone and strengthen the prostate gland. Its fatty acids and sterols have been clinically tested and can safely enhance the health and healing of the prostate. It is also used to treat coughs from colds, as well as asthma and bronchitis. May be beneficial for both sexes to balance the hormones. Studies show saw palmetto can alleviate prostate enlargement, support prostate healing and repair, aid in eliminating the buildup of harmful hormones in both males and females, and relieve urinary discomfort.

Senna Leaf

Senna is a powerful laxative, and is most effective when combined with herbs such as cardamom, ginger or fennel. These aromatic herbs seem to increase regularity and reduce the chance of bowel cramps, due to their strong action.

Slippery Elm

One of nature's best herbs, slippery elm is used for numerous ailments including sore, scratchy throats, mouth irritation and constipation. It aids digestion and helps cleanse the colon. It is a remedy for kidney and lung problems. Some herbalists use it to relieve the pain of ulcers.

Suma

First discovered by Brazilian indian tribes, this herb is called the South American Ginseng. Named "para todo", meaning "for all things", it is used as an overall tonic and may relieve chronic fatigue syndrome. It is also said to relieve the symptoms of menopause and to treat exhaustion from viral infections.

Thyme

During the middle ages, thyme was thought to increase courage, and was given to knights as they went into battle. Today, in addition to its culinary uses, Thyme is used as an expectorant and a disinfectant, and is also known for its antifungal properties. It may bring relief to migraine headaches and help clear the lungs and respiratory system.

Uva Ursi

Also known as bearberry, uva ursi is one of the best remedies for kidney and bladder infections. It's use as a folk remedy has been confirmed by modern research showing its effectiveness in treating urinary tract infections. It is also as excellent diuretic and digestive stimulant

Valerian

For centuries, valerian has been used to treat nervous tension and panic attacks. A wonderful herb, valerian is said to be calming and quieting to the nervous system, and may help relieve insomnia and improve circulation. It ranks among the ten most widely used herbs in world, and if you have trouble falling or staying asleep, this is an excellent alternative to sleep aids. It also eases muscle tension and pain. Women find it soothing during their monthly cycle, relieving menstrual and intestinal cramps. It is also recommended for promoting balance in times of high stress.

White Deadnettle

Has been known to reduce enlarged, benign prostate glands. Has an astringent and soothing action on the reproductive system, acts as a uterine tonic; good to use after prostate surgery.
Use as a simple or with cornsilk, hydrangea, or couchgrass as a healing diuretic and to enhance the action on the prostate.

White Oak

A powerful astringent herb, white oak bark is used for hemorrhoids and to remove kidney and gall stones. It is useful for gum infections and sore throats. It is high in bioflavonoids, and is used to strengthen the capillaries, to aid in treating varicose veins and chronic nosebleeds, gingivitis and loose teeth.

White Willow

This is another herb that was prescribed by Hippocrates to treat pain and fever. A natural form of salicin, white willow is useful for stomach troubles and heartburn, but particularly used for headaches, arthritis, and the reduction of inflamed joints. It may also be used for hayfever and is useful for bladder infections.

Wild Yam

Botanical Name: Dioscorea villosa.
Common Names: Colic Root, China root, yuma, devil's bones.
Medicinal Properties: Antispasmodic, antibilious, diaphoretic, hepatic.
Known to be very relaxing and soothing to the nerves. Useful in all cases of nervous excitement. Will expel gas from the stomach and bowels. Good in cholera. Useful in neuralgia of any part. Excellent for pains in the urinary tract. One of the best herbs for general pain during pregnancy. Take during the whole period of pregnancy. Will allay nausea in small frequent doses. Excellent for cramps during the latter part of pregnancy.

Combined with ginger will greatly help to prevent miscarriage. Use a teaspoonful of wild yam, one-fourth teaspoon ginger. Also good to combine with squaw vine for use during pregnancy. Valuable in affections of the liver, spasms, and rheumatic pains. Steep a heaping teaspoonful in a cup of boiling water thirty minutes. Drink cold one to three cupfuls a day, a large swallow at a time. Children less according to age.

Wood Betony

Betony is often used to treat stomach ailments such as heartburn, indigestion, and stomach cramps. It cleanses the blood of toxins, thus greatly benefiting the liver and spleen. It is also widely used to treat headaches.

Yellow Dock

A wonderful blood purifier which will be of use in most skin problems. High in digestible iron, it helps tone the entire system. It is useful in ulcers, constipation, rheumatism, and in addition, is used to build strength and endurance.

Yerba Mansa (Matte)

Yerba mansa is considered by folk healers to have many properties similar to goldenseal. Thus, it is used to treat colds and fevers, arthritis and allergies. Considered by many to be an effective herbal antibiotic, it is also used for bleeding gums and herpes simplex.

Yerba Santa

American Indians were known to chew or smoke the leaves of this herb to treat asthma, bronchial problems, and hayfever. Modern herbalists still use it for all chest conditions. It is also reputed to be good for rheumatism and arthritis.

Yucca Root

This herb has been used for hundreds of years by the Southwestern Indians for pain and inflammation caused by arthritis and rheumatism. It is also said to reduce joint inflammation, and has been used with success for allergies and to strengthen the immune system.

Chapter 23 – *Hardcore Supplements*

SOURCES

1) Pedersen, M., : Nutritional Herbology, Wendell W. Whitman Company,
2) *The Healing Herbs,* by Michael Castleman.

REFERENCES

1) Vandenberghe, K., et al., Long-Term Creatine Intake is Beneficial to Muscle Performance During Resistance Training. *Journal of Applied Physiology*, 83 2055-2063, 1997.
2) Jacobs, I., et al., Creatine Ingestion Increases Anaerobic Capacity and Maximum Accumulated Oxygen Deficit. *Canadian Journal of Applied Physiology*, 22 (3), 231-243, 1997.
3) Kreider, R., et al., Effects of Creatine supplementation on body composition, strength and sprint performance. *Medical Science in Sports*
4) Whey Protein, *www.greaterpower.com*
5) Batterman, W., Whey protein for athletes, *Dtsh Milchwirtsch*, 37 (33), 1010-1012, 1986.
6) Newsholm, EA., Biochemical mechanisms to explain immunosupression in well-trained and overtrained athletes. *International Journal of Sports Medicine*, 15 (3) s142-s147, 1994.
7) Padgett, D.A., Loria, R.M., In vitro potentiation of lymphocyte activation by dehydroepiandrosterone, androstenediol, and androstenetriol. *Journal of Immunology*, 153 (4) 1544-1552, 1994.
8) Blaquier, J., et al., The amount of testosterone formed upon incubation in human blood., acta, *Endocrinology*, 55, 697-704.
9) Batcheldor, B., and Wright, J., New-age ergogens, *Flex Magazine*, Dec 1998, 227-231.
10) Sahelian, R, Lipoic Acid: The Unique Antioxidant, *www.raysahelian.com*
11) Alpha Lipoic Acid Information, *www.nutrimart.com*
12) Packer. L., Alpha Lipoic Acid Review, *Free Radical Biology and Medicine*, 19, 227-250, 1995
13) Mogher, K., et al., Lipoic Acid reduces glycemia and increases muscle Glut4 content in streptozotocin-diabetic rates. *Metabolism*, 46 (7) 763-768, 1997.
14) Study Confirms That Chromium Picolinate Aids In Body Fat Loss, *www.pslgroup.com*
15) Brichard, S.M., et al, Marked Improvement of Glucose Homeostasis in Diabetic Mice given Oral Vanadate. *Diabetes*, 39, (11), 1990.
16) Brichard, S.M., et al., Long-term improvement of glucose homeostasis by vanadate treatment in diabetic rats, *Endocrinology*, 123 (4), 1988.
17) Momordica charantia – Bitter melon: A fact sheet from Seattle Treatment Education Project, *www.thebody.com*
18) Pushpa, K., Gourdin: A wonderful effective way to reduce blood sugar level, *www.wwindia.com*
19) Edwards, DJ, et al, Identification of 6"7"-dihydroxybergamottin, a cytochrome P450 inhibitor, in grapefruit juice. *Drug Metab Dispos*, 24 (12), 1287-90, 1996.
20) Grapefruit Enhances Medications, *www.people.virginia.edu*
21) The Grapefruit Juice Effect, *www.pharminfo.com*
22) Ameer. B, Weintraub, RA, Drug Interactions with Grapefruit Juice, *Clinical Pharmokinetics*, 33 (2) 103-21, 1997.
23) Mechanism of interaction for GJDIs, *www.powernetdesign.com*.
24) Chan, WK, et al, Mechanism-based inactivation of human cytochrome P450 3A4 by grapefruit juice and red wine. *Life Science* 62 (10) PL 135-42, 1998.
25) Bailey. DG, et al, Grapefruit juice-drug interactions, *British Journal of Clinical Pharmacology*, 46 (2), 101-10, 1998.
26) Khajuria, A, et al., Permeability characteristics of piperine on oral absorption-an active alkaloid from peppers and a bioavailability enhancer., *Indian Journal of Experimental Biology*, 36 (1) 46-50, 1998.
27) Allamech, A, et al., Piperine, a plant alkaloid of the piper species, enhances the bioavailability of aflatoxin B1 in rat tissues., *Cancer Letters*, 61(3) 195-9, 1992.
28) Piperine, The Cochran Foundation of Medical Research, *www.cochranfoundation.com*

**Jason Arntz and
Amy Fadhli**

CHAPTER TWENTY-FOUR

Cardio – The Key To Total Muscularity

For some it's a passion, for others it's the lowest form of contempt. What we are referring to of course is cardiovascular training or "cardio." Besides the increased mass of today's bodybuilders, the other area of great improvement is body fat percentage. The eight to ten percent of thirty years ago has given way to bodybuilders sporting physique's with their body fat level down in the two to four percent range. It's even conceivable that Amet Zutula and the late Andreas Munzer, approached one percent in peak condition. We will be the first to admit that "cutting" drugs and a closer attention to diet has accounted for much of the increased vascularity, but a third variable has also taken on new importance in recent years, that being aerobics or cardio.

Lee Apperson

> **"You must train strenuously and force your body to use stored bodyfat for energy. This means both training with weights and aerobics. Your energy output must be greater than your energy intake."**
>
> – Robert Kennedy, *MuscleMag International* publisher and editor commenting on pre-contest training.

THE CARDIOVASCULAR SYSTEM

The center to the human cardiovascular system is the heart, a four chambered organ located just slightly to the left of the center chest cavity. If you want a guide as to your heart's size, simply make a fist. This relatively small structure will beat an average of 2.5 million times during its lifetime, and pump 225 to 230 million liters of blood.

Milos Sarcev

The heart is really a double pump in that the right side pumps deoxygenated blood to the longs, while the left side pumps oxygenated blood to the entire body.

If the heart is analogous to a water pumping station, the blood vessels are the water ducts. The body has three primary types of blood vessels. Arteries are named as such because they carry oxygenated blood to the various body tissues. Arteries appear red in color because of the high amounts of oxygen-binding hemoglobin pigment contained in red blood cells. Because they are subjected to the heart's pumping pressure, arteries have thicker, more elastic walls than veins.

Once the oxygen rich blood reaches the body tissues it doesn't pass straight into cells but passes through a progressively smaller set of blood vessels called capillaries. From the capillaries the oxygen passes into the cells were it is used in cellular respiration. Waste products are then dumped into an opposite set of capillaries, which then lead to the large blood vessels called veins that lead back to the heart.

Veins are the arteries' opposite number and appear blue in color because of the lower level of oxygen bound to hemoglobin. Veins are not subject to the same pressure as arteries and as such their walls are thinner and less flexible. The blood returning to the heart, called venous return, moves much slower than the blood being pumped away from the heart, and in extreme cases may pool in the lower extremities leading to fainting. Besides moving the body, the contracting thighs and calves act as pumps to push the blood back to the heart. Sentries and soldiers who stand still for extended periods of time are at special risk for fainting. Incidentally fainting is the body's way of getting the upper body down to the level of the lower body!

CARDIOVASCULAR FITNESS

The two most important variables associated with cardiovascular fitness are intensity and duration. Intensity refers to the level at which the heart and lungs are operating, while duration is the length of time the body is subjected to the particular cardio exercise. The two variables are interrelated as high intensity necessitates a shorter duration, while lower intensities can be maintained for longer durations.

Cardiovascular training has numerous benefits to health. Bodybuilders focus primarily on fat loss as it's the most visible benefit while on stage. The lower the bodyfat level the greater the degree of muscle definition and vascularity. A secondary benefit to having low bodyfat is that it greatly reduces the odds of cardiovascular disease – the number one killer in North America. Long before fat begins accumulating on the outside of the body it has started to build up around the heart, other organs, and blood vessels. So while your innards won't make any difference to short term bodybuilding success, they play a major role in determining if you will be around to compete in any masters events.

"I admit that going to the gym and sweating for half an hour on the boring treadmill or bicycle is not the greatest. I don't blame you. What you have to do is make aerobics fun. There is no reason why you shouldn't be enjoying the activity."

– Frank Sepe, *MuscleMag* columnist and top model responding to a readers question about how boring cardio training can become for many die-hard bodybuilders.

Frank Sepe

A second benefit to cardio training concerns blood volume. Regular cardio exercise can increase blood volume by as much as a liter in an adult male. More blood means more oxygen-carrying red blood cells, which in turn allows for longer, more intense workouts, both weight training and cardio.

Another benefit to cardio training is that it increases the number of blood vessels. This is in response to the increase in blood volume. From a training point of view it means more oxygen to the muscles, but from a bodybuilding point of view it increases what bodybuilders refer to as "vascularity." To the average person it looks "gross," but to bodybuilders extra veins only add to that freaky defined look.

If weight training is the primary stimulation for skeletal muscle growth, cardio is the primary heart "builder." The heart is composed of muscle tissue remember, and the individual muscle fibers will strengthen and grow slightly in response to regular exercise. The result is a stronger organ capable of pushing more blood throughout the body.

"Contrary to what most may believe, doing aerobics - within reason – does not cannibalize lean muscle mass. What I have observed is an increased recovery from weight workouts and an increased vascularity throughout my physique, more than what would be expected from a decrease in bodyfat."

– Edward K. Wietholder, *MuscleMag* contributor assuring bodybuilders that moderate cardio is not only not counterproductive, but is in fact essential.

With all the attention focused on the heart's role in oxygen transport, it's often forgotten that the heart also plays an equally important role in waste transport. As the body's cells carry out cellular respiration they give off carbon dioxide and other metabolic products as waste. The body is extremely sensitive to such wastes so it tries to get rid of them as quickly as possible. A cardiovascular system running at peak efficiency is capable of faster waste removal than a system that borders on sluggishness.

A final benefit to cardio exercise is believe it or not, relaxation. Most individuals who engage in regular cardio exercise report that they sleep better at nights, and can deal with stress more efficiently.

Hopefully by now we've convinced you that cardio is not just for wimps. It has a legitimate role in bodybuilding and long-term health. So let's get to it!

CARDIO TRAINING

Although no perfect system has been devised to determine the best level to exercise at, a number of guidelines do exist.

Exercise physiologists use the term "target heart rate" to predict the best level to exercise at. A person's theoretical maximum heart rate is 220 minus his or her age. For example a 40-year old would have a theoretical maximum heart rate of 180 (220-40 = 180). Likewise a 20-year old's would be 200 (220-20 = 200). Now it is possible for individuals to reach their theoretical maximum heart rate, but they would only be able to maintain this level for a very short period of time – a couple of minutes at the most. Physiologists have devised a range of upper and lower heart rates that provide adequate cardio stimulation without overstressing the heart. It's called the target heart rate zone and can be easily calculated by taking 60 percent and 90 percent of the individual's maximum theoretical heart rate. In our two previous examples the values would be:

Mike Francois

40 year old
60 percent x 180 = 108 for lower
90 percent x 180 = 162 for upper

For a forty-year-old the training zone would be between 108 and 162 beats per minute. Anything much below 108 would not be stimulating the heart that effectively, while above 162 could place too much stress on the individual's heart.

20 year old
60 percent x 200 = 120 for lower
90 percent x 200 = 180 for upper

For a twenty-year-old the range is 120 to 180.

No doubt many readers are wondering how they measure their heart rate or pulse. Most modern cardio machines these days have heart sensors built into the handles. Others have an attached strap that you place around your wrist (if not you can buy one at most better athletic stores). If all else fails use the old stand-bye of placing one of your fingers on the wrist, about a half-inch back from the base of the thumb. Simply count the number of beats in a ten-second period and multiply by six. For example if you count 26 beats in a ten second period your heart rate would be 26 x 6 = 156.

Most newer cardio machines have target heart rate zone charts attached to them so you don't have to manually calculate your target zone. In fact most machines nowadays require you to input your age at the beginning as part of the initially programming sequence. The machine then takes care of the calculating for you. Finally if you work out at a large fitness facility that has a running or aerobics area, odds are there will be a large target heart rate zone chart on the wall somewhere.

THE CASE FOR AND AGAINST TWO ZONES

In the late eighties and early nineties the concept of having two training zones became popular. It was found that a lower intensity zone in the 65 to 75 percent of theoretical maximum was best for fat burning, while the higher 75 to 90 percent was best for cardio stimulation. This is true to an extent but here's the problem. While the lower level burns more fat calories, the higher level burns more calories total. And even though the higher level burns less fat calories as a percentage, it burns more fat calories over all. In addition the higher level does a better job of stimulating the cardiovascular system.

Another benefit of staying in the higher zone is that it contributes more to what exercise physiologists call "afterburn." As soon as you start exercising there's more than just an elevation in heart and respiration rate. The whole metabolic process speeds up as well. And what's nice from a fat burning point of view is that it doesn't stop as soon as you cease exercising. It continues for many hours afterwards. The research shows that high intensity exercise (75 to 90 percent of theoretical maximum heart rate) maintains this elevation or "afterburn" for a longer period of time than the lower intensity (60 to 75 percent) zone.[1] We should add that weight training produces the longest afterburn. This is why the smartest personal trainers these days encourage their overweight clients to "hit the weights." Both the activity of weight lifting and the stronger better conditioned muscles produced, elevate the body's metabolism thus contributing greatly to the fat loss process.

WHEN, HOW MUCH, HOW OFTEN?

Now that we've got the nitty gritty out of the way it's time to look at the basic concepts.

The first issue concerns the best time to do your cardio. And you may be happy to hear that it doesn't matter. You can do your cardio first thing in the morning or the last thing at night. You can do it on the same days as your weight training or on opposite days. We will add that most individuals perform their cardio right before their strength training. Besides working the cardio system, it helps warm the body up for the strength training workout.

A couple of people have suggested that by doing cardio the first thing in the morning, before breakfast, the body will burn more fat as a fuel source. Now there is limited evidence to support this, but it's not conclusive. The advantage to early morning training is so slight that it's not really a consideration.

Although there's much flexibility in terms of when to do cardio, the same cannot be said for duration and frequency. Time after time research has found that in order to adequately stimulate the cardiovascular system and promote fat loss, the heart rate must be kept elevated for a minimum of 25 to 30 minutes. Notice we said minimum as most bodybuilders average 45 to 60 minutes per cardio session. In terms of frequency the accepted minimum is three times per week. Once again most pre-contest bodybuilders increase this to four to six.

TYPES OF CARDIO TRAINING

Cardio training can be subdivided into three broad categories; outdoor activities, organized aerobic classes, and cardio machines. Let's look at all three in detail.

ANYTIME ANYWHERE

Outdoor physical activity, has been a part of human society since earliest times. Whether it was for fun (the ancient Greeks and the first Olympic games), for survival (running down a wild animal for food), or during war (try swinging a fifty pound club or throwing a heavy spear if you don't believe us), it still amounted to physical activity in the form of muscle contraction and an elevated heart rate. While hunting animals with spears, and engaging your enemies with clubs, tends to be considered old-fashioned these days, the use of sports for physical activity is an integral part of most societies. In fact you don't need to become involved with organized sports to obtain your cardio exercise. Go for a run, swim, bike ride, etc. Outdoor activities are both relatively cheap, and not counting those in large cities, provide you with fresh air while you do it. You don't need fancy, hi-tech equipment to stimulate the heart and lungs.

ONE AND A TWO AND A THREE....

For those who either hate outdoor activities, or live in climates that don't always cooperate, most large fitness facilities offer organized cardio classes. They go by many different names: cardio- pump, body-shaping, spinning, step-to-health, etc. The common denominator to all is a highly motivated instructor who will put you and twenty or thirty others through your paces for 45 to 60 minutes. Cardio classes are great for those who lack the motivation to push themselves when the sweat starts rolling and lactic acid starts building. Of course as a future competitive bodybuilder, we doubt that motivation is a problem for you. Further, most bodybuilders tend to prefer doing things on their own. Spending endless hours in the gym training essentially training on one's own and then all of a sudden jumping into a class of fifty jumping and cavorting individuals just doesn't appeal to most aspiring Ronnie Coleman's. This is why most bodybuilders opt for the third category – the stationary cardio machine

EVERY WHICH WAY YOU CAN

In a manner of speaking cardio training has mirrored weight training in terms of the equipment available. The modern bodybuilder has at his or her disposal an almost endless variety of cardio machines that bear little resemblance to the old stationary bikes of twenty or thirty years ago. You can run, skate, step, or row the extra fat off now days. Further, most of the new machines can be programmed to optimize your time. No more haphazard guessing as to the best target heart rate, intensity, tension, etc. The machine takes care of everything, you simply go for the ride (or step, or row, or skate, or...). The following is a brief

André and Rune Nielson

introduction to the cardio equipment found in most modern gyms. It is by no means complete as every month sees something new come on the scene. For convenience we have divided the machines into categories. Keep in mind there may be twenty different models of a particular rowing or stepping machine.

STATIONARY CYCLES OR BIKES

Stationary bikes were probably the first mass-market indoor cardio "machines." We use the term machine lightly as the first bikes were nothing more than a simplified outdoor bike that had the wheels elevated off the floor. To increase the tension the user tightened a knob or pushed down on a small lever. Calorie counting and heart monitoring were far in the future. But the simplicity of these bikes was also their selling point. You didn't need a degree in computer programming like some of the newer machines. And their small size meant you could put large numbers in a small area of the gym.

As the computer chip began taking over society, it was inevitable that it would make its way to cardio machines. Most of the newer cardio cycles these days have consoles that would rival that on the starship Enterprise! It seems a simple tension lever won't cut it any more. Anything with less than five steps of programming it considered obsolete.

Despite out tongue-in-cheek comments on the latest cardio cycles, we will be first to admit that the hi-tech programming provides a more efficient workout. As soon as you enter all the information, the "onboard" computer will keep track of your heart rate, integrate it with the other information you entered, and then adjust the tension to keep your heart rate within the target heart rate zone. The guesswork has been eliminated.

Abbas Katami

There are two basic types of cardio cycles; standard and recumbent. Standard cycles are the familiar, sitting up straight, ten-speed shaped bikes. Whether the simple $200 version or the $3000 state-of-the-art jobs, the basic shape hasn't changed much from thirty or forty years ago.

In recent years a new shape has emerged on the scene, the recumbent bike. Recumbent bikes were first developed for physical therapy rehab. Instead of sitting up straight, you sit back with the legs out in front, in an almost vertical position. The advantage is that most of the body's weight is supported by the large hip muscles, and less stress is placed on the knees and ankles. Further, most users report less stress on the lower back. There is no difference between the two bikes with regards to efficiency. If after all those years of squat-ting, rowing, or dead-lifting, your knees or lower back is a tad contrary, you might want to opt for the recumbent bike for your cardio.

TREADMILLS

Treadmills are probably the most popular cardio machines in gyms across North America. Treadmills allow you to go for a walk, jog, or run, irregardless of the climate outside.

Treadmills allow you to go for a walk, jog, or run, irregardless of the climate outside.

There are two basic types of treadmills; motorized and unmotorized. As most gyms use the motorized versions we will be brief discussing the unmotorized models.

Unmotorized treadmills are primarily aimed at the home market. They usually consist of a simple upright frame consisting of two long cylindrical wheels connected to a conveyor belt. As the user pushes back with his or her feet the belt revolves around the wheels. Most gyms refrain from using such treadmills as their cheap construction would not stand up to the heavy volume of usage. Their one redeeming feature, however, is cost. You can buy a decent model for about $500 to $1000. Used for an hour a day, four or five days a week, such a machine should last for years.

It is because of the relative flimsiness of unmotorized treadmills that most gyms use motorized versions. Such models which range in price from $1500 to $15,000 or more, offer numerous advantages over unmotorized models.

First of all the presence of a motor necessitates a much sturdier construction. This means that the machine is able to withstand the daily punishment inflicted on it by 200-pound individuals. How long do you think a $200 home job would last with 280-pound Paul Dillett bouncing up and down on it? Not long we assure you. But most motorized units are rated for between 300 and 400 pounds.

A second advantage is comfort. Most commercial treadmills have a shock absorbing system that cushions as you run or jog. This means much less stress on the joints, particularly the knees and ankles. For those of you who have never run before, or weigh in excess of 200 pounds, we strongly urge you to experiment with the various treadmills available in your gym (assuming your gym has more than one model). Some will have a better cushioning mechanism than others. This means less wear and tear for you in the long run.

Another major benefit to commercial treadmills is the motor itself. Instead of having to physically push the belt with your feet, you simply keep up with it. Not only is this more comfortable in terms of running, but motorized belts don't have the same friction as unmotorized models.

The final major benefit to motorized treadmills is the advanced console. Some units can only be used in the manual mode. This means you set the speed, angle, and time. Others allow you to program in a specific course that mimics a run outside. The machine will automatically speed up or slow down, and incline to various degrees (usually up to 15 degrees on most models) to simulate running across outside terrain. There may even be an attached heart sensor (on the front or side handles, or a strap) that will take your pulse and keep you in the target heart rate zone.

We should add that some of the more expensive unmotorized treadmills also have electronic consoles, but you usually have to go upwards of $1000 or more to get the full spectrum of features found on commercial models.

The downside to motorized treadmills is cost. The cheapest you can buy is about $1500, with middle of the road models going up to $5000 to $7000. For those who see money as no object (you lucky bastards!) you can throw $10,000 to $15,000 on the latest Quinton or Orbitar model. Such machines have the best of everything and will probably become obsolete before they physically wear out.

We know that cost is not really an issue as treadmill usage is included in the cost of the gym membership. But many of you may decide to purchase one down the road. At least now you know the basics for when you get confronted by an overeager salesperson.

Before moving on, we need to raise the issue of safety for first-time treadmill users. When you run outside, the brain becomes accustomed to the scenery passing you by. But on a treadmill everything is stationary. It takes the brain a couple of sessions to get used to having the legs moving fast but nothing else. Even experienced runners have found themselves disoriented the first time they use a treadmill. We suggest you spend your first session doing nothing more than a brisk walk. Then after a few sessions you can increase to a jog and finally a run.

Steppers give you a great cardio workout.
– Brad Baker

STEPPERS

Steppers are named as such because they require you to place both feet in separate steps and make an up and down stepping motion. Steppers have two main selling points; they are very simple to use, and they give you a terrific cardio workout. Stepping is one of the most basic of physical movements and you can't go through life without doing it on a regular basis. It's also very demanding as the entire lower body (fifty percent of your muscle mass) is continuously in motion. There are two basic versions of stepping machines. One form requires a short stepping motion that forces you to push more from the calves. The other requires long full steps that primarily stress the hips and thighs. There is a misconception among many people that the latter version is better for "slimming" the hips and thighs, but this is simply not the case. Slimming is basically burning more calories than you take in and forcing the body to draw on fat deposits for energy. Both forms of stepping machines burn approximately the same number of calories per unit time.

If stepping machines have a drawback it's that some people find them hard on the knees, ankles, and lower back. Basically the entire body weight is pivoting on the knees and ankles, in a repetitive manner, for 30 minutes or more. Those with knee or ankle problems, or those on the heavy side may want to give the stepping machines a pass.

ROWERS OR ERGOMETERS

Rowers, also called ergometers, evolved from the old-time rowing machines that allowed university crews to keep in shape during the off-season. Such machines were so popular around the turn of the century that even the gym on the ill-fated luxury liner, the Titanic had one.

What makes rowing so effective is that it involves just about the whole body. Unlike most cardio machines, which primarily use the legs, rowing forces the upper and lower body to do an equal share of the movement. Rowing is also an easy movement to learn. An absolute beginner can be rowing in comfort within a matter of minutes. Finally, and this is more of a practical than physiological benefit, for some reason, rowing machines don't receive the same volume of usage, of say treadmills or cycles. This means you will probably never have to wait long to gain access to one.

ELIPTICALS

Next to treadmills, ellipticals are fast becoming the most popular cardio machines in gyms. They are similar to steppers in that you place both feet on steps. But instead of making an up and down stepping motion, you make a circular or elliptical motion. This type of stepping places less stress on the knees and ankles than the up and down stepping motion.

Chris Cormier, Kevin Levrone, Flex Wheeler and Ronnie Coleman know the importance of having low bodyfat levels while onstage.

There are two basic types of elliptical machines. One version just has the leg motion with the arms holding on to a set of stationary handles. The other has a set of handles that you move forward and backward with the arms as the legs move in the circular motion. These machines are very popular with skiers as the movement is very similar to cross country skiing.

SKATERS OR SLIDERS

For those who workout at a large, well equipped facility, you may have access to one of the newest forms of cardio equipment – skaters or sliders. These machines are similar to ellipticals in that you place your feet in a set of steps and make a circular motion, but instead of moving in a vertical arc, you move in the horizontal, as if ice or roller skating. Skate machines are not for everyone as they take time to get the coordination down. And the image of a 250-pound bodybuilder on one of these things could be grounds for a chuckle or two! But for those looking for something different in the way of cardio, don't be afraid to give one a try.

THE BEST CARDIO MACHINE?

Comparing and ranking cardio machines tends to stir up the same controversy as the barbell versus dumbell debate. In other words everyone has his or her favorites. The basic question to be asked is "Is one cardio machine better than another?" And the simple answer is "generally speaking, no." Most of the machines fall within 50 calories or less burned per unit time. On paper the rower and elliptical machines with moving handles should be the best as they involve both the upper and lower body muscles. And the more muscles in motion the greater the energy demand placed on the body. But in practice rowers and ellipticals don't seem to burn significantly more calories. What's the bottom line to all this? Try all the cardio machines at your gym and see which ones feel most comfortable. And we don't mean easiest on the cardio system either. We mean the ones that place the least stress on the joints. If you don't notice any difference between the various units, treat them like you would weight training exercises. In other words, alternate things around. Just as the muscles become accustomed to the same exercises, so too will the cardiovascular system adapt to the same cardio machine. Every couple of weeks try a different movement.

SUGGESTED CARDIO ROUTINE

For those new to cardio exercise or just getting back to it after a layoff, we suggest easing into it. Don't think because you can squat 500 pounds you can run for a "wimpy" thirty minutes from day one. We doubt the first time you walked into the gym you put 500 pounds on your shoulders and started squatting. The same holds true for cardio, you work up to a 30-minute run or cycle at 75 to 90 percent target heart rate. Try the following:

	Time (in minutes)	Frequency	Target Heart Rate
Weeks 1 and 2	10 to 15	3 to 4 per week	60 to 70 percent
Week 3	20 to 25	3 to 4 per week	60 to 70 percent
Week 4	20 to 25	4 to 5 per week	75 to 90 percent
Week 5	30 to 45	4 to 5 per week	75 to 90 percent

REFERENCE
1) *International Journal of Obesity*, 22, 489-493, 1998.

Just as muscles become accustomed to the same exercises, so will the cardiovascular system adapt to the same cardio machine. Try a different form of cardio every couple of weeks.
– Jason Arntz

Dorian Yates, Nasser El Sonbaty and Paul Dillett get ready to battle it out.

BOOK NINE

COMPETITION

CHAPTER TWENTY-FIVE

You've Arrived!

As that old familiar song goes "it looks like we made it." After countless sets and thousands of hours slaving away in the gym, you've developed a physique that keeps gathering attention and compliments. Odds are, hardly a day goes by that someone doesn't come up and suggest you try your hand at a bodybuilding competition. And you know something, we agree. Let's face it you've earned it. Of course some readers have no intentions of ever competing. Developing a great physique is reward enough. You've already accomplished more than most people. Only a select few individuals have the dedication and desire to hit the gym on a regular basis for years on end. So to those readers who bodybuild for the mere health and enjoyment of it, we say congratulations and well done! To those seriously giving competition a go, or even those mulling it over, read on. Hopefully by the end of this chapter your competitive juices will be flowing. And more important, we hope we can provide you with enough ammunition to make your competitive experience as productive and rewarding as possible.

Paul Dillett, Shawn Ray and Flex Wheeler

"The number one characteristic all champions have in common is their dedication to training and eating properly. A couple of other factors common to all champions are good genetics, ability to build muscle and confidence in their ability to build muscle and compete at a high level. They are champions not just physically but also emotionally. They hate to lose, and love to win, and nothing else much matters."

– Robert Kennedy, *MuscleMag International* publisher and editor, summing up the common characteristics of all great bodybuilding champions.

Aaron Baker

WHY COMPETE?

If you've read this far then odds are you are seriously considering strutting your stuff on stage. For those still a tad apprehensive, see if the following reasons don't cement your commitment.

Probably the biggest advantage to competing is what could be termed the acquisition of knowledge. This is a fancy way of saying you'll learn more. Competitive bodybuilding is an art form all by itself. You don't simply slap a few poses together and hit the stage. A few do, but their placings usually demonstrate the folly of such foolishness. It takes months to adequately prepare for a bodybuilding show and get it right. And often two or three attempts are needed before you, what the pros like to say "dial it in." By this we mean getting your diet right, putting a posing routine together, readjusting your training, and all the little things that complete the package. Most bodybuilders pay little attention to the previous until they decide to compete. Then it's a frantic couple of weeks trying to get everything ready. The smart ones usually start preparing at least three months out from the show. But even then it's a learning experience. There's nothing wrong with this. In fact the knowledge you gain will stay with you for the rest of your life whether you decide to compete again or not.

Another benefit of competing is that you may actually make progress preparing for the show. As discussed in the chapter on advanced training techniques, switching exercises and rep ranges is one of the best ways to shock the muscles into new growth. In peaking for a show the general philosophy is to replace compound, basic exercises, with isolation movements. Further, rep ranges of 6 to 8 are generally replaced with reps in the 10 to 15 range. So despite doing extra cardio and following a reduced calorie diet, many bodybuilders report that they actually gain quality muscle during the pre-contest phase of training.

If the possibility of making improvement exists before competition, it definitely exists afterwards. Virtually every bodybuilder reports making the best gains of his life in the couple of months after the show. Switching from both a calorie reduced diet and isolation back to compound exercises shocks the muscles into new life. There's also the rebound effect to consider. The body not only gains back the small amount of muscle you may have lost during the precontest phase, but seems to want to add even more muscle than normal. The couple of months immediately following a contest can be termed anabolic overdrive. It seems no matter what you do, the muscles keep responding. Granted this will only last for a couple of months. But to someone stuck in a plateau for years, the alternating of diet and training styles before and after a contest may be just what the doctor ordered.

Another benefit derived from competition falls under the category of injury rehabilitation. Granted the pre-competition period has its own risks, but for the most part increasing the reps and decreasing the weight is a great way to give all those minor aches and pains a chance to heal. Let's face it, no matter how strict your training style and technique, hoisting literally tons of weight can play havoc with the various soft connective tissues of the body. If you are like most bodybuilders, as soon as you detect a slight injury you modify your routine and try to train around the injury rather than give it a complete rest. We agree that if you take time off every time you get a minor ache or pain you'll probably never workout again. But facts are facts. Major injuries usually start out as minor injuries that are never given a chance to heal. Even by switching exercises the odds are you still attempt to handle as much weight as possible. And even though you may think you are training around the injured area, you are not. It's virtually impossible to remove all the stress from the injured area, especially with basic compound exercises. So while the lighter weight and isolation movements of the precontest season are not a guaranteed cure for minor injuries, they go a long way to improve things.

A final reason for competing is because it's fun! The authors have yet to meet a bodybuilder who didn't find the whole competitive experience enjoyable. Sure many disagreed with the judges decision, or found one of the competitors rather obnoxious backstage, but for the most part virtually everyone who takes the competitive plunge has

Chris Cormier and Kevin Levrone

nothing but positive memories of the event. Conversely, talk to "older" bodybuilders who never competed and you'll find a high percentage that regret never having stepped up to the posing dais. Granted the number of "masters" shows means that it's still not too late, but let's face it most individuals would like to have competed at least once while in their "prime."

Hopefully by now those of you who were undecided about competing now find the competitive juices flowing. To quote Robin Williams in the movie *Dead Poets Society*, you have to "seize the moment." We promise you, you won't regret it.

YOUR FIRST SHOW – A VIEW FROM AFAR

It may surprise you to hear that your first show should not be the one you compete in. Your first competition is for viewing purposes only. There are many things you can do cold turkey, but competitive bodybuilding is not one of them. Our advice is to attend a local or regional show and see how things are done. This way when your turn comes there won't be any major surprises.

A typical bodybuilding contest is divided into three sections; weigh-in, prejudging, and evening show. We are going to go into each in more detail in the next couple of chapters. For our purposes now we'll give you a general introduction as to what to expect during each phase.

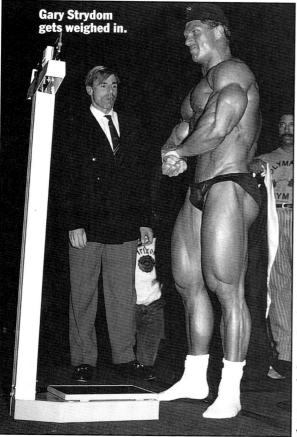

Gary Strydom gets weighed in.

WEIGH-IN

Bodybuilding is similar to many sports in that rather than an open free-for-all, the competitors are divided into classes based on bodyweight. Men's bodybuilding is usually divided into five classes:
Bantam weight
Lightweight
Middleweight
Lightheavyweight
Heavyweight.

Women's shows are usually divided into light and heavyweight, but it often comes down to the number of competitors entering the show. As women's weights usually fall within a 20 or 30 pound range, there's less flexibility for the judges to subdivide into more than two categories. Conversely men's weights may go from the low 100s (i.e. 120 to 130) up to the high 200s (250 to 280). In fact at the pro level every year sees a preponderance of competitors weighing 280 to 300 pounds or more. It's probably only a matter of time before the judges add a superheavyweight category like in Olympic weightlifting and boxing.

As the name implies, the purpose of the weigh-in is to check and see if the competitors make their weight class. Although it varies, most weigh-ins are scheduled the night before the prejudging. In most cases this is Friday night, with the prejudging and evening shows on Saturday. There's nothing complicated about weigh-ins, each contestant steps on the scales wearing nothing but their posing trunks. If they fall within the required range then they can leave and get ready for the prejudging the next morning. If they are a few pounds over, many bodybuilding federations will allow them an hour's grace to lose the weight. This is why you'll see contestants wearing rubber suits, going for a run, or hitting the sauna, in a frantic effort to lose that pound or two to "make their weight."

The object in bodybuilding is to come into the show at the top of your weight class. By this we mean being the biggest and more important, best conditioned athlete in the division. It's one thing to be the heaviest, but this means nothing if that extra five or ten pounds is water or fat. Numerous 185-pounders have beaten out of shape 198-pounders. So don't misunderstand when we say you should come in at the top of your weight class.

If by chance the athlete misses his or her peak, they may arrive at the weigh-in carrying more weight than (five pounds is usually the limit that can be lost in the form of body fluid in an hour) can be comfortably lost in an hour. In this case they have no choice but to move up a category. Now if they are in shape then they still stand a chance of winning, but the odds have turned against them. For a lightheavyweight who misses his peak by one or two pounds (say 200 versus the desired 198) it's an uphill battle to square off against 240-pounders, especially if the natural heavyweights are in shape.

As a final note, missing your weight class may have another practical consideration. If you are representing a team, then missing your peak may deprive the whole team. Most sports federations only allow one competitor per division. As soon as one competitor screws up, the whole team suffers. The bottom line is that you must time things perfectly so that you don't show up on weigh-in day carrying excess baggage.

PREJUDGING

Most prejudgings take place on Saturday morning starting around 10:00 a.m.. Depending on the number of contestants you could be out of there in an hour, or be there till mid afternoon. Although the evening show sounds more glamorous, most contests are won and lost at the prejudging. The prejudging can be considered the most analytical part of the show, and for the most part it's all business. As a future competitor it's an absolute must that you attend the prejudging.

Flex Wheeler, Ronnie Coleman and Chris Cormier set up for the relaxed round.

Generally speaking the order of appearance at the prejudging is:
Men's bantam weight
Men's lightweight
Women's lightweight
Women's heavyweight
Men's middleweight
Men's lightheavyweight
Men's heavyweight.

Once each class is called out on stage they will be arranged in a straight line by the emcee or head judge. The first order of business is the relaxed round. The competitors will be asked to face the judges, turn to the right, turn around, turn to the right again, and finally face the judges once more. Although it's called the relaxed round you'll notice that the competitors try to tense every muscle as much as possible, with special emphasis on flaring the lats for width, and keeping the abs tight.

"I agree with you and so obviously do the IFBB judging hierarchy. That's why they have a relaxed judging round where the competitors are viewed from the front, back and sides in the normal position."

– Robert Kennedy, *MuscleMag International* publisher and editor responding to a reader's question about why some bodybuilders look better standing relaxed than others.

In round two you'll see the competitors comparing what are called compulsory poses. Most of these are very familiar and odds are you hit them frequently in front of your mirror every morning. If you don't, we suggest you start this practice as the compulsories must be executed perfectly on stage or you'll never find yourself in the winner's circle.

Round three is the free posing round and each competitor comes out individually and performs a posing routine set to music. The free posing round allows mediocre physiques to gain ground on more complete physiques. All things being equal, the best physique usually wins, but there have been numerous cases where contestants lacking in the physique department have beaten better competitors because of a great posing routine. As you watch each contestant go through their routine, pay close attention as to how they move from one pose to the next. Some competitors simply stick a few shots together with little or no coordination. Others, however, look like poetry in motion.

The final round is called the posedown and may or may not take place at the prejudging. In any case all the competitors are lined up on stage and at the signal launch into what's popularly called a posing free-for-all. You'll see the favorite being "challenged" by the underdogs. You'll see everyone jockeying for position, each doing his or her best to highlight his or her best points. After time is up the competitors are asked to exit the stage.

THE EVENING SHOW

Ronnie Coleman, Achim Albrecht and Flex Wheeler

The evening show has two main purposes; to give the judges one last look at the competitors, and to entertain the audience. Although most placings have been determined during the prejudging, there will invariably be one or two divisions where the quality is such that a second look is warranted. When you attend your first show you'll notice that competitors who looked unbeatable in the morning only look average during the evening show. You'll also see a few contestants who didn't seem to stand a chance earlier in the day, all of a sudden show up sporting a vastly improved physique. What happened?

"I have a lot of respect for Ronnie both as a friend and as a competitor. He did a great job, and was rewarded for it, and I congratulate him because he deserved it."

– Flex Wheeler, top pro bodybuilder commenting on placing second to Ronnie Coleman at the 1998 Mr. Olympia.

Peaking is an art form and few competitors hit it dead on the first try. Some competitors peak a day or two early, while others look vastly superior a couple of days after the show. Then there are those who misjudge things by a couple of hours. Although peaking during the prejudging probably makes more sense as this is where most contests are won or lost, peaking during the evening show has the advantage of getting the audience on your side. This is why you often hear a chorus of boos when a seemingly better looking competitor loses out to someone who doesn't look as sharp. What's probably happened is one competitor peaked during the morning show while the other hardened up over the afternoon. As most in the audience don't attend both rounds, they attribute the final placings to bad judging when in fact it was the competitors that changed.

Speaking of the audience, where the prejudging tends to be semi-civilized, the evening show borders on manic. There's nothing quite like a bodybuilding audience. A couple of minutes sitting in the audience will confirm that you are definitely not at the opera.

What makes bodybuilding shows so entertaining is the audience is usually subdivided into "camps." Most gyms have competitors in the show and the patrons of the various gyms actively encourage them on. Encourage is a polite way of saying yell, scream, shout, and just about any other form of verbal participation. Things really get interesting when two competitors from different gyms are in the running for first and second. While the audience rarely gets into fisticuffs, the verbal abuse traded back and forth is alone worth the price of admission. Chances are you'll get caught up in the excitement. Great, because you can feed off the audience when your time comes to step on stage.

Besides the larger, more vocal audience, the only other major difference at the evening show is the presence of a guest poser. Depending on the size of the show (i.e., local, regional, national) the guest poser may be a top amateur or pro. Most guest posers perform two routines, one about half way through the show, and the other towards the end. If you've never seen a pro bodybuilder before you're in for a treat. Most are twenty or thirty pounds above contest weight, and while a couple have reputations for being down right fat during the off-season, most come

Chris Cormier and Flex Wheeler

in looking pretty darn good. And did we say massive? It's nothing out of the ordinary for a bodybuilder who competes at 250 to guest pose at 280 to 300. What you'll see is the epitome of just how far the human body can be taken with regards to musculature. From 55 to 60-inch chests to 22 to 23-inch arms, you'll see it all. If the pro is one of the top bodybuilders in the world, you'll see the other contestants sneaking a peak from the wings as well. After all this is what they are aiming for. And while most don't have the genetics to reach this level, there's nothing wrong with dreaming. You can bet that as the behemoth hits each and every pose, most of the competitors are right there with him, fantasizing about the day when they'll be the guest poser.

There's nothing quite like a bodybuilding audience. A couple of minutes sitting in the audience will confirm that you are definitely not at the opera.

POST SHOW FESTIVITIES

Although some shows end when the trophies are handed out, the better promoters usually invite the competitors and audience to a post-show get-together. This may be a formal, everything supplied free event, or simply show up at a rented club or social hall. If you have the time, we strongly encourage you to attend these after-show gatherings. You'll basically be surrounded by a couple of hundred people all talking about one topic – bodybuilding. If you manage to come away from such a gathering without learning something then you weren't listening very well. The amount of knowledge exchanged is almost endless. Odds are you'll hear tips and techniques that will make a big improvement in your training. More important you'll get a chance to size up the future competition! After all that's what you'll be at next year's social – a bodybuilding competitor.

All right we've got you hooked. It's time to get down and dirty so to speak. The next couple of chapters are going to lead you step by step to the posing platform. We won't guarantee these few chapters will turn you into the next Arnold, but we are confident they'll make the most of your individual genetics and desires. Let's do it!

CHAPTER TWENTY-SIX

What You Are Shooting For

As with most sports, bodybuilding has a hierarchy of contests. You don't just decide to compete in the Mr. Olympia or Arnold Classic. You first must earn the right to appear in such prestigious shows. At the lower end of the competitive ladder we find the city championships. In smaller states and provinces you may be able to start your bodybuilding career by going right to the state or provincial shows. Most shows are divided into novice, teen, women's, men's, and masters.

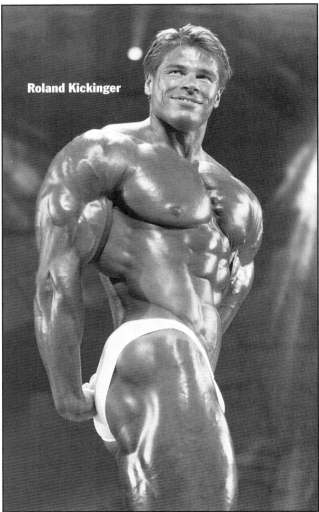

Roland Kickinger

Depending on the size of the city, the quality can range from mediocre to outstanding. The level of competition at the New York City or Los Angeles championships, rivals, if not surpasses many state and provincial shows. A very high percentage of U.S. amateur champions are previous winners of the larger city contests. The winners of each class at a city show are then eligible to compete in the state championships. Once again the population of the state usually determines the quality of competition. The California state championships are very prestigious and bodybuilders know that if they add this state title to their belt, they will be one of the favorites at that year's Nationals.

After winning your class at the state or provincial championships you can go directly to the Nationals, or compete in a regional show. As the name implies, regionals take in a number of adjacent states or provinces. For example Canadian bodybuilders can compete in the Atlantic, Central, or Western championships. U.S. bodybuilders have available such shows as the Western, Southern, Mid-West, and NorthEast Championships. Such shows are not pre-requisites, but any bodybuilder who wins or places at one of these shows will get special consideration at the Nationals.

Chris Cormier, Flex Wheeler and Kevin Levrone

All of this brings us to each countries' National Championships. The U.S. or Canadian Nationals are the jewel in the crown of any North American amateur bodybuilder. Winning such a show not only establishes you as the best amateur bodybuilder in the country, but also earns you that valuable piece of paper affectionately called a "pro card."

WHAT'S IN A NAME?

For those new to the sport, the term "championships" makes perfect sense. After all this is the same terminology used by most sports. But to the "older" readers among you, the name "National Championships," doesn't carry the same prestige as "Mr. America." Up until the early 1980s, bodybuilding was unique in that the winners were not called champions but "Mr.'s." Such titles as Mr. California, Mr. America, and Mr. Universe, were the goals of every competitive bodybuilder. Bill Pear, Larry Scott, Lou Ferrigno, and Dave Draper, all won the Mr. America title. In the early 1980s, in an attempt to bring bodybuilding in line with other sports, the "Mr." titles were replaced by the term "championships." Now days, the U.S. National champion competes in the World Championships which was once known as the amateur Mr. Universe. The only "Mr." title left today is the granddaddy of all bodybuilding titles, the Mr. Olympia. And to win this you must be a pro bodybuilder.

PRO BODYBUILDING – MUSCLING IN ON THE BIG BOYS

Once a bodybuilder has conquered the amateur ranks, the next step is to turn pro. Before going any further we should warn you that few bodybuilders have the genetics to make it to the pro level. In fact such is the competitiveness of today's bodybuilding that winning a state championship is out of reach for most individuals. To make it as a pro you need all four primary variables in abundance. By this we mean great genetics, proper eating habits, long hours in the gym, and as much as we hate to admit it, a moderate to severe devotion to pharmacology. If you are deficient in one of these areas, the chances of going all the way to the pro level are almost nonexistent. Still, the pro ranks have seen individuals a tad deficient in the genetics department, so go for it. You have nothing to lose by trying and as the old saying goes, if you are going to dream, dream big!

Bruce Patterson

Twenty years ago the big three on the pro bodybuilding stage were the Mr. World, Mr. Universe, and Mr. Olympia titles. With the reorganization of bodybuilding in the early eighties, the Mr. World and Mr. Universe titles have been replaced by such shows as the IronMan Invitational, Arnold Classic, and New York Night of Champions. These three form the nucleus of the winter/spring bodybuilding season. Then come September or October, the top pros savagely fight for the one remaining Mr. title, the Mr. Olympia.

The Mr. Olympia or "Olympia" as it's affectionately known, was created back in 1965 by Joe Weider to establish once and for all who was the greatest bodybuilder alive. Such has been the dominance of the Mr. Olympia by certain individuals that in 35 years, there have only been ten different winners. As an example, the three greatest Mr. Olympia's, Arnold Schwarzenegger, Lee Haney, and Dorian Yates, have won 21 titles between them.

In recent years the Mr. Olympia has been followed by a series of Grand Prix shows usually held in Europe.

If there's one area where bodybuilding falls far short of most other pro sports it's prize money. The winner of the Mr. Olympia or Arnold Classic takes home around $100,000, with second and third pocketing $50,000 and $25,000 for their efforts. This may seem like a lot of money but the average golfer claims $300,000 to $400,000 for winning a PGA event; and tennis players can earn $500,000 to $1,000,000 for a single tournament. Once a bodybuilder places out of the top three, he or she takes home a paltry $5000 to $10,000 for their efforts. When you factor in, eating, supplements, and yes, drugs, a bodybuilder would have to win a couple of big shows to make what could be called big bucks. Even by placing third on three or four occasions, the individual is still only making a middle class salary. The fact that the current Mr. Olympia, Ronnie Coleman, still works as a police officer in Texas, should give you an idea of how things stand with regards to bodybuilding as a source of income.

What we are trying to say here is that if you have visions of turning pro and earning "millions" of dollars, you may have to re-evaluate your thinking. Yes some top pros make seven figure incomes, but not from prize money. They earn most of their money from seminars, posing exhibitions, and supplement endorsing. (For a list of winners of the major pro and amateur contests please see the Appendix at the end of the book).

Ronnie Coleman

The Rounds

ROUND 1

Although called the "relaxed round" you'll be anything but relaxed. The purpose of this section of the contest is to compare physiques based on symmetry and overall body proportions. This not to say size and muscularity don't count here. We assure you they do! But initially the judges want to see what the competitors look like just simply standing there. Then in the next two rounds the judges will start focusing more on size, muscularity, etc.

As soon as you come out on stage you'll be instructed to form a straight line across the stage. For convenience each competitor is given a number back stage which he or she attaches to their posing suit. This means things will be rather impersonal on stage. From now on you are nothing more than a number. So don't expect to hear your name called. If there are less than five or six competitors in the class, the judges will have everyone go through the comparisons together. If it's a large class, the judges will ask three or four competitors to step forward. Although not conclusive, at most contests the first competitors called forward are usually the ones who will fight for the top spots. If, however, you don't make the first call out, don't despair. The authors have attended shows where the eventual winner was hardly ever called forward. The judges took one look and decided he or she was the best and didn't require a lengthy battery of comparisons with the other competitors.

As soon as you take your place in the line up, the contest begins. Don't assume that because you are not posing you are not being judged. From the moment you walk on stage, until the moment you leave, assume at least one judge is watching you. In a close contest, you could win or lose based on just how you looked entering and exiting the stage.

Nasser El Sonbaty and Kevin Levrone

"From any angle, in any pose, it's hard to find a single flaw in them. They're like rare diamonds. Each muscle is perfectly shaped, seamlessly tying into the next with grace and magnificence. Such development is unrealistic for the majority of us."

– Ron Harris, *MuscleMag International* contributor commenting on the physiques of Flex Wheeler, Lee Labrada, Shawn Ray, and Ronnie Coleman.

The "relaxed" round can be subdivided into four general poses; front, rear, and both sides. Here's how it goes. Once in the lineup, the judges will take a good look at each competitor from the front. The head judge or emcee then asks the competitors to take a quarter turn to the right so that the left side of the body is facing the judges. It's at this point that at least one competitor turns to the left. This is usually the result of nervousness and if it happens to be you, don't panic. Simply smile and turn the right way round. You won't be penalized for such a simple mistake. In fact you may be doing everyone a favor as it helps to lighten things up. Let's face it both the competitors and judges are probably a tad nervous and a momentary break in the proceedings goes a long way to relax everyone.

Front double biceps

After a good look at the left side, the competitors are asked to make another quarter turn to the right so that their backs are visible to the judges. Another quarter turn presents your right side to the judging panel. Finally you will be asked to turn back to the front.

In round two the contestants will be required to execute seven mandatory or compulsory poses.
Here, Lee Priest demonstrates them for us.

As we alluded to earlier, you don't stay completely relaxed during this round. For starters, make a slight V with the feet and push down with the heels and balls of the feet. Also curl the toes back slightly. Although it seems trivial, such little variations help flex the thighs and calves. When you are facing or back on to the judges, try to keep the lats flared as much as possible. This helps augment the all-important V-shape. When side on to the judges, keep the triceps as tight as possible. Finally, and perhaps most important, keep the abs sucked in and tight at all times. This is something even the top pros forget to do. Of course it doesn't help matters when many have large, distended stomachs brought on by heavy growth hormone and diuretic use. After you complete all four poses you will be asked to step back in the main line up, or if it's a small class, begin the second round.

ROUND 2

The second round is often called the compulsory round, as the contestants will be required to execute seven mandatory or compulsory poses. Although female bodybuilders are only required to perform five of the seven poses, many judges either out of not knowing the rules, or mere curiosity, have the competitors execute all seven. For this reason we are going to go into all seven in detail, and female readers should be familiar with them all.

FRONT DOUBLE BICEPS

The front double biceps is without a doubt the most popular of all the bodybuilding poses. You'll even see five-year olds hamming it up doing this one. As Arnold once said if you can hit this pose early in your routine and look good, it establishes your domination over the other competitors and almost assures you of a top placing. In a manner of speaking the name "double biceps" is misleading as the biceps only contribute a small part to the overall effect. Just about every muscle is on display in this pose and this is why it's one of the compulsories.

There are generally two ways to hit this pose. You can hit it straight on with everything square with the floor so to speak. Or you can add a touch of artistry by bending one knee slightly, twisting the torso, and raising one arm slightly higher than the other. Although there are no set rules, the larger competitors usually hit the pose straight on, while the smaller bodybuilders add the variations. Take a look at old pictures of Arnold, Sergio Oliva, and Lou Ferrigno, or recent photos of Nasser El Sonbaty, Ronnie Coleman, or Kevin Lervone. All six men are famous for their huge arms and don't really need to do anything fancy to appear effective in this pose. On the other hand smaller competitors need to draw attention away from their lack of mass by adding slight variations. Guys like Frank Zane and Lee Labrada routinely beat larger bodybuilders by following such a practice.

As a word of advice, make a point backstage of sizing up your competition. One quick glance is usually enough to determine how you stack up in the arm department against the other competitors. If you have size in abundance hit the pose straight on and let the judges take a good look. Conversely if you are giving away size, adopt a page from Zane's or Labrada's book and add the slight variations.

Here are few additional pointers to get the most out of the front double biceps pose. As soon as the judges call for the pose, set your thighs first. As you raise the arms concentrate on flaring the lats as much as possible. And don't forget to keep the abs sucked and tight. As we said earlier, despite the name, the judges will be comparing more than just biceps. In fact two of the sport's greatest names, six-time Mr. Olympia, Dorian Yates, and eight-time Mr. Olympia, Lee Haney, regularly won this pose despite lagging in the biceps department. Yet because the rest of their physiques were so overwhelming they still managed to dominate this pose.

Back double biceps

BACK DOUBLE BICEPS

Most of what we just said about the front double biceps applies to the rear version. The obvious difference is that you perform the pose with your back facing the judges. As with the front version, the back double biceps pose is dominated by other muscles, in this case the shoulders, back, and triceps. As a matter of fact this shot also reveals any weakness in the calves and hamstrings.

As soon as the call is given to hit the pose, start by setting the legs. In fact most contests require that one leg be extended behind you with only the toes resting on floor. The purpose of this is to show the judges the calves. Once the legs are set, slowly raise the arms upward, trying to flare the lats as much as possible. Once you have everything in place slowly move the arms forward and backward, contracting and retracting the shoulder blades. You should also contract the lower back muscles by sticking the glutes back slightly and arching. There's nothing quite like a well-developed set of spinal erectors to enhance this pose. If you don't believe us take a look at Dorian Yates performing this pose. His spinal erectors appear python-like as they run up the lower back. Dorian is a perfect example of what we said earlier about the pose being sort of misnamed. From the rear Dorian's biceps are virtually invisible. His triceps and brachialus practically hide his average-sized biceps. Yet this pose would regularly earn him points as his back, triceps, and calves were in most respects superior to the other competitors.

FRONT LAT SPREAD

The front lat spread is another pose where the name is not really reflective of the primary muscles displayed. The lats are not that visible from the front even among the larger members of the sport. This pose is dominated by the chest, shoulders, arms and thighs. The lats may or may not be visible between the arms and chest up close to the armpits. Guys like Lee Haney, Ronnie Coleman, and Paul Dillett literally dwarf other competitors with this shot. And what's ironic about Dillett is that he has a mediocre back as compared to the other pros on the scene. But his chest, shoulders, and arms are so humungous that you don't notice his lat weakness, at least from the front.

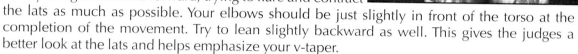

Front lat spread

As with the biceps poses, start by setting the legs with a v-shaped stance, heels pushing on the floor. Rest the thumbs on the lower torso, just under the ribs, and keep the elbows back behind you. Now pivot on the thumbs and slowly bring the elbows forward, trying to flare and contract the lats as much as possible. Your elbows should be just slightly in front of the torso at the completion of the movement. Try to lean slightly backward as well. This gives the judges a better look at the lats and helps emphasize your v-taper.

As a word of caution, many bodybuilders bring the arms way to far in front of them thinking that it's flaring the lats even more and making them appear wider. In actuality they appear narrower and to be honest, rather stupid. Once the elbows are in line with the chest, or slightly in front (one or two inches) the lats are flared as much as possible. You either have them, or you don't. No amount of flexing is going to bring them out. Only extra time in gym can accomplish this.

Rear lat spread

REAR LAT SPREAD

This is the first pose we've discussed were the name accurately describes the primary muscle being displayed. Although you can hide weak lats from the front, forget it on this one. Any weakness will immediately stand out. We hate to keep picking on Paul Dillett, as he's one of the top pros in the world (most recently the winner of the 1999 New York Night of Champions). From the front and side he appears almost unbeatable and can stand next to anyone. But as soon as he turns around his less than great back lets him down. Paul has what bodybuilders call "high lats." This means the bottom of his lats, attach higher on his torso than most bodybuilders. So even though the mass is there, it covers nowhere near the surface area of other bodybuilders. It doesn't help matters either by having probably the largest shoulders in pro bodybuilding! Conversely guys like Dorian Yates, Ronnie Coleman, and Flex Wheeler, have full, complete lats that cover the whole back of their torsos. And then there's Franco Columbu. Even by today's standards Franco is considered by many to have the greatest set of lats of all time. When Franco flared his lats outward from the rear, images of manta rays came to mind. His lats had probably the most width and thickness of any pro then or now.

Once you get the go ahead, set the legs with the now familiar v-shaped stance. You may or may not have to extend one leg back and flex the calf. Rest the thumbs on the lower, outer section of the ribs and begin flaring the arms forward, stopping with the elbows in line or slightly forward of the chest. As with the front version, don't force the arms too far in front of the body. It doesn't add anything to lat width and it only makes you appear amateurish on stage.

Side triceps

SIDE TRICEPS
In most cases the judges will allow you to pick your favorite side, but they may make all the competitors execute it from the same side so practice both. As soon as you turn sideways bend the knee of the leg closest to the judges (the same side as the arm you are showing) and pivot on the toes with the toes pointing slightly away from the judges and heel pointing towards the judges. This gives the panel a clear view of your calves, which make up a major portion of this pose. Next reach behind with the non-posing arm and grab the hand or wrist of the displayed arm. The arm you are flexing for the judges should be slightly bent with the triceps flexed as much as possible. Finally keep the abs tucked in as far as possible to make the waist appear as small as possible.

Side chest

SIDE CHEST
There's only one way to sum up this pose, check out page 620 of the soft cover version of Arnold's Encyclopedia of Bodybuilding. That my dear friends is a side chest pose. And those are the most famous pecs in bodybuilding history. Even Arnold's good buddy Franco, seen in the background, is looking on in awe. That's the effect Arnold had on spectators and competitors alike when he hit one of his trademarked side chest poses. Even by today's standards we doubt there's anyone that can duplicate that shot on page 620.

As with the side triceps, you may or may not be allowed to pick your side for this one. The legs are set identical to the side triceps, with the calves and hamstrings very much on display. There are two variations you can use on this pose. You can keep the torso square with the floor and draw the clasped hands back tight against the lower rib cage. This was the most common version back in Arnold's day. The trend now is to lean the torso towards the judges and squeeze the pecs as hard as possible to bring out as much striation and muscularity as possible. If you know you have the largest chest in the contest, adopt Arnold's version. If on the other hand you have an average-sized, but very defined chest, try the second version.

THIGH AND ABDOMINAL

Although the chest and arms tend to get the most reaction from the audience, few competitors who win this pose place far from the top. Having a great midsection means more than a great set of abs. It also means that you have a very low bodyfat percentage. The midsection is the first

Thigh and abdominal

place fat accumulates and the last place it leaves. So having a great set of abs is indicative of overall conditioning.

The only choice you may have on this pose is which thigh you have forward. As with the side chest and triceps the judges may be flexible or rigid. In any case put one leg in front of you pivoting on the toes so that the knee is facing outward. This gives the judges a good look at the calves as well as making the thigh look as large as possible. It also helps bring out the separation between the four thigh heads. Once the legs are set place both hands behind the head and push light to moderately on the back of the skull. This flexes the lats, chest, and abs, all of which are being given a good scrutiny by the judges. If you have good control over your abs, alternate contracting and relaxing to draw attention towards your midsection. This also gets the audience on your side, as every one of them knows how hard it is to develop a great looking midsection. If your abs are average but your thighs are the strong point, then flex the extended leg as much as possible. In short emphasize your strong points while minimizing your weak points. We will say more on this in the next section

ROUND 3

Round 3 is often called the free posing round and allows each competitor the chance to do his or her own thing so to speak. Unlike the previous rounds, which involve direct comparison with other contestants, in this round you have the stage all to yourself. You'll be given around 90 seconds to come out on stage and perform a posing routine set to music. In a manner of speaking this round is similar to the free posing rounds in figure skating and gymnastics.

Our first suggestion in preparing your free posing routine is to sit back and watch a video of various pro bodybuilding contests. If you haven't taped one off one of the sports channels, either rent one out at a bodybuilding store or even better, order one through the mail. It may set you back $30 or $40 but it's worth every penny especially if you plan on competing on a regular basis. Put the tape in the video player, mix up a protein or creatine drink and sit back for an hour. Although not necessary, we strongly encourage you to take out a notebook and jot down a few observations.

Chapter 27 – *The Rounds*

The first thing to observe is the way the competitors enter and exit the stage. Some casually walk out to the sound of silence and then start posing as soon as the music kicks in. Other bodybuilders incorporate the entrance and exit into their routines with the music starting before they make their appearance. The next thing to notice is what poses each performs and how they move – called transition – from one pose to the next. The object is to highlight strong body parts and try to cover up weaker ones. This is why you'll see Nasser El Sonbaty hitting a lot of most musculars, Dorian Yates showing his back at every opportunity, and Ronnie Coleman raising his arms on more than one occasion. Such bodybuilders know that from these angles they are almost unbeatable. Conversely Paul Dillett doesn't perform an overabundance of back shots, as this muscle group is not up to the standard of other areas. From the front and side, however, Paul takes a back seat to no one.

Ronnie
Coleman

"Oh yes. In fact I practiced two. I didn't know how the stage would be set up, and how I'd have to enter, so I practiced coming in from the side and also coming in from the back. I wanted to be ready for any eventuality."

– Ronnie Coleman, 1998 Mr. Olympia commenting on how he prepared for his posing routine entrance.

Another thing to observe is how each bodybuilder "carries" his or herself on stage. By this we mean facial expressions, body posture, and interaction with the other competitors. Some bodybuilders almost cringe ever time they are asked to engage in direct comparisons with other contestants. Others relish the opportunity and it shows on their faces. If you are the shy type that feels uncomfortable stepping on stage wearing a skimpy posing suit in front of a couple hundred or thousand people, then you have two choices. Either grab the bull by the horns and learn to adapt, or change sports. We know this sounds rather blunt but bodybuilding competition is not for the meek and mild. It can be war out there and without sounding like an advertisement for some soldier of fortune magazine, only the strong shall survive. We should add that most bodybuilders feel nervous on their first outing. That's only human nature. But if after a couple of shows you still hate the thought of stepping on the posing dais, you may want to rethink your entire bodybuilding philosophy. To be successful in bodybuilding you need to be confident, self-assured, and perhaps most of all, charismatic. From the moment you step on stage until you exit your face should convey to the judges that you are the best and they needn't bother looking at any other competitors!

MUSIC SELECTION

It may seem trivial but selecting the right piece of music can make or break your posing routine. Choose wisely and both the judges and audience will drop their lower jaws in awe. Choose incorrectly and you are just another competitor on stage. It's that important.

From watching the video or live shows you'll see that just about every type of music can be used for a posing routine. From opera and classical, to rap and mainstream rock, anything goes. A few words of caution just the same. Unless you have an overwhelming physique and are one of the largest most muscular people on stage, stick with music that has an upbeat flavor. A small, symmetrical bodybuilder may look graceful posing to classical music, but they tend to put both judges and audience members alike to sleep. Even within the pro ranks you'll see the smaller bodybuilders posing to rap, middle of the road rock, or dance music, rather than classical or opera. Very few so-called "symmetrical" bodybuilders can get away with posing to the latter groups. Guys like Arnold, Lee Haney, Nasser El Sonbaty, and Kevin Lervone, can pose to Wagner, Strauss, etc, because they had (or have) over-powering physiques that were usually the largest onstage. Of course Nasser and Lervone routinely pose to upbeat rock and dance music as well. Although not etched in stone, as a general rule of thumb, anyone can pose to fast tempo rock and dance music, but leave the classical and opera to the big boys.

One of the best ways to choose your music piece is to visualize posing every time you hear a favorite song on the radio or video channel. Let's say you are sitting in traffic and a popular tune comes on the radio; start visualizing what it would be like to be on stage posing to that song. You'll quickly notice that some songs practically lend themselves to a posing routine while others just don't cut it. No problem, just file the workable songs away in your memory banks for future reference. Now all you need to do is build your posing routine around one of them. Think of your poses as the words, which you are setting to music. The best posers can bring their personalities across just by posing on stage. No words are needed. They are that in tune with their posing routine.

Roland Cziurlok

ROUTINE DEVELOPMENT

The primary purpose of a free posing routine is to display your physique to the judges in the most favorable manner possible. You want to show the judges that your physique is the best. Therefore you want to tailor your routine to emphasize your strong points and minimize your weak areas. Although not a necessity, you should include some of the compulsory poses in your routine. As mentioned earlier, these poses display the full body to the judges and a bodybuilder who looks good from these angles is almost certain to place at or near the top.

"Yes, to make sure they looked the way I wanted. Then I'd practice them away from a mirror. That's very important because you don't want to become dependant on it. There's no mirror on stage. I tried to develop muscle memory of what each pose felt like."

– Ronnie Coleman, 1998 Mr. Olympia commenting on one of the biggest mistakes bodybuilders make; relying too much on mirrors while they practice their posing.

Generally speaking you start your routine with one of your best poses. This gets the audience on your side and makes the judges sit up and take notice. Speaking of the audience you must do everything possible to get them on your side. The judges are only human after all and a competitor who gets the audience "a-hootin-and-a-hollerin," will almost certainly score higher than someone who poses to near silence. And to reiterate what we said earlier this is another reason to stick with popular upbeat music. Most bodybuilding audiences fall in the 15 to 40-year old age group. Few are classical or opera fans. In fact such music tends to put most attendees to sleep. We know the classical and opera fans reading are getting hot under the collar about now, but facts are facts.

PICTURE PERFECT

You will need two important allies in helping you put together your free posing routine; the camera and a trusted friend. No matter how many times you look in the mirror you are still only getting one person's opinion – yours! And no matter how much you flatter yourself, this is not adequate enough. We strongly suggest you shoot a couple of rolls of film posing to thirty or forty poses. There's nothing complicated about selecting poses. Just flip through old copies of *MuscleMag International* or other popular bodybuilding magazines and take a look at the hundreds of different poses, both studio and contest. If you have a large collection of magazines you'll discover that the bulk of the poses haven't changed much over the years. Ronnie Coleman's, Flex Wheeler's, and Dorian Yates' pictures from the nineties, are not that different from Arnold's, Franco's, and Lou's pictures from the seventies. Another thing you'll notice is some bodybuilders look better from some angles than others do. A few have become famous for a particular pose leading to the term of "signature" pose. Arnold's three quarter back and front, single biceps poses (check out the cover of *Arnold: The Education of a Bodybuilder*) are his trademark shots. Franco's back lat spread, Lou Ferrigno's most muscular, Dorian Yates' single biceps/thigh pose, and Sergio Oliva's two hands above the head, hands facing outwards; have all become part of bodybuilding legend.

Once you get the film processed, divide the pictures into three categories; good, fair, and throw away. As a rule of thumb you will need to hold each pose for about five seconds. As you only have 90 seconds to perform your routine, this works out about 18 poses in your entire routine. If you plan on including a couple of compulsories, you are left with time for about 12-15 additional poses. Now you see where the pictures come in. Go to your "good" pile and sub-divide them into front and back views. Unless you have a glaring weakness from the front or back, try to balance your routine about fifty-fifty. Only resort to selecting poses from your "fair" pile if you can't complete the routine using poses from the "good" pile. This is where your trusted friend comes in (preferably not another competitor in the same contest!). In fact obtain the opinions of as many different people as possible. Your best case scenario would be some one who judged bodybuilding in the past. They know exactly what to look for. They can give you an unbiased comment as to what poses would impress a judging panel.

Once you have the poses selected the next step is to sequence them with your music selection into an evenly flowing routine. We mentioned earlier how a good routine should be split evenly between front and back poses. Although this is the level you strive for with your physique, it's a fact that most bodybuilders look better from either front or back. This is where creativity comes in. If your back is not up to the standard of your front, tailor your routine accordingly. Instead of a fifty-fifty split, perform about 70 to 75 percent of your poses from the front. This way you are still showing the back, even if it is a tad weak, and at the same time putting your best foot forward so to speak. Some readers may wonder why they need to show the back at all. Well, the judges are not stupid. They assume because you are afraid to turn around then you have something to hide. And you know something, they're right! After all they saw you in the compulsories and trust us, have a pretty good idea of what you look like from the rear. What you are trying to do with a posing routine is not so much hide a weak area completely (let's face it you can't) but emphasize your strong points. The odds are most of your opponents will have weaknesses as well. Few bodybuilders are perfectly balanced. Hopefully at the end of the day your strong points out-muscle your weak points and earn you the winner's trophy. If not, there's always next year.

Lee Priest and
Paul Dillett

Here's a sample routine to give you an idea as to how a posing routine may look. As soon as you walk out on stage squat down with one leg straight out to the side, the other knee bent, and bow your head. As the music starts raise your head and place the thumbs on your lower rib cage and hit a front lat spread. From here you can stand up and do a front double biceps. Next hit a three-quarter back shot either one or two arms (check out pictures of Arnold) flexed in the traditional biceps pose. Hold for three to five seconds, and then turn around and do a back lat spread. From here you could hit a back double biceps or turn to one side and do a side triceps or chest pose. Follow with an abdominals pose, either the hands behind the head compulsory version or hands clasped behind the lower back and one leg extended. If you do the traditional version, you can easily move into a single biceps pose. From here you can go in just about any direction. You could turn around and throw in a few artistic arms over the head poses, or remain front on and start your finale. Although not a requirement, most bodybuilders conclude with a series of most muscular poses (nicknamed the "crab"). You need look no further than Lou Ferrigno or Nasser El Sonbaty for inspiration in this regard. If you have these guys on tape notice how that don't just hold the pose but actually raise the arms above the head and crunch down three or four times to fully get the traps, chest, and arms flexed to the max. They also alternate flexing both biceps as they hold the pose at the bottom. When a bodybuilder is in shape (i.e. very low bodyfat) the most muscular makes it appear as if they will explode all over the first couple of rows!

Please keep in mind the previous is just a rough sample as to how to put poses together in a sequence. As with training styles, there is an infinite number of ways to select and combine poses. You may find that by taking a couple of poses from each your favorite bodybuilding stars gives you the routine that best suits your individual physique.

VIDEO AND TRANSITION

Once you have a series of poses set to music, the final step is to be able to move from one pose to the next. If the still camera was a great help for picking poses, the video camera will be invaluable for making things flow. The movement from one pose to the next is called transition. Executed properly, you look like poetry in motion. Done improperly and your routine looks pasted together at the last minute. If you don't have a video camera odds are a video store near you will rent one for $20 to $30. Once again a moderate financial investment but well worth it. Set the camera up and run through your routine. Throw the tape in the video recorder and sit

Andreas Munzer

back and watch yourself on TV. You are now seeing yourself from the judges' viewpoint. You may be impressed or you may want to change sports. Don't panic as most people are embarrassed the first time they see themselves on video film. If your routine looks like a collection of separate poses, then you need work. On the other hand if one pose moves into the next without any noticeable stoppage or break, then you are well on your way. A great posing routine allows smaller bodybuilders to compete on an even footing with bodybuilders who outweigh them by thirty or forty pounds. It's not surprising then that the best posers tend not to be the largest bodybuilders on stage. Guys like Frank Zane, Lee Labrada, and Shawn Ray, can't out-muscle larger bodybuilders like Mike Mentzer (Zane), Lee Haney (Labrada), and Ronnie Coleman (Ray). Instead they have taken posing to the next level. In Zane's case it garnered him three Mr. Olympia titles, Labrada came very close to beating Lee Haney, and Shawn Ray has beaten or placed higher on several occasions than most of the current crop of bodybuilding pros including Ronnie Coleman.

The great posers make posing appear almost effortless. Notice how they open the hands between poses and then close tightly just as they hit the next shot. Opening the hands gives the illusion of grace while closing adds an element of power. Without making it sound that only "smaller" bodybuilders have mastered posing, some of the greatest posers were also among the largest. The one and only Arnold was probably the first large bodybuilder to combine mass and presentation into one neat package. His great rival from the seventies, Sergio Oliva, while matching Arnold in size, appeared almost amateurish on stage. Lee Haney's record eight Mr. Olympia's were due in no small part to his outstanding stage presence. Today, guys like Ronnie Coleman, Flex Wheeler, and Kevin Lervone, spend as much time on their posing routines as training, in the weeks leading up to a contest. All of which leads us to Vince Taylor.

Pavol Jablonicky

In the late 1980s and early 1990s Vince established a reputation as the greatest poser on the scene and his patented robot routine never failed to bring the house down. Even now as a master competitor (twice Masters Mr. Olympia winner) Vince can still hold his own against guys literally half his age. While we don't expect you to dominate the posing scene like Vince, suffice to say you can't go wrong if you try to imitate some of Vince's moves.

PRACTICE, PRACTICE, PRACTICE

If there's one piece of advice to give you it's that you need to start your contest preparation at least two to three months before the show. Slapping a posing routine together at the

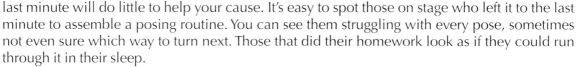

last minute will do little to help your cause. It's easy to spot those on stage who left it to the last minute to assemble a posing routine. You can see them struggling with every pose, sometimes not even sure which way to turn next. Those that did their homework look as if they could run through it in their sleep.

There's another reason to start a couple of months in advance. Ninety seconds doesn't sound like much, but it's the equivalent to the hardest set of squats you've ever done. Holding and moving between poses is very tiring. If you don't believe us try holding a front double biceps under full tension for ten seconds. See what we mean. Now do the same for all the compulsory poses. The fifteen to twenty minutes you'll spend on stage will be as physically draining as any workout. Those that practice months in advance can make posing look very relaxing while those that leave it till the last minute will be huffing and puffing.

As a final comment, there's another benefit to practicing your posing months in advance. Posing is one of the best ways to harden the physique. By this we mean the muscles will take on a more rugged look and make it appear as if you've been chiseled out of granite. Posing will give you that extra striation and vein which will be a great asset once you step on stage.

CONCLUSION

Once you have your posing routine put together, the next step is to address all the finer points that will complete the package so to speak. In the next chapter we will show you how to remove body hair, tan, select a posing suit, apply posing oil, and just about anything else that fully prepares you for the big show. So hang in there, we are almost there!

CHAPTER TWENTY-EIGHT

The Finer Points

REMOVING BODY HAIR

Legend has it the great biblical strongman, Samson, lost his great strength after the Philistines removed his hair. In a manner of speaking athletes have come full circle these days as most tend to remove all body hair in the weeks leading up to a contest. As a matter of fact more and more are shaving the head bald as well. For swimmers the less body hair makes for less water resistance and may take a fraction of a second off their times. Wrestlers often do it to cut down on mat burns and give their opponent less to grab on to. As a bodybuilder you will want to remove all body hair to give the judges a better view of your hard-earned muscles. In addition less body hair allows the body to tan easier.

There are numerous ways to remove body hair. As all have advantages and disadvantages we are going to go into some of the more popular ones in detail.

Brad Baker

SHAVING DOWN

By far the most popular method men use for removing body hair is to shave it off with either a straight edge or electric razor. The advantage of the straight razors is cost (a couple of dollars for a few disposables) and closeness of shave. Most straightedges now days have two or three blades and believe it or not the ads are correct. They not only cut the hair off at the surface, but in many cases below the surface. Most of you have seen the ad that says how the first blade lifts the hair while the second and third cut it off so that when the root snaps back it's below the skin surface. The advantage of this for bodybuilders is that once shaved in such a manner it appears as if the skin is totally devoid of any body hair. In fact it looks as if you had no hair in the first place. Of course nothing comes without a price. Most individuals who shave down the first time using a straight edge develop a mild to moderate rash. This is a combination of the skin not being conditioned to having a piece of sharp steel scraped over it and the hair roots literally sticking in to the surrounding skin. In a manner of speaking straight edges are too efficient.

If you decide to shave down using a straight edge, we suggest doing it about one to two months in advance. Then every week or two give it a touch up. This allows any nicks and cuts to heal, and gives the skin a chance to toughen up.

For those with sensitive skin, or no patience to use a straight edge, the second option is your best bet. For $40 to $50 you can buy an electric razor. You may already have one as most electric shavers have an attached moustache trimmer on the back. All it takes is five to ten minutes and you can shave the whole body. The upside is that because it doesn't shave as close to the skin as a straight edge, you don't have to worry about cuts or skin rashes. Of course this is also the downside as where you could go a week or more between shaves with a straight edge, you will only get two to three days between electric shaves.

The best option is probably a combination of the two. Take most of the heavy hair off with the electric razor and then do touch ups with the straight edge.

HAIR REMOVAL CREAMS

For the male readers among you, this is another area where women are far more knowledgeable. As the name implies, hair-removing creams are just that; creams that are applied to the desired area and after a period of time, a quick wash and off it comes. The most popular brand is Neet, which comes in a tangy smelling white lotion. You simply smear it on the area, wait about fifteen to twenty minutes and then wash it off. The lotion works because of active ingredients, which literally break down the hairs' protein structure. The hair is practically digested and easily crumbles and falls away. No razors, cuts, or weekly touch ups. You can do it a day or two before the show.

Notice we didn't include the word rash in our list of things not to worry about. As with any foreign substance, a certain percentage of the population may be allergic to the active ingredient in hair removal creams. Don't smear the whole body without first doing this little test. Cover a small area of the back of the arm, say a one-inch circle, and wait 15 to 20 minutes. If you are allergic you'll find out pretty quick. In fact you'll probably start developing a rash in less than an hour. It makes far more sense to discover you are allergic to a particular skin lotion this way than being covered head to foot with the stuff.

If you are allergic, you may be able to experiment with different brands, but always run the same simple test first. Without discouraging you, however, most brands use the same active ingredients and the odds are you'll have to resort to the good old straight edge or electric razor.

For those looking for something extra, a new company called Lex, may offer just what you're looking for. Lex's new hair removal system is a three-product approach that removes hair, helps keep it off and fully moisturizes the skin to give it a smooth, healthy look.

The first stage contains calcium thioglycolate as the main ingredient. This substance completely destroys hair protein.

Lex's second stage contains ingredients to actually retard the hair growth. This helps hair from regrowing.

Finally to smooth and moisturize the skin, Lex offers a moisturizing lotion that combats dry blotchy skin. All three products come as a kit and make an ideal contest preparation skin care package.

ELECTROLYSIS

Although shaving and creams are the most popular methods of hair removal, there is another option – electrolysis.

As the name suggests electrolysis involves using and electrical current to literally destroy the hair root. In the same manner a tree depends on its root system for survival, so to will hairs die if their roots are destroyed. At one time electrolysis was only popular with older, menopausal women who wanted to remove the sparse upper-lip hair that sometimes accompanies changes in hormone levels. But in recent years, everyone from models and actors, to swimmers and bodybuilders are opting for this form of hair removal.

Electrolysis has two big disadvantages; cost and speed. In fact the two go together. Each hair must be destroyed separately, and as one might guess, it doesn't come cheap. For a male bodybuilder to undergo electrolysis for the entire body, the bill could run into the hundreds of thousands of dollars. Even if money was no option, it would take hundreds of sessions to get rid of the thousands of body hairs. For most, the cost and time involved rules out electrolysis as a viable means of hair removal. It may only make sense for females who grow facial hair from steroids to resort to it.

One of the myths about electrolysis is that it's permanent. This is not entirely true, however. Many individuals who have had the procedure report that it takes multiple treatments to finally terminate the little suckers. For a male bodybuilder with the equivalent of a shag coat on their legs, electrolysis is not really an option.

WAXING

At one time waxing was the exclusive domain of females, but not any more. When male bodybuilders heard about the advantages of this time-tested technique, they began adding it to their pre-contest preparations.

Waxing involves applying a coat of hot liquid wax to the skin and allowing it to cool. Once it hardens the wax can be ripped off in sheets pulling the hair with it. Take a look at a Band-Aid the next time you remove one from a cut. Notice the hairs? The same thing occurs with wax. You can "mass-murder" a couple of hundred of the little scoundrels with one swipe. Of course waxing is not all fun and games. As might be expected hot wax can be a tad uncomfortable. And ripping must be done in one quick stroke. Trying to pull the wax off the skin slowly not only increases the amount of pain involved, but is in fact less effective as it takes a quick rip to tear the hair loose. Pulling slowly may only pull the hair free of the wax, leaving it still attached to the skin.

The primary advantages of waxing are cost and speed. Waxing kits are relatively inexpensive, and you can rid the body of most hair within an hour or two.

BODY SUGARING

Although it's been around for thousands of years, it's only in recent years that body sugaring has begun to be taken seriously by bodybuilders. It's called "sugaring," and was originally an Egyptian concept, introduced to Rome by captives following Emperor Octavian's defeat of Cleopatra and Mark Anthony. It works very simply. A paste made from sugar and citric acid is applied to the skin, then a strip of cloth is pressed firmly against the skin over the sugared area. With a quick pull the hairs and dead skin cells are removed. There are no harsh chemicals, which can harm or irritate your skin. For bodybuilders who may have acne on their chests, backs and shoulders, body sugaring is safe for even the most sensitive skin. In fact, it will improve it! Unlike shaving which only works for a few days and can cut up acne-contoured skin, body sugaring may only need to be used every couple of weeks. And since body sugaring pulls out the hair follicle (around which the acne blemish forms, as well as removing the dead cells and debris that block the pores), your skin will get a deep cleaning that will show an immediate visible improvement!

Does it hurt? We're not going to sugarcoat it for you (sorry we couldn't resist!). Yes, the first few times are going to be painful, but not as painful as waxing. If you can, have a friend pull the cloth strips and then press their hand on the cleaned area, it won't hurt quite as much. But it works, and it works well

FRANCO'S WAY!

We mentioned this story in our *Bodybuilding Encyclopedia*, and thought it a great way to conclude the section on hair removal. In one of his books, two-time Mr. Olympia, Franco Columbu tells of his unique approach to hair removal. Instead of wimping out and using a razor or straight edge, Franco used to let it grow long and then rip it out with his hands. Whether it's something in the Italian diet or spending all those years in Arnold's shadow, no

Justin Brooks

one knows for sure if the story is true (Franco swears it is). But unless you are descended from the KGB or Gestapo, we advise you to take the wimp route and use one of the less painful means of hair removal!

TANNING

It only makes sense to follow hair removal with tanning as they both have similar functions, to highlight the musculature as much as possible. Tanning has become a bad word in recent years given the depletion of the ozone layer and consequent reduction in the atmosphere's filtering properties. This is one reason why sun-block lotions now have high double-digit figures. Excessive sunlight damages the skin and can lead to skin cancer.

The light you see is only part of what physicists call the electromagnetic spectrum. Your eyes can only see a fraction of the various energy rays that continuously bombard the atmosphere. Even some of the "colors" that we use for painting are only partially visible to the naked eye (infra-red and ultraviolet) in their purist form. Some energy waves like am and fm radio are harmless, while others like microwaves and gamma waves can be deadly.

Tanning is a defense mechanism developed by the body to protect it from some of the sun's ultraviolet radiation. In its simplest form, tanning involves a darkening of the skin due to the release of specialized compounds called pigments. Our ancestors who evolved close to the equator developed very dark skin in order to protect them from the intense sun radiation that hits this part of the earth. As humans spread north where the sunlight wasn't as intense, over millions of years the skin lost some of its protective dark coloring. This is why people from northern countries have very pale skin, while those of African decent have much darker skin. But here's the important thing; individuals of northern ancestry have not lost the ability to darken their skin. As soon as they are exposed to intense sunlight, the skin releases dark pigment as a protective mechanism. And while someone from say, Sweden, could never develop the same degree of skin pigmentation as someone from central Africa, they can darken to a deep brown color.

WHY TAN?

We've given you the biological reason for tanning, now comes the bodybuilding applications. All things being equal, a dark skinned individual will look larger and more muscular than a pale individual. The bright lights on stage are in a manner of speaking a double edge sword. On one hand they enable the audience to see the competitors better, but on the other they "wash" the skin out. By this we mean the light makes one muscle run into the next, and sort of hides any separation between the muscles. Conversely dark skin preserves the body's natural contours and reveals the individual's true size and muscularity. All things being equal, an African-American bodybuilder will look more muscular than a very pale-skinned Caucasian. Which is why white bodybuilders need to add "skin coloring" to their list of precontest preparations.

Before discussing tanning in detail we should add that our African-American readers might want to add a few hours lying in the sun as well. Tanning you see not only darkens the skin, but also dries it to an extent making it hug the muscles more closely. The result is a harder, more muscular looking physique. This is why many of the top African-American IFBB pros routinely hit the beach for a few "rays" in the weeks leading up to a big show. At that level of competition they need every little bit of extra hardness to be competitive.

JOURNEY INTO DARKNESS

There are two primary light sources that can be used to tan or darken the skin – natural sunlight, and artificial tanning lamps. Let's look at both.

The nice thing about sunlight is that it's free, easily obtainable, and available for an average of 12 to 18 hours a day (with our apologies extended to our readers in Alaska!). Of course the downside is that sunlight contains the full spectrum of electromagnetic radiation – both the waves that only tan the skin and the waves that may destroy it leading to skin cancer.

> **"After many years, exposure to the sun's rays can suppress the skin's immune system and permanently damage its cell structure and function. The result can be growth of red or brown scaly patches which may be pre-cancers, indicating the development of skin cancer itself."**
>
> – Kerrie-Lee Brown, *MuscleMag International* contributor outlining the potential danger of prolonged exposure to the sun.

If you have pale, fair skin (i.e. northern European ancestry), we suggest limiting your time in the sun to an hour or less. At least until you have a good, protective base tan. Even then, you should wear a heavy – SPF 10 or more – sunscreen and apply it frequently throughout the day especially if you are swimming or doing a lot sweating. For those not familiar with the SPF system of sunscreens, it's a rating scale indicating how much longer you can stay out in the sun before burning with the sunscreen as opposed to not wearing any sunscreen. Some individuals mistakenly believe that the numbers are measured in hours. Let us

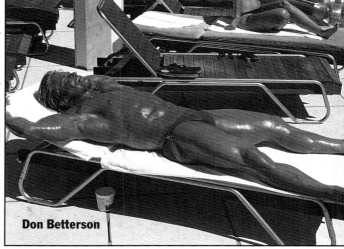

Don Betterson

Tanning beds are very convenient and will do a nice job if used properly.

stress that an SPF of 10 does not mean you can stay in the sun for ten hours. It means that if you start to burn at around 20 minutes, then an SPF of 10 should protective you for 200 minutes or about three hours. Now this sounds great in theory but as we said earlier, body sweat and water will reduce much of the lotion's effectiveness. And keep in mind the SPF numbers are a guide only. Everyone's skin responds differently. You may need an SPF of 20 to get the same protection as someone using a 10.

BAKE EVENLY ALL OVER

If you are playing sports or working in the sun, then chances are you will get a good tan over the entire body. If on the other hand you are lying on a blanket, don't make the mistake of only lying front and back on. It's easy to tan the large muscles of the body like the chest, shoulders, back, and thighs. But the smaller muscles like the biceps and triceps tend to require special attention. The insides of the arms, close to the torso, are well hidden and you will need to lie on your side with the arms stretched out overhead to get direct sunlight on the area. The next time you are at a contest take a look at the competitors when they do a front double biceps pose. There's bound to be one competitor who forgot to tan the armpit/inner arm region. Standing relaxed they may appear to be tanned all over, but as soon as they raise their arms, the over-sight becomes all too obvious.

The best times to tan are mid morning and late afternoon. Midday provides the most direct sunlight, and for most the risk of sunburn is not worth it. Our suggestion is to gradually increase exposure time up to a maximum of a couple of hours a day. For those in northern climates this may mean starting with five or ten minutes and adding a couple of minutes a week. Even then there may be those who don't turn brown but red. For these individuals one of the next two options may be the solution.

FAKE N' BAKE

Let's face it not everyone can leave Gold's gym after a workout and stroll down to Venice Beach. With the exception of Florida, California, and a few southern and lower mid western states, most individuals don't get year round tanning temperatures. Try suntanning in Michigan or Canada in January and you'll be quickly hauled off to the local psychiatric hospital! It doesn't help matters either when most local contests are usually in the fall or late winter. Thanks to the miracle of modern science you can get a great tan without having to go outside.

> **"Many people think that artificial tanning methods (tanning beds, booths, lamps) are safer than the sun. Not true. Getting a tan indoors can damage your skin too!"**
>
> – Kerrie-Lee Brown, *MuscleMag International* contributor warning readers that artificial tanning methods have their own risks.

They go by various names including tanning lamps, tanning beds, and solariums. No matter what you call them, they all accomplish the same thing, use artificial light to induce a tan. Tanning lamps have most of the harmful light rays removed leaving only the rays that increase skin pigmentation (to satisfy the anti-tanning groups we will agree that "harmful" is a relative term and prolonged exposure to tanning lamps can cause sunburn and skin damage).

There are two primary types of tanning booths. Some are shaped like a giant waffle iron and require you to lie down flat on the bed and close the cover. The new models allow you to stand up with the lamps encircling you about 300 degrees. You only have to turn slightly to expose the whole body.

If tanning by solarium has a disadvantage it's cost. A ten-package pass costs anywhere from $30 to $50. For those with little or no skin color to begin with it will probably cost you $100 to $150 to darken adequately enough for a contest. On the bright side (no pun intended!) tanning beds are very convenient and will do a nice job if used properly.

LIQUID SUNSHINE

For those who can't seem to get a decent tan from light, natural or artificial, there is still one option remaining. In fact even those who have a good tan come contest day, rely on tanning creams to add the finishing touches.

Artificial tanning creams have been around for decades, but it's only in the last decade or so that quality products have come on the scene. Tanning creams are smeared on like regular sunscreen or tanning oil, but instead of blocking out the sun, or enhancing its effects, artificial creams create the tan themselves. They do this by reacting with enzymes in the skin and turning brown. The first generation creams were flawed in that instead of brown they usually left the individual yellow and jaundiced looking. For the most part the newer products create a decent brown color, but since everyone responds differently, you may want to test a small area of skin first (this also establishes if you are allergic to the product.)

"I start the Thursday before the contest with one coat of Pro Tan. My second coat of Pro Tan goes on Friday morning, the third coat Friday night. A helpful hint is to use old sheets on your bed and wear old clothes because everything will be stained and smell like Pro Tan."

– MuscleMag International columnist and top physique model, offering advice on artificial tanning.

The last category of tanning lotions, are to all intents and purposes, dyes. They usually come in small bottles and you simply spray the liquid on and presto, instant tan. Tanning dyes allow even the palest of competitors to step on stage sporting the California look. If they have a disadvantage it's they are a tad messy. They won't just color your skin, but everything it comes in contact with, including clothes, bed sheets, and towels, etc. If you have very pale skin with no base tan, you will probably need four or five coats to darken the skin. This is a lot of dye and you may want to choose your clothes and bed sheets wisely for this time period.

One practical piece of advice concerning tanning dyes, either have someone else apply the liquid or do it yourself wearing a pair of plastic gloves (check any hair salon or body products section of a drug store). The skin on your hands has a thick, dead outer layer that seems to soak up tanning dye likes it going out of style. You may have trouble darkening the rest of the body, but not the hands. They will go virtually black! How often have the authors seen competitors step on stage revealing the telltale signs of self-application. Remember the goal is to have the entire body sporting the same degree of color. The best way to do this is to use sunlight or a tanning bed to get a good base tan, and then touch up with either artificial tanning lotion or dye.

STRETCH MARKS

Dave
Palumbo

We could discuss this topic in just about any chapter but since it relates to appearance we thought it would fit in here. Stretch marks are those unsightly purple streaks usually found where two or more muscles come together. They are most commonly seen in what bodybuilders call the pec-delt tie-in region. This is the area in the front shoulder where the chest, shoulders, and biceps, all come together. In extreme cases they appear as long red rips in the skin. They are produced when the underlying muscles grow faster than the overlying skin. In effect the skin can't keep up and stretches and rips. While most natural trainers have mild cases in the pec-delt region, they are really a characteristic of steroid users. It's very uncommon for natural trainers to experience muscle growth that outpaces skin growth. Conversely you'll see ghastly stretch marks on the biceps, chest, and thighs of regular steroid users.

If the cause is straightforward, the cure is not. Once you have stretch marks, you have them for life. If your muscle size diminishes, your stretch marks may fade to an extent, but rarely disappear. Stretch marks are a case where prevention is far more effective than treatment. The primary goal in prevention is making the skin more pliable and stretchable in the areas where stretch marks mainly occur. Creams high in coconut oil and vitamin A have been found to very effective in reducing the size of stretch marks. You don't need to spend a fortune for some prescription drugs either. Most of the common sun tanning lotions containing coconut oil will suffice quite nicely. As soon as you detect the first sign of the skin weakening in a particular area (the previously mentioned pec-delt region being the most common) start rubbing the coconut cream into the area once or twice a day.

For those who have them and plan on competing, the first thing to realize is that you won't be penalized. Further, a good tan will hide most stretch marks. Still for those with very prominent marks, we suggest using either the artificial tanning lotion or dye to sort of camouflage them. Two of the biggest names in the history of bodybuilding, Mike Mentzer and Paul Dillett, are famous for their stretch marks in the chest region. Yet both have won major championships (Paul the Arnold Classic and New York Night of Champions and Mike the Mr. America and Mr. Universe).

As a final comment on this topic, some of you may wonder if stretch marks are dangerous. The answer is a guarded no. By this we mean we have never heard of a body-builders developing an infection from such. But keep in mind the skin is the body's first line of defense. It separates you from the external environment, which contains a host of pathogens (germs). As soon as the skin is ripped you run the risk of letting something unwanted in. At the first sign of infection in a stretch mark see your physician.

HAIRSTYLE

We just spent a couple of pages telling you how to get rid of hair, now we are going to offer suggestions on improving its appearance! What we are referring to is scalp hair, not body hair.

The odds that a contest could be won or lost on hairstyle alone, are pretty remote. But given the competitiveness of today's contest, you don't want to step onstage looking like something left-over from Woodstock (with all due respect to the scraggly-looking members of the sixties generation!) Nothing detracts from a great looking physique like a mound of unkempt scalp hair. You spent years changing the appearance of your body, so why not take a couple of minutes and make your hair presentable.

Whether you wear your hair long or short is your choice. In fact the speed with which fashions keep changing, means that specific advice we give here could be outdated by the time this book hits the shelves. Whatever length you wear, make sure it, neatly trimmed and clean. Spend $15 or $20 on a haircut. You've certainly spent far more on your physique. Grab a couple of back issues of *MuscleMag International* and look at the hairstyles of the pros and top amateurs. Ask your wife, girlfriend, or female acquaintance to offer advice as to how to style it. As much as we hate to admit it, most women know far more about hairstyles than most men. Conceal your pride and take advantage of such knowledge.

LOSE ONE, LOSE ALL

For those who either hate hairstyles, or don't know much about them, you have one other option remaining – get rid of it!

A quick glance at a pro line up and you'll see numerous competitors sporting the cue-ball look. By this we mean bald. Guys like Flex Wheeler, Shawn Ray, Ronnie Coleman, and Kevin Levrone, all have made the bald look very fashionable in the last couple of years. Others such as Nasser El Sonbaty, Paul Dillett, and Dorian Yates, stop just short of the bald look and go for the military crew cut.

The nice thing about shaving all or most scalp hair off is it's one less thing to worry about on contest day. And for those who've worn long locks for most of their life, take comfort in knowing that most who shave their head bald, later report that they wished they'd done it sooner.

Vegetable oils absorb into the skin and give the body that much desired sheen.

POSING OIL

As mentioned earlier, the bright lights used at bodybuilding contests can make it appear as if competitors are less muscular than they really are. The old time strongmen found that by rubbing the body with oil they could preserve much of the body's muscular appearance. Of course like anything, there are right and wrong ways to "oil up."

For those about to grab the bottle of baby oil we suggest otherwise. Baby and other petroleum-based oils don't absorb into the skin but mainly sit on top of it. This will reflect virtually all the light and make you appear as some great walking firefly! Vegetable oils on the other hand absorb into the skin and give the body that much desired sheen. In addition as you start to sweat, the oil slowly rises to the surface. So in a manner of speaking it's self- monitoring. The most popular oils you'll see backstage are olive and almond, but most vegetable oils will suffice.

Lee Priest

As most promoters allow contestants to bring a "coach" backstage, have them apply the oil for you. It may seem trivial but you can't always trust the other contestants. There have been cases were a rival put too much oil on one part of a fellow competitor's back, and left another area dry! Most bodybuilders will gladly help you out, but we strongly urge you not to ask the person who you think is your closest competition to oil up. Look at it another way. Would you really want to help another competitor look better than you do? We think not.

Determining how much oil to use is a case of trial and error. This is another reason to have a few trial runs a few days in advance, and preferably with the same person who will accompany you backstage. This way there's no guessing on the day of the contest. Generally speaking you want to apply enough oil to highlight the muscles without drowning them. Some competitors are literally dripping backstage and the places where they stand resembles a Texas oil field. You are going for that sheen look, not an advertisement for the glimmer man!

POSING SUITS

The official "uniform" of bodybuilding is a small pair of posing briefs. For females there is also a top. There are two things to look for in posing trunks, color and style. Let's look at both.

THE COLOR PURPLE?

Posing suits come in a wide variety of colors with the most popular being, red, purple, black, brown, and blue. Generally speaking select your posing suit based on skin color. If you are of African-American ancestry, stick with red, purple, or blue. Dark colors like brown and black practically disappear and blend in with the skin. Conversely Caucasians should avoid light colors like white, pale blue, etc. Also, light colors tend to make the waist look larger than it really is – something to be avoided at all costs.

Jason Arntz

Although we said that ultimately the color you wear is your choice, there are a few exceptions. IFBB rules state that competitors may not wear trunks that are more than one color (i.e. symbols, two-tone, etc.) or metallic (i.e. silver, gold, fluorescent).

THE IN STYLE

Given the skimpiness of posing suits, it's hard to believe that style comes into play. But in fact it's the skimpiness that is governed by IFBB rules. Although you may satisfy the curiosity of some of the audience (and a few judges we dare say), there are standards to be followed in terms of what must be covered. If your posing briefs cover to little of the gluteus (the butt for those who skipped Chapter Two) you could be penalized. For female competitors the breasts must be kept partially covered. Now as much as we'd like to define "partially" we can't. To quote one U.S. senator "I can't define pornography but I'd recognize it when I saw it." The same applies here. As a rule of thumb if the nipples are visible, you need to add more material to your top.

Besides keeping the naughty bits covered, there's a practical side to posing suit style. By the property of optical illusion, you can make short legs appear longer by wearing what is called a "high cut" posing brief. This means the trunks are cut higher and expose more of the legs. Now we are not suggesting Lee Priest is going to match Lou Ferrigno, but for anyone with short legs, a high cut suit will help balance your symmetry. The opposite holds true as well. If your legs are proportionally longer than your torso, opt for a fuller set of posing briefs.

WHERE TO BUY

There's really not much difference between posing suits and swimming suits, with the possible exception of advertising logos (i.e. Speedo) and decorative emblems attached. Most sports stores have a good selection of swimming trunks so this is the first place to look. If your town or city has a specialty bodybuilding store, then odds are they'll have posing suits in stock (the smarter ones will order in extras for the contest and advertise at the local gyms). If all fails order a pair from one of the many advertisers in *MuscleMag International*, or other bodybuilding publication. Prices vary but men should be able to get a decent pair for $30 to $40, and females will spend $60 to $80. These are baseline average numbers of course. If money is no object there are retailers only too happy to charge you hundreds of dollars for top of the line brands. Our advice is to opt for the cheaper pair for your first contest, and then if you think you have a career in the sport, fork out the extra bucks.

CARB LOADING AND DEPLETION

Carb loading and depletion is a perfect example of cashing in on the concept of illusion. The primary goal of every bodybuilder is to step up onstage as large and as cut as possible. The judges don't care how much you can bench press or how fast you can run the 100-meter dash. They only call it as they see it.

Carb loading and depletion has two purposes. The first is to help you shed subcutaneous water so your muscularity stands out. The second is to supersaturate the muscles with carbohydrate making them appear bigger and fuller. Here's how you do it.

DEPLETION

The first step is to deplete the muscles of most of their carbohydrate stores. For large bodybuilders (over 200 pounds) this will take four to five days. Smaller bodybuilders can probably do it in three to four days. As loading takes about the same time, you will need to start depleting about six to eight days out from contest day. Females can probably deplete in two days so they would start about four days before the show.

There are two primary ways to deplete stored carbohydrate (glycogen) levels. The first is to cut down on intake. The general rule of thumb is to cut your carb intake by 50 percent. Assuming an average of 350 to 400 grams per day, the individual would drop his or her carb intake to 175 to 200 grams. Now there may be those who are tempted to cut carb intake by more than 50 percent but we advise against this. As it is you will be treading a fine line between adequate carbs for energy, and inducing catabolism. Once carb levels drop too low the body starts burning muscle tissue as a fuel source. This is the last thing you want. There's also the brain to worry about. The brain's primary fuel source is carbohydrate. When levels drop your cognitive abilities may suffer. You probably have noticed how irritable and confused some bodybuilders get while on a pre-contest diet. This is often due to low carbohydrate levels.

The other method for carb depletion is to burn up existing supplies, and this means exercise. Take two exercises per body part and perform three sets of each for 15 to 20 reps. Over a three or four day period this will burn off just about any stored glycogen.

We should add that carbohydrate depletion can be bloody murder. And this is being polite! Few bodybuilders go through the depletion phase feeling any better than lousy. It's ironic that something designed to make you look better will in all probability make you feel a whole lot worse!

LOADING

About three or four days before the show you switch gears and start the loading phase. By this point you will have noticed the muscles literally shrinking and becoming flat. Don't worry in a couple of day's time they'll be fuller and larger than you thought possible. There's nothing complicated about carb loading. You simply do the opposite of what you did during the depletion phase.

The first step is to increase you carb intake. The general rule is to take in 50 percent more than you did before you started depleting. Using our example of 400 grams per day, you would load on 600 grams per day. The reason for such a high intake is to take advantage of what's popularly called the "rebound" effect. After three or four days of depletion the body is begging for carbohydrate. And when it finally gets it, it will store proportionally more of it than normal (the body treats fat the same way, which is why going long periods of time without eating only triggers fat storage mechanisms). This over-storage of carbohydrate swells the muscles to the point of bursting. In addition it takes extra water to facilitate the process. You'll be happy to know that most of the water comes from under the skin. This has the effect of thinning the skin and making it hug the muscles. Within three to four days the muscles are not only larger, but also more defined and vascular.

To keep carbohydrate levels high we suggest little or no training during the three or four days leading up to the show. Training burns glycogen and you'll only impede the loading process by working out. Spend your gym time practicing your posing and taking care of last minute details.

IT'S ALL IN THE TIMING

Before leaving this topic we should point out that timing is everything when it comes to carb loading. Few bodybuilders get it dead on the first time. It may take you two or three attempts to figure out how long it takes to deplete and/or load. This is why you should keep detailed notes during both phases. If find yourself looking much better on the day after or before the show, you know that you will have to readjust your schedule for the next show.

Carb loading and depleting can be so precise that a competitor could look average during the prejudging but appear unbeatable during the evening show. But because most of the judging takes place during the morning session, the competitor may not win the show. This comes as a shock to most of the audience who were not present during the prejudging. They feel the judging panel robbed the individual. But in fact the competitor simply missed his or her peak by about six hours. The opposite can also occur where a bodybuilder peaks for the prejudging and has enough points to win the whole show despite not looking the best on stage during the evening show. Once again the audience is puzzled by the judges' decision.

Carb loading and depletion are like many other facets of bodybuilding. It takes time to get them perfect, but when you do, it can make the difference between cracking the top three or not making the finals.

Markus Ruhl

CHAPTER TWENTY-NINE

Contest Day

If you've done everything correctly, a few hours from now will see you on stage in your first bodybuilding contest. Before we go any further we'd like to say congratulations and no matter what the judges think you are already a winner. Few people have the physique or guts to get up on stage and compete. So once again, well done!

The purpose of this chapter is to help you wade through the murky waters that collectively fall under the category of contest day. You may think it's only a matter of showing up and following directions, but it's very easy to get lost in the confusion that surrounds a bodybuilding contest. We are going to see if we can smoothen things out for you.

Chris Cormier, Flex Wheeler and Kevin Levrone

ARRIVING ON TIME

Unless you have been given specific instructions as to what time to show up, give yourself at least an hour. If the prejudging starts at ten, then time it so you are pulling into the venue parking lot no later than 9 to 9:15. For those from out of town you may want to conduct a trial run a day or two before the contest. Keep in mind weekday traffic is much heavier than weekends, so if won't take you as long on Saturday morning.

As soon as you check in you will be given a number to attach to your posing suit. This is your identity for the next couple of hours. We suggest memorizing it, as you will only hear numbers from now on. If you are in the lightheavyweight or heavyweight class, you may be able to sit in the audience and watch the lightweight and women's classes go through the prejudging. But don't be surprised if the promoter or head judge ushers everyone backstage.

The best way to describe backstage at a bodybuilding contest is organized confusion. Depending on the facility there may be separate men's and women's change rooms and a common warm-up room, or two completely separate areas for the sexes. Once you've found the correct preparation area, take out your "contest kit" and get yourself ready. Your starter kit should contain the following:

1 water bottle
1 bottle of artificial tanning solution or cream
2 pairs posing suits
2 cassette tapes of your posing music

Vince Taylor

Let's look at each in detail.

The water bottle as simple as it may sound will be one of your best friends over the next couple of hours. It's ironic that the more in shape you are the closer to dehydration you probably are. The nervousness combined with the bright lights will only add to the problem by causing you to lose additional water (nervousness increases urination, and hot lights increase the amount of water lost by sweat). Fainting and cramping are all too common at bodybuilding contests and there's no need for you to join the ranks of the best-built body-builder lying on a stretcher! You should be sipping water periodically backstage. Notice we said sipping not gulping. Drink too much and you run the risk of stomach distension and gas. You also have to remember that the body likes to conserve water for later use, and one of the storage sites is between the skin and under-lying muscles. There have been numerous cases of bodybuilders being shredded for the prejudging but appearing "smooth" for the evening show. Often the problem is related to excessive fluid intake throughout the day, which robs the competitor of their much-prized definition. Your goal is to consume enough water to keep from suffering the symptoms of dehydration, without going overboard and ruining your appearance.

The next item on the list is a towel to wipe off any excess sweat and posing oil, both before and after you enter and exit the stage. For the sake of a couple of bucks you can pick up a plain beach towel that you can discard after the show. You don't want to use one of mom's good designer towels given the tanning and posing oil you will be wiping off.

Unless you are 100 percent naturally tanned, bring along a bottle of instant tanning spray to carry out last minute touch ups. This is especially true if much of your tan is artificial to begin with. Something as simple as getting out of bed or putting on clothes could wipe off some of the tanning solution. Even oiling up may reveal a few lighter areas of your body. A few sprays with the tanning dye quickly takes care of that.

You noticed we said to bring two pairs of posing trunks. Competitors have been known to play some cruel tricks backstage, and stealing another's posing suit is one of them. Ken Waller's stealing of Mike Katz's shirt in the documentary *Pumping Iron* has become legendary. All it takes is for you to turn your back for a split second and some rival could go off with your posing attire. Even something as simple as excess tanning dye could ruin your day. Our sugges-tion is to wear one pair to the contest, and have an extra pair stored safely in your gym bag.

Most bodybuilders usually perform a mini-workout backstage to try and pump up the muscles to make them appear larger.

Just as household dryers have been known to eat socks, so too have tape decks been known to digest competitors' posing music at bodybuilding contests. Unless you are one of those rare individuals who can improvise on the spot and pose to nothing but the audience's shouting, we suggest bringing two copies of your posing music to the show. You won't be penalized for something beyond your control, but let's face it there's enough to worry about without having to rely on the audience for your background music!

In addition to the previous, there are a few optional items you may want to bring along. Give your height of anxiety, the odds are you skipped or had little for breakfast. If there's a large number of competitors in the show you may end up going three, four, even five hours without eating. Bring along a small snack such as a granola bar, piece of fruit, bran muffin, etc. There doesn't need to be much food in the stomach to nullify the feelings of hunger.

You may also want to bring along a tracksuit. With most contests held in the fall or early spring, many venues cut down on costs by turning the heating system down or off on weekends. Keeping warm on stage is no concern, but it could get chilly standing around backstage for any period of time. Keep your tracksuit on until you are ready to begin pumping and oiling up.

HERE WE GO!

Most contest organizers will give you two primary warnings. The first will be the approximate time your class is to be judged. Keep in mind that bodybuilding judging is a very fluid entity. Judges can only guess as to how long each class will take depending on the number in each class. If the quality of competition is high, it means the judges will need to spend more time scrutinizing. As you wait backstage, keep track of what class is being judged on stage.

The second warning is usually the five-minute warning and by this point you should be ready to hit the stage.

About thirty minutes before curtain time you should begin your final preparations. The first thing to do is what has fashionably become known as the backstage "pump-up." Hopefully by now the word "pump" doesn't throw people off. Most bodybuilders usually perform a mini-workout backstage to try and pump up the muscles to make them appear larger. Bodybuilding is as much illusion as substance, remember. A lighter competitor can look larger than a heavier competitor if they have a low body-fat percentage and fuller muscles. Forcing extra blood into the muscles is one way to create the illusion of size. Most bodybuilders don't pump up the abs as the extra blood and associated tightness makes it difficult to flex them.

As backstage preparation rooms are not commercial gyms, you will need to be creative with your exercises. If you are lucky there may be a few light dumbells and a barbell or two. But that's usually it. Still with a bit of ingenuity you can give the whole body a good pumping workout and here's how.

MUSCLE	EXERCISE
Thighs	Sissy squats
Hamstrings	Dumbell curls or stiff-leg deadlifts
Calves	One-leg standing calf raises
Chest	Push-ups
Side shoulders	Dumbell lateral raises
Rear shoulders	Bent-over lateral raises
Back	Chins, pullovers, one arm rows, rope pulls
Biceps	Narrow chins, dumbell or barbell curls
Triceps	Bench dips, narrow pushups, one arm extensions

Note – each exercise is performed for 2 sets of 15 to 20 reps.

With regards to the thighs, there are two schools of thought. Some bodybuilders find pumping the thighs makes them difficult to control. The extra blood also may take away some of the thigh's sharpness. Others treat the quads like any other muscle and find that the extra pump actually brings out more vascularity. Our advice is to conduct a trial run a couple of days before the show.

You'll notice that we've included two of the best non-weight exercises, pushups and chinups. These two exercises will pump up the entire upper body. Pushups work the chest, shoulders, and triceps, while chins target the lats, biceps, and forearms. We won't elaborate on pushups as they can be done literally anywhere. Chins on the other hand may require that creativity we alluded to earlier. Unless the contest is held at a gym, odds are there won't be a chinning bar backstage. But if you look around you may find something that can be used as a substitute. Older buildings tend to have exposed plumbing, and this means an abundance of pipes. Most one-inch or larger pipes will support your weight and make great chinning bars. In fact many gyms use one-inch pipe for this very purpose. If there's no piping around, you could use a door. Open the door, stand directly end

Towel pulls are a good back stage pump up because they provide just enough resistance to work the lats and biceps.

on, and grab the top. From here pull yourself up as if doing a narrow chinup. The obvious disadvantage to this is that the lower torso will chafe against the door. For this reason you may want to keep your sweat suit on. Even then your family planning may be put in jeopardy! Still, as the old saying goes, any port in a storm.

A third option is to invest a few dollars and buy one of those portable chinning bars that fit between doorframes. If two or three of your friends are in the same contest then you could all split the cost.

If chins are not your cup of tea, try rope pulls. This is an exercise that is almost exclusively reserved for backstage pump-ups. Have a partner grab one end of a towel and you the other. Adopt a runner's stance, bend slightly at the waist, and pull the towel into the lower rib cage as if doing a seated row. Your partner serves as the "weight stack" and provides just enough resistance to make you work the lats and biceps. Watch any bodybuilding documentary or flip through any magazine and you are guaranteed to see bodybuilders performing rope pulls backstage.

Although it varies, we suggest doing two sets of 15 to 20 reps of each exercise. This should be enough to pump up the muscles without tiring you out. Remember that you'll need most of your energy on stage so don't do a full workout before hand.

OIL READY!

Once you have everything pumped, primed, and ready, your final step is to oil up (or down depending on how you look at it!). Have your partner apply a thin coating of oil over the entire

body. Have him or her massage it in well so there's nothing dripping off you. With the possible exception of the hands and feet the whole body surface should be oiled. And don't forget the inner thighs and under the arms either. You can't see these areas standing relaxed, but they become very obvious when you start posing. Once you are satisfied that you have a good coating applied (get a second and third opinion on this as well) take your towel and gently wipe off any excess oil on your body. It's also good etiquette to clean up the floor area where you were standing. This prevents anyone from slipping on, what more than likely is a hardwood floor.

SHOW TIME

About five minutes before your class is to go on, a representative, usually a backstage usher, will lean in the door and yell a five-minute warning. By this point you should be ready to go. If you feel nervous, don't worry, we assure you virtually every other competitor feels the same way. Even many of the sport's top pros get the butterflies before a big show. Not only is it human nature, but healthy. A dose of nervousness increases adrenaline output, which in turn increases mental alertness – something that will come in handy on stage.

With the possible exception of the hands and feet the whole body surface should be oiled.

"Judges are human. They sometimes make mistakes. They have personal likes and dislikes both in the type of physique they prefer and whether they like a competitor's personality. They can be influenced by reputations, good and bad, and a host of other factors that have nothing to do with bodybuilding."

– John Simmons, *MuscleMag International* contributor offering his views on bodybuilding judges.

The first thing you'll notice as you walk on stage is the intensity of the lights. Stay focused and appear as confident as possible.
– Darrem Charles

The walk to the stage will be both one of the shortest and longest of your life. By short we mean physical distance, as most backstage prep areas are located close to the stage. By long we are referring to the feelings of apprehension you are no doubt feeling. All we can say is trust us, as soon as you get out onstage, things will be happening so fast that you won't have time to dwell on nervousness.

HEARD BUT NOT SEEN

The first thing you'll notice as you walk on stage is the intensity of the lights. If you've never been on stage before the feeling is reminiscent of staring into the headlights of an oncoming car, and you my friend are the deer! The second thing you'll notice is that with the exception of the judging panel and first couple of rows, you can't really see the audience. For those who are nervous in front of large groups of people, this is a godsend.

The most important person for the next couple of minutes is the emcee or head judge. He or she will be your guide and will pass along the requests of the judging panel. Don't let your mind wander while on stage. Try to stay focused at all times and appear as confident as possible.

"Don't be disheartened if you aren't chosen for a modeling job, and don't get discouraged if you don't place in the top three at a competition. You can't get stressed out. Take it all in stride."

– Frank Sepe, *MuscleMag International* columnist and top model offering advice on any aspect of bodybuilding that involves a judge's opinion.

As we discussed each round earlier, there's no need to rehash everything once again. Suffice to say the number of competitors will determine how long you are on stage. Five or less and you'll probably be out of there in ten or fifteen minutes. On the other hand if your class has ten competitors or more, you might as well be prepared to spend 30 minutes or more on stage. The authors have seen contests where the quality of competitors was so high that the judges needed nearly an hour to sort them out. Even if your are not officially being judged, assume you are! Even how you stand in the line-up can raise or lower you a few positions in the contest.

IT'S OVER ... FOR NOW

As soon as your class is finished go backstage and dry off the excess sweat and posing oil. We assure you there will be plenty of both after all the flexing and posing under the hot lights. What you do from here is up to you. If you were in one of the lighter classes you can probably sneak into the audience and view the remaining classes (the odds are you won't be able to do the same thing at the evening show as it's probably sold out). If on the other hand the pre-judging is complete, you can either head home or back to the hotel; or take in the seminar.

Most promoters bring in a top amateur or pro bodybuilder to guest pose. In many cases the individual will conduct a seminar Saturday afternoon between the pre-judging and evening show. Unless you are dead tired, we urge you to attend. Such individuals are storehouses of knowledge, having trained for five, ten, even twenty years or more. As most conclude their seminar with a question and answer session, you may be lucky enough to have one of the sport's best directly answer your question. Just think what it would be like to discuss biceps training with Ronnie Coleman or chest training with Jean Pierre Fux? Does it get any better?

Nasser El Sonbaty

If seminars are not your thing, head home or back to the hotel room. With most evening shows starting around seven (with the competitors being required to show up at six) you have four or five hours to kill. Chances are a lack of sleep the night before and the rigors of the pre-judging have left you exhausted. You can't go wrong by hitting the sack for a few hours. As a matter of fact we highly recommend it. You have another grueling session ahead of you, and although we may be wrong, more than likely a late night as well. Before you crash (which is probably what you'll do.) have a trusted means to wake you up around 4:30 or 5:00. If at home rely on a friend or relative. If you are at a hotel, buzz the front desk and leave a wake-up call notice.

As soon as you wake up have a small meal or snack. Try a bran muffin or granola bar, a small piece of fruit, and a glass of skim milk or juice. In place of juice you can substitute one of the popular athletic drinks. Basically eat enough to get you through the evening show, but not enough to cause stomach distension.

ACT TWO – THE EVENING SHOW

Barring something unexpected, the evening show will progress in a similar manner to the pre-judging. The two major differences are the size of the audience and the presence of a guest poser.

Most pre-judging audiences are small and consist of die-hard bodybuilding types, people like you, the authors, and Bob Kennedy! But the make-up of the evening show is more varied. You'll find wives, husbands, girlfriends, boyfriends, media reporters, and the usual assortment of curiosity seekers. Because of this, most evening shows are sold out or close to it.

Besides size, most evening shows are more boisterous, and it's not just because there are more people. Pre-judging audiences are very analytical and most act in a similar manner as the judges. During the evening ,however, reservation and analysis goes out the window, and it becomes a free for all with people yelling and screaming support for their favorite bodybuilder. Take advantage of this and if possible have a few "plants" in the audience to yell support for you.

The other major difference is usually the presence of a guest poser. Although it varies most promoters usually put the guest poser on just before the light heavyweights or heavy weights. If the individual is slated to do a second appearance he or she will usually go on after the heavyweight class, just before the awards are announced.

"In the past few years I think bodybuilding has been judged more on the name, reputation, and last contest entered. I mean let's judge a show based on what's happening on the day of the competition not on the one that was decided six months ago."

– Paul Dillett, top IFBB pro voicing his opinion on bodybuilding judging.

By the evening show the judges have a good idea of the placings. But don't assume you've won or lost. Treat the evening show like the pre-judging and give it all you got. In a weight class with a number of high-quality physiques, the odds are good to excellent that the evening show will determine the winner. And as mentioned earlier, competitors who looked

By the evening show the judges have a good idea of the placings. But don't assume you've won or lost. Continue to give it all you've got.

No matter what the outcome, accept it with poise and dignity.
– Flex Wheeler and Joe Weider.

good in the morning, may have lost it by the evening show. If you happen to be running a close second, a good showing at the evening show plus the audience's input, may push you over the edge and give you the title.

AND THE WINNER IS...

Now for the moment of truth. We are by no means guaranteeing the information in the previous chapters will hand you the winner's trophy, but we are confident that provided you've done your homework, you'll step on stage in the best shape of your life. No matter what the outcome, accept it with poise and dignity. As soon as your name is called, smile, offer handshakes to the other competitors, and diplomatically leave the stage. Don't moon the judges, throw a tantrum, or storm off in a huff. You'll do both yourself and the sport a greater service by being a good sport than a sore loser. And from a more practical perspective, if you compete again next year, the odds are you'll face most if not the entire judging panel once again. Bodybuilding is a small family and if you alienate the judges by giving them the finger or dirty stares and they'll pay you back next year. Whether their decision was sound or not we assure you their memories are quite good.

If you happen to place second (a respectable showing in any contest) congratulate the winner, and raise his or her hand in the air. This shows tremendous class on your part, and endears you to the judges, audience, and other competitors.

POST CONTEST FESTIVITIES

Whether you win or lose, chances are your first priority is to ingest calories. We are talking a major pig-out here. Even the top pros engage in mega-eating in the hours after a show. Most promoters help you in this regard by arranging a post-contest get together. This could be a banquet, nightclub, or restaurant. Unless you are ready to drop from exhaustion, we urge you to attend. There's nothing like a couple of hundred bodybuilders all talking shop. Even the most heated rivals will be observed exchanging friendly dialogue. Don't be afraid of over indulging either. Let's face it, you've earned it. In fact once the floodgates open you'll probably do little else over the next few couple of days. Most bodybuilders pack on twenty or thirty pounds in the weeks following a contest. Rumor has it former Mr. America, Gary Leonard, gained an incredible 60 pounds in two weeks following his Mr. America win.

There is one exception to the previous. If you were lucky enough to win your class, chances are you will be eligible to compete at the next level. Most contests are arranged so that if you win at one level, the next contest is held one or two weeks later. For example win the city championships and you are off to the state championships. This means holding your shape for another week or two. There's no way you could regain your competitive shape after a two or three day pig-out. But for the rest of you – PIG OUT!

If you happen to place second (a respectable showing in any contest) congratulate the winner, and raise his or her hand in the air. This shows tremendous class on your part, and endears you to the judges, audience, and other competitors. – Kevin Levrone and Nasser El Sonbaty

"Of course! I stayed at the backstage photo shoot until the last picture, and then went to the banquet and stayed until the last person walked out."
– Ronnie Coleman, 1998 Mr. Olympia enjoying every minute of post-contest festivities.

Bodybuilding Bucks

Bodybuilding has come along way since winners received a tin of protein powder for their efforts. It's now possible for a select few pros to earn a decent living from bodybuilding. And this doesn't include the hundreds of thousands of individuals who earn money from the sport in other ways. Thanks to the promotional efforts of such individuals as the Weider brothers, Robert Kennedy, and Arnold Schwarzenegger, there are literally dozens of avenues that people can use to make a living from the sport of bodybuilding.

> **"Well, when I won the Mr. America, I thought the whole world would be at my door, but I was disappointed. I remember looking in my mirror at 2 a.m. in the morning saying "This is it? This is all there is?"**
>
> – Larry Scott, former bodybuilding great commenting on the less than lucrative side of competitive bodybuilding.

Aaron Baker

In the following chapter we are going to look at bodybuilding as a business. Some of the topics apply strictly to competitive body-builders (i.e. guest posing, prize money, photos and videos), while others can be undertaken by just about anyone with a knowledge of bodybuilding (contest promotion, book and article writing, gym instructing.)

PRIZE MONEY

As we alluded to earlier, prize money is probably the most well known but least lucrative way to earn money in bodybuilding. Even if a bodybuilder was to win every major show of the season, his income would still only equal what a typical golfer or tennis player makes for one tournament. And as for the rest of the pros out there, forget it. With second and third place paying $50,000 and $25,000 respectively, and the rest of the field receiving a $5,000 to $10,000 appearance fee, relying solely on prize money is a short cut to starvation. That's why most focus their energy on the other sources of income that bodybuilding has to offer.

"Have a look at any muscle magazine and read the final paragraph of any interview with a bodybuilder or fitness star. You'll probably find contact information for guest posing, seminars, autographed pictures, etc. Are these stars providing services and products just because they are dedicated to their fans? The truth is that they are trying to earn money from bodybuilding. It is not an inherently lucrative sport for any but the top competitors."

– Dom Mochrie, *MuscleMag International* contributor commenting on the lesser known side to bodybuilding; financial return.

Kevin Levrone and Flex Wheeler

GUEST POSING

It's difficult to nail down just when guest posing became a legitimate source of income. Certainly the old-time strongmen could be called "posers" in the technical sense. With the naughty bits covered by nothing more than a fig leaf, guys like Charles Atlas and Sig Klein, would entertain audiences with their outstanding muscle control; usually after a demonstration of their strength.

In the 1950s and 1960s Mr. America and Mr. Universe winners would routinely appear at amateur events to boost ticket sales. In a manner of speaking things haven't changed much as putting Ronnie Coleman or Flex Wheeler's name on a contest poster almost assures a sell out.

"Bodybuilding is not really financially rewarding. Only a very small percentage of athletes make a living at it. My father always told me that if you want to do bodybuilding, fine. But you should finish your college degree in case you break a leg."

– Gary Guinn, NABBA, USA Champion commenting on some fatherly advice he received concerning career choices.

From the pro's perspective things have improved considerably since the mid 1970s and it's chiefly due to the efforts of two individuals: Franco Columbu and Arnold Schwarzenegger.

Up until Arnold and Franco came on the scene, guest posing was more of a hobby than a legitimate profession. But Arnold and Franco's popularity in the '70s meant that they were in a position to charge promoters for their efforts. Arnold and Franco helped bring bodybuilding respectability, and they used their personalities to establish guest posing as a lucrative business venture.

Ronnie Coleman

Guest posing received a second boost in the late '70s and early '80s from the Incredible Hulk, Lou Ferrigno. Big Lou brought bodybuilding to the masses and into the homes of mainstream North America.

"Tremendously! The phone's been ringing off the hook for guest posing and appearances. There's a high demand for advertisements and TV. Radio, and magazine interviews. I'm leaving tomorrow for California to do a new commercial for my sponsor, Met-Rx."

– Ronnie Coleman, 1998 Mr. Olympia responding to a *MuscleMag* interviewer's question about life after winning bodybuilding's biggest show.

Most pros these days charge between $2500 and $5000 for a single appearance. If this sounds steep, keep in mind the hundreds of extra audience members such pros will draw. Promoters know they'll more than make up for the cost with the extra spectators that show up.

We should add that some of the most in demand guest posers have never won a major show. In fact two of them, Canadian colossus, Greg Kovacs, and California behemoth, Vic Richards, have never placed in the top ten of a pro contest. But their 350 and 280 pounds respectively, appeals to the mass-above-all-else freaks out there. Both these guys are among the strongest and most massive bodybuilders around. Their schedules are booked far in advance with requests for guest posing and appearances.

With the possible exception of the top five or six bodybuilders, most pros make far more money guest posing than competing. Of course like any professions, there are bodybuilders who have reputations for consistently showing up in shape and others who are downright fat. Given that the bodybuilding family is fairly close-knit, word quickly gets around as to whom promoters can depend on, and who to avoid. All it takes is for a pro to turn up out of shape a couple of times and they can pretty well kiss his or her guest posing career good-bye. For those readers who are nearing the top of the amateur ladder and feel they have a career in bodybuilding, you owe it to the fans to appear at guest posing appointments in decent shape. No one expects you to be rock hard and in contest shape. But there's no need to carry thirty or forty extra pounds of fat like a few of the top pros do when they guest pose.

SEMINARS

It only makes sense to follow the topic of guest posing with seminars. Most pros are not contracted just to guest pose. For an extra thousand or two most will throw in a seminar. Even Arnold, despite the lofty heights he's reached in the entertainment world, conducts seminars at his annual Arnold Classic Weekend.

Most seminars are held Saturday afternoon, just after the prejudging and before the evening show. They are usually two to three hours in duration, but may extend into the following Sunday. Seminars are big business these days and some of the more dedicated pros will work thirty or forty weekends a year just doing seminars.

For those who are starting to make a name for themselves at the amateur ranks, it's only a matter of time before you'll be asked to conduct a seminar, if not already. If you have a background in teaching or some other occupation involving public speaking, then the transition to giving seminars is very easy. But most readers probably fall into the category of dreading to give a five-minute speech in high school. For such individuals we suggest paying close attention to the next few paragraphs.

"But seriously, I'm 30 years old, bodybuilding is treating me well. I'm single but I hope to be married with a kid in five to ten years. I hope something positive will come out of bodybuilding, like having my own business. I don't want to work for anyone else again. I just want to be happy in the future."

– Johnny Moya, IFBB pro expressing the same dreams as most 30 year olds.

One of the best ways to learn how to do something is by watching others. In this case it means attending as many different bodybuilding seminars as possible. Even if the person conducting it is only one or two contests above you on the bodybuilding ladder. You may not pick up much in the way of knowledge, but we are sure you'll learn various techniques for conveying it. Some of the best lecturers in the world are only moderately knowledgeable in

Thomas Zechmeister

their field, but are outstanding when it comes to teaching it. Conversely most of us have had teachers and professors who were brilliant in the lab but were totally lost in front of a class of students. The same holds true for pro bodybuilders. Some are great at conducting seminars while others struggle for every word.

Another suggestion is to take a few public speaking courses. The most well known is the Dale Carnegie course, but most colleges and universities offer excellent courses as well. For the cost of a couple of containers of creatine you'll become proficient in public speaking. Even if you never use it for bodybuilding purposes, it's something the business community values when they see it on a resume.

We'll be the first to admit that there is a certain degree of natural ability involved in public speaking, but with practice and determination, almost anyone can become quite proficient.

PHOTOS

With the increased number of glossy magazines these days, mail-order photos are not that popular anymore. Twenty or thirty years ago most of the top bodybuilders had an ad in one or more of the popular bodybuilding magazines offering 8X10 photos for sale. For around $5 you could get an autographed picture of your favorite star. But with most of the major magazines now being offered in full-color, many with full-page studio photos, the popularity of personalized photos has taken a nosedive. About the only regular ad you'll see these days is the one featuring the Cuban-born "Myth," Sergio Oliva. Sergio is one of the enduring legends of the sport and his battles with Arnold back in the late sixties and early seventies have become part of bodybuilding immortality.

We should add that while the number of bodybuilders offering photos through the mail has declined, there is an overabundance of fitness models and competitors offering their wares. Ads for such stars as Vicky Pratt, Monica Brant, and Marla Duncan, can be regularly seen in the pages of *MuscleMag International.*

Lest we give the impression that you can't buy photos of your favorite bodybuilders anymore, we assure you, you can. Take in any pro bodybuilding show or convention and you'll find plenty of booths selling photos. If the owner is not competing, odds are they'll be behind the booth. For $5 to $10 they'll be more than happy to sell you a personalized, autographed photo.

For those readers on the verge of entering the pro ranks, or even competing in top amateur shows, selling photos is another option for bringing in a few bucks. If you are seriously considering this, the following tips will come in handy.

The first order of business is to hire a photographer. If you live in a small town the odds are there won't be anyone with experience in physique photography. Shooting a sunset and shooting a bodybuilder are two separate entities. Everything from lighting to positioning must be taken into account. Unless someone local has the expertise in this area, we suggest making contact with a professional photographer, and more than likely this means heading to a larger center.

One of the best places to start looking for a photographer is at a large gym. Most better establishments have photo-posters of bodybuilders adorning the walls. In most cases they'll have a few pros and any top amateurs from the local scene. If the photographer's name is not on the picture (down on the bottom in much the same manner as painters signing their work) contact the gym

Craig Titus

owner or manager and ask where the pictures came from. Nowadays most photographers will leave their card wherever their work is being featured. The odds are good to excellent that before you leave the gym you'll have the name or names of a couple of quality contacts.

In terms of contact, we suggest phoning ahead of schedule as most photographers (at least the better ones) do things by appointment. This may seem inconvenient but it's actually a benefit to you, as you won't have to worry about interruptions when you finally meet.

Female bodybuilders and fitness competitors have been taken advantage of, both financially and physically, by men posing as photographers. If you get approached by anyone claiming to be a photographer, do a background check on him first. – Bob Kennedy and Torrie Wilson

If the photographer in question is experienced in this area, then he or she will simply set up the photo shoot and work out any minor details. If on the other hand they have limited experience, your first order of business is explaining exactly what you want. At this stage it wouldn't hurt to have a roll or two of your own photos to give the person an idea as to what poses and angles you are looking for. Your preparation and contest photos are an excellent starting point. From here it's just a matter of showing up at the photographer's studio or whatever background setting you two decide on.

A WORD TO OUR FEMALE READERS

Before leaving this topic we would like to pass along a word of caution to any female bodybuilder or fitness competitor reading this book. As most females know the world is filled with males whose sole purpose in life is taking advantage of unsuspecting females. The sports of bodybuilding and fitness are no exception. If you are in the middle of a workout and some guy comes up to you claiming to be a "photographer," under no circumstances sign anything or go anywhere with the individual until you do a background check. For $10 a guy can pick up a Kodak disposable and call himself a photographer. They may initially take a few pictures, but we think you know what his ultimate goal is.

There are numerous stories about female bodybuilders and fitness competitors being taken advantage of, both financially and physically, by these unscrupulous characters. If you get approached by anyone claiming to be a photographer, ask for the following:

1) His business card
2) Samples of prior work
3) References from other girls he's worked with
4) His business address

If the individual is legitimate, he will have no objection to supplying all the previous. In fact he'll probably offer it before you get a chance to ask.

There's always someone taking photos backstage at a contest.

We are by no means trying to make you paranoid about the issue, but in this day and age you need to be careful. The odds are if someone approaches you out in the open in the gym, then he is probably who he says he is, a photographer. But run a simple background check just to be on the safe side.

BODYBUILDING PHOTOGRAPHER

Instead of being the model in the photos you have the option of being the one who takes the pictures. Thanks to the pioneering work of such bodybuilding photographers as Russ Warner, Art Zeller, John Balik, and Chris Lund, literally hundreds of individuals make a decent income from physique photography. Even *MuscleMag International's*, Robert Kennedy, has been known to take a picture or two. And despite his modesty, has developed a reputation as one of the best photographers around.

Although there's no formal training criteria for taking pictures, most of the best photographers around have completed a college or university degree majoring in the arts. At the very least they have taken a few courses in creative photography.

Most of the names you see in bodybuilding magazines started their careers as every day photographers, taking pictures of weddings, graduations, wildlife etc. Then one day someone came along, either a bodybuilder or publisher, and asked them to shoot a few rolls of film featuring a contest or two. Eventually word gets around and before they know it they are in the "physique shooting business."

"My photography was still just a hobby back then though. My bodybuilding was most important to me. I never thought of making a hobby out of it, but I was a bodybuilder and photographer and eventually I put the two together."

–The late Artie Zeller, one of the sport's greatest photographers, commenting on how he got started in the business.

If you monkey about with the camera on occasion, and would like to get into things more seriously, start by developing your portfolio. By this we mean having a collection of your work available for potential clients. Remember the advice we gave to women in the last chapter about sleaze-balls, well, you are now on the opposite side of the fence. You will be the one checked out so you want to be as professional as possible.

The best way to start your portfolio is to shoot pictures of close friends and acquaintances. Let's face it you will make mistakes (too much light, not enough light, poor background choice, wrong angles) and it's better to learn on friends than complete strangers. Another thing, you will do most of your initial work for free. Your primary concern at this stage is developing a reputation for quality, and the only way to accomplish this is by practice. As you improve in your trade, word will get around, and before long a snowball effect takes place. The more pictures taken, the better you get, the more requests come in. After you've shot a couple of hundred rolls of film, and a couple of dozen bodybuilders, you should have a decent level of competence. In a manner of speaking, one leads to the other. If your reputation is poor then you won't have to worry about buying film! On the other hand if you start getting requests from strangers, then you are on your way. One of the authors found this out at a local contest. What started as a favor for a friend quickly led to nearly a dozen requests from other competitors to take their picture back stage. Before it was over, nearly 200 photos had been taken. As the author in question had no intentions of getting into the physique photography business, he only charged for developing costs and film. But that's how fast things can happen.

Jason Mathas and Darin Lannaghan

HOW THE PROS DO IT

It's safe to say that the popularity of the major bodybuilding magazines like *MuscleMag International*, *Flex*, *IronMan, Muscular Development*, etc., owes much to the high quality pictures spread throughout their pages. In fact such is the importance placed on pictures that most of the big magazines have their own staff of photographers. Such people are the best in the world and rival photographers in any other profession. Perhaps only underwater photographers have it harder as in their case some of the models may object to being photographed and decide to bite off a limb or two!

Most of the best physique photographers either live in California or spend a great deal of their time visiting there. California is the Mecca for bodybuilders with Venice Beach, Santa Monica, being perhaps the most popular physique shooting setting in the world. All the greats in bodybuilding history have their portfolios stuffed with beach shots. Arnold and Franco's pictures from the seventies are classics.

Besides Venice Beach, Santa Monica is home to three of the most famous gyms in the world, Golds', World, and Powerhouse. The original Gold's Gym from *Pumping Iron* fame is closed but a newer, larger facility is located a few blocks away. Just about anyone who's anyone in bodybuilding can be found working out at one of these three gyms; and as would be expected this is where the best photographers take their pictures.

Photography, bodybuilding, and the gym business are so interwoven in California that many of the big gyms have separate areas designated solely for picture taking. And it's not done in a haphazard manner either. Even the best photographers in the world don't just walk into Gold's and start shooting pictures. In most cases they set up a photo shoot in advance with both the gym and the bodybuilder/fitness model in question. In fact strangers who walk into Gold's and World will be asked to check any camera equipment at the front desk. You don't just start snapping away at Flex Wheeler or Paul Dillett without first getting their permission.

Besides the photographers employed by the magazines there are numerous free-lance photographers who frequent the major gyms. They follow the same rules as the magazine staffers but are not guaranteed that their work will be published. Instead they'll submit what they feel are their best shots to the major magazine publishers and if the publisher likes what he or she sees, money will exchange hands and the photo or photos will appear in the not too distant future.

Given its Canadian location, *MuscleMag International* relies heavily on free-lance photographers based in southern California. The works of such photographers as Irvin Gelb and Jim Amentler are regularly featured in *MuscleMag International* magazine, *Oxygen* magazine, and *MuscleMag's* growing library of books (including this one).

For those who feel they have what it takes to be a bodybuilding photographer, keep in mind that the profession is in many respects similar to bodybuilding itself. You don't just start shooting the top stars and have Joe Weider or Robert Kennedy pounding on your doorstep. Instead you start at the local level, establish a reputation and work your way up. It also helps if you know a local competitor who looks like they could go somewhere in the sport. As they work his or her way up the ladder you can do likewise. Then if the individual gets "discovered" by a major bodybuilding publication, you will be in a good position to get noticed yourself.

As a final piece of advice don't limit yourself to male bodybuilding. Female fitness is booming, and the top bodybuilding magazines are constantly on the lookout for the next "cover girl." If you know someone in your area that you feel has the "look," it would be in your best interest to make contact, at least on a professional basis. A series of good photos could be the start of something big for both of you. Just make sure you follow the rules of etiquette laid down in the previous chapter.

VIDEOS

Although the mail order sale of 8X10 photos has declined in recent years, that of videos has gone through the roof. This is not surprising given today's MTV video generation. In a manner of speaking videos are the end result (at least for now) of the consumers quest for realism. First came paintings, which were replaced by the more realistic photos. Then came 8-mm film, which put movement to pictures. And now we have video, which is even more realistic.

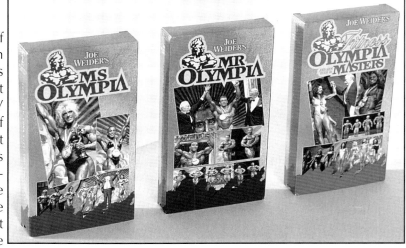

You can still buy 8mm home movies of the great champs from the fifties, sixties, and seventies. Most of the major magazines have ads for such films. But how many readers know how to use a film projector? In fact many of you probably haven't even seen one up close with the possible exception of a peek through the window at the local cinema. It's far simpler these days to throw a tape in the old VCR and press play. The machine takes care of everything else.

Bodybuilding videos come in three forms; documentaries, contests, and instructional. Let's take a closer look at all three.

Without a doubt the most popular bodybuilding documentary of all time is the now classic *Pumping Iron.* This was the first documentary to treat bodybuilding in a serious manner. Although it featured numerous bodybuilders, the dominant personality by far was Arnold Schwarzenegger. In fact this one documentary launched Arnold's film career and helped propel him to the top of the Hollywood movie industry. Other bodybuilders such as Franco Columbu, Lou Ferrigno (who in a few years would be seen by millions as *The Incredible Hulk*), Ken Waller, Mike Katz, and Robby Robinson, also had prominent roles.

Markus Ruhl

Pumping Iron followed these bodybuilders as they prepared for the 1975 Mr. Olympia and Mr. Universe contests. But rather than set the camera up in the audience, the film's creators, George Butler and Charles Gaines, went behind the scenes. They showed the human side to bodybuilding and the sacrifices made in the quest to be the best. Because of this one film, millions of people don't say they are going to lift weights, they say they are going to "pump some iron."

Since the release of *Pumping Iron,* numerous other documentaries have been produced. *Pumping Iron II,* followed the women as they prepared for the Ms. Olympia. In 1996, 1997, and 1998, three documentaries were released that profiled the top bodybuilding stars as they trained for each year's Mr. Olympia titles.

By far the biggest selling video category in bodybuilding are those that cover contests. Thanks to modern technology you can watch virtually every Mr. Olympia, Arnold Classic, and New York Night of Champions, since the early eighties onward. For $29 to $39 you can see Lee Haney's domination in the 1980s, Dorian Yates' terror in the 1990s, and perhaps the start of Ronnie Coleman's dynasty, starting in 1998.

Besides the big pro events, most of the top amateur shows are also available on video. Not only are they great entertainment, but as we discussed earlier in the book, they make excellent teaching tools for learning how to pose and conduct one's self on stage.

If contest videos are the best sellers, instructional videos are the fastest rising. Leading the way in this regard is Dorian Yate's great video, *Blood and Guts.* With a title like that it better deliver, and it does. Big time. Up until the release of *Blood and Guts,* most instructional videos where rather tame and fluffy. That is they showed models using pitifully light weight, heavily choreographed, and fake beads of sweat. You won't find any of that in Dorian's video. Instead you see Mr. Yates and his training partner go through real, hardcore, ball-busting, workouts. Dorian doesn't take time to explain what a set or rep is. His intensity and actions are his instruction. Just as *Pumping Iron* set the standard for documentaries, so has *Blood and Guts* established the new parameters for instructional videos.

Chapter 30 – *Bodybuilding Bucks*

When word of sales of *Blood and Guts* got around, many of the other big names in the sport released their own videos. If Dorian's is tops, Canadian behemoth, Greg Kovacs, is a close second. Weighing anywhere from 350 to 400 pounds (320 in contest shape!), Kovacs is one of the largest and strongest bodybuilders around. And despite never having placed in the top ten of a pro show, is one of the most popular draws at any convention or show. His video *Colossus* was shot in a similar manner to *Blood and Guts* and focuses more on Kovac's workouts than instructional tips.

Supplement endorsing is big business for pro bodybuilders. – Garrett Downing

For those who actually want advice and not merely to see some 300-pound brute go through a life and death experience, there are numerous quality, pure instructional videos available. Such bodybuilders as Flex Wheeler, Shawn Ray, Lee Priest, and Kevin Lervone, have all released excellent instructional videos that demonstrate correct exercise technique. The fact that all three are in tremendous shape as they work out can't but help boost your motivation levels.

SUPPLEMENT ENDORSING

Supplement endorsing is one of the oldest means by which bodybuilders can obtain extra rewards from the sport. But where today's bodybuilder can command hundreds of thousands of dollars, thirty years ago the payoff was probably a few tins of whatever they were endorsing. Some things do change for the better after all.

The theory behind endorsing is simple: show your product being held aloft by a top pro and the buying public will assume that that's how the individual built his or her physique. Psychologists would use the term guilt by association. This is the theory anyhow, but today's readers are far more knowledgeable than their counterpart twenty or thirty years ago. Back in the good old days steroids and other performance enhancing drugs were a bonafide secret to all but those closest to the sport. Showing a 220-pound bodybuilder on the beach, promoting Brand X protein powder carried tremendous weight. All it took was a caption saying "I built my physique entirely with Brand X" and sales went through the roof. The teens and novices reading the magazines and seeing the ads didn't know the whole story.

This all changed in the early 1980's with the release of Dan Duchaine's *Under Ground Steroid Handbook*. The genie was out of the bottle so to speak, and the magazines had no choice but to follow suit and fess up. Those 250-pound bodybuilders praising the muscle-building properties of Brand X were no longer the guaranteed investment of twenty years ago. A different approach was needed. That's why you rarely see ads these days showing body-builders claiming that their physiques are the sole result of Brand X. Instead they say how the product made a "big difference" (probably true for some current supplements), or "helped me make the best gains of my life" (a more debatable point).

Although the approach taken by advertisers has changed since the days of Muscle Beach, let us assure you supplement endorsing is big business for pro bodybuilders. So big that the old freelance approach has been replaced by lucrative contracts committing the body-builder to one company. In fact many pros focus more on the potential for a contract than the prize money the contest may provide. That $25,000 or $50,000 won at the Arnold Classic or Mr. Olympia, may translate into hundreds of thousands or millions of dollars from supplement endorsing.

At the top of the supplement contract mountain is bodybuilding businessman supreme, Joe Weider. It was Joe who really started the whole contract issue and many of the biggest names in bodybuilding are under contract to Weider Enterprises. This gives Weider exclusive rights to use the individual's image and name to promote his products. As would be expected many of the other major supplement players got in on the act and started signing up body-builders themselves. As examples: Lee Priest is under contract to Pro Lab; Ronnie Coleman endorses Met RX, and Greg Kovac's promotes Muscle Tech. The next time you go to a large convention or contest, if the bodybuilders in question are not competing, chances are you'll find them "manning" the booth. In Kovac's case you'll observe the Canadian Colossus consum-ing thousands of dollars worth of Muscle Tech products over the three or four days. Greg is one bodybuilder who practices what he preaches.

CLOTHING

It was only a matter of time before bodybuilders started cashing in on the fashion conscious nineties. It seems working out in a T-shirt and pair of shorts is no longer chic. Thou must look thy best, says the fashion industry.

Bodybuilding clothing is not a new concept, but things have evolved considerably since the days of iron-on transfers. From designer T-shirts and shorts, to sweatshirts and track pants, whatever article of clothing you are looking for, there's someone only too happy to step up and sell it to you.

Bodybuilders have always been difficult to "dress" given their shapes and sizes. Most off the rack clothes are tailored to fit the "average"population, and here lies the problem. The "average" Joe, who has a 48-inch chest, also has a 40+ inch waist! As a mater of fact we are probably being generous by allowing for an 8-inch chest-waist differential. Most out of shape individuals sport the same size waist and chest. On the other hand most bodybuilders have a 15 to 20-inch size difference between waist and chest. There's also the leg size to consider. For a bodybuilder with 28-inch thighs to find pants that fit he'd need to go up to 40-inch + waist size. So now the legs fit, but there's enough material left over in the waist to make a set of sails for the Bluenose or USS Constitution.

Besides chest, legs, and waist differences, you have those massive arms to consider. Most over-the-counter clothes won't go near a set of 18-inch+ arms. Even a muscular 17-inch arm will be hard pressed to fit into a normal jacket or shirt.

Recognizing that bodybuilders needed tailor-made clothing, such former stars as Mike Christian and Gary Strydom, launched their own lines of specially designed bodybuilding wear in the late 1980s. Since then the clothing industry has nearly mirrored the supplement industry with each month seeing a new line popping up out of nowhere. In fact as the book went to press, Robert Kennedy was launching a clothing line to complement his best-selling Formula One supplement line.

MAIL ORDER COURSES

This is another form of income that was at one time lucrative, but has taken a nose-dive in recent years. Back in the sixties and seventies, there was a limited amount of information available for aspiring bodybuilders. With only a few decent magazines (*Muscle Builder Power, IronMan, and Muscular Development*) and books (i.e. Bill Pearl's *Keys To The Inner Universe*) available, bodybuilders were often left to their own devices for increasing their knowledge. For those lucky enough to work out at a large gym, they had contact with more experienced bodybuilders. But for someone in a small town, they were pretty much on their own.

In true capitalist fashion, the top bodybuilders of the day helped fill this niche. Guys like Larry Scott, Bill Pearl, Sergio Oliva, Arnold, Franco Columbu, and Boyer Coe, all marketed training booklets and pamphlets. For around $5 you could get Arnold's chest training secrets, Larry Scott's tips for biceps building, and Oliva's routines for enlarging the back. In most cases you could buy each champ's entire package for $25 to $30.

Mail order courses reached their peak in the late seventies and early eighties, which not surprisingly is when the number of bodybuilding books and magazines exploded. Instead of $5 for a small booklet devoted to training one muscle, bodybuilders could now buy 250 page books and magazines that covered the full spectrum of bodybuilding – training, nutrition, supplements, etc. As it stands right now there are 15 to 20 quality magazines available each month, and literally dozens of top notch bodybuilding books.

Most of the current generation of pros don't offer mail order courses. Instead they rely on seminars, videos, and in many cases, their own books, to convey information and increase their income.

For those of you who have some of the old training pamphlets, hold on to them. While they'll never be worth the same as, say a Joe Dimaggio rookie card, nevertheless bodybuilding is like most sports in that as time goes on the nostalgia element creeps in. Collectors have been known to spend big bucks on items related to the golden era of any sport. For bodybuilders this would be the glory days of Muscle Beach, the late fifties, sixties and early seventies. Mint condition, original courses by guys like Larry Scott, Dave Draper, Arnold, etc., increase in value every year. Given Arnold's popularity his booklets from when he first came to America, will eventually fetch a tidy sum. Of course this is assuming you decide to sell. If you are a collector yourself, try checking out basement flea markets on Saturday mornings. Mixed in with old comic books and *Popular Mechanics* magazines you'll often find some of the old training courses. The odds are good to excellent you can pick them up for literally cents a copy. Over the space of a summer you could have a collection containing hundreds that down the road might be worth thousands of dollars. Stranger things have happened.

MAGAZINE ARTICLES

Many bodybuilders supplement their incomes by writing for the major bodybuilding magazines. In some cases it's one or two articles per year, while in others they have a monthly column (i.e. Dorian Yates, Mike Mentzer). We have to be honest, however, in that many of the

Many bodybuilders supplement their incomes by writing for the major bodybuilding magazines.

articles attributed to such and such a bodybuilder, were in fact ghost written by staff writers who may contact the pro for advice, or who may create the entire article from scratch. Now you may ask why any publisher would do this, but keep in mind that with things being as competitive as they are in the magazine business, having a top pro "write" an article exclusively for your magazine is one way to boost sales.

This is not to say that none of the top pros pen their own material. Guys like Frank Zane, Mike Mentzer, and the late Vince Gironda, are among the best writers in the business. In Mike's case he's probably accomplished more as a writer, than as a competitor; and this is saying something as he won both the Mr. America and Mr. Universe titles. Many may disagree with Mike's one-set-to-failure training philosophy, but his theories on overtraining have influenced millions in the last two decades.

> **"An article will take several hours to compose, and probably some months to hear back from the publishers once you submit it, but you may be well on your way to becoming a freelance writer. This is a great small business which requires very little overhead."**
>
> – Dom Mochrie, *MuscleMag International* contributor offering his views on how to get started in the bodybuilding writing game.

As a final note on this topic, a few bodybuilders who started out writing for the magazines, eventually published their own. Joe Weider went from amateur bodybuilder/part-time writer, to establishing Weider Enterprises. Every month, three of his magazines, *Muscle and Fitness, Flex,* and *Shape,* battle it out with rivals for sales (with *Muscle and Fitness* being the number one bodybuilding magazine in terms of sales).

Robert Kennedy's story is similar to Weider's. Bob quickly recognized that he didn't have the genetics to go that far as a competitor so he went into the writing game. From a few articles in *IronMan* to *MuscleMag International, Oxygen,* and over thirty books, Bob is one of the sport's most prolific writers.

BOOKS

In a manner of speaking the mail order booklets discussed earlier were small books, but it wasn't until the late seventies and early eighties that bodybuilding books came into their own. Bodybuilders can thank three individuals for this, Arnold you-know-who, Joe Weider, and Robert Kennedy.

Chris Cormier, Darrem Charles and Nasser El Sonbaty

Arnold was quick to recognize the potential of books and once established as the best bodybuilder around, released his first book, *Arnold The Education Of A Bodybuilder.* The book tells Arnold's complete story, from his early days in Austria and Germany, to his immigration to the U.S. in the late sixties, to his domination of the sport in the seventies. For those that have or have seen the book, that one picture of Arnold on the cover has probably done more to entice people to start weight training than any other. Even by today's freaky standards, no one has been able to duplicate that pose.

Following the success of *Education of a Bodybuilder,* Arnold released books on strength training for both men and teens, and then set the standard for all time with his 700+ page *Bodybuilding Encyclopedia.*

In the early eighties, bodybuilding businessman extraordinare, Joe Weider, put his thirty odd years in the business to good use by releasing *Bodybuilding – The Weider Approach.* The book was really a great summary of all the information contained in *Muscle and Fitness* magazine (originally *Muscle Builder Power*).

In the early eighties, *MuscleMag International's* Robert Kennedy decided to get in on the act and released the best-selling *Hardcore Bodybuilding.* This book was so successful that he followed up with *Beef It!, Cuts!,* and *Unleashing The Wild Physique* (with the late Vince Gironda). To date Bob has written over 40 bodybuilding books and is recognized as one of the most knowledgeable individuals in the game.

Bodybuilding books generally fall into two broad categories; autobiographical and instructional. Besides Arnold's *Education of A Bodybuilder,* such stars as Franco Columbu (*Coming on Strong*) and Lou Ferrigno have released their own autobiographies.

As expected most bodybuilding books fall into the instructional category. Besides Weider's and Kennedy's series of books, such stars as Tom Platz, Samir Bannout, Dorian Yates, and Lee Haney, have released their own publications. In addition the owners of the famous Gold's Gym franchise, have added to the growing bodybuilding library. And we'd be remiss if we ignored our own humble contributions, *The MuscleMag International Encyclopedia of Bodybuilding, Anabolic Primer, BodyFitness for Women, Anabolic Edge,* and this book.

Writing books is another area where having a competitive background is not necessary. In fact most bodybuilding books are written by individuals with little or no competitive experience. Joe Weider and Robert Kennedy competed early in their careers but never won any of the major titles. Even the books released by Tom Platz, Arnold, Lee Haney, etc, where primarily written by professional writers (with input from the stars of course). The late Bill Reynolds wrote dozens of books for the top stars. In some cases he included his name on the book's cover (i.e., "with Bill Reynold's" down at the bottom), while in other cases he was pure ghost-writer, and received no public recognition.

ME, A WRITER?

For those who think they have what it takes to write professionally, both books and magazine articles, we offer the following advice. There's an old saying, first we crawl, then we walk, and finally we run. Writing works the same way. Rarely do you go from never been published to writing a book. Your first step should be to take a few creative-writing courses. Unless you completed a major in English at college or university, you'll need to hone your writing skills. Most colleges and universities offer evening courses for non-majors who just want to sharpen their writing techniques.

The nest step is to get published any way you can. Try writing a couple of short articles and see if any of the bodybuilding magazines will publish them. Don't limit yourself to just the big periodicals either (*Flex, MuscleMag International, Muscle and Fitness,* etc). Every month sees a new publication hit the magazine stands. In fact the new magazines are trying to get established themselves and constantly look for new blood to help them in their cause. Getting published by one of the smaller periodicals may not only get your name in print but could set you up long-term if the magazine in question makes it big-time down the road.

Another thing, don't expect to get paid for your efforts, at least early on. Sending in your first article with a request for money is the surest way NOT to get published. Your primary goal at this stage is to get that first article published. In a manner of speaking you are like a struggling actor or actress waiting for that first big break – even if it means playing a dead person!

Once you have a series of articles published, you may be in a position to request payment for your services. We say may because you don't want to alienate the magazine's publisher. Remember there's a lot of competition out there. Start overpricing yourself and the publisher may turn to someone who's just as hungry and will work for free.

We will admit, however, that it also works the other way. If you establish a reputation for delivering quality work on time, then publishers will come knocking on your door. This is how the authors of this book first got started in the writing business.

After the limited success of our first, self-published book, *Steroid Myths,* in the early nineties, we assumed our humble writing careers had reached a plateau. But as luck would have it, Robert Kennedy (owner and publisher of *MuscleMag International*) had just started a sub-division of *MuscleMag* for book publishing. He read our book and contacted us about writing a series of books for *MuscleMag*. It was an easy decision on our part and the book you hold in your hands is number five. Sometimes small things lead to bigger and better things. It certainly did in our case.

THE GYM INDUSTRY

BODYBUILDING CAMPS

It's nice to read books and magazines featuring the advice of the stars, but something entirely different to workout next to them.

Paul Dillett

> **"I decided to open the business. It's a one-on-one personal training studio consisting of about 2000 square feet, 28 pieces of equipment. I cater to everyone from housewives wanting to get back in shape to business executives."**
>
> – Paul Dillett, top IFBB pro commenting on his personal training facility.

In the early eighties, three-time Mr. Olympia, Frank Zane, and his wife Christine, started Zane Haven, which to all intents and purposes could be called a bodybuilding resort. Where some individuals go to so called "fat farms," bodybuilders could fly to Palm Springs, California, and spend one or two weeks basically eating, sleeping, and talking bodybuilding. Such a "vacation" didn't come cheap with a one to two-week package costing a couple of thousand dollars. Still, most that attended such camps felt it was worth every penny. What made Frank such a great host was his background in teaching and his unsurpassed knowledge – something he continuously improved on given his limited genetics.

> **"Well, I'll tell you, these gyms take a lot of time. You would think I'd get a life, but there's a lot of intricacy here. The relationships you build in the gym as an owner are many and varied. My wife works with me so we get to spend a lot of time together."**
>
> – Dave Draper, bodybuilding legend commenting on the gym business.

Following on the success of Zane Haven, a group of enterprising individuals started the annual series of camps called Bodybuilding Expos. Instead of one top pro, they assembled a whole team of bodybuilding personalities, each an expert in one particular field.

In recent years, such bodybuilders as Paul Dillett and Michael Francois, have started their own training camps. Modeled on Zane Haven, they give bodybuilders an opportunity to train and learn from the top people in the sport.

> **"It's not a hardcore gym per se, but has a wide range of members and a lot of good equipment. People mind their own business there, and no one is snotty or cliquish, which is more than I can say for a lot of places. I have to pass three or four gyms to get there myself, but it's worth the drive."**
>
> – Will Brink, *MuscleMag* columnist commenting on how the atmosphere of a gym is part of the training experience.

ACTING

To those new to the sport, we assure you Arnold Schwarzenegger was not the first bodybuilder to step in front of the camera lens, and he won't be the last. Hollywood has always had a need for "heavies" in the movies. You know, the guys who start out inflicting terror but eventually get their asses kicked by the male lead. Bully trashed, fair maiden rescued, all live happily ever after. That sort of thing. Check out the old Errol Flynn and Douglas Fairbanks Jr. movies and you'll see what we mean. Granted the "heavies" in the twenties and thirties were no Greg Kovacs or Nasser El Sonbatys, but for their time they were considered "beefy."

> **"I was there less than a year. Guys in the muscle game got small acting parts here and there. A lot of them worked as extras. Channel nine was the popular channel back then and they were introducing male muscle types of films, pirates and swords, gladiators, any tough male roles. Everyone would show up at the cattle calls for these films."**
>
> – Dave Draper, bodybuilding legend reminiscing about the movie industry back in the 1960s.

Despite the bit parts obtained by bodybuilders and other well-built actors (i.e. swimmers Johnny Wisemueller, Buster Krabb) it wasn't until the late '40s and early '50s that a true bodybuilder managed to slay the bully and get the girl for himself. Steve Reeves changed the way Hollywood looked at bodybuilders. He proved that well-built could be transformed into big box office returns. For a number of years, Steve Reeves and his series of *Hercules* movies were the top box office draws in the world.

Following on the success of Reeves was South African born Reg Park, who appeared in his own *Hercules* movie. By the 1960s such stars as Dave Draper, Larry Scott, and many other regulars of "Muscle Beach" were appearing regularly in a series of beach movies staring Don Rickels, Annette Funichello, and Frankie Avalon.

The 1970s saw the emergence of the one bodybuilder who would build on Reeves' success and take acting to unheard of heights – Arnold Schwarzenegger!

Arnold's first movie was not *Pumping Iron* or *Conan The Barbarian*. No, Arnold appeared as Arnold Strong in the immensely forgettable 1971 movie *Hercules in New York*. Of course using the same dedication and perseverance that made him king of the bodybuilding world, Arnold started a string of box office smashes in 1980 with *Conan The Barbarian*. From Conan to *The Terminator*, to *True lies*, Arnold regularly battles with Harrison Ford, Bruce Willis, and other action stars for the top spot in Hollywood.

We would be remiss if we ignored the other great bodybuilders who made their mark in the TV and film industry.

Arnold's main rival in the documentary *Pumping Iron*, Lou Ferringo, became one of TV's biggest stars with his portrayal of the *Incredible Hulk* in the late '70s and early '80s. He also appeared in a few movies, most notably a remake of *Hercules*, and *Cage*.

Other bodybuilders who have had small parts in major movies, or lead roles in B movies include Serge Nubret, Sergio Oliva, Frank Zane, Franco Columbu, Tom Platz, The Barbarian brothers, and Cory Everson. And in recent years, top pros Roland Cziurlok and Gunter Schlierkamp, have begun making a name for themselves in both the movies and TV commercials.

FROM LOCAL THEATRE TO HOLLYWOOD?

Making it as an actor or actress is just as difficult as climbing to the top of the bodybuilding hierarchy. In some respects perhaps more difficult as there is much more competition. A big bodybuilding class may have 15 or 20 competitors whereas a role in a movie may be contested by hundreds if not thousands of hopefuls.

The best piece of advice we can give you concerning Hollywood is not to go there – at least not yet. Every year thousands of Harrison Ford or Sharon Stone wannabe's arrive at LAX, with nothing more than the shirt on their backs. They have one thing in common, a lifelong desire to be discovered. But the reality is most of them aren't. After a couple of weeks when the glamour starts wearing off and the few hundred dollars are spent, reality sets in. Daily life consists of working as a waiter or waitress and trying out for auditions. Most eventually give up and go back to home. A few unlucky ones end up on the street; and we don't need to go into detail on how they make ends meet. Life can be cruel that way.

If you have a great desire to be a performer, then check out the local scene first. The competition is much less, you have a support group of friends and relatives, and perhaps most of all, you get to find out if acting is really in your blood. It may sound great to see celebrities on Leno or Letterman talking about their latest movies, but what you don't see are all the 20-hour days that went into the movies' production.

> **"I sometimes do television commercials or print ads for the newspapers. I did work for a cookie company, for a bank, and also appeared in some music videos."**
>
> – Thomas Zechmeister, IFBB pro, discussing some of the occupations he's had over the years.

If you manage to break into the local theatre scene and establish a name for yourself, then you are in much better position when it comes to landing bigger and better roles. Like any job you now have a resume. You may go to Los Angles as the State bodybuilding champion, but trust us, that means little or nothing in Hollywood. If, however, you have a combination of theater work, a few local TV roles, and maybe a few bit parts in a few minor movies, then you stand a better chance when you go role seeking in Tinseltown. Look at it another way, three of the biggest gyms in the world, Gold's, World, and Powerhouse, are all located about 20 miles outside of Hollywood in the Santa Monica/ Venice Beach area. Between them they have thousands of members with hundreds of titles, many far more prestigious than yours, and many of these individuals would sell their grandmother and her dog just to land a small movie role. If you hope to compete with that you need something besides your muscles going for you.

We know we've been blunt in the last few paragraphs, but as the old saying goes, the truth hurts. We are trying to save you a world of hurt. The acting profession is great for those that make it. But Hollywood has a bad habit of chewing up and spitting out those who fail to make the grade. All we can say is seek your fortune on the local scene first, and if you develop a reputation as a quality actor or actress, then Hollywood will come looking for you!

CONTEST PROMOTION

It's inevitable that sooner or later many bodybuilders decide to try their hand at running the whole show or contest promotion. In a manner of speaking it's like an actor who finally decides to go behind the camera instead of in front of it. The best example of a bodybuilder turned contest promoter is Arnold.

When Arnold retired in 1975 he formed a partnership with Jim Lorimer, and the two of them started promoting contests in Columbus, Ohio. After promoting a number of Mr. Olympia's in the late seventies and early eighties, they created their own contest, the Arnold Classic, in 1989 (formerly the Pro World Championships).

Other bodybuilders that have established great reputations as contest promoters include Nimrod King, Bev Francis, and Kevin Lervone.

Shawn Ray

WHERE TO START

For those who decide to wet their beak at contest promotion, the first thing to tell you is you don't just up and hold the Nationals or Regionals. Contest promoting is similar to competitive bodybuilding in that you must start at the bottom rung and work your way up. Once you pay your dues at the local level, and establish a reputation as someone who can run a quality show, then you may get your chance at the big time.

The first step in contest promotion is to become affiliated with a major bodybuilding federation. Although there are other federations, by far the largest is the International Federation of Bodybuilders or IFBB. Most states and provinces have local affiliates with the IFBB and all it takes is a phone call to a local gym to get the address or phone number of the local representative. Registering is a simple process that involves filling out a few forms and paying the $25 or $30 yearly fee. That's it, you're in!

Technically you could jump into the contest bidding from day one, but we advise against it.

Chapter 30 – *Bodybuilding Bucks*

Unless you have a reputation in the community as a successful businessperson, few people know you. Why do bodybuilders spend so much time trying to get into the various bodybuilding magazines? It's because they know the exposure will guarantee them points on contest day. Bodybuilders can never have too much exposure. Contest promotion is similar. You don't just come from nowhere and start promoting.

Our advice is to undergo a sort of apprenticeship program. That is, volunteer your services to a local promoter for a few years. The experience you gain will be invaluable down the road. In addition volunteering gives you an opportunity to hone your skills and make a name for yourself as someone who can get things done.

Vince Taylor

After a couple of years working behind the scenes, you can start seriously considering about promoting a show yourself. The first thing to do is size up the local situation. Most federations hold only one show per year. Unless you live in a large population center, odds are your community will experience one contest a year. If the promoter who has run that same show for years is still interested in promoting, and more important, has been doing an excellent job, you may want to reconsider your plans. Look at it this way, why would any federation bypass seasoned experience in favor of a relative newcomer? Yes, you could submit a proposal just to let them know you are interested, and who knows you may get lucky. But as the old saying goes, if it ain't broke, don't fix it. Don't be too shocked if the contest is awarded back to the original promoter.

Your best opportunity for grabbing a contest is when the original promoter decides to step down (or is asked to step aside for one reason or another). It still doesn't mean you will get the rights to promote the show, but at least the playing field has leveled.

Let's say you land the rights to put on your first show. Congratulations! Now the fun starts.

YOUR WIZ KIDS

No matter how efficient your organizational skills there's no way you can run the show yourself. You need help. Think of yourself as the President-elect and your are setting up your first government cabinet. You need to surround yourself with a group of individuals who are willing to give you their time and expertise. Odds are there will be many hangers-on from previous shows. If they offer their services, jump at the opportunity. Likewise there will also be people at your gym who will jump at the chance to become "part of the show."

Another person you may or may not want to talk to is the previous promoter. We say may or may not because it all depends on why the person stepped down and your relationship with that person. If they retired under happy circumstances and your relationship with him or her is cordial (or neutral), then by all means give him or her a call. They'll more than likely be only too happy to offer advice. On the other hand if the individual was asked to step aside (legal or organizational problems) or your relationship with him or her is less than ideal (maybe you did in fact manage to steal the contest rights away from him or her after all), then making contact may not be in your best interests.

Start preparing for the contest as soon as possible. Many promoters start gearing up virtually as soon as this year's show ends. Certainly you will need to book the venue far in advance. This is not so much out of convenience as necessity. Most venues are in steady operation year round. This is especially true on Friday and Saturday nights. The odds that you could book a venue a couple of weeks before the contest date are slim.

There are three primary concerns when booking a venue: size, cost, and location. Let's look at all three.

SIZE DOES COUNT!

Generally speaking the size of the venue will be determined by the size of the contest. A local city show will draw hundreds, while a state or regional contest will pack in thousands. Of course with bodybuilding growing in popularity every year, even local shows may draw thousands. So you may want to take a close look at how many tickets were sold in previous years for the contest you are promoting. Some of the most popular venues include high school auditoriums, hotel convention centers, and musical concert halls.

COST

Besides size, another practical concern is cost. High school auditoriums are the cheapest and can usually be had for a couple of hundred dollars. Of course it depends on the school and facility. Some high schools have concert halls that rival any civic center. As expected such facilities are in big demand and don't come cheap. On the other hand a typical high school gymnasium won't be that expensive.

Hotel convention centers and concert halls are comparable in cost and will set you back thousands of dollars for a one day rental. Once again the level of your contest determines whether or not you really need to spring for such a facility. The more prestigious the show the more spectators it will probably draw and the higher the ticket cost you can get away with. Thus you will be in a position to afford the more pricey facility. Of course successfully putting on a city championship in a classy facility will go a long way in furthering your reputation as a promoter. It becomes a balancing act between the contest, the facility cost, and the impression you want to make.

WHERE OH WHERE

The final major selection variable in picking a venue is location. Generally speaking there are two groups of people to take into account, the competitors and the audience. It only makes sense to hold the show as close to the bulk of the population as possible. For a city show it's not really an issue, as the contest will have to take place within the city boundaries. But for a state or provincial show you may have a number of cities to choose from. If the bulk of the competitors live in one city then that's where you should pitch your tent so to speak. If things are evenly split, then you'll have to start weighing such factors as where the contest was held in previous years, the quality of the venues in each city, and even the opinions of the various people helping you out.

PROMOTION

Once you have the venue selected and contest date fixed, it's time to start letting people know about it. This means promotion of course. There are a number of different means to get the word out about your show. Some methods are small in audience but virtually everyone who sees it is a potential competitor or audience member. Other methods are mass market and hit the full spectrum of society. Let's see what we can do about letting people know about that great contest of yours.

Perhaps the easiest way to advertise your contest is to go to the places where bodybuilders hang out; and this means gyms and supplement stores. Print off a number of flyers containing the important points about the contest, i.e. date, show level, time, location, etc. Then hit all the hardcore and middle of the road gyms in your area. Most gym owners will be only too happy to help you out, as many are bodybuilders themselves. You may also want to mail out flyers to any gyms outside of comfortable driving distance. You notice we left out the third category of training establishments, fitness spas. You'll find very few hardcore bodybuilders at such places, and the owners won't exactly jump at the opportunity to help promote a bodybuilding show. Bodybuilding is not a sport, right? In the meantime it doesn't hurt to check just the same. There may be a few potential audience members working out there.

Besides gyms, hit the various supplement stores. Every Nutrition House, GNC, MuscleMag International store, is fair game. Let's face it, these are the places where most bodybuilders buy their creatine, glutamine, protein, etc.

Once you've hit what we call the target areas, it's time to go mass market. There are three primary forms of mass market media, newspapers, radio, and TV.

The cheapest of the three is newspaper advertising. For a couple of hundred dollars you can get a decent ad in the weekend edition of most local newspapers. For a few extra dollars you can have your ad placed in the sports section, which is after-all the part of the paper that most potential competitors and spectators read the most. There may even be a way to get some major advertising without paying!

Most sports reporters are getting tired of covering the mainstream sports day after day, especially at the local level. Sure the sports reporters at the *New York Times* probably don't get bored interviewing the New York Yankees or New York Knicks. But Joe or Jill average at your local paper is looking for something different than the city softball league. And this is where you come in.

Despite their ignorance of the sport, most mainstream sports reporters find bodybuilding interesting. All it takes is a phone call to the sports department and you may talk your way into getting free coverage. If one or two of your competitors have national potential, then even better. The reporter can do a feature profiling them and your upcoming contest. We are by no means guaranteeing a major write up in the paper, but you have nothing to lose by trying.

In terms of popularity the next step up the ladder in media promotion is the radio. An ad on the radio will cost more than the newspaper but you will hit a much larger audience. And unlike newspapers, which can be biased in terms of readership, virtually everyone listens to the radio. If you have the cash you could put a 30-second spot on all the radio stations in your area, but we have a better suggestion. The population pool that most of your competitors

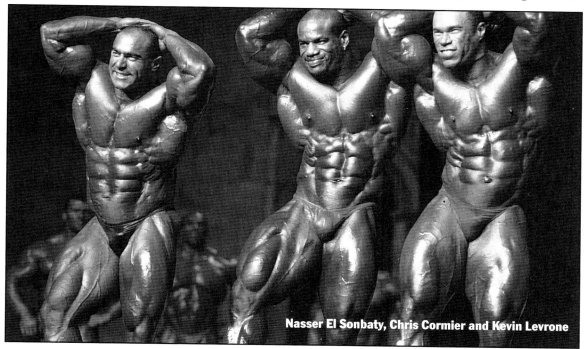

Nasser El Sonbaty, Chris Cormier and Kevin Levrone

and audience members will come from is the 15 to 40 year-old age group. Although there are exceptions, the bulk of this age group listens to top ten middle of the road pop rock. Yes the southern states have a devoted country music following, and there are those who love classical or jazz, but for the most part, top ten AM and FM radio stations are the most popular. This is where you should spend your ad money. That way you'll hit more potential competitors and spectators.

For obvious reasons television is the most visually appealing of media sources. Of course it's also the most expensive. Once again it's a balancing act between finances, reputation, and precedent. If previous promoters by-passed TV and still had a good turn out, then perhaps you can do the same. But if numbers were low for the past couple of years, and you want to make a good impression, and you have the cash, then check out one of the local TV affiliates. You can even try the approach we discussed earlier involving the newspaper sports reporter. See if one of the local TV sports anchors is interested in covering your contest or profiling one or more of the competitors. Once again the answer may be no, but it's worth a shot. And if by chance he or she goes for it, the dividends reaped will be enormous. In most cases a full house for the evening show and a much bigger turn out for the prejudging.

A final option for promoters of bigger shows (large cities and up) is to drop a line to one of the major bodybuilding magazines. Most have a monthly listing of upcoming shows. As an example *MuscleMag International* has a monthly section called *What's On*. Just send in a typewritten sheet highlighting your contest's main points (time, place, level, and who to contact for more information) and they'll put it in for you.

IS IT NECESSARY?

Before leaving the topic of promotion we need to re-emphasize the importance of doing so. If the biggest name in bodybuilding – Arnold Schwarzenegger – has to advertise in magazines and on TV to promote his Arnold Classic, what makes you think your show will be a success just by word of mouth. Odds are it won't. Spend the few extra dollars to get the word out. We assure you, you'll get it back plus more, by having a successful show.

ALMOST THERE!

Besides venue, contest date, location, promotion, etc, there's a host of smaller items that must be taken care off. We use the word "small" lightly as failure to address any one of them can derail your contest big-time.

As soon as you select the venue make a close inspection of the lighting system. In fact lighting is so important that you may want to add it to your venue criteria list. Most high school auditoriums and concert halls are designed with plays and music shows in mind; not highlighting partially nude bodies! This means the lighting system at such facilities may or may not need to be modified. When you do your check, bring along one or two individuals to serve as models and someone who's familiar with judging. You may find the lights wash the physiques out, produce distracting shadows, or are just not powerful enough. If the lighting system available can't be modified, you will need to hire a private lighting contractor. Yes it will set you back a few dollars but it's an absolute must. It's not just the judges you are trying to please. You have the competitors, the buying public, and from a long term perspective, federation representatives who may be considering you for bigger and better things. It doesn't make sense to have everything come crashing down because of a few light bulbs. And let's face it, you can't cover up a poor lighting system. The first weight division won't even get to their first pose when judges and audience alike will start voicing their displeasure.

Unless you have very deep pockets and a philantrophy streak

Gunter Schlierkamp

running through you, you will need to charge an admission fee. And this means tickets. Contact a few local printers and get quotes on printing. Perhaps the most important piece of advice we can give is print exactly the number of tickets as seats. Unlike the airline industry, which assumes a certain percentage of no-shows, most individuals who buy tickets will in fact attend the show. The airlines will deliberately oversell and in most cases things work out. But occasionally more passengers turn up than expected. The airlines usually offer a few incentives to get a couple of passengers to give up their seats. But you have no such option. There is no repeat bodybuilding contest in a few hours. There have been cases were promoters oversold a contest by a couple of hundreds seats. The end result was a large number of angry individuals left standing at the door. Can you say roid rage?

If your venue seats 1000 then you print 1000 tickets. It's that simple. Don't forget that you'll need tickets for both morning and evening shows. You could take the chance and only print 500 tickets for the prejudging as in most cases it won't sell out. But for what an extra 500 tickets would cost to print, it's probably just as well to run them off. Better safe than sorry.

THOSE INVALUABLE HELPERS

Earlier we mentioned that you will need to surround yourself with staff. These helpers will be invaluable in the days leading up to the contest. And as for the day of the contest, they will be worth their weight in gold. Here's a partial list of duties that should be delegated to helpers:

1) Audience ushers
2) Lighting assistants
3) Backstage ushers
4) Ticket punchers
5) Parking lot attendants
6) Judges assistants (obtain water, run messages, etc.)
7) Garbage collectors
8) One or two personal assistants
9) Guest poser assistants
10) Floaters (to move around as needed.)

This list is by no means complete. Your job will be to oversee the whole operation. It will be the most frenzy-filled day of your life! It will start a couple of hours before the prejudging and run until the end of the early morning festivities. If everything runs smooth, the odds are you'll not only get to run the same show next year, but there's a good chance that in a few years you will be bidding to hold more prestigious contests. And one final piece of advice; if there are a few minor glitches during the show, don't panic. Few shows go perfect. As long as the problems are dealt with in an efficient manner and don't interfere with the actual contest itself, you have nothing to worry about. Best of luck.

Frank Sepe

BOOK TEN

SO, YOU WANT TO KNOW MORE?

Bodybuilding Resources

"Many so-called experts rely mostly on anecdotal information and practical gym experience when it comes to training information, but Charles, because he is an Olympic coach speaks directly with many bodybuilding and strength experts throughout the world."

– Greg Zulak, *MuscleMag International* columnist commenting on top strength coach, Charles Poliquin.

As much as we'd like to claim this one book is the key to your bodybuilding success, let's face it, there's a whole spectrum of information out there. Our humble attempts are just a small addition to the total knowledge pool. In the following chapter we are going to look at the four broad sources where you can obtain further information to add to your bodybuilding library. Some of the sources have been around for decades while others are just now emerging on the scene.

BODYBUILDING FOLK

In Chapter One we gave you a brief history of bodybuilding particularly as it related to those who shaped the sport. This chapter is going to add names to the list. In a matter of speaking it's a who's who of bodybuilding. And as many of these individuals routinely give seminars, we urge you to attend one or more.

Rather than simply list the top bodybuilders over the last fifty years or so, we try to give examples of people from the many different facets of the sport. For example Joe Weider and Robert Kennedy never won a major bodybuilding title, but few individuals have shaped or contributed to the sport in the manner both of these guys have. For obvious reasons we include Arnold, but the name Oscar Heidenstam is probably unfamiliar to most readers. Finally as with any list, this one is incomplete. We say this not out of purpose, but practicality. No matter how many rewrites or additions, someone's name will get left out. To those whose names we've omitted (you know who you are), our sincere apologies.

THE MOVERS AND SHAKERS

"I was working for Joe Weider back in the late '50s/early '60s. He asked 'What do you think of this kid?' The photo was a side chest pose of Arnold when he was about 18. I looked at it and I quickly had a funny feeling. I said 'You know Joe, he's going to be the next great star in bodybuilding.' Joe replied 'Well he's coming next week and I'd like you to go to the airport and pick him up.'

– The late Artie Zeller, commenting on his first impression of a young Austrian kid named Arnold Schwarzenegger.

Scott Abel – At last count, Canadian Scott Abel's clients had won over 100 contests. Throughout the eighties and nineties Scott has developed a reputation as one of the sport's top coaches and trainers. Among those who have profited from Scott's advice are Laura Creavalle, Vince Taylor, and Laura Binetti.

Chris Aceto – Like Scott Abel, Chris has made his mark in the coaching and training arena. His clients include Bob Paris, David Dearth, and Vince Comerford.

Charles Atlas – Probably the first individual to bring the benefits of strength training to the masses. Charles' simple little "don't kick sand in my face" ad in the backs' of comic books has sold over 6 million courses of Dynamic tension. Although not a true bodybuilder in the modern sense, Charles nevertheless entertained crowds with his excellent muscle control in the 1920s and 1930s.

Doris Barrilleaux – Doris is one of the true pioneers of women's bodybuilding and has been promoting the benefits of weight training for women for nearly forty years. Her efforts in the late seventies were a major influence in the IFBB creating the first Ms. America and Ms. Olympia contests.

Kim Chizevsky – Kim is a three-time and the current reigning Ms. Olympia winner. She has also won the 1993 Ms. International contest.

Ronnie Coleman – This Texas police officer is currently the number one bodybuilder in the world having won the 1998 Mr. Olympia. Ronnie has also won the New York Night of Champions, Toronto Pro Invitational, and numerous Grand Prix titles.

Franco Columbu – is one of the sport's all time greats having won the Mr. Europe, Mr. Universe, and twice Mr. Olympia contests. A former native of Sardinia, Franco is also a practicing chiropractor and nutritionist.

Laura Combes – Laura was another pioneer in womens bodybuilding and won the 1980 Ms. America contest sporting a degree of muscularity that was about ten years ahead of its time. She passed away in 1989.

Candy Csencsits – Candy was one of the more versatile members of the sport having worked as a model, teacher, IFBB official, and pro bodybuilder. She also held degrees in psychology and nutrition. Her death of breast cancer in 1989 at just 33 was a shock to the bodybuilding world.

Chris Dickerson – Chris was bodybuilding's first African American Mr. America and is believed to have won more titles than any other bodybuilder has. His long career reached a climax by winning the 1982 Mr. Olympia. Chris was famous for his symmetry and posing, and routinely beat competitors outweighing him by forty or fifty pounds.

Dr. Mauro Di Pasquale – With numerous books and articles on drug use in sports to his credit, Dr. Mauro is one of the well-known individuals in bodybuilding and athletics. Unlike many writers who simply tell how to use drugs, DiPasquale takes a medical approach and after first advising against using performance-enhancing drugs, he then provides information on how to avoid serious side effects. His Doctor's Corner column was a staple in *MuscleMag International* for years.

Bill Dobbins – Bill is one of the sport's most prolific writers having written books for Arnold Schwarzenegger, Bruce Jenner, and Gold's Gym. He's also an accomplished photographer, and has contributed to numerous bodybuilding magazines.

Dan Duchaine – Dan has become known as the "steroid guru" in bodybuilding thanks mainly to his best-selling *Underground Steroid Handbooks 1* and *2*. He has also been a regular contributor to such magazines as *MuscleMedia 2000, Pump,* and most recently the online magazine testosterone.net . His latest book is *Body Opus.*

Carla Dunlap – Carla is another women's pioneer having won the 1983 Ms. Olympia contest. She is also an accomplished broadcaster and is featured regularly on TSN and other sports networks as a bodybuilding commentator.

Cory Everson – Cory became the first superstar in women's bodybuilding, having won the Ms. Olympia title six times. She combined the best qualities of shape, proportion, definition, muscle development, and perhaps most of all, femininity. Although retired since 1990, Cory regularly promotes the sport through her books, videos, and TV commentating.

Lou Ferrigno – After Arnold Schwarzenegger, Lou is probably the world's most well-known bodybuilder. In his heyday, Lou carried about 265 pounds on his 6' 5" physique. He won the Mr. America, Mr. Universe, and placed third to Arnold and Serge Nubret in the 1975 Mr. Olympia, featured in the documentary, *Pumping Iron.* After staring as TVs *Incredible Hulk* for numerous years, Lou came out of retirement to compete in the 1992 Mr. Olympia weighing in excess of 300 pounds. Although he placed out of the money, he won the hearts of the audience and followed up next year by placing second at the newly formed Masters Mr. Olympia.

Bev Francis – This former native of Australia was for six straight years the strongest female in the world (world powerlifting champion from 1980 to 1985) and one of the first women to officially bench over 300 pounds in competition. After switching to bodybuilding she placed second to Cory Everson at the 1990 Ms. Olympia.

Vince Gironda – The "Iron Guru" was one of the most colorful characters in the sport. His death in 1998 brought to an end over sixty years associated with the sport of bodybuilding. His gym in Hollywood, "Vince's" featured some of the most well-known celebrities in the world. Vince started his career as a stuntman and after switching to bodybuilding became famous for his muscularity, which was deemed too muscular by the judges at the time. In 1984 he teamed up with *MuscleMag's* Robert Kennedy to write the best-selling book, *Unleashing The Wild Physique.*

Lee Haney – In 1990 Lee accomplished what many thought, impossible tying Arnold's record of seven Mr. Olympia wins. A year later he broke the record with his eighth consecutive win and established himself as the sport's most dominant Mr. Olympia winner ever. Lee used his sheer size, all 250 pounds, to swamp the competition. Since retirement he has opened a gym, done TV commentating, and helped train numerous athletes including boxing great, Evander Holyfield.

Oscar Heidenstam – Considered one of the true pioneers of modern bodybuilding, Oscar helped found the National Amateur Bodybuilding Federation (NABBA), edited and published *Health and Strength* magazine, and won the 1937 Mr. Britian title and placed second at the 1952 Mr. Universe. His passing in 1991 signaled the passing of an era.

Manfred Hoeberl – Manfred was one of the top stars on the strongman circuit in the early nineties. He became famous for his size sporting a 60-inch chest, 25+-inch arms, and 320-pound frame. A car accident brought his strongman career to an end but he managed to regain most of his size and still is a huge draw at conferences and exhibitions.

Bob Hoffman – Bob is considered by many to be the "father" of weightlifting in America and helped form both the American Athletic Union (AAU) and *Strength* magazine.

Dr. Arthur Jones – Dr. Jones has been one of the most influential people in bodybuilding, both for his one set to failure theories of training and for inventing the Nautilus line of equipment. In addition to weight training he has one of the largest private collections of wild animals in the world.

Robert Kennedy – British-immigrant Robert Kennedy is the embodiment of the American Dream, even if it was Canada he decided to settle in! Since coming to Canada in the late sixties, Bob has become one of the most influential figures in the sport. Besides publishing *MuscleMag International* and *Oxygen* magazines and the new *American Health and Fitness*, Bob has written over forty books on the subject of bodybuilding, not to mention hundreds of magazine articles. He's also one of the best photographers in the business, although he won't admit it!

Rachel McLish – Rachel won the very first Ms. Olympia contest and was one of the pioneers of the female bodybuilding movement.

Mike Mentzer – Although he won both the Mr. America and Mr. Universe titles, Mike is perhaps more famous as a writer, particularly in endorsing his Heavy Duty style of training; an expansion and modification of Dr. Arthur Jones' theories of one set to failure training. In recent years Mike had a column in *Muscular Development* magazine.

Andreas Munzer – One of the most tragic figures in bodybuilding, Andreas Munzer died in 1996 from what physicians called "massive internal hemorrhaging." Munzer became famous for his shredded contest condition, and while never winning a major show, managed to crack the top five on a number of occasions. His death helped confirm something assumed for years, the extent of drug use in pro bodybuilding.

Lenda Murray – Six-time Ms. Olympia, Cory Everson was no sooner off the stage when the reign of Lenda Murray began. Lenda won six Ms. Olympia titles from 1990 to 1995. Before bodybuilding Lenda had dreams of becoming a Dallas Cowboy Cheerleader, but despite making it to the final 45, she was told her thighs were too big!

Serge Nubret – Serge will forever be remembered for coming from nowhere to place second to Arnold at the 1975 Mr. Olympia, featured in the documentary *Pumping Iron*. Considered by many to be one of the sport's all-time greats, Serge was famous for his miniscule waist and humongous chest.

Sergio Oliva – Even by today's standards Sergio Oliva was and still is a bodybuilding freak! After defecting from Cuba in the early 1960s, Sergio switched from weightlifting to body-building and won the Mr. Olympia from 1967 to 1969. Sergio was famous for his unbelievable size, which earned him the nickname "The Myth." Sergio made a return to bodybuilding in 1984 and despite being up against guys 20 years his junior, placed a respectable 8th.

Reg Park – Reg Park was one of the top bodybuilders of the 1950s, having won three Mr. Universe titles, as well as appearing in the movie *Hercules*. His 6'2" 220-pound physique served as an inspiration for Arnold Schwarzenegger, who was then a young lad growing up in Austria.

John Parrillo – John has developed a reputation as one of the most knowledgeable individuals in bodybuilding. Besides his regular column in *MuscleMag International*, John has his own line of supplements called Parrillo Performance.

Bill Pearl – Another of bodybuilding's all-time greats, Bill's competitive career lasted from 1952 to 1971. During that time period this native American won the Mr. America title and four Mr. universe titles. Today in his early seventies, Bill sports a physique that could still hold its own in a bodybuilding contest.

Bill Phillips – Bill is owner and publisher of *Muscle Media* magazine as well as the immensely popular EAS line of supplements. Bill started his career by writing the best-selling *Anabolic Reference Guide* book in the mid eighties. The periodic updates to this book eventually became *Muscle Media 2000* magazine, and eventually *Muscle Media*.

Tom Platz – Tom was one of the top bodybuilders in the late seventies and early eighties. He won both the Mr. America and Mr. Universe titles, and many feel he should have won the 1981 Mr. Olympia. To this day most in the game feel Tom had the greatest legs in bodybuilding history – past or present.

Charles Poliquin – Charles is currently one of the most sought after strength coaches in the world. His clients include some of the best amateur and professional athletes in the world. Besides writing for *Muscle Media* magazine and *Testosterone.Net*, he has authored the very popular *The Poliquin Principles* book.

Steve Reeves – The late Steve Reeves won both the Mr. America and Mr. Universe titles as well as starring in a number of highly successful *Hercules* movies in the 1940s and 1950s. Steve was the first bodybuilder to carry his physique over to the entertainment industry. Steve wrote for *Muscular Development* magazine as well as his own book *Building The Classic Physique*. Steve's death was mourned by the entire bodybuilding world.

Bill Reynolds – The late Bill Reynolds was one of bodybuilding's most prolific writers. Besides the hundreds of magazine articles he penned, he wrote numerous books for Weider Enterprises, Lee Haney, Tom Platz, and Samir Bannout.

Robby Robinson – Robby is one of the most enduring bodybuilders around having started his career back in the early seventies. In that time he has won the Mr. America, Mr. Universe, New York Night of Champions, Masters Mr. Olympia, and numerous Grand Prix titles. Robby still does battle with guys half his age and his arms are considered to be among the best of all time.

Don Ross – Don was nicknamed "Ripper" for his outstanding muscularity and helped usher in the extremely low bodyfat look. Besides winning the Mr. America title, Don was also a successful writer having written the very popular *Muscleblasting* book.

Larry Scott – Larry was bodybuilding's first Mr. Olympia, having won the title in 1965 and 1966. Famous for his arms, Larry had small roles in a number of "beach" movies that were popular in the 1960s. The preacher bench is often called the Scott Bench in his honor.

Arnold Schwarzenegger – Arnold is unquestionably bodybuilding's greatest star. Like Muhammad Ali in boxing and Michael Jordan in basketball, Arnold's popularity transcended the sport. During his career Arnold won five Mr. Universe titles and seven Mr. Olympia titles. After staring in the 1975 documentary *Pumping Iron*, Arnold began a movie career that saw him become the top box office draw in the world. In addition he has released a number of best selling books including *Arnold The Education of a Bodybuilder* and *Arnold's Encyclopedia of Modern Bodybuilding* (revised in 1998).

Vince Taylor – Vince is one of the most successful bodybuilders in history having won the Mr. America, World Championships, Masters Mr. Olympia, Arnold Classic, New York Night of Champions, and numerous Grand Prix events. A former member of the U.S. military, Vince is one of bodybuilding's all-time great posers.

Rick Wayne – Rick was one of the top bodybuilders in the 1960s and 1970s. Yet despite winning such titles as Mr. World and Mr. Universe, Rick is best known for his literary talents. Rick has written hundreds of magazine articles over the past thirty years and co-authored the very successful *Three More Reps*, series of bodybuilding books. His book *Muscle Wars* is considered one of the best behind-the-scenes bodybuilding narratives ever written.

Ben Weider – Ben is the IFBB's elder statesman and he has devoted most of his life to promoting the sport of bodybuilding. His efforts finally paid off with bodybuilding being granted Olympic status, although the drug issue will need to be addressed before final implementation takes place.

Betty Weider – Betty has been active in the fitness industry for most of her life and is one of the pioneers who championed weight training for women. With a number of books and magazine articles to her name, Betty is recognized as one of the most knowledgeable individuals in the area of physical fitness. She is the wife of publisher and IFBB founder Joe Weider.

Joe Weider – Despite the recent challenge from various newcomers, Joe is bodybuilding's most successful businessman. His corporation, Weider Enterprises, publishes *Muscle and Fitness, Flex, and Shape*, magazines. In addition Joe has written thousands of magazine articles and numerous books during his long career. Joe was one of the founding members of the International Federation of Bodybuilders – IFBB.

Ken "Flex" Wheeler – During the 1990s Flex had won just about every bodybuilding title available. Only the Mr. Olympia has escaped his grasp and he has placed second on two occasions. Flex is considered by most to have the best combination of size, shape, and symmetry, of any pro currently competing.

Dorian Yates – Most of the 1990s belonged to Birmingham, England, native, Dorian Yates. At 265-270 pounds, Dorian was the largest Mr. Olympia ever, and his run of six straight titles established him as one of the greatest bodybuilders in history. His training video *Blood and Guts* became a best seller, and set the standard for all future training videos.

Frank Zane – Three-time Mr. Olympia, Frank Zane, is another of bodybuilding's all-time greats. In addition to his three Mr. Olympia wins, he won the Mr. America, Mr. Universe, and was one of the few bodybuilders to defeat Arnold in competition (the 1968 Mr. Universe). Frank is long retired from competitive bodybuilding but is still active in writing, promotion, and running his highly successful bodybuilding camp, Zane Haven.

MAGAZINES

Every month there are dozens of magazines published that cater to the full spectrum of physical fitness. Of these there are a dozen or so aimed specifically at bodybuilding. Some such as *IronMan* and *MuscleMag International* cover the full scope of bodybuilding, while other such as *Flex* or *Muscular Development*, cater to specific areas. Still others are nothing more than an ad for a particular supplement line.

> **"The only way you can hope to make continuing progress throughout your bodybuilding career is to keep learning new ideas, methods and techniques. There are magazines, books, and now even Web sites."**
>
> – Ron Harris, *MuscleMag International* contributor offering a few suggestions on how to improve your bodybuilding knowledge.

MuscleMag International – First started by British immigrant, Robert Kennedy, *MuscleMag International* is one of the "middle of the road" bodybuilding magazines. Every month the magazine features articles covering every facet of bodybuilding from drugs and supplements to training articles and contests. Although based in Ontario, Canada, most sales are in the US. *MuscleMag International* was one of the first bodybuilding magazines to take an unbiased stance on drug use in sports, and rather than preach horror stories like other magazines, *MuscleMag* looked at both sides of the issue.

Muscle and Fitness – *Muscle and Fitness* is the top selling bodybuilding magazine and is a direct descendant of the old *Muscle Builder Power* magazine of the 1960s and 1970s. *Muscle and Fitness* is published by Joe Weider, and since the introduction of *Flex* magazine in the early eighties, has shifted focus from hardcore bodybuilding to bodybuilding as a way of life. The magazine still covers the top contests and personalities, but the serious issues such as drugs, supplements, and advanced training play a secondary role to the topics that promote bodybuilding as a form of fitness.

Flex – Another of Joe Weider's publications, *Flex* is an offshoot of *Muscle and Fitness* magazine. *Flex* is devoted to hardcore bodybuilding and each issue features the latest information on drugs, supplements, contest coverage, and training information. In addition *Flex* contains probably the best training photos of any bodybuilding magazine.

IronMan – *IronMan* is published by John Balik, and is one of the oldest publications in bodybuilding. *IronMan* is similar to *MuscleMag International* in that it covers the full spectrum of bodybuilding topics. *IronMan* is one of the best magazines available for cutting edge supplementation and training.

Muscular Development – Of all the current bodybuilding magazines, *Muscular Development* seems to be having the most trouble finding an identity over the past five years. Initially they were hardcore bodybuilding, but then switched to an "all natural" format. When sales took a drop, they switched to their present format catering to athletes who use bodybuilding principles to improve their performance. *Muscular Development* is shallow on contest coverage and bodybuilding profiles, but they are the best magazine when it comes to supplement information and the latest scientific studies. *Muscular Development* is owned by the huge supplement company, Twin Lab.

Muscle Media – Published by Bill Phillips, *Muscle Media* grew out of a series of updates to Bill's highly successful *Anabolic Reference Guide. Muscle Media* was initially called *Muscle Media 2000* and at the time was the best source of supplement and drug information. Within a few months *Muscle Media* jumped to the top of the magazine heap, and had a huge loyal following. But in the space of a few issues, Bill switched the format from hardcore drug and supplement information to the natural sports looks. In addition the magazine became heavily laced with advertising for Bill's EAS line of supplements. To most readers it was a sell-out and despite shrinking sales, Bill seems content to keep the current format.

Oxygen – *Oxygen* is another publication of *MuscleMag International* and its main focus is women's fitness; although women's bodybuilding plays a secondary role.

Shape – *Shape* is another Weider publication that looks at women's fitness. Shape is currently the top-selling magazine in its class and features the top women in the fitness and entertainment industries.

Powerlifting USA – Although not a bodybuilding magazine, many bodybuilders buy the journal given the overlap between the two sports. Although the magazine features nutrition and supplement articles, the main focus is strength training and profiles of powerlifters. For those bodybuilders interested in increasing their strength (which is most we assure you!), this magazine has some excellent suggestions.

Pump – *Pump* is one of the new kids on the block and is published by JDC Publishing. This over-sized glossy magazine is basically a supplement catalog filled in with some swimsuit pictures and training information. Although the occasional decent article makes it to the table of contents, about three quarters of the magazine consists of ads for their line of So Cal Sports Supplement (SCSS) and others.

BODYBUILDING BOOKS

The days of only having mini-training booklets and one or two full-length books are over. You now have at your disposal literally hundreds of fine bodybuilding publications to add to your library. Some are written by top competitive bodybuilders, while others are penned by recognized experts in the field. Bodybuilding books can be divided into four broad categories: biography, training, nutrition, and drug and supplement books. The following is a comprehensive list of some of the better books out there. We should add that many are out of print, but can easily be obtained at flea markets or used bookstores. If all else fails contact the online bookstore www.amazon.com. If they can't get it, no one can!

For convenience we have listed the books by author or publisher. We do not review every book, as it would take too long. Instead we limit our comments to the most popular books. Most of the books are reviewed at www.amazon.com.

MUSCLEMAG INTERNATIONAL PUBLICATIONS

First started in the early 1990s, MuscleMag International's book publishing division is now one of the largest bodybuilding publishers in the world.

Anabolic Muscle Mass. The Secrets of Anabolic Reinforcement Without Steroids
By Dennis B. Weis and Robert Kennedy.
One of the best mid-sized hardcore books available. The book primarily focuses on advanced training techniques.

Anabolic Primer. An Information-Packed Reference Guide To Ergogenic Aids For Hardcore Bodybuilders
By Phil Embleton and Gerard Thorne.
This is the largest full-spectrum supplement and drug reference guide currently available. It covers just about every conceivable substance used by bodybuilders to increase muscle size and lose body fat.

Anabolic Edge. Secrets For That Extra Lean Muscle Mass
By Phil Embleton and Gerard Thorne.
The sequel to *Anabolic Primer, Anabolic Edge* looks at the latest hardcore drugs and supplements to come on the scene in the latest couple of years.

Animal Arms. Ultimate Size and Shape Training for Building Monstrous Arm Muscles
By Robert Kennedy and Dwayne Hines.
A mid-size book that focuses on arm building techniques.

Awesome Abs! The Gut Busting Solution For Men And Women
By Paul Chek. A mid-sized book aimed at strengthening and reducing the midsection.

Bodyfitness For Women. Your Way To Physical Perfection
By Gerard Thorne and Phil Embleton.
A large book that covers the full spectrum of women's physical fitness. The book gives a special emphasis on weight training.

MuscleMag International's Encyclopedia of Bodybuilding.
The Ultimate A-Z Book On Muscle Building! – By Gerard Thorne and Phil Embleton.
One of the largest and most comprehensive bodybuilding books currently available. The book contains over 750 photographs and takes the reader from the beginner to the competitive level of bodybuilding.

Fast Lane To Fitness. The Busy Woman's Guide To Building A Sleek Physique
In A Limited Amount of Time. By Robert Kennedy and Dwayne Hines.

Hot Legs! Shaping a Tight and Trim Lower Body.
By Robert Kennedy and Dwayne Hines.

The Magic of Fat Loss. Lose Fat and Double Your Energy for Life.
By Robert Kennedy and Dwayne Hines.

Massive at Last! How to Build More Muscle Mass Than You Ever Thought Possible.
By Robert Kennedy and Dwayne Hines
A mid-sized book that looks at the fundamentals of building large powerful muscles.

Muscle Building 101. The Fundamentals of Shaping Your Physique
By Robert Kennedy and Dwayne Hines.

Priming the Anabolic Environment. A Practical, Scientific Guide to
the Art and Science of Building Muscle. By Will Brink.
A mid-size no nonsense book by regular *MuscleMag International* columnist, Will Brink. The book goes into both the training and ergogenesis of building muscle mass.

Six-Pack Abs in 60 Days. The Easy Way to a New, Slimmer Midsection.
By Robert Kennedy and Dwayne Hines.
Small, but highly informative book that shows you how to reduce the midsection in the shortest time possible.

Super Routines of The Super Stars.
Hot Training Cycles for Ultimate Muscle Growth!
By Robert Kennedy and Dwayne Hines
A collection of advanced training routines from bodybuilding superstars.

BY ROBERT KENNEDY

Besides writing for his own company MuscleMag International, Robert Kennedy has written for other publishers including Sterling Publishers of New York.

Awesome Arms, By Robert Kennedy. Another in the successful body art series.

Barn Door Shoulders. **Superstriated, Melon-sized Delts!**
From the body art series.

Mass. **New Scientific Bodybuilding Secrets**

Super Chest. Deeper, Thicker, More Ripped-Up Pecs
MuscleMag body part series.

Hardcore Bodybuilding. The Blood Sweat and Tears of Pumping Iron
One of the first hardcore books to be released, this publication made the best-sellers lists in the early eighties.

Cuts! Gain Muscle! Lose Fat!

Built – The New Bodybuilding For Everyone

Rock Hard! Supernutrition for Bodybuilders
One of the first books to dive deep into the science of bodybuilding nutrition.

Beef It! Upping The Muscle Mass
The sequel to *Hardcore Bodybuilding, Beef It!* elaborated on the advanced training principles needed for maximum muscle growth.

Bodybuilding Basics
One of the simplest yet straight-forward books aimed at beginner and intermediate level bodybuilders.

Hardcore Action Bodybuilding. Pumping Iron to Sculpt a Winning Body

MuscleBlasting. Brief and Brutal Shock Training, with Don Ross.

Natural Bodybuilding for Everyone

Natural Bodybuilding For Men and Women

Posing! The Art of Physique Display

Pumping Up! Super Shaping the Feminine Physique, with Ben Weider

Raw Muscle!

Reps! The World's Hottest Bodybuilding Routines!

Rip Up! Get Rock Hard and Super Cut Now!

Savage Sets! The Ultimate Pre-Exhaust Pump Out

Stack It! The Ultimate New Strategy for Mass!

Start Bodybuilding

Unleashing The Wild Physique, with Vince Gironda

The World Gym Musclebuilding System , with Joe Gold.

BY FRANK ZANE

Frank Zane has won every major title in bodybuilding including the Mr. America, Mr. Universe and three Mr. Olympia titles.

Frank Zane: Mind, Body, Spirit

A combination biography and training book, this publication reveals all Frank's secrets obtained over 40 years in the bodybuilding field. Besides training, Frank goes into such topics as meditation, psychology, and motivation.

BY FRANCO COLUMBU

Two-time Mr. Olympia Franco Columbu is one of the best under 200-pound bodybuilders ever. Besides his two Mr. Olympia wins he won the Mr. Europe, Mr. World, and Mr. Universe titles. He also holds degrees in nutrition and chiropracty.

The Bodybuilders Nutrition Book

This book is almost exclusively devoted to nutrition and was one of the first of its kind ever released.

Coming On Strong

Similar to Arnold Schwarzenegger's *Education of a Bodybuilder*, this book covers Franco's early life in Europe and his rise to bodybuilding stardom in the mid seventies.

Franco Columbu's Complete Book of Bodybuilding

This mid-sized book covers the full spectrum of bodybuilding topics.

Redesign Your Body: The 90-Day Real Body Makeover

A small, easy to read book aimed at those who have limited knowledge about physical conditioning.

Starbodies: The Women's Weight Training Book

Weight Training and Bodybuilding: A Complete Guide for Young Athletes

Winning Bodybuilding

BY BILL DOBBINS

Bill is one of the top writers and photographers in the field of bodybuilding.

The Women: Photographs of The Top Female Bodybuilders.

Arnold's Bodybuilding For Men

First published in 1984, this book was co-written with Arnold Schwarzenegger and covers the full spectrum of bodybuilding.

The Encyclopedia of Modern Bodybuilding

Mega-sized book by Arnold Schwarzenegger and Bill Dobbins that became a huge international best-seller. At over 700 pages it was and still is the largest book of it kind on the sport of bodybuilding.

The New Encyclopedia Of Modern Bodybuilding

The updated (1998) version of Arnold's original Encyclopedia. It contains an additional 100 pages and is probably the most complete book ever written on the sport. It is currently only available in Hardcover so the $35-$40 ($80 Cnd) may be its only drawback.

The Gold's Gym Weight Training Book

First published in 1991, this mass-market paperback book looks at bodybuilding from the point of view of the most famous gym in the sport, Gold's Gym.

Hi-Tech Training

BY DR. ELLINGTON DARDEN

Dr. Ellington Darden is another of bodybuilding's most prolific writers. Most of his bodybuilding books focus on the Nautilus theory of strength training (i.e. one set to failure), but many of the books are worth the price for the photography alone.

Grow: A Crash Course For Getting Huge

The Nautilus Book

A very thorough book that covers Dr. Arthur Jones' Nautilus theory of training.

Nutrition and Athletic Performance

One of the first books that looked at the role nutrition plays in improving athletic performance.

100 High Intensity Ways To Improve Bodybuilding

Big Arms In Six Weeks

High Intensity Bodybuilding: For Massive Muscles Fast

Nautilus Training Principles Applied to Free Weights and Conventional Equipment.

High Intensity Strength Training

Massive Muscles in 10 Weeks

Nautilus Advanced Bodybuilding Book.

Super-High Intensity Bodybuilding

BY MIKE MENTZER

Like Ellington Darden, Mike Mentzer is a proponent of one set to failure training. In fact he won't even consider any other type of training. Still the books are a valuable source of information pertaining to overtraining and advanced training techniques.

Mike Mentzer's Complete Book of Weight Training

Mike Mentzer's Spot Bodybuilding:
A Revolutionary New Approach to Body Fitness and Symmetry.

The Mentzer Method To Fitness: A Revolutionary Weight Training System for Men and Women.

BY RICK WAYNE

Besides winning both the Mr. World and Mr. Universe titles, Rick was at one time editor of *Muscle and Fitness* magazine. His book *Muscle Wars* is considered a classic.

Muscle Wars: The Behind The Scenes Story Of Competitive Bodybuilding.
This book was probably the first of its kind to look at the personality side of bodybuilding and show how psychology plays a major role in bodybuilding success.

Posedown: Muscletalk With the Champs
This book co-authored with George Snyder looks at the training philosophies of the top body-builders from the seventies and early eighties.

BY BILL REYNOLDS
The late Bill Reynolds ranks up there with Robert Kennedy and Bill Dobbins for the number of bodybuilding books published. He also wrote hundreds of articles for most of the major body-building magazines.

Bodybuilding For Beginners
Co-written with Mr. International winner, Andreas Cahling, this book introduces to beginners the fundamental concepts in bodybuilding.

Gold's Gym Nutrition Book
One of the best books that examines nutrition as it relates to bodybuilding.

The Gold's Gym Training Encyclopedia
Very complete book that covers the full spectrum of bodybuilding topics.

Joe Weider's Ultimate Bodybuilding: The Master Blasters Principles of Training and Nutrition
Written for businessman supreme, Joe Weider, this book goes into detail on the various Weider Principles that virtually all the top bodybuilders have followed over the years.

Supercut: Nutrition for the Ultimate Physique
Another pioneering book that looked at nutrition and bodybuilding success.

The Weider System of Bodybuilding
One of the first books of its kind, this book outlines and describes the Weider approach to bodybuilding, with a special emphasis on training tips from the sport's top bodybuilders.

Competitive Bodybuilding
Sequel to *The Weider System of Bodybuilding*, this book looks at advanced bodybuilding and what it takes to be successful in the sport.

Joe Weider's Mr. Olympia Training Encyclopedia
Another book written for Weider Enterprises, this one looks at the training strategies of the top bodybuilders over the last thirty years.

Freestyle Bodybuilding

Mr. Olympia's Muscle Mastery: The Complete Guide To Building and Shaping Your Body
Written for 1983 Mr. Olympia, Samir Bannout, this mid-sized book takes the bodybuilder from the beginning to the competitive level of bodybuilding.

Peak Physique: Your Lifetime Guide To Muscle And Fitness
This book was written for the "ageless wonder," Albert Beckles, a man who was winning pro bodybuilding contests while in his fifties!

Pro-style Bodybuilding
Written for Tom Platz, this book looks at Tom's theories of training including how he built the greatest legs in bodybuilding history.

Solid Gold. Training the Gold's Gym Way
Another book in the Gold's Gym training family.

BY ARNOLD SCHWARZENEGGER
We had to mention Arnold as he has probably sold more bodybuilding books than any other writer. We hesitate to use the term writer as in most cases the books were co-authored with others. Still the image of the "Austrian Oak" sitting down at a typewriter or computer does raise a few eyebrows! Most of Arnold's major books have been covered under other authors.

Arnold: The Education of a Bodybuilder
Co-authored with Douglas Kent Hall, this book is bodybuilding's best-selling biography, and the picture on the cover has probably introduced more people to bodybuilding than any other.

BY CHARLES POLIQUIN

Charles is one of the top strength coaches in the world today, and some of his clients pay up to $300 per hour. He is also an accomplished writer, having written for numerous magazines including *Muscle Media 2000* and the online magazine *testosterone.net*.

The Poliquin Principles

This 151-page book is probably the most comprehensive book of its size around. Rather than just list routines, Charles goes into the science behind sets, reps, and frequency.

BY LARRY SCOTT

Larry won the first two Mr. Olympia titles and was famous for his outstanding arm development

Loaded Guns

Sporting two of the best arms ever in bodybuilding, Larry shows you how in this mid-sized book.

CHARLES GAINES AND GEORGE BUTLER

In some respects these two guys are the most important people in bodybuilding history. They certainly rank up there with Arnold, Joe Weider, and Robert Kennedy. Yet most people never heard of them. But their 1973 book *Pumping Iron* changed bodybuilding forever.

Pumping Iron

The first book to look at bodybuilding in an objective manner. It introduced Arnold Schwarzenegger to the American public and helped take bodybuilding from high school gyms to respectable concert theaters. The success of the book lead to the documentary of the same name. Released 1977, it followed Arnold, Lou Ferrigno, and others as they prepared for the 1975 Mr. Olympia. *Pumping Iron* has the authors' vote as the most influential and important book in bodybuilding history.

WEB SITES

As little as five years ago, this category didn't warrant attention in a book such as this. Yet in that short time period the internet has become one of the biggest sources of information on any topic. And we mean ANY topic! Whatever you are into, you can be sure there is someone else out there with the same interest who has put up a Web site. The Internet is a treasure chest of goodies for bodybuilders, but like Halloween, you have to watch out for those one or two apples containing needles or razor blades.

There are numerous categories of Web sites available for bodybuilders to browse or "surf." Some are nothing more than advertising pages for a given supplement brand. Nothing wrong with that mind you, but let's face it, anyone pushing his or her line of supplements is probably going to be a tad biased.

Another category of sites are those put up by individuals who want nothing more than to see their names in print. These are by far the most numerous types of sites and it's up to you to weed through the information and separate legitimate information from utter garbage.

A third category are the large, expensive, on-line magazines that rival the best paper magazines. They have large, highly knowledgeable staff writers who dish out top quality information on a monthly basis. Some are free while others require a monthly fee.

Chapter 31 – *Bodybuilding Resources*

The following is just a sample of the wide assortment of Internet sites available. And as the "net" is probably the fastest growing information medium out there, you'll quickly notice that every month will see a whole new selection appearing for the first time in your search engines. Finally most sites offer links to other sites. It becomes the proverbial snowball effect, two sites lead to four, four leads to eight, eight leads to sixteen, and so on. In a matter of seconds you can be hitting hundreds of sites all related to bodybuilding.

www.testosterone.net – One of the largest and most extensive sites available. *Test.net* was started by a group of ex-*MuscleMedia 2000* writers who felt *MuscleMedia 2000* was going too "softcore" and selling out. *Test.net* features the writings of T.C. Luoma, Charles Poliquin, and Tim Patterson. *Test.net* is primarily aimed at hardcore bodybuilders who want the latest information on hardcore drugs, supplements, and training. Without sounding like a paid advertisement, the authors consider this the best on-line site for hardcore bodybuilding information.

www.mesomorphosis.com – Ranking right up there with *Test.net*, *Meso.net* is another site aimed at no nonsense bodybuilders. There's no topic they won't touch, and they always make a point of referencing their information. In 1999, *Meso.net* became available by subscription only, but given the quality of information they present, they are definitely worth the monthly fee.

www.getbig.com – Another great site that covers the full bodybuilding spectrum. *Getbig.com* features everything from training and nutrition, to supplements and contest coverage. As of this writing it's free.

www.bodybuilding.com – As with *Getbig.com*, *bodybuilding.com* takes the *MuscleMag International* approach; try to cover as much ground as possible in each edition. As of this writing bodybuilding.com is free.

www.bookworld.com – Bookworld is a major distributor of books based in Florida. They distribute the full line of *MuscleMag International* books and other great publications. Besides distributing to the major bookstores, they have their own site where you can buy online.

www.amazon.com – The net's largest outlet for books, amazon.com carries just about everything that is available in written form. They even have an extensive tracking system for out of print books.

www.barnesandnoble.com – Another huge online book outlet. Barns and Noble sell both new publications as well as track down out of print editions.

www.heavyweights.com – One of Canada's fastest growing, online supplement stores. Heavyweights is run by provincial middleweight bodybuilding winner (Newfoundland) Rob King and carries just about every hardcore bodybuilding supplement available. It also has a Forum where bodybuilders can write in and express their opinions on a host of topics.

Amy Fadhli

MR. OLYMPIA WINNERS

1965 – Larry Scott
1966 – Larry Scott
1967 – Sergio Oliva
1968 – Sergio Oliva
1969 – Sergio Oliva
1970 – Arnold Schwarzenegger
1971 – Arnold Schwarzenegger
1972 – Arnold Schwarzenegger
1973 – Arnold Schwarzenegger
1974 – Arnold Schwarzenegger
1975 – Arnold Schwarzenegger
1976 – Franco Columbu
1977 – Frank Zane
1978 – Frank Zane
1979 – Frank Zane
1980 – Arnold Schwarzenegger
1981 – Franco Columbu
1982 – Chris Dickerson
1983 – Samir Bannout
1984 – Lee Haney
1985 – Lee Haney
1986 – Lee Haney
1987 – Lee Haney
1988 – Lee Haney
1989 – Lee Haney
1990 – Lee Haney
1991 – Lee Haney
1992 – Dorian Yates
1993 – Dorian Yates
1994 – Dorian Yates
1995 – Dorian Yates
1996 – Dorian Yates
1997 – Dorian Yates
1998 – Ronnie Coleman
1999- Ronnie Coleman

MASTERS MR. OLYMPIA

1994 – Robby Robinson
1995 – Sonny Schmidt
1996 – Vince Taylor
1997 – Vince Taylor
1998 – Vince Taylor
1999 – Vince Taylor

IFBB PRO MR. UNIVERSE (CHANGED TO ARNOLD CLASSIC)

1975 – Bob Birdsong
1979 – Roy Callender
1980 – Jusup Wilkosz
1981 – Dennis Tinerino

IFBB PRO WORLD CHAMPIONSHIPS

1982 – Albert Beckles
1983 – Mohammed Makkawy
1984 – Albert Beckles
1985 – No contest
1986 – Rich Gaspari
1987 – Ron Love
1988 – Mike Christian
1989 – Robby Robinson

ARNOLD CLASSIC WINNERS

1989 – Rich Gaspari
1990 – Michael Ashley
1991 – Shawn Ray
1992 – Vince Taylor
1993 – Flex Wheeler
1994 – Kevin Lervone
1995 – Michael Francois
1996 – Kevin Lervone
1997 – Flex Wheeler
1998 – Flex Wheeler
1999 – Nasser El Sonbaty

IFBB MR. AMERICA

1949 – Alan Stephan
1959 – Chuck Sipes
1960 – Gene Shuey
1962 – Larry Scott
1963 – Reg Lewis
1964 – Harold Poole
1965 – Dave Draper
1966 – Chester Yorton
1967 – Don Howorth
1968 – Frank Zane
1969 – John DeCola
1970 – Mike Katz
1971 – Ken Waller
1972 – Ed Corney
1973 – Lou Ferrigno
1974 – Bob Birdsong
1975 – Robby Robinson
1976 – Mike Mentzer
1977 – Danny Padilla

AAU MR. AMERICA

1938 – Bert Goodrich
1939 – Roland Essmaker
1940 – John Grimek
1941 – John Grimek
1942 – Frank Leight
1943 – Jules Bacon
1944 – Steve Stanko
1945 – Clarence Ross
1946 – Alan Stephan
1947 – Steve Reeves
1948 – George Eiferman
1949 – Jack Delinger
1950 – John Farbotnik
1951 – Roy Hilligenn
1952 – Jim Park
1953 – Bill Pearl
1954 – Dick DuBois
1955 – Steve Klisanin
1956 – Ray Schaeffer
1957 – Ron Lacy
1958 – Tom Sansone
1959 – Harry Johnson
1960 – Lloyde Lerille
1961 – Ray Routledge
1962 – Joseph Abbenda
1963 – Vern Weaver
1964 – Val Vasilieff
1965 – Jerry Daniels
1966 – Bob Gajda
1967 – Dennis Tinerino
1968 – Jim Haislop
1969 – Boyer Coe
1970 – Chris Dickerson
1971 – Casey Viator
1972 – Steve Michalik
1973 – Jim Morris
1974 – Ronald Thompson
1975 – Dale Adrian
1976 – Kalman Szkalak
1977 – Dave Johns
1978 – Tony Pearson
1979 – Ray Mentzer
1980 – Gary Leonard
1981 - Tim Belknap
1982 - Rufus Howard

1983 – Jeff King
1984 – Joe Meeko
1985 – Michael Antorino
1986 – Glenn Knerr
1987 – Richard Baretta
1988 – William Norberg
1989 – Matt Dufresne
1990 – Peter Miller
1991 – Joe DeAngelis
1992 – Mike Scarcella
1993 – Billy Nothaft
1994 – Andy Sivert
1995 – Terry Hairston
1996 – Doug Rieser
1997 – Bill Davey
1998 – Harvey Campbell

IFBB AMERICAN NATIONAL WINNERS

1982 – Lee Haney
1983 – Bob Paris
1984 – Mike Christian
1985 – Phil Williams
1986 – Gary Strydom
1987 – Shawn Ray
1988 – Vince Taylor
1989 – Troy Zuccolotto
1990 – Alq Gurley
1991 – Kevin Levrone
1992 – John Sherman
1993 – Mike Francois
1994 – Paul DeMayo
1995 – Don Long
1996 – Willie Stalling
1997 – Tom Prince
1998 – Jason Arntz

NEW YORK NIGHT OF CHAMPIONS

1978 – Robby Robinson
1979 – Robby Robinson
1981 – Chris Dickerson
1982 – Albert Beckles
1983 – Lee Haney
1985 – Albert Beckles
1986 – Lee Labrada
1987 – Gary Strydom
1988 – Phil Hill
1989 – Vince Taylor
1990 – Mohammad Benaziza
1991 – Dorian Yates
1992 – Kevin Levrone
1993 – Porter Cottrell
1994 – Mike Francois
1995 – Nasser El Sonbaty
1996 – Flex Wheeler
1997 – Chris Cormier
1998 – Ronnie Coleman
1999 – Paul Dillett

IRONMAN INVITATIONAL

1990 – Shawn Ray
1991 – J.J. Marsh
1992 – Vince Taylor
1993 – Flex Wheeler
1994 – Vince Taylor
1995 – Flex Wheeler
1996 – Flex Wheeler
1997 – Flex Wheeler
1998 – Flex Wheeler
1999 – Chris Cormier

IFBB PRO MR. UNIVERSE

1975 – Bob Birdsong
1978 – Roy Callender
1979 – Roy Callender
1980 – Jusup Wilkosz
1981 – Dennis Tinerino

IFBB MR. UNIVERSE

1959 – Eddie Sylvester
1960 – Chuck Sipes
1961 – Chuck Sipes
1962 – George Eiferman
1963 – Harold Poole
1964 – Larry Scott
1965 – Earl Maynard
1966 – Dave Draper
1967 – Sergio Oliva
1968 – Frank Zane
1969 – Arnold Schwarzenegger
1970 – Franco Columbu
1971 – Albert Beckles
1972 – Ed Corney
1973 – Lou Ferrigno
1974 – Lou Ferrigno
1975 – Ken Waller
1976 – Robby Robinson

NABBA MR UNIVERSE

1947 – Steve Stanko
1948 – John Grimek
1950 – Steve Reeves
1951 – Reg Park
1952 – Mohamed Nasr
1953 – Bill Pearl
1954 – Enrico Thomas
1955 – Mickey Hargitay
1956 – Ray Schaeffer
1957 – John Lees
1958 – Earl Clark
1959 – Len Sell
1960 – Henry Downs
1961 – Ray Routledge
1962 – Joseph Abbenda
1963 – Tom Sansone
1964 – John Hewlett
1965 – Elmo Santiago
1966 – Chester Yorton
1967 – Arnold Schwarzenegger
1968 – Dennis Tinerino
1969 – Boyer Coe
1970 – Frank Zane
1971 – Ken Waller
1972 – Elias Petsas
1973 – Chris Dickerson
1974 – Roy Duval
1975 – Ian Lawrence
1976 – Shigeru Sugita
1977 – Bertil Fox
1978 – Dave Johns
1979 – Ahmet Enulu
1980 – Bill Richardson
1981 – John Brown
1982 – John Brown
1983 – Jeff King
1984 – Brian Buchanan
1985 – Tim Belknap
1986 – Charles Clairmonte
1987 – Basil Francis
1988 – Victor Terra
1989 – Matt Dufresne
1990 – Peter Reid
1991 – Rainer Gorbracht
1992 – Mohammad Mustafa
1993 – Dennis Francis
1994 – Nick Van Beeck
1995 – Grant Clemesha
1996 – Federico Focherini
1997 – Grant Thomas
1998 – Gary Lister

IFBB WORLD AMATEUR CHAMPIONSHIPS

1978 – Tom Platz
1981 – Lance Dreher
1983 – Bob Paris
1985 – Peter Hensel
1995 - Agathoklis Akathokleous
1996 – Jeno Kiss
1997 – Ahmed Haidar

IFBB MR. WORLD

1962 – Lenee Castaneda
1963 – Jorge Brisco
1965 – Kingsley Poiteir
1966 – Sergio Oliva
1967 – Rick Wayne
1968 – Chuck Sipes
1969 – Frank Zane
1970 – Dave Draper
1971 – Franco Columbu
1972 – Mike Katz
1973 – Ken Waller
1974 – Bill Grant
1975 – Robby Robinson
1976 – Darcy Beccles

NABBA PRO MR. UNIVERSE

1952 – Juan Ferrero
1953 – Arnold Dyson
1954 – Jim Park
1955 – Leo Robert
1956 – Jack Delinger
1957 – Arthur Robin
1958 – Reg Park
1959 – Bruce Randall
1960 – Paul Winter
1961 – Bill Pearl
1962 – Len Sell
1963 – Joseph Abbenda
1964 – Earl Maynard
1965 – Reg Park
1966 – Paul Winter
1967 - Bill Pearl
1968 – Arnold Schwarzenegger
1969 – Arnold Schwarzenegger
1970 – Arnold Schwarzenegger
1971 – Bill Pearl
1972 – Frank Zane
1973 – Boyer Coe
1974 – Chris Dickerson
1975 – Boyer Coe
1976 – Serge Nubret
1977 – Tony Emmott
1978 – Bertil Fox
1979 – Bertil Fox
1980 – Tony Pearson
1981 – Robby Robinson
1982 – Edouardo Kawak
1983 – Edouardo Kawak
1984 – Edouardo Kawak
1985 – Edouardo Kawak
1986 – Lance Dreher
1987 – Olev Annus

1988 – Charles Clairmonte
1989 – Charles Clairmonte
1990 – Charles Clairmonte
1991 – Victor Terra
1992 – Peter Reid
1993 – Edouardo Kawak
1994 – John Terelli
1995 – Brian Buchanan
1995 – Gianpiero Cataldi
1995 – Shawn Davis
1995 – Marco Falcone
1995 – John Terelli
1995 – Warren Treasure
1995 – Colin Wright
1996 – Shawn Davis
1997 – Eddie Ellwood
1998 – Eddie Ellwood

WOMEN'S CONTESTS

MS. OLYMPIA

1980 – Rachel McLish
1981 – Kike Elomaa
1982 – Rachel McLish
1983 – Carla Dunlap
1984 – Cory Everson
1985 – Cory Everson
1986 – Cory Everson
1987 – Cory Everson
1988 – Cory Everson
1989 – Cory Everson
1990 – Lenda Murray
1991 – Lenda Murray
1992 – Lenda Murray
1993 – Lenda Murray
1994 – Lenda Murray
1995 – Lenda Murray
1996 – Kim Chizevsky
1997 – Kim Chizevsky
1998 – Kim Chizevsky

NPC AMERICAN NATIONALS

1980 – Laura Combes
1981 – Carla Dunlap
1982 – Carla Dunlap
1983 – Lori Bowen
1984 – Cory Everson
1985 – Diana Dennis
1986 – Cathey Palyo
1987 – Renee Casella
1988 – Laura Beaudry
1989 – Susan Myers
1990 – Nikki Fuller
1991 – Kim King
1992 – Drorit Kernes
1994 – Michele Ralabate
1995 – Paula Suzuki
1996 – Gayle Moher
1997 – Nicole Bass
1998 – Brenda Raganot

AAU MS. AMERICA

1980 – Carla Dunlap
1981 – Laura Combes
1982 – Tina Plakinger
1983 – Kerrie Keenan
1984 – Jill O'Connor
1985 – Joone Hopfenspirger
1986 – Connie McCloskey
1987 – Teresa Nordaby
1988 – Cathy Butler
1989 – Mary Adams
1990 – Linda Slayton
1991 – Theresa Locicero
1992 – Kathi Costello
1993 – Karla Nelsen
1994 – Midge Shull
1995 – Betsy Briggs
1996 – Cynthia Barker
1997 – Denise Richardson
1998 – Denise Richardson

JANA TANA CLASSIC

1991 – Sue Gafner
1992 – Nikki Fuller
1993 – Denise Rutkowski
1994 – Sue Price
1995 – Michele Ralabate
1996 – Melissa Coates
1997 – Chris Bongiovanni
1998 – Lesa Lewis
1999 – Gayle Moher

Glossary

Abdominals – Series of muscles along the front and lower region of the torso. The abdominals are flexors that draw the torso towards the legs. They also play a major role in keeping the body in an upright position.

Aerobic exercise – Form of exercise involving oxygen. Aerobic exercise allows the body to maintain low to moderate levels of activity for extended periods of time.

AFWB – The American Federation of Women Bodybuilders is responsible for the promotion, organization, and running of female bodybuilding contests in the US.

Agonist – The muscle that contracts to produce the desired movement during an exercise.

Amino acids – The 20-24 individual subunits that form the links in peptide chains. Peptide chains in turn form larger units called protein.

Anabolic – Term used to describe chemical reactions where smaller molecules are combined to former larger units. Amino acids combining to form peptide chains and ultimately protein, is one such example.

Anaerobic exercise – Form of exercise that takes place when there is insufficient oxygen available. The chief by-product of anaerobic exercise is lactic acid. Anaerobic exercise allows the individual to exercise intensely for short periods of time.

Androgenic – Series of physiological effects associated with testosterone and testosterone derivatives. Examples include facial hair growth, masculinization of the vocal chords, and development of the reproductive system.

Antagonist – The muscle opposite the agonist that relaxes during an exercise.

Anticatabolic – Term used to describe any drug or compound that reduces or impedes catabolic (breakdown) reactions.

APC (American Physique Committee) – Bodybuilding federation that is affiliated with the IFBB and is responsible for organizing and running amateur bodybuilding contests in the US.

Asymmetric training – Type of exercise that involves training one side of the body at a time. Examples include one arm dumbell rows, one arm cable laterals, and concentration curls.

Back – Common name for the large collection of muscles located on the dorsal (rear) region of the torso. The back includes the latissimus dorsi, teres major and minor, rhomboids, and trapezius.

Biceps – The two-headed muscle located on the front of the upper arm bone (humerus). The biceps are flexors that contract and draw the forearm towards the upper arm.

Biofeedback – Psychological term used to describe the self-monitoring abilities of the human body. Biofeedback can take the form of both psychological and physiological symptoms.

Biological value scale – Measuring scale used by biochemists and nutritionists to compare the nutrient composition of two or more food substances.

BMR (Basal Metabolic Rate) – The baseline metabolic rate of an individual. It is the sum total of all the biochemical reactions that take place during rest.

Bulking up – Old bodybuilding term used to describe the process of training heavy and eating large amounts of food in order to gain bodyweight. After "bulking up" the individual would then increase cardio and decrease calorie intake to shed excess bodyfat. With the number of contests and endorsement appearances these days, bulking up is not as popular as it once was.

Burns – Partial reps performed at the end of a set when no additional full reps are possible.

Bursae – Fluid-filled sacks that surround the body's joints. They provide lubrication and support to the joints. Bursae may become inflamed leading to bursitis.

Calves – Small muscles located at the back of the lower leg bones (tibia and fibula). The calves consist of the larger upper gastrocnemius and smaller lower soleus.

Carbohydrate – Nutrient compound that serves as the body's primary fuel source during exercise. Carbohydrates may be simple or complex in nature. The common name for carbohydrate is sugar.

Carbohydrate loading – Technique used by competitive bodybuilders to increase muscle fullness and reduce water retention. It involves four to five days of carb depletion (reducing carb intake and increasing high energy exercise) followed by four days of loading (increasing carb intake and reducing high energy exercise).

Cartilage – Specialized type of tissue found between two bones. Cartilage acts as a type of shock absorber.

Cheating – Training technique where other muscles are brought into play after the primary muscles become fatigued.

Chest – Large muscles located on the front of the upper torso. The chest consists of the pectoral majors and pectoral minors, whose primary function is to draw the arms forwards and together.

Compound exercise – Any exercise that involves movement at two or more joints. Compound movements are also called basic exercises and should form the bulk of beginner and intermediate training programs.

Compulsory poses – Series of seven poses that bodybuilders must execute during the second round of a bodybuilding contest.

Cortisol – Catabolic hormone released by the adrenal glands in response to stress. Prolonged elevation of cortisol leads to a breakdown in muscle tissue.

Cycle training – Training style where individuals alternate heavy intense workouts, with less intense training. Cycles can be daily, weekly, or monthly.

Definition – Bodybuilding term used to describe the level of body fat. A "defined" bodybuilder would have a very low (-6 percent) body fat percentage.

Density – Bodybuilding term used to describe the amount of clearly visible muscle mass carried by an individual.

Descending sets – Training technique where the individual reduces the amount of weight after going to positive failure on a set.

Dislocation – Type of injury that occurs at a ball and socket joint. A dislocation involves the partial or full slipping of the ball on one bone out of the socket on the adjacent bone.

Diuretics – Natural or synthetic substance that causes the body to lose water. Bodybuilders use diuretics to shed water in the days leading up to a contest so their musculature stands out better. Diuretics can be dangerous as they also increase the loss of charged atoms called ions or electrolytes which are involved in many essential reactions including heart contraction.

Down the rack – Training technique where the individual uses progressively lighter dumbells on an exercise. In its purest sense down the rack involves dropping the weight a couple of times within one set of a particular exercise.

Ergogenic aids – Any substance that increases an individual's athletic performance. Popular bodybuilding ergogenic aids include creatine, glutamine, anabolic steroids, and growth hormone.

Fast twitch muscle fiber – Type of muscle fiber designed for high intensity short-term usage.

Fat – High-energy food nutrient that serves as a form of energy when carbohydrate levels are low. Fat also insulates the body and is the precursor for the production of many hormones.

Flexibility – Physiological term used to indicate the degree of pliability or stretchability of a muscle or group of muscles.

Forced Reps – Technique where additional reps are performed with the help of a spotter after no additional positive reps are possible.

Fractures – Type of injury involving a partial or complete break in one of the body's bones.

Free posing – Posing routine performed in Round Three of a bodybuilding contest. It involves a series of poses set to music.

Giant Sets – Training technique where four or more different exercises for the same muscle group are performed consecutively with little or no rest in between.

Glycogen – Biochemical term used to describe the stored form of sugar. Glycogen is primarily stored in the muscles and liver.

Growth Hormone – One of the body's primary anabolic hormones. Unlike steroids, which mainly increase the size of skeletal muscles, growth hormone causes other structures including internal organs to enlarge as well.

Gynocomastia – Medical term used to describe the feminizing of the nipple region in males due to an excess of testosterone or anabolic steroids converting into the hormone estrogen.

Hamstrings – Flexor muscle group located on the back of the upper legs. The hamstrings are more properly called the biceps femoris.

Heavy Duty – Training style popularized by Mr. America and Mr. Universe, Mike Mentzer, that involves performing one all out, highly intense set to failure.

Hypertrophy – Physiological term used to describe the enlarging of a muscle due to an enlargement of individual muscle fibers.

Glossary

IFBB (International Federation of Bodybuilders) – The IFBB is the largest bodybuilding federation in the world and is responsible for organizing and running the various professional bodybuilding contests around the world. The IFBB was started by Ben Weider in Montreal in 1946.

Instinctive training – The training philosophy whereby an individual trains according to biofeedback. Instinctive training takes years to master but is the most highly evolved of training principles.

Isolation exercises – Exercises that place most of the stress on the targeted muscle group.

Isometric – Type of muscle contraction where the muscle tenses but does not shorten in length. An example would be pushing against a stationary wall.

Isotonic – Type of muscle contraction whereby the muscle shortens in length. Most bodybuilding exercises are isotonic in nature.

Joint – The point or space where two bones meet.

Lactic acid – The chief byproduct of anaerobic respiration. The build-up of lactic acid leads to both the unpleasant burning sensation and muscular fatigue.

Latissimus dorsi – The large fan-like muscles located on the upper dorsal region of the torso. The lats draw the arms downward and backward from the overhead position.

Layoff – The time period spent away from training. Bodybuilders should take a layoff for 4 to 6 weeks every year to allow minor injuries to heal and the recovery system to recharge.

Ligament – The fibrous connective tissue that joins one bone to another.

Metabolism – The sum total of all the biochemical reactions that take place in the human body.

Muscle (skeletal) – The type of tissue that produces movement, aids in support, and helps regulate body temperature.

Negatives – Type of training involving the slow lowering of weight that is too heavy to lift in a positive manner.

Mr. Olympia – The top professional men's bodybuilding contest first held in 1965.

Ms. Olympia – The top professional women's bodybuilding contest first held in 1980.

Off-season – Period of the year where bodybuilders focus their energy on gaining mass and strength. The off-season comprises the bulk of the year for bodybuilders.

Overtraining – State where the body's recovery system cannot keep pace with the physical demands placed on it.

Peaking – Bodybuilding term used to describe pre-contest preparation.

Placebo effect – Psychological term that refers to the effects obtained from a drug due the belief the drug will work.

Plateau – The point at which a bodybuilders training routine no longer yields results. The "cure" for a plateau is a total revamping of the individual's training approach.

Posedown – The free-for-all posing routines displayed by the top bodybuilders in Round Four of a contest.

Positive nitrogen balance – The term used to describe the ratio of nitrogen to other elements in the body. In order for protein synthesis to occur, nitrogen levels must be in a certain ratio with other compounds.

Pre-contest – The time period where bodybuilders devote their energy to shedding bodyfat, preparing posing routines, and finishing their physiques. Most bodybuilders start their pre-contest training about three months before the contest.

Pre-exhaust – Training technique first described by Robert Kennedy where an isolation exercise is performed prior to a compound exercise.

Pre-judging – The first judging session that takes place at a bodybuilding contest. It is usually held on a Saturday morning.

Priority training – Training technique where a bodybuilder trains his weakest muscles first in his workout.

Proportion – Term used to describe the balance of a bodybuilder's physique. It refers to the relative size of each muscle group.

Protein – Nutrient group primarily used in the building of the body's tissues including muscle tissue.

Pump – Bodybuilding term used to the swelling of a muscle due to an influx of blood during and after a few sets of an exercise.

Pumping Iron – Slang term used by bodybuilders that refers to lifting weights for bodybuilding purposes. Pumping Iron was also the name of the popular 1975 bodybuilding documentary starring Arnold Schwarzenegger and Lou Ferrigno.

Pumping Up – The series of exercises bodybuilders perform backstage at a contest to swell the muscles with blood before going on stage.

Pyramiding – Training technique where the weight is increased and the reps decreased with each successive set.

Quadriceps – The four large extensor muscles in the upper leg that are commonly referred to as the thighs.

Reps – Abbreviation of the word repetition that refers to the series of lifts performed during each set of an exercise.

Rest/Pause – Training technique involving going to positive failure during an exercise, waiting ten seconds, and then resuming the set.

Ripped – Bodybuilding term that refers to any competitor showing a low level of body fat.

Set – Term that refers to one group of reps of a particular exercise.

Shocking – Any change in training style that kick-starts the muscles into new growth after a plateau is reached.

Shoulders – The three medium-sized muscles located at the top of the arms and base of the neck that elevate the arms to the front, side, and rear.

Slow twitch muscle fiber – Type of muscle fiber designed for medium intensity, long-term usage.

Spinal erectors – Series of muscles located on the lower and mid dorsal region of the torso. Their primary function is to help keep the body in an upright erect position.

Split routines – Training style that involves training different muscles during workouts.

Spot – The term used to describe the assistance another member provides during a set.

Staggered sets – The alternating of exercises for two different muscle groups. Staggered sets are usually performed for the calves and forearms.

Steroids – Group of compounds designed to mimic the anabolic properties of the male hormone testosterone.

Sticking point – Position during an exercise where the muscle is at its weakest.

Stretching – Series of exercises that help loosen and lengthen muscles.

Stretch marks – The reddish/purplish marks located in areas of fast muscle growth. Stretch marks are in fact tears in the skin that occur when the underlying muscle grows faster than the overlying skin.

Strict form – Type of training where only the target muscle group performs the lift. Associated muscle involvement is kept to a minimum.

Strip sets – Training technique where plates are removed from a barbell after positive failure is reached, and the set continued.

Supersets – Training technique where one set of two exercises is performed back to back with as little rest as possible between the sets. Supersets may be for the same muscle group or opposing muscle groups.

Supination – Kinesiology term used to describe the rotating of the hands to a palms up position.

Supplements – Any natural, synthetic, legal, or illegal substance used by bodybuilders to boost performance.

Symmetry – Term used to describe the relative size of an individual's muscles.

Synergism – The biochemical process where two or more substances taken together magnify each other's effects.

Tanning – The process of using natural or artificial light to darken the skin.

Tendon – The long chords of connective tissue that connect muscles to bones, or muscles to other muscles.

Tendonitis – The inflammation that occurs in and around tendons due to injury or overuse.

Glossary

Testosterone – The primary anabolic hormone in the human body. It produces such effects as increased muscle size, aggression, and the development of the secondary sex characteristics.

Training to failure – Term used to describe the process where a set is carried to the point that no further lifting can occur due to muscular fatigue.

Triceps – Three-headed muscle located on the back of the upper arms. The triceps are the primary extensor muscles of the arm.

Trisets – Training technique where one set of three different exercises are performed back to back for one muscle group.

Twenty ones – Training technique where an exercise's range of motion is divided into two halves and seven reps for each half are performed followed by seven full reps.

Vascularity – Another term used to describe a low level of body fat. It also refers to the prominence of veins on a bodybuilder's physique.

Warm-up – The series of light exercises and cardio that prepares the body for more intense training.

Weight class – The weight divisions within a bodybuilding contest. The weight divisions in a men's contest are bantamweight, lightweight, middleweight, lightheavyweight, and heavyweight. Most women's shows are divided into light and heavyweight classes.

Workout – The entire series of exercises and cardio training that an individual engages in during one training session.

Index

446

Index

Contributing Photographers
Josef Adlt, Jim Amentler, Alex Ardenti,
Garry Bartlett, Paula Crane,
Ralph DeHaan, Skip Faulkner,
Jerry Fredrick, Irvin Gelb,
Robert Kennedy, Jason Mathas,
Mitsuru Okabe, David Paul,
H. Rosenkranz, Rick Schaff,
Rob Sims, Doug White, Art Zeller